CHRIS WRIGHT
ONE WAY OR ANOTHER
MY LIFE IN MUSIC, SPORT & ENTERTAINMENT

CHRIS WRIGHT

ONE WAY OR ANOTHER

MY LIFE IN MUSIC, SPORT & ENTERTAINMENT

OMNIBUS PRESS

London / New York / Paris / Sydney / Copenhagen / Berlin / Madrid / Tokyo

Cover designed by Fresh Lemon
Picture research by Jacqui Black

ISBN: 978.1.78305.228.8
Order No: OP55528

Exclusive Distributors
Music Sales Limited,
14/15 Berners Street,
London, W1T 3LJ.

Music Sales Corporation
180 Madison Avenue, 24th Floor,
New York,
NY 10016,
USA.

Macmillan Distribution Services
56 Parkwest Drive
Derrimut, Vic 3030,
Australia.

Every effort has been made to trace the copyright holders of the photographs in this book but one or two were unreachable. We would be grateful if the photographers concerned would contact us.

Typeset by Phoenix Photosetting, Chatham, Kent
Printed in the EU

A catalogue record for this book is available from the British Library.

Visit Omnibus Press on the web at www.omnibuspress.com

Contents

Acknowledgements

A great many people deserve my gratitude for the impact they have had on my life. Unfortunately, not everyone's involvement is recorded in *One Way Or Another*, and I apologise to those who ended up on the cutting room floor during the editing process.

To those many individuals that I do mention, perhaps I should take this opportunity to apologise in advance for the candour in which I have written about everything and everyone. I have tried to call the lines as I saw them and no doubt there will be the odd occasion when I have judged the ball to be in when it was out. I have treated myself with the same degree of self-deprecation as I have adopted in my approach to everyone else, so happily we are all in the same boat when it comes to my recollection of the facts, good or bad.

I would like to acknowledge the role played by my wife, Janice, in helping me keep my feet on the ground, though sometimes it required superglue to make them stick. Also for having to put up with me disappearing into the study at 11 o'clock in the evening for a five minutes that turned into over two hours, just as I thought of something else I felt an immediate urge to record for prosperity.

Thanks also to my first wife, Chelle, for being so understanding of the time I spent in the early years away from home in order to build the business that became Chrysalis.

We can never put the clock back on all of those times I was away at vitally important moments in the lives of all my children, often at the other side of the world at the behest of a musician or his representative who urgently needed my presence on that one particular day when something equally important was happening in the lives of Tim, Tom, Chloe or Holly. I appreciate their understanding for the way I somehow juggled these competing responsibilities, and find it hard to express in words the pride I feel at the way they coped with my absences and matured into adulthood.

Thanks also to my sister Carol for taking responsibility of looking after my mother and father in Lincolnshire, single-handedly, in their old age, something that I feel guilty about even today.

The story would have been very different were it not for the support and friendship of my former business partner Terry Ellis. We achieved so much together in almost 20 years sharing the helm of Chrysalis. We were as brothers, sometimes fighting, sometimes stubbornly incommunicado, but more often than not pulling hard in the same direction.

I need also to mention the late Charles Levison who was the nearest thing I had to a second partner as we re-built the company together in the Nineties and into the early years of the 21st Century. Even now when I am confronted with a difficult situation, I ask myself: "What would Charles' advice have been here?"

My thanks to editorial aide Pierre Perrone without whom the book would surely not have happened, and his partner Em Irvine for transcribing many hours of tapes. Pierre's painstaking attention to detail was amazing, as was his ability to remember things that even I had forgotten. Similarly, my thanks also to editor Ian Gittins for judiciously reducing the book by almost half without, seemingly, detracting enormously from the story. And my appreciation is also due to Omnibus editor Chris Charlesworth for understanding the whole concept of the book, making further editorial suggestions and being prepared to accept it in the form in which it is supposed to be read.

There are many more and I am sure you all know the various contributions you have made, not least Alan Edwards whose enthusiasm for the book has been vital in its passage from initial idea to printed page. My life has been made rich by the wonderful people that have crossed my path on this incredible journey. Long may it continue.

Chris Wright, June 2013.

Foreword

By Sir George Martin

I cannot think of anyone more suitably qualified to write about the music business and how it developed from the late sixties onwards than Chris Wright. He was no bystander gazing at rock heroes; instead he took hold of them, shaped them and made them successful, transforming the lives of scores of young musicians who became rich and famous as a result. His book *One Way Or Another* offers a vivid account of his life and times, following his career from the time he left university and plunged himself into the murky and turbulent world of music management to the eventual sale of his company, Chrysalis.

We had parallel lives. As a music producer I was lucky to have signed The Beatles but I knew that I would be hopeless if I tried to act as their manager. I watched Chris Wright in those early days and could see the mountain he had to climb to get recognition for his acts, especially in the USA. But he had the knack. More, he had the determination to succeed, and in no time became one of this country's most respected music entrepreneurs. Then he translated that success into other fields, sport, radio and TV. His book, one of the best I have read about the workings of the music business, tells you how and why he did it – and doesn't flinch at describing in detail the trials and tribulations he encountered along the way.

Chris has been a good friend for many years and we have had a lot of laughs together. Isn't that what it's all about?

CHAPTER 1

This Was

I was born as World War II was drawing to a close, on September 7, 1944, in the local hospital at Louth, a small market town about 10 miles inland from Britain's east coast on the edge of the Lincolnshire Wolds. As I grew up it often seemed to me that this was where the world ended, for the area is totally exposed; barren, isolated and unforgiving. When the icy winds blow in from the North Sea, it is said to be the coldest place in England, with no hills between here and the Ural Mountains in Russia.

Between the Wolds and the North Sea is the Marsh, totally flat and with large dykes running across. We lived in the middle of the Marsh, in a village called Grimoldby that was home to a few hundred people, with a pub and post office. It was halfway between Louth and Mablethorpe, a small seaside resort whose large beach was enclosed by sand dunes. I remember the tides could run three or four miles out to sea at any one time, and such was its isolation that the RAF had established a bombing range on the coast where they could practise aerial manoeuvres above land that was far away from civilisation.

The Lincolnshire coast is shaped like a bow with Louth roughly in the middle where you'd place an arrow. Over the centuries, the currents from the North Sea have eroded the southern part of the coast and in turn deposited material on the north side. There are villages under the sea on the southern part and inland villages that used to be major ports on the north side. In mediaeval times the small port at Saltfleet Haven, five miles from the sea, was one of the largest ports in the United Kingdom, well-positioned for trading with Germany and Scandinavia.

Once the Roman settlement of Luda, Louth was an attractive town in a county that bears the hallmarks not only of the colonising Romans – who established Lincoln, then called Lindum, as one of their major bases in England – but also of the Vikings and Danes who invaded later. The strange names of Lincolnshire's towns and villages echo the Roman, Danish and Viking civilisations that once prospered there.

I was a farmer's son, born into a farmer's life, and not a particularly prosperous one. My father came from a long line of farmers and I was expected to follow in his footsteps. Well-liked locally, he was strict and if I stepped out of line I got whacked, but that's how it was for most children in those days. My mother, however, was untypical for a farmer's wife and she encouraged me to study, to read books and do well at school.

When my grandfather was alive Grove Farm occupied over 500 acres about one mile outside Grimoldby, on the road to Louth, but by the time I was born an unfortunate chain of events had reduced it by half, and it would shrink even further in due course. My grandfather had two sons: the elder, Norman, after whom I was christened with my second name, and my father, whose name was Walter Reginald but was always known as Reg because his father was also called Walter. When Norman married, my grandfather divided the farm into two so that his elder son, with his new wife, could farm half of it. Soon afterwards, in 1938, Norman died of tuberculosis and his half of the farm passed into the estate of his wife. So, in one fell swoop, what would have been a relatively productive arable farm of 500 acres became a much smaller and less economically viable farm half that size.

My grandfather's wife, my paternal grandmother, also died six months later, before I was born. Tragically, my grandfather thus lost one son, his wife, and half his farm all in the space of a few months.

The situation was further complicated by World War II. As the closest area of the UK to Germany, Lincolnshire became a major base for the RAF with bases built all over the county, including one right next to our farm in the adjacent village of Manby. The famous Dam Busters raid originated from RAF Scampton, and I can recall planes crashing on to our land after missing their take-off or landing.

Proud to be patriotic, my grandfather was fully committed to supporting the war effort and was only too happy to allow the RAF to build Manby Aerodrome. Unfortunately it didn't stop there. The government also requisitioned much of the farm for dispersal runways where aircraft could be concealed during the night. Having bombed their intended target, German planes would dump any spare ammunition on airbases beneath their flight path on the return journey. Dispersing the aircraft prevented such an eventuality.

After the war, the airbase remained RAF property but the land was returned to us in a poor condition for farming. One consolation for me was that from a very young age I could drive my father's car on the abandoned runways.

A remarkable man, my grandfather survived many hardships and lived to be nearly 100. He was born December 8, 1874 and died in May 1974, and even at the ripe old age of 99 dressed immaculately from his bowler hat to his Gladstone bag. He would catch the bus into Louth once a week to do his shopping, and he never missed chapel on Sunday.

The community was divided between Methodist and Church of England, with very few Roman Catholics, and the annual football match between Church and Chapel inspired fierce rivalry. My grandfather was a strict Methodist, my mother C of E, a conflict that undoubtedly scarred their marriage.

The farmhouse itself was a lovely old building at the end of an impressive driveway that meandered past a duck pond. My grandfather continued to live there while my parents, who married in 1943, lived in a modern semi-detached house in the village which itself had a fair amount of land, enough for my father to develop a substantial chicken-breeding unit there. My sister, Carol, was born two years after me.

Father worked the farm each day with very little help apart from the occasional farm hand or, during the war, POWs from the local camp, a couple of whom he became quite pally with. I went to the local primary school which had two rooms, one for children from five to eight, the other for the eight to 11 year olds.

Most of my relatives in different parts of East Lincolnshire were also farmers. On Sundays, I sang in the church choir, and in the afternoon we would visit these distant relations for tea. Some spoke in a Lincolnshire dialect I could barely understand, almost a language of their own. If you were starving you were cold, not hungry!

My grandfather was originally from the Wolds village of Tealby, near Market Rasen, and had many relatives there. One family had a rookery next to the farm house, and each year in the late spring they would host a rook shoot, an important social occasion attended by many branches of the family from all over the county.

In those days, it seemed like everyone in our village kept a pig, even families not remotely connected to the farming industry. Every once in a while an awful squealing noise heralded the imminent death of a local porker, its throat about to be slit as it hung from the executioner's tripod. When a family pig was slaughtered, bits of it were always dished out to others in the village.

Screaming pigs aside, the Lincolnshire Wolds was an idyllic place in which to grow up. Even though the war had just ended and other parts of the country suffered rationing, we were never short of food. Living on a farm helped, of course, but toast and dripping, bread and butter pudding, honey, poultry and game, were all plentiful. Being so close to the major fishing port of Grimsby, we had plenty of seafood.

I was nine when the great floods of 1953 wreaked havoc on the coast. A freak combination of Moon and tide allowed the sea to breach coastal walls and surge miles inland, almost as far as the village of Grimoldby. In the next village saltwater was deposited over agricultural land, causing enormous economic hardship for the farmers. Suddenly our sleepy area was overrun by a constant stream of lorries bringing slag from the coalfields of Yorkshire and Nottinghamshire to rebuild the sea defences. Someone in the village was killed after being hit by one of these trucks.

From about the age of 10, I worked on the farm after school, and even drove a tractor. Not many kids learned to drive so young but in those days, tractors were exposed to the elements, and it was bitterly cold. A year later, I started at the local grammar school, King Edward VI Grammar School for Boys in Louth.

Shortly after I changed schools my grandfather decided the time had come to leave the farm and move to a small cottage he owned in the village. So we decamped to the farmhouse, which at the time had electricity but no running water, no plumbing, no central heating and no bathroom. We bathed in a huge metal tub filled with hot water boiled on the stove. The loo was outside, a two-seater in a purpose-built shack in the garden. In those days, this wasn't a huge problem, though it was a bit of a step down from our modern semi in the village. Somehow, living in the midst of a farm made up for the deprivations.

I rode my bike a mile to catch the bus to school. Cycling was crucial for it was the only means of getting around. We would go to Lincoln and visit the Castle and famous Cathedral, which contains one of only four surviving copies of the Magna Carta. We would cycle down to the coast to pick samfire or fish for dabs. The bicycles gave us a huge amount of freedom.

I thought nothing of cycling the 35-mile round trip to and from Cleethorpes to watch Grimsby Town play football. I'm not sure many people today would be prepared to cycle 35 miles to watch Manchester United, but there was little alternative, as public transport was very limited. My fondness for football, which culminated in me buying Queens Park Rangers FC in 1996, began here. I have many happy memories of my father taking me to watch Grimsby Town as a child, and standing with my back to the elements, protected from the cold by the mass of humanity behind me.

Years later, when I was the owner of QPR, Rangers played away at Grimsby as both clubs were in the Championship. It had been many years since I'd watched a game there, too long perhaps for I'd forgotten about the cold that my fellow directors warned me about. It was only the middle of October so I didn't think it could be that bad. Anyway, I thought I was used to it because of all the games in my childhood and teens. How wrong was I? In the directors' box, on the opposite side of the ground, you were fully exposed to the bitter wind, and it was freezing, even in the middle of October.

Back in the village, I converted one of our redundant outbuildings into a youth club where my friends and I could get together. We decorated it and put in a little snooker table and, more importantly, a table tennis table. Together with Victor, my friend who lived opposite our house, and another friend, Dai, from the air force base, we practised constantly and became rather good. We entered a team in the third division of Louth & District Table Tennis League, and won our matches so easily that, instead of promoting us to the second division, we were promoted straight to the first, which we also went on to win, and we soon ended up representing Louth in the county league. Table tennis became an important part of my life, much more so than any other sport. We even considered entering the national championships.

Sport played a central role in our family life. My father turned out regularly for the village cricket team, as did my uncle and myself when I was old enough. In the winter, we'd wake up in the middle of the night and listen to Test cricket broadcasts from Australia on an old valve radio, and trips to Headingley or Trent Bridge in Nottingham to watch Test matches were a highlight of the year. I also played tennis on a court at the airbase in Manby that we were able to access, though I didn't play competitively, just for fun.

At the grammar school in Louth, teachers who had taught my father were still there. Strangely, there were about 225 boys, with probably the same number of girls at the girls' school a few hundred yards away, but of those 225, about 50 boarded in a lodge. Quite why people would send their sons from all over the country to a little grammar school in Lincolnshire, I have no idea, but they did. So, the school was a mixture of boarders and day boys.

My father rode to school on horseback, four miles there and back. The deputy headmaster, a complete sadist called Hemmings with the nickname of Stitch, had taught my father, and most pupils lived in fear of him. When the headmaster was away, he would invent every excuse to get boys in for caning, dishing out punishment to such an extent that on Friday mornings a huge queue of boys lined up for six or 12 of the best. I tried to keep out of trouble as much as possible and never suffered the same fate as some of my friends. The punishment was meted out quite randomly, so God knows how I managed to avoid it.

The same cannot be said about similar treatment from my father when he thought I thoroughly deserved it, and two occasions when he was really cross with me spring to mind. Every week, someone would come round to check the sex of newborn chicks by picking them up, squeezing them, turning them upside down under a light and then tossing them into different baskets for boys and girls. Once, a couple of friends and I decided to test all the chicks. We went through the whole procedure but, of course, had no idea which was male or female, and in picking them up we killed them all. Sexing was something that had to be done delicately, and professionally. My father was furious.

Another time, I thought it would be a nice idea to let our little ducklings go for a swim. So we filled up this huge old metal bath with water and put all the ducklings in, then went back to playing table tennis. The ducklings might have swam happily for the first few minutes but soon got tired, could not get out of the bath and drowned. So one week I killed all the chicks and the next killed all the ducklings. My father didn't let me forget that in a hurry.

A friend of my mother's from her nursing days lived in London and we visited her occasionally. I was always fascinated by the Southern Electric railway line at the bottom of her garden. She and her family had decided to emigrate to Australia on the £10 ticket. I overheard conversations between my parents about going to Australia or Africa, which many people did after the war, but my father was unwilling to go because he felt an obligation to his father. Otherwise, I think we too would have gone to Australia.

My earliest recollection of summer holidays was when, in my early teens, we bought a caravan which we towed down to Devon and then to Cornwall, a three-day trek there and back. After a while, my father decided he could avoid the towing and rent a much better caravan when we arrived. We had some splendid holidays, especially at Dodman Point near Mevagissey. One summer, I went on a school trip to Perpignan in the South of France, near the Mediterranean border with Spain. That was exciting, my first time out of the country.

As I got older, my horizons became broader. I must have been 15 when I went off cycling around the North Yorkshire Moors, staying in youth hostels with Edward Green, a family friend from near Grimsby. We did that again the following year, except we hitchhiked – which we'd discovered was far quicker than cycling from place to place!

This set me up for the following year, when I was 17. My friend Geoffrey Baker, whose father was headmaster of the village school in Grimoldby, and I entered a competition wherein the winners had to come up with the most enterprising holiday scheme. Given our experience of hitchhiking around Yorkshire and staying in youth hostels, we came up with the idea of going much further afield and hitchhiking from the north of Norway around Europe and back home to England, again staying in hostels.

We won the competition and the two of us hitchhiked to Newcastle to catch a boat to Bergen, arriving later that afternoon with the evening and the night to kill before boarding. We went to the cinema and watched the classic British movie *A Kind Of Loving,* a gripping, emotional film set in the era before birth control which was enough to put a young man off sex for life! We spent the night on benches in the railway station until the police moved us on, by which time we could make our way to the port.

It was quite a trip. From Bergen we continued across the Norwegian fjords down through Sweden, across Denmark, Germany, Holland, Belgium, back over across the English Channel and then up from Dover to Lincolnshire, hitchhiking the whole way. It sounds pretty mundane these days but, in the summer of 1962 with transportation being what it was, no mobile phones and few having flown in an aeroplane – I certainly hadn't – it was probably tantamount to having a gap year away and going to Thailand or trekking in the Andes.

At the age of 15, I finished the equivalent of what are now called GCSEs, and informed my parents I intended to stay on at school to take A-levels and go on to university. My father wasn't happy. He'd always assumed that I would take over the farm but I had seen enough of farming to last me a lifetime. I had come to realise there was a better way of making a living than getting up at five o'clock every morning in the freezing cold to milk cows and chase sheep that had escaped, and then spend an hour or so getting a recalcitrant tractor to work to plough fields before repeating the process again with the animals in the afternoon. My dad had actually wanted to be a livestock auctioneer, but his father wouldn't allow it – especially after he had lost half his farm through the untimely death of his eldest son.

Determined to sit A-levels, go to university and pursue another career, I stood my ground and turned my back on farming. Fortunately, my mother took my side. She had been brought up in London, although her family came from that area of Lincolnshire. For my part, I had spent the first 12 years of my life in a normal village house rather than a farmhouse, and deep down inside I think my mother preferred that to living in the farmhouse. When I declined to take over the farm, my mother seemed relieved, and maybe sensed an opportunity to persuade my father to sell up and retire or find something else to do.

In the event, this is precisely what happened. The farm was sold and they moved to Woodhall Spa, about 25 miles away from Grimoldby, a town famous for its spa water and for one of the best inland golf courses in the UK. My sister, Carol, went to live with them because she was two years younger than me; she still lives in the area.

It was proposed that I move into the lodge at school and become a boarder, but since I was used to having a fair amount of freedom and flexibility in my life, I refused. My best excuse was that I was playing competitive table tennis several nights a week and if we were playing in the county league we could be miles away, with late nights in the process. In the end, I won that argument and went to stay with my aunt, uncle and cousin in Grimoldby, Sunday night to Friday night, and continued as a day boy, going home to see my parents at the weekend.

It was around this time that I decided that I wanted to become a journalist. I had secured a part-time job as a reporter for the local newspaper, the *Louth And District Standard,* and had to file copy on local issues once a week. With ambitions to become a sports or political journalist, I was encouraged to go to a secretarial college and learn shorthand and typing but I refused as it seemed too much of a girlie thing to do.

By the start of the 1960 term, I was old enough to drive a motorbike so my father bought me a little 50cc machine. Halfway between what today would be a scooter and a moped, I used it to commute weekly from my aunt's house in Grimoldby to where my parents were living in Woodhall Spa. I remember many times riding the motorbike across the Wolds in the winter and ending up on a Sunday afternoon at my aunt's house frozen to the bone. You couldn't feel any part of your body; it took about an hour or two to thaw out in front of the fire. I have no idea if being semi-frozen once a week for an hour does any lasting damage.

This continued until I managed to pass my motorbike test a couple of months later. Then my father bought me a baby blue three-wheeler Bond Minicar, a weird contraption with a motorbike engine that qualified as a motorbike not as a car. With its 198/197 cc Villiers motorbike engine under the bonnet, two seats at the front and two little bench seats under a canvas roof at the rear, it could fit six people. If the electric starter motor didn't turn the engine over, you'd lift up the bonnet, stand inside it and kick-start it like a motor bike.

So, from the age of about 16 years and two months I was the only one in my peer group who had a car; we would use it to go to table tennis matches, go to the pub, or go out partying. In rural Lincolnshire, where public transport was sorely lacking, it was marvellous. I was fully mobile and it put me in a position to enjoy my last two years at school, living at my aunt's house, weekending at my parents, playing a lot of sport and having fun.

On my 17th birthday, at about 10 o'clock in the morning, I took my driving test for a car and passed. I know two others who passed their driving test on their 17th birthday, both of whom I was professionally associated with. One was Mick Abrahams, the original guitarist in Jethro Tull, who then had the group Blodwyn Pig and claims in his autobiography to have done the same thing. The other is Anna Ford, the newsreader, whose music career I helped with in her student days. It's not quite as unusual as it sounds.

The night that I passed my driving test, I went out in my Bond Minicar and managed to overturn it in the middle of a dyke, going too fast around a bend. My uncle was with me, and I nearly killed the both of us. I daren't tell my father. We managed to crawl out by cutting open the canvas roof and scrambling through, and I arranged for a local farmer to pull it out of the dyke. Somehow I got it fixed. Whether my uncle told my father I have no idea. I had sworn him to secrecy.

The accident was probably a blessing in disguise as it meant I was a little bit more careful when I got a proper car soon after. My father bought me a Fiat 500 Belvedere station wagon, like a midget version of the real thing.

While at school, I joined the CCF, the Combined Cadet Force. The chap who ran it, Major Meade, the French teacher at the school, put me in charge of administration, distributing uniforms and handling equipment. This entitled me to my own office, but if growing up on the farm had put me off wanting to be a farmer for the rest of my life, my time in the CCF, with the annual summer camps, did the same for me in terms of a military career. Fortunately, the concept of national service was abolished in the UK before my time came.

It might seem unusual in view of the path my life would follow but my interest in music at the time was rather limited. There wasn't a music scene in Lincolnshire but my tennis teammate Victor Cooper had a record player – an ancient model with a big funnel speaker and stylus that played shellac 78 rpm singles. We couldn't afford the needles, which wore out very quickly, but there were cactus plants in his house and we discovered that their needles made a pretty good substitute. So I would listen to records on his old gramophone by skiffle king Lonnie Donegan, who had started out with Chris Barber's Jazz Band, and Elvis Presley, soon to become the biggest rock'n'roll star of them all.

I also listened to Tommy Steele and Chuck Berry and remember Paul Anka's number one hit 'Diana', released in 1957. I first heard that on my friend's gramophone with its cactus needle and many years later my company, Chrysalis Music, ended up owning the whole Paul Anka catalogue, including 'Diana'. One night in London, Paul and I were having dinner and I told him that the first time I heard 'Diana' was on a wind-up gramophone with a cactus needle. He couldn't believe it.

Music was far from an important part of my life when I lived in Lincolnshire. Little was I to know that was all about to change.

CHAPTER 2

19

It was all very well saying I wanted to go to university but my little country grammar school was not about to give me a great deal of help. I would have to do it all by myself.

In school, I started A-levels in History, Geography and French. For French, I had to go the local girls' school, as so few boys did it, but the French teacher took a dim view of boys being there so my Gallic studies were binned and replaced by English Literature.

At the same time, I got hold of books and reference materials, read through the brochures and prospectuses in the school library and began applying to various universities. I'm not sure if I could have got into Oxford or Cambridge. People from Louth Grammar School did occasionally go to Cambridge, as opposed to Oxford, but the school never saw me as Oxbridge material.

Like most farmers, my father hadn't been to university, nor had anyone from my immediate family for that matter. I was flying blind on this one. I applied to Durham and to Queen Mary College in London to read History but both turned me down. I was beginning to despair. The only institution that appeared minded to accept me for History was the University of North Wales in Bangor.

I had also applied to Manchester University to join its new Politics and Modern History course, which I thought looked really interesting. Unbeknownst to me, this was in the process of becoming its flagship course, as the university was trying to develop a programme for 25 students along the lines of the Philosophy, Politics and Economics degree at Oxford and downgrade the bottom third at the end of the first year. This obviously made it a very high pressure course. Those who didn't make the cut would be given places on another course but without the same prestige.

After reading the prospectus, I was keen to go to Manchester. I had always taken an interest in politics, and furthermore the city was the cultural centre of the north of England. At home, we always watched Granada TV and BBC North from Manchester. Also, after the Munich air disaster in 1958, Manchester United became everyone's favourite football team, so the idea of being able to watch Manchester United was a bonus. It seemed as good as being in London.

To my surprise, when I returned from my Scandinavian jaunt in 1962 I received a letter from Manchester University saying I had been accepted. It was all very short notice, and there was very little time to register and find accommodation. My father came with me to help out and I moved into digs in Longsight where the landlady, a middle-aged spinster called Miss Sampson, always insisted on the Miss! It was pretty cold and depressing, and my roommates and I often took to burning newspapers in the evenings to stay warm.

In those days the smog in Manchester was terrible, like a low black cloud through which nothing could be seen. If you breathed through a handkerchief it would be black within five minutes. Walking home from the bus, you genuinely did not know if you had put the key in the right door, and I remember going into the house and being unable to see from one end of the room to the other.

Nevertheless, at 18 I was living in Manchester and ready to start a new chapter in my life. I still had my Little Fiat 500 Belvedere estate car, perfectly formed and half made of wood, so I was able to drive home to Lincolnshire fairly regularly. I had three friends on the course from the Hull area so I would also drive there, taking the A57 Snake Pass across the Pennines which, in the days before motorways, was pretty dangerous and often closed.

I went regularly to football matches, starting off with United at Old Trafford but I soon shifted my allegiance to Manchester City at Maine Road, the old City ground on the edge of Moss Side. This was quite close to the university which, oddly, I'd chosen partly so I could watch Manchester United. It soon became apparent to me that the teams were split on sectarian grounds, as in Liverpool, Glasgow, Edinburgh and Dundee. United was the Catholic team and City the Protestant side. Coming from a Methodist Protestant background, my father had threatened to disown me if I married a Catholic. So Manchester City it was.

To stay on my course at the end of the first year, I had to pass the equivalent of A-level French. Thankfully, I had spent part of the summer driving around Switzerland and France in my little car with my Grimoldby friend Geoffrey Baker and a tent. This was great for my language skills so I managed to pass with ease and make the cut for the second year of the Politics and Modern History course.

I had always worked during school holidays, and pre-university I had worked in a hotel bar in Boston. After my first year at uni, I did night shifts in a bakery in Lincoln and the following year found a job in the offices of a grain depot in Odense in Denmark. It paid so little that I had to save all week to treat myself to a hot dog, although I did manage occasional weekends in Copenhagen, and even one in the south of Sweden.

Nearer to home, in 1965 I drove a small truck delivering fizzy drinks, or pop, around Greater Manchester. The by now mainly West Indian-populated Moss Side was always lively, and I recall knocking on one door to be greeted by someone shouting, "Can you get the police, the bloke on the next floor has just shot his wife!"

For my second year at Manchester University, I was able to find better digs next door to my best friend, a fellow student called David

Townsend. Life was beginning to get better, much more fun, not least because music had returned to my life in a big way.

Before I went to university, I had never been to a proper gig. The only major venue in Lincolnshire was the Boston Gliderdrome, which in the fifties put on dances with big bands led by Joe Loss and Ted Heath but I was too young and never went. In the sixties, after I had left, they would present the hot pop acts of the day, like the Walker Brothers and PJ Proby, but in my day there was nothing to turn me into the music junkie I would have been if I had grown up in London.

This all changed in Manchester, where going to Saturday night gigs at the union was a staple of many students' lives. The Beatles released their first single, 'Love Me Do', in October 1962, a month after I arrived in Manchester. Liverpool, of course, was right next door. It all triggered an immediate and somehow instinctive interest in me… God, this is exciting!

In September 1962, however, most of the entertainment on offer at Manchester University was still old-school dance bands, with local bandleader Jack Kirkland playing most weekends. Later on, we had trad jazz groups like Acker Bilk, Kenny Ball, the Mike Cotton Jazzmen and Humphrey Lyttelton, and male students were particularly fond of the Ivy Benson All Girls Band. Aside from a Swinging Blue Jeans gig I recall in December 1962, Manchester University seemed to be stuck in a time warp.

Interestingly, many of the smaller groups were supplied by an agency from north Manchester called the Bookbinders, run by a musical family that included a girl of about my age called Elaine Bookbinder. She would eventually find fame as Elkie Brooks.

On January 27, 1963 – 16 days after 'Please, Please Me' was released – The Beatles played in Manchester at The Three Coins coffee bar, a long, narrow cellar that held something like 200, though 650 squeezed inside that night with about 2,000 outside who couldn't get in. I would have loved to have gone, but didn't find out about it until the next day. The music, the clothes, the vibe – everything about the scene seemed exciting, and I knew I wanted in.

My friends and I began complaining about the uni gig schedule. David Townsend agitated on my behalf, claiming I was the right man to revitalise the college music scene. Was I? I didn't know, but I went along with the idea.

Although I had never been on the student council, David proposed me for union president on a platform of improving the entertainment, getting in top-class pop groups and – crucially – allowing non-student girls into the union. This was to be my election platform.

The serving president of the student union was David Clark, who years later became a cabinet minister under Tony Blair and is now in the House of Lords as Lord Clark of Windermere. Clark told me: "There is a very strong chance that you will be elected President and it could destroy your life. It is very time-consuming, you won't have the experience to do it and you have your finals coming up. I would advise you to withdraw and just stand for the Union Council and get yourself involved with running the entertainment." I took his advice and did exactly that.

The presidential election was won by Dan Brennan, now also a Labour Peer, while a friend from Birmingham, Keith Mallett, and I were both elected to the student council. Keith became social secretary and appointed me as his assistant. My friend and cheerleader David Townsend was debates secretary, and ITV-newsreader-to-be Anna Ford became lady vice-president.

Incidentally, Dan Brennan's successor as the president of the student union was a guy called Mike Costello. He was later exposed as a hard-line communist with links to Moscow who'd been helped into the role by the International Union of Students in Prague. His father was a diplomat in Moscow and Mike had been recruited by the KGB as an agent and planted at Manchester University to instigate demos and student protests and infiltrate the British student movement. The university authorities got wind of this and made Mike an offer he couldn't refuse: resign or else.

By the autumn of 1963 things were changing fast. The days of the dance bands were gone. We booked Carl Wayne & The Vikings, a

Birmingham group later to became The Move; Wayne Fontana & The Mindbenders; Johnny Kidd & The Pirates; The Merseybeats; and Lonnie Donegan who was still going strong in the face of the beat boom. We snapped up The Spencer Davis Group with Steve Winwood for £50 before they'd had a hit. We even booked Little Eva from the US, who'd just hit big with 'The Locomotion'.

One of our coups was locally based Herman's Hermits. We'd booked them for a mere £17 but by the time the gig came around, they were riding high in the charts with their first hit 'I'm Into Something Good'. That was a major feather in our cap.

Halfway through 1964, Keith Mallett resigned and left the university and I took over as social secretary. The fun continued with wild acts such as Rev Black & The Rocking Vicars, and Screaming Lord Sutch & The Savages. The Pretty Things brought about 20 girls on their coach. Dealing with some of the biggest acts of the day was an amazing experience.

Blues aficionados were delighted when we booked The Cyril Davies Allstars, the first ever British group to play blues, and soon after Alexis Korner, always regarded as the father of the British blues scene. Later on in 1964 we had Brian Poole & The Tremeloes, The Searchers and Them, with singer Van Morrison, whose record 'Here Comes The Night' was high in the charts.

This was arguably topped in March 1965 when for £160 we booked The Yardbirds, making what I believe was their first appearance after Jeff Beck took over from Eric Clapton on guitar. The following week, on the first of their many visits we had The Graham Bond Organisation, one of my personal favourites, with Jack Bruce on bass and Ginger Baker on drums, both of whom went on to form Cream with Eric Clapton.

When Clapton left the Yardbirds to join the uncommercial but highly regarded John Mayall in his hugely influential Bluesbreakers, he laid the foundations of a career that would last for 50 years. I saw the Bluesbreakers at the Manchester Domestic Science College, in a building called the Toast Rack, because that is what it had been designed to look like. With Mayall on organ and guitar, Clapton, John McVie on bass, and Aynsley Dunbar on drums, it was an amazing night, a gig I will never forget.

The Who played the university for £325 on October 30, 1965, just after 'My Generation' was released. The following month, The Moody Blues appeared for £200, a year after they topped the British charts with 'Go Now'. Manfred Mann were paid £425, and The Small Faces £300. (Later on, when I was supplying the groups as an agent, we would pay Pink Floyd £450, Jimi Hendrix £500 and Stevie Wonder £650.)

Once a week we would also audition around 10 local groups, mainly soul bands. They would all run through their numbers and we would ask them to finish with 'Knock On Wood' by Eddie Floyd. Whoever did the best version, we booked.

Largely due to the rapidly changing nature of the live music business that the sixties ushered in, being social secretary at a university the size of Manchester soon became a major undertaking. We had to come up with serious money to pay the emerging groups. So it was that, as a student aged just 20, I was becoming one of the biggest music promoters in the country. Nobody else appeared to be doing what we were doing. In time, becoming a Students Union social secretary would be a recognised route into the music industry, and looking back I can see now that I was blazing a trail into uncharted territory.

Outside of the university, during my last year there I also started to help run a venue called the J&J Club in Longsight. In reality it was a working men's-style club where comedians and strippers were the regular fare but another student, Keith Bizeret, had taken over Thursday nights and brought in blues groups to play there specifically for students.

With hindsight, I'm not sure that Keith Bizeret really needed my help but he felt he did, and asked me to be his partner. He did most of the work, designed and printed the posters and collected the money, while I would simply organise the bookings and look after the groups on the night. For me, this was easy but by then I was probably becoming more aware about what was happening musically than most people, and Keith maybe understood this.

Tellingly, I had realised that Thursday nights offered an opportunity to book good groups for less than the big fees they commanded on Friday, Saturday or Sunday nights. This was because they had a hole in their booking sheet that night.

The J&J Club was a great gig to play, a place where the groups and the audience just naturally connected. It was quite tiny, holding about 300 students, and the temperature probably touched 50°C with perspiration dripping from the ceiling, but everybody wanted to play it. Though we may have paid them only as little as £15, the bands would do it because they enjoyed it so much. All of the best northern blues groups played there, and quite a few from London too. We would go back to Keith Bizeret's digs at the end of the night and divvy up the proceeds. For me, as a student, it was a lot of money.

Keith was from London and was well connected. He knew Giorgio Gomelsky, who was involved with The Rolling Stones and The Yardbirds in the early days, as well as Hamish Grimes and Harold & Barbara Pendleton, who ran the Marquee Organisation. Keith would design all the posters for the J&J Club in weird graphics, not unlike what I would later see at the Fillmore in San Francisco.

In theory, after my finals in the summer of 1965 I was to leave the university but I had no idea what to do. My specialist subject had been American Politics, and the head of Manchester Uni's American Studies Department was Professor Maudling Jones, who'd been visiting professor at the University of Chicago.

Unbeknownst to me, Chicago at the time was the leading university for social sciences in America. Milton Friedman taught economic theory. The Chicago School of Economics doctrines were later embraced by both Margaret Thatcher and Augusto Pinochet in Chile. I was pretty left wing in those days, so God knows what would have happened to me if I had ended up there.

Manchester was a bit of a hotbed of left-wing politics and Labour Party leader Harold Wilson felt like the shock of the new, certainly compared with stuffed-shirt old Tories such as Sir Alec Douglas-Home. During the 1964 General Election, I campaigned door to door for Labour and I was delighted when they won and Harold Wilson became Prime Minster.

Nevertheless, I was intrigued by the idea of going to America, and especially to a university in Chicago. At the same time, I didn't want to give up what I had going in Manchester. I loved organising the university entertainment and I was making good money with the J&J.

I discussed my predicament with Michael Lee, my tutor in the Politics and Modern History department. He suggested I apply to the Manchester Business School, which had opened a year earlier. This sounded like a more suitable idea and I secured a place, which gave me another year as a Manchester student, thereby allowing me to maintain my social secretary role.

So, armed with a degree in Politics and Modern History, I started at the Business School. It was a big deal at the time because it was one of only two institutions in the UK that were offering a programme similar to that offered by the Harvard Business School in the US, the other one in England being the London Business School. The School was located not on the university campus, but in the centre of the city.

I moved into a three-bedroom house with some mates in Cornbrook Street close to Whalley Range, a pretty dilapidated area of Manchester. The bathroom was through one of the bedrooms, and the only toilet was outside in an alley. I had one bedroom, Dave Townsend took over the dining room and a friend called Doug D'Arcy, who would succeed me as university social secretary and play a major role in my life, took another bedroom.

Doug shared his room with a friend called Charles whom he knew from Hull. Unlike us, Charles was not a student and had a proper job. He used to go to bed fully dressed, with a bowl of cornflakes and a bottle of milk by his bedside, so he could wake up in the morning, eat his cornflakes and one minute later leave for work. As a strategy, it had a very low success rate.

Maybe I was spreading myself too thin because at the end of the academic year, in summer of 1966, the Manchester Business School decided not to award me a business diploma. It was the first thing I had ever failed in my life and I was gutted. Admittedly, I hadn't turned up to many lessons, but I thought I had been really lucky with the exam questions and performed brilliantly. Clearly I was wrong.

At this point, the realisation dawned on me that the life of pleasure I'd been leading would have to come to an end. In fact it didn't so much as dawn on me as slap me in my face. I was hanging about with a few mates one morning when the conversation turned to what we were all planning to do in the vacation.

Someone asked me, "How about you, Chris? How are you spending your vac?"

The penny dropped. It's not vac, is it? I'm not coming back.

What *am* I going to do?

CHAPTER 3

Hear Me Calling

Suddenly, I had no job to go to and absolutely no idea how I was going to pay next month's rent. Up to that point, I had survived on a combination of student grants, occasional money from my family, vacation jobs and what I made from putting on gigs at the J&J.

Obviously, I could not ask my family for any more money. I'd finished my education and was now of a working age so my thoughts turned to getting a proper job. I scoured the newspaper ads looking for firms taking on trainees. I applied for every possible position that I could think of.

One big advantage of job-hunting back then was that if you went for an interview, the prospective employer would pay your expenses. It soon became my only means of survival. I would travel to London from Manchester, eating breakfast on the train, and lunch while I was down there. Suddenly I was in London for interviews a lot. Failing my business diploma didn't seem to make any difference; indeed, some employers saw it as a plus as they were sceptical of the benefit of business courses.

I applied to be a trainee manager with C&A, the big Dutch-owned clothing chain, and for a similar job at Marks & Spencer.

Yet I was more intrigued by the idea of working in an advertising agency, which I thought sounded interesting and would play to my creative tendencies.

For one London interview, which I thought was with an advertising agency, I found myself in a very formal office near London Bridge talking to a small, balding guy with short black hair and little glasses on the end of his nose. He was almost hidden behind a huge desk and spoke with a very strong Eastern European accent.

I told him a little bit about myself and how much I wanted to work in advertising. Clearly, if I'd known anything, I would have noticed that this place did not look like an advertising agency, but I had my speech worked out and I just got on with it. Halfway through, he interrupted me and said: "Mr Vright, I think I had better tell you vat this company does. Ve are the largest importer and exporter of steel in the United Kingdom."

Thinking on my feet I did a quick shuffle and explained how desperately keen I was to work in the steel import-and-export business. I thought I had blown it but clearly I hadn't because, a little later, he said to me: "Mr Vright, how vould you like to go to America?"

"Well, I have always wanted to go to America. I would be very interested," I replied.

"Good, because ve are recruiting for our American office also. The head of the American office vill be over here next week and I vould like to put you forvard to him as a potential candidate to join *that* office."

"Where is it based?" I asked him.

"Florida."

"Oh it sounds great. How long would I go to America for?"

He looked at me perplexed and said: "Vell, for good of course."

"Well, I would love to come back on Monday and be considered," I said.

On the train back to Manchester, I was kind of shaken by the whole prospect. The idea of a job that sent me to America was obviously attractive, but at heart I was far away from knowing what

I really wanted to do. Making a decision that important so quickly seemed wrong somehow.

Back home, I wandered along to the pub outside the office of the Ian Hamilton Organisation, one of Manchester's largest booking agencies. I had booked many music acts through them, specifically from their junior partner Roy Williams.

Roy happened to be in the pub and asked me if I had found a job yet. I told him I had just been for an interview in London and been offered the chance to go to America but that I didn't know if that was what I wanted.

Ian Hamilton arrived and came over to join the conversation. He said: "Well, if you can't decide what you want to do, whilst you are making up your mind you can come into our office. I will give you a desk and a telephone. You know all the universities and the colleges, most of the social secretaries. Why don't you see if you can organise some bookings for our acts? Anything you can manage to sell to them, I will give you half the commission."

Now *this* sounded interesting. The next morning I turned up at the office in Kennedy Street. I had a phone, a desk… and nothing else. Ian wasn't paying me anything, so straight away I started getting on the phone to social secretaries and arranging to go for a drink. I got a pretty good response from them, probably because as an ex-student I spoke their language.

I would get in my car and trundle off to Durham, Leeds or Sheffield – basically all the universities around the North of England – and try to persuade social secs to book groups from me, both the local outfits we represented such as The Toggery Five with Paul Young, later of Sad Café and Victor Brox's Blues Train, and all the big groups from London. I was pretty successful, too, so much so that I called up the steel company and cancelled the interview for the position in the States. I carried on applying for jobs, of course, because if I didn't have any interviews, I didn't eat.

There were days when I had to choose between going to a job interview and getting fed, or meeting a social secretary to talk about bookings, but before too long I realised there was more potential for making money from selling the groups to the universities than from getting a proper job. That this could actually become my job had not quite dawned on me yet. Indeed, I had serious cash flow problems. In fact, I had no money at all. It was June 1966 and the bookings were all for September at the earliest. My commission wouldn't be paid for months and with no more interview expenses, I was finding food hard to come by.

Some days I would not eat at all. Occasionally, it would happen two or even three days in a row. Once, having not seen me for weeks, my parents came to visit. They arrived with my sister, Carol, and her boyfriend, Richard, who later became her husband. I believe it was the only time they ever came to Manchester, so they must have been concerned about my welfare. They didn't take well to Moss Side. When they arrived outside the Cornbrook Street house they were too embarrassed and probably even scared to come in. They sent Richard to come and get me, and we drove off somewhere for lunch.

Doug D'Arcy and myself had become friendly with a local disc jockey called the Mad Baron who worked the clubs and ballrooms. He looked and performed like a young Jimmy Savile but with thick black hair that looked like it had been backcombed. Baron – I never knew his real name – had a heart of gold and helped keep my spirits up. He knew Jimmy Savile well, and was able to source the records he needed to play from him. The deal was one cigar, or snout as Jimmy called them, for one record. The arrangement worked for both of them, especially Jimmy, who would have been given the records free anyway.

Baron told me stories about Jimmy's extra-curricular activities, especially what happened backstage after the weekly Sunday evening disco at the Top Ten Club at Belle Vue. It seemed Jimmy had a penchant for young girls, and it was thus no surprise to me when the paedophilia scandal erupted around Savile after his death 40 years later.

Once, as a joke that I struggled to see the funny side of, Baron and Doug got into my unlocked car and wheeled it around the corner from outside my house. They were helped by a group of children who happened to be nearby. I thought it had been stolen and was beside myself. (Twenty years later, when Doug D'Arcy was talking to Morrissey about a possible record deal, the former Smiths singer admitted he had been one of the culprits!) Another time, just as I was about to drive to a college booking meeting, they tied a load of empty bottles to it.

Occasionally we would go to the local casino, Mr Smith's club, and play roulette, hoping to make enough money to eat. I would wait for three reds or blacks in a row, and then put something on the other colour. It might have made no sense mathematically but it seemed to work, to a point, and we usually ended up ahead. Yet it took many hours to win enough to buy a meal.

I knew that things could only get better, but I had no idea how. My situation then reminds me of the Bob Dylan song 'Like A Rolling Stone': "When you've got nothing, you've got nothing to lose." I explained my situation to Ian Hamilton, but he couldn't pay me until he himself got paid. I asked him if there was anything I could do and he came up with an idea.

Ian had booked a week of dates for an act from London called Dr Crock & His Crackpots, a group of oldish musicians who did a comedy act. They were to play two shows a night for one week, the first at the Cleveland Arms, a large pub in Wolverhampton, and the second at the Riverboat Club in Salford.

Dr Crock & His Crackpots were terribly disorganised and Ian asked me to pick them up from their digs, drive them to Wolverhampton, make sure they got on stage, collect the money, and get them up to Salford in time for the second gig, quite a trek in the days before the M6 went beyond Cannock.

This, effectively, was my first paid job in the music business: roadying for Dr Crock & His Crackpots. They weren't a complete handful, and they were pretty good fun. The dates coincided with the famous World Cup of 1966 and I watched England beat Germany on TV in Wolverhampton at the home of Dai Clarkson, a friend and former member of my old table tennis team from Lincolnshire.

Whatever else was going on, I soon learned that the main task was always to make sure you picked up the cash as this was the only way you could get your commission. This was the real bottom line: the groups needed the money to live and the agents had to get their share and pay their bills as well. And so, armed with this knowledge, I decided that my next career move would be to start managing groups myself. Ian Hamilton was happy for me to do so, and for the groups to be signed to me personally, which looking back was pretty unorthodox and extremely generous of him.

The first group I picked up were The Cockahoops, from Birmingham, whose name I changed to Cock-a-Hoop. They were a four-piece, jazz-blues group who played Nina Simone and Mose Allison numbers. They were probably the only group in the country doing this kind of material at the time and they were very, very good but it wasn't what people wanted.

However, their piano player was a young black guy called Frank Spencer (no, he didn't wear a beret) who had two thumbs and six digits on one hand. He would throw in a few American R&B numbers that were popular at the time, records by Sam & Dave and Eddie Floyd, the kind of stuff Geno Washington was doing. Washington & his Ram Jam Band specialised in a non-stop medley of raunchy R&B covers and were probably the biggest act on the club circuit at that time.

Consequently, things were looking up for Cock-a-Hoop. The audience tolerated the Mose Allison stuff because when Frankie got up off his stool to lead the band they were extremely exciting. They started generating quite a following, playing the universities, other clubs and venues like the J&J.

As I hung in there during my penurious summer of 1966, I knew that when the students came back in September I would have the J&J Club going for me as well and might therefore be doing quite well for someone my age. So I took the plunge, stopped going to wild-goose-chase job interviews altogether and just carried on working out of the agency.

On the last weekend in June, I went to Aberystwyth University. My companion was a girl called Lee who worked at the Twisted Wheel, the famous and prestigious rhythm'n'blues and soul club in Manchester. The Wheel was just one spoke of a very vibrant Northern club scene at the time. The Manchester Cavern was the Wheel's main rival, while the Liverpool Cavern was the home of Merseybeat and Peter Stringfellow was running the Mojo Club over in Sheffield. London bands would often drive up and play all three cities in one night.

They would host British soul groups such as Geno Washington and Jimmy James & The Vagabonds as well as visiting US artists like Wilson Pickett and Ben E King. There were also frequent appearances by sound-a-like versions of older groups such as The Drifters and The Coasters whose ever-changing personnel seemed not to matter so long as the material was performed with a smile and sounded like the records. The famously wily agent Roy Tempest would bring them over from the States and insert the word 'Original' to their name.

Soul bands played these venues but home-grown British blues stuck to the college circuit or the blues clubs that sprung up in leafy London suburbs. This changed around 1965, when groups such as John Mayall & The Bluesbreakers, The Yardbirds and Steam Packet, with Rod 'The Mod' Stewart on vocals, began to appear regularly at the Twisted Wheel.

Lee worked at the Twisted Wheel with her friend, Heather. In truth, I fancied Heather more than Lee but I thought that Heather was far too pretty for me. She probably was, although I did meet up with her in London a year or two later. By then she was a bunny girl in the Playboy club and we had a brief encounter one night that was evidently less memorable for her than for me because I never saw her again, which was a shame.

So Lee came to Aberystwyth with me. I organised the university students' union entertainment for the coming winter, and the next day the two of us drove to the coastal town of Aberdovey. With not a cloud in the sky and a brisk breeze gusting in off the Irish Sea, the two of us lay on the beach all day. These were the days before anybody knew anything about sun tan lotions and protection factors, and on the drive back to Manchester we got as far as Rhyl or Prestatyn before realising that we had the most unbelievable sunburn. Mine was particularly bad, and I should probably have been hospitalised. My meetings the following day with a succession of agents in London were fairly mortifying.

This was around the time I began managing – or, at least, representing – Anna Ford. Having served with me on the student union committee at Manchester University, she was now a folk singer. You don't need me to tell you that she was also very beautiful.

Her dark hair combed back into a ponytail, Anna sat on a stool, played the guitar and sang American folk songs, some of which were very, very good. I have always thought there is something really sensual about an attractive girl playing a guitar. Joan Baez was very big at the time and Anna was just like her, except prettier.

Anna worked best for students' union gigs or as a filler between two groups but I started finding her other bookings, too. For some obscure reason, I secured her a week's work at a very big cabaret club, Mr Smith's in Stoke on Trent. There were two Mr Smith's then – one in Manchester and one in Stoke.

The Smiths' clubs regularly played host to the likes of Ken Dodd, Roy Castle and Tommy Cooper. Anna and I drove to Stoke every evening for a week. They had eight acts or so on each night, and we turned up on the Wednesday to discover it was stag night but she was still expected to perform, whereas most of the other female acts weren't.

Anna went on first, totally unfazed, performing her songs with such assurance that nobody shouted "Gerrem off!" as usually happened to female acts on stag nights. The rest of the night's bill consisted of strippers and blue comedians. I know Anna remembers the week too, as she mentioned it on *Desert Island Discs*, explaining that she was upset that the strippers were paid more than she was! I don't think she ever wrote her own material, but, impressively, she was the first person I ever heard sing 'Guantanamera'.

Anna was a very beautiful girl and everyone fancied her. Like most men she met, I would have loved to have started a relationship with her, but I never got any sign that she was remotely interested, so to my regret our relationship remained strictly professional. I still see her from time to time.

As September neared, Ian Hamilton took pity on me and subbed me a few quid so I could eat, but there were still days when I simply went hungry. I had to buy petrol to get to the universities and I had to buy copious amounts of beer for the ever-thirsty social secretaries. But then autumn came around and suddenly I was rolling in it.

By now, I knew how to get big acts like Cream and The Who from the agents in London because I had booked them myself when I was at Manchester University. I had a good relationship with most of the big agents and they knew that I was a good client. I could get anybody, for any university, and I was able to negotiate a good price. From a standing start, I developed quite a good business.

When the J&J started up again, I moved out of the run-down house near Moss Side to a flat in posh Cheadle Hulme in the Cheshire suburbs, but I wasn't happy there so I moved back to Fallowfield, near the university, and within walking distance of Maine Road. I lived there for the rest of my time in Manchester.

I was still booking the blues groups. I could give them the J&J Club on Thursday and university work on Friday and Saturday. One band that called me were The Jaybirds, from Nottingham. The bass player, Leo Lyons, was looking after their bookings and he kept bugging me for a gig. They specifically wanted to play the J&J.

The Jaybirds wanted to be a blues band but to make ends meet at the time they were backing The Ivy League, who had a string of hits in the sixties. Essentially two songwriters, John Carter and Ken Lewis,

The Ivy League had a constantly changing cast of musicians. Their previous incarnation had been as Carter-Lewis & The Southerners, with Jimmy Page on guitar, and they later briefly became The Flower Pot Men. In fact the next time I saw The Jaybirds was as the backing group for The Ivy League at the Oceans Eleven cabaret club in Manchester.

It was a parlous semi-existence for The Jaybirds. Sometimes they would be booked to perform as themselves only to arrive to find they were expected to be somebody else. In the days before artists were on television, no one really knew what American groups looked like. Unscrupulous promoters would advertise a US band with a current hit and sell tickets as if they were appearing, and when The Jaybirds or some other Brit band turned up, they would have to learn the hit song pretty quickly or face a bruising confrontation with the venue's bouncers.

The Jaybirds played the J&J Club for £15, our normal rate, and they went down brilliantly. Keith Bizeret was impressed by their fantastic guitarist and vocalist, Alvin Lee, and suggested I try to manage them, but initially I was sceptical. Eventually, at Keith's insistence I took them out for dinner, got on well, and in a move that would change my life forever I became The Jaybirds' manager. Keith and I sadly lost touch – I last saw him in 1967, when he and I drove his little bubble car with the steering wheel in the door down to Cornwall to see his girlfriend – but I certainly owe him an enormous debt.

Around the same time, someone else who would prove equally important to me joined the Ian Hamilton Organisation. Don Read, who joined with a similar arrangement to mine, was a jazz buff from Nottingham. He and I soon developed a very strong rapport.

Ian Hamilton's attitude was that artists were just commodities, to be bartered and sold like any other commodity. On my first day working for him, Ian said, "If you want to be successful in this business there's only one thing you've got to remember: it's them against us and if you ever forget that you will never make it." Don's attitude was very different. He loved his acts and he did a lot for them. He would travel down to London to hang out in the pubs in Soho, and try to get them stories in *Melody Maker*.

Don had a family. He and I would go out every Friday evening to where his groups were playing to try and get some commission money so his wife could put food on the table. We would drive along the East Lancashire Road to places like Wigan and Warrington to pick up cash from the promoter.

The group would tell the promoter they weren't going on until they had the cash in their hand. Don would say he had to have the cash: the group was probably working for £20 and might owe Don £20 commission from the week, but would need petrol to get to their next gig in Leeds or Sunderland the following night. Negotiations would take place over the £20, and in the end they would probably split the fee. That was the way the world was in those days.

Soon after I signed The Jaybirds, we changed the group's name to Ten Years After. Chick Churchill, their organist, came up with it. Having spent weeks thinking of a new name, he suggested it after seeing a newspaper headline: "Ten years after the Russian revolution". Later, the band would claim it was because they had started 10 years after Elvis Presley's breakthrough in 1956.

Through my now growing connections on both the college and the club circuit, I was able to secure a date for them at the Marquee in London. The manager, John Gee, was a real jazz buff and particularly loved Frank Sinatra, especially the album he made at the Sands Hotel in Las Vegas with the Count Basie Orchestra. He was totally blown away by Ten Years After's version of 'Woodchopper's Ball', a Woody Herman, and therefore a jazz, number.

I was amazed at how Alvin Lee was able to play the guitar as fast as he did, and I wasn't the only one. The group went down a storm at the Marquee and soon after John Gee was on the phone offering them a weekly residency – an accolade that was accorded only to the most accomplished blues groups.

As well as the Marquee, Ten Years After played all the other blues clubs around the country and they soon developed a real buzz. Peter

Green's Fleetwood Mac came out at about the same time and the two groups were in serious competition with each other.

And of course there was Cream. I saw the first ever Cream gig, a secret show at the Twisted Wheel in Manchester in July 1966. I was totally privileged to have been there. I had met both Ginger Baker and Jack Bruce from the Graham Bond Organisation dates at Manchester University. In fact, they were probably my favourite group at the time. That was a couple of days before Cream made their official debut at the Seventh National Jazz & Blues Festival at Windsor, where they brought the house down.

Because Ten Years After, who were now starting to do very well, were living in London, I became concerned that unless I moved there too my relationship with them would suffer, along with my ability to manage them. This became a real concern of mine, especially as I was already spending much of my time in London anyway.

About the same time, I became aware that someone called Terry Ellis was doing the same thing in the south that I was doing in the north: booking college gigs. More and more frequently, I would try and get business, especially in the Midlands, and find out that this Terry Ellis chap had got there before me.

Terry was always undercutting me on prices. I didn't know who he was but I discovered he had been a social secretary at Newcastle University and had written about music for the university paper. He even showed up trying to interview Bob Dylan in *Don't Look Now*, the D.A. Pennebaker documentary filmed in Britain in 1965.

Terry had left to work for Michael Jeffery, who managed The Animals and then later Jimi Hendrix in partnership with Chas Chandler, The Animals' bass player. Jeffery started the Anim agency, which he asked Terry to run, but it hadn't worked out as Terry found him impossible to work for. Mike Jeffery, about whom rumours of skulduggery persist to this day, ended up dying in a Spanish plane crash in 1973, three years after Hendrix died.

Terry was a year older than me. I was always a year ahead of myself but then I had done an extra year at the Manchester Business School.

So when I was at the Business School, Terry was already working for the Anim agency. The year I spent at the Ian Hamilton Organisation, Terry had a proper job working in industry for a salary, but he still kept some university contacts and he was running that business from a phone-box during his lunch break.

Typical of our competitiveness was the time that I tried to book Cream into Birmingham University. The fee was £300, but the agency, the Robert Stigwood Organisation, would not split its commission. You had to make what you could on top. I quoted £330, but the social secretary told me he could get them from Terry for £320. I countered with £310, really making very little on the booking. Terry then reduced it to £300. I knew he would not be making a penny on the deal.

I realised that if we continued to compete like this, we would both be losing money so when Ten Years After next played at the Marquee Club, I arranged a meeting with him. We appeared to get on. He said his business was going well and he was thinking of leaving his regular job to start up independently. We talked about sharing an office.

I wasn't totally convinced. It was a big move from Manchester to London and I was still only 22 years old. Plus I had other options. I knew Bryan Morrison, who also had an agency in London, which he ran with Tony Howard and Steve O'Rourke. This was before Steve started to manage Pink Floyd. O'Rourke had big horn-rimmed glasses, and Tony Howard would come in with a bottle of milk every morning and drink the whole bottle himself. I found it all quite bizarre. Bryan offered to let me work out of his office and I was sorely tempted.

Yet overall, moving to London seemed to be the obvious course of action. Ian Hamilton didn't really book my kind of acts – he was a pop person – but in the summer during college holidays I asked him to do me a favour and see if he could get Ten Years After a few pop club bookings. He secured one at a venue called The Place, in Hanley, Stoke-on-Trent, owned by Kevin Donovan. It was the kind of venue where girls come to dance around their handbags.

The morning after the gig, Ian was furious. He told me, I've just had Kevin Donovan on the phone threatening never to book another group from us. He said your group Ten Years After died a death. "Ten Years After? Ten Years too bloody late!" he said. "It's ridiculous, you have to get rid of them. Either they go or you go."

I said: "OK, well, they're not going, so I am."

So I just upped and left the Ian Hamilton Organisation. I think he was quite surprised. Yet we remain on good terms. Ian now lives in Australia but came to see me a couple of years ago and pointed out that he was the only person ever to have given me a job, and also the only person ever to have sacked me. Both of these claims happen to be entirely true.

But my mind was made up. After five great years in Manchester, I was leaving. It was the summer of 1967 and I was on my way to London.

CHAPTER 4

Butterfly Boys

Terry Ellis and I agreed to get together, not as an actual business partnership but simply sharing facilities. I would carry on doing my thing and Terry would do his, although he was not as yet managing any artists.

Instead, he had a few projects such as a Spanish all-girl group who vanished without a trace, and a tour with the sultry French chanteuse Françoise Hardy who had been a sensation with 'Tous Les Garçons Et Les Filles' and 'All Over The World' a couple of years earlier. He also booked a couple of tours for Reparata & The Delrons, a trio of Italian-American girls who had a hit with 'Captain Of Your Ship'. Terry ended up having a relationship with one of the girls, Lorraine. This was the only thing he got out of the tours as I doubt they made much of a profit!

We called our new arrangement the Ellis-Wright Agency. This was years before the days of the telex, never mind fax or e-mail; urgent written communication was by telegram, and we needed an address for that. We put my first name and his last name together and came up with Chris-Ellis. Which, in time, obviously became Chrysalis.

We started working from Terry's flat on Blythe Road in Shepherd's Bush. I had nowhere to live in London. Terry was sharing with a friend called Clive Walter so I slept on the floor in their passageway until I was able to find a bedsit. We had a telephone. That was it.

Terry had a holiday booked. He was going off to Morocco for three weeks. Before he left, we prepared a brochure with all the acts we were able to supply. We sent it out to every social secretary at every college in the country, explaining what we did, and told them to call us to book their entertainment. Terry then left for his holiday.

Almost immediately, everything went mad. The phone was ringing off the hook. I had to go out and buy a table and put it in the flat, immediately converting it into an office. I hired a girl, then two, just to type the contracts and post them to the colleges.

One of the girls was Dawn Ralston, an intelligent and sensible soul. She quickly became the Ellis-Wright agency's PA, office organiser and all-round mother hen. Her brother, Chris, would later play regularly in the second row for the England rugby team.

When Terry came back from his holiday a couple of weeks later, and saw what had happened he hit the roof. "You've got to get rid of the table. It's my flat!" he said, "And I am not having strangers in my home!" But we had nowhere else to go, and the staff were due to arrive for work the next morning. He genuinely could not understand the magnitude of what had happened in his absence. When the next day dawned, he quickly understood.

Clearly we needed a new base to house our operation. We set out to get proper offices and found a room in a building called Carrington House at 130 Regent Street. Terry knew that the rock group agencies were in Soho and the Baker Street area. He thought that one day we might be doing business with Americans and having a Regent Street address sounded quite posh. It wasn't quite in Regent Street, it was on a side street, but the postal address was Regent Street. We decided we were going to need more help so we hired a guy called Dave Robson, a former social secretary at Sheffield University.

Between us we had the college gig business pretty well sewn up by now and my next major achievement was securing a record deal for Ten Years After with Decca. Mike Vernon, who'd seen the group at the Marquee and knew a thing or two about blues guitarists, offered us the deal, and the contract incorporated a £1,000 advance. We made an album at the Decca studios in West Hampstead, produced by Mike, who had previously produced British blues groups like John Mayall's Bluesbreakers with Clapton and then Peter Green. It was quite an illustrious team: the engineer was Gus Dudgeon who later produced Elton John, and the tape operator was Roy Thomas Baker who went on to produce Queen and The Cars.

Decca released the debut album, simply called *Ten Years After*, on its Deram label in October 1967 without even putting out a single. As far as I know, TYA were the first group ever to do that. Word of mouth among their devoted live following meant the album sold out in a day, all 10,000 copies as I recall.

Decca was delighted as it was trying to establish Deram as its hip, counterculture imprint. Of course, Decca was the label that famously turned down The Beatles in 1962, and had been trying to repair its reputation ever since, though it had signed The Rolling Stones in 1963. Neither Decca nor the wider music industry could understand how a supposedly unknown group like Ten Years After could be so successful so quickly.

Soon after we signed TYA to Decca, Don Read, my former jazz-buff friend and colleague from the Ian Hamilton Organisation, turned up unexpectedly in our offices having driven down from Manchester. He said: "I've been watching you, I think you're doing a great job with Ten Years After. One of my groups, the John Evan Band, have real potential." The John Evan Band was a seven-piece blues band from Blackpool whose singer, Ian Anderson, played the harmonica – but not yet the flute – and had a two-man brass section.

Don asked if I would like to take over the band as he didn't think he could take them any further. He felt they needed management in London. Don even said: "Ian, the lead singer, has the ability to write fantastic songs. What I would like you to do is to give me the publishing on every other song that he writes. That's all I want out of it."

In truth, I had no idea what he was talking about. Back then, I didn't know what publishing was. The people I was involved with mostly didn't write songs but covered B.B. King and Muddy Waters numbers. It was a very canny request by Don but unfortunately for him it didn't happen, mainly because we didn't understand what he was asking for.

I was aware of the band from my Ian Hamilton days and went up to see them play at Manchester University. In those days, it was all about guitarists: Eric Clapton, Jeff Beck, Jimmy Page, Pete Townshend, Peter Green, Keith Richards and Alvin Lee, with Jimi Hendrix about to give everyone a run for their money. I thought the John Evan Band guitarist, Neil Smith, was weak and told them I would take them on only if they replaced him. Ian and John Evan agreed and we brought in Mick Abrahams who had been in a Manchester group called The Toggery Five.

The John Evan Band moved down to Luton where Mick lived and began rehearsing with him but we knew they needed a new name. They considered Candy-Coloured Rain but settled on Bag O' Blues. After several weeks of rehearsals, I booked them into two college gigs over a weekend. Unfortunately I couldn't get to the shows, so after the weekend, I called up the social secretary from the first gig and asked, "What was the group like?"

"Fantastic!" came the reply. "They went down a storm, I loved them – amazing sound for a four-piece!"

"No, that's the wrong group," I explained. "The Bag O' Blues is a seven-piece."

He was adamant. "No, they were just a four-piece."

I couldn't believe it. I called up the next college booker, who had exactly the same story. And they both wanted to book them back.

Completely mystified, I phoned Ian Anderson and bluntly asked him: "What the hell is going on? I've just spoken to the two social secretaries from the weekend and they both said that you are a four-piece group with no Hammond organ, no sax, and that you're not playing the harmonica, you're playing the flute! What's it all about?"

"Stop," said Ian. "Did they want us back?"

I exploded: "I don't give a damn whether they want you back or not! I want to know what's going on. I have other dates booked on the basis that you are a seven-piece band."

Ian confessed. When the six original band members had moved down from Blackpool to Luton, four had quickly got homesick and went back up north. Only Ian, bass player Glenn Cornick and new guitarist Mick Abrahams remained, so they had brought in a mate of Mick's called Clive Bunker on drums and played the gigs anyway.

"Why didn't you tell me?" I asked Ian.

"Because you'd have sent us back to Blackpool!"

I went to see the new line-up of Bag O' Blues and they were great. Thinking we might go the Ten Years After route, I booked them a gig at the Marquee but still felt they needed a better name. Dave Robson in our office suggested Jethro Tull, the name of an 18th-century agricultural pioneer who invented the seed drill.

They were still playing mainly blues, driven by Mick Abrahams, but live, Ian Anderson was becoming more and more focal, playing the flute on one leg in his long shabby overcoat. He had long straggly hair, grew a beard and started handing out cigarettes to the kids in the audience. He looked like a tramp, which meant that Jethro Tull definitely made sense as a name.

Before handing the band over to me, Don had lined up a record contract with MGM Records, the UK recording division of the label attached to the American film company. Tull had already been in the studio and cut 'Sunshine Day' and 'Aeroplane' but the contract wasn't yet signed, so Terry and I went to see Rex Oldfield, MGM's UK chief. We said, "You've got this contract, we made a record, it's ready to be released. That's all fine but we want an advance."

"We don't pay advances," Rex told us.

I said, "Well, it need only be £1,000, that's what we got for Ten Years After."

Rex wouldn't budge. We said £500, came down to £100, £50. It was just the principle of the matter. He kept saying no. Eventually, I said, "Well, we won't sign the contract, then," and we walked out.

MGM had basically turned the band down for the sake of £50. They had all the singles pressed and had to withdraw them. A few escaped and reached the market place. The band name was spelled wrong on the label as Jethroe Toe. These singles are incredibly collectable now. I wish I had one.

Meanwhile, Ten Years After's career was developing outside the UK, especially in Holland and Scandinavia. We flew to Rotterdam from Southend airport in one of the original Freddie Laker converted planes that operated as car ferries with seats in the back and cars in the front. It was my first time ever on an aeroplane, and it flew so low it seemed to be skimming the sea.

After the show we flew back in a proper jet and in early 1968 toured Scandinavia. It was a select tour party: the group, a roadie and me in a transit van with all the equipment in the back. I believe they call it paying your dues.

I had always liked Scandinavia, having had a few university vacation holidays there, and life on the road was certainly fun at times, especially when you were playing cool venues like the Star Club in Copenhagen. However, there were many long nights spent sitting in the van, sharing the driving to the next gig.

A major hazard was the risk of being beaten up by local louts or by jealous boyfriends who didn't appreciate their girls taking a fancy to Alvin Lee, especially in the more rural venues. In one town we had just finished loading all the equipment into the van when Leo, the bass player, picked up a chair and smashed it over the head of a huge guy who was hanging around with his mates. The group yelled at me to run, we all jumped in the van and roared off. I was in shock, but they'd realised that the gang of lads were about to attack, and decided on a pre-emptive strike. They'd been on the wrong end of too many similar incidents in the past.

Hamburg was another great tour stop. Like most English musicians from The Beatles down, the group was familiar with the city, having spent weeks honing their craft in the Star and Top Ten clubs, playing from 10 p.m. until 4 a.m., with 45 minutes on and 15 minutes off. Hamburg could make or break a group; it's a pity such gruelling apprenticeships aren't de rigueur for today's emerging groups. Ten Years After relived their memories and introduced me to the lurid delights of the Reeperbahn and Grosse Freiheit.

While we were busy building up the fanbase in Europe, Decca had released the *Ten Years After* album in America on the London label, its US imprint. Little did we know what was about to happen there as I had never been to the States and really knew nothing about the record business on the other side of the Atlantic beyond the fact that it was huge and lucrative.

So, in February 1968 I was dumbfounded to receive a letter (which I still have on my office wall) from San Francisco's top rock promoter Bill Graham. Bill was asking if Ten Years After could play the famous Fillmore Auditorium and a similar venue he was opening in New York. Make no mistake: this was a key moment in the development of our company. It totally and utterly redefined our history.

In the days before tight formatting became the norm on American radio, FM station DJs played whatever they wanted, and it transpired that both KSAN and KMPX in San Francisco had been playing the *Ten Years After* album on a regular basis. It had got a real buzz going. Terry Ellis's hunch that we might be doing business with Americans had proved correct.

Bill and I negotiated a deal for Ten Years After to play his Fillmore theatres in both San Francisco and New York, booking them for two consecutive weekends in California, which was fairly unprecedented. We needed a US booking agency and I signed them to General Artists Corporation [GAC], with an agent called Jackie Green who was more used to booking cabaret acts. They probably weren't quite the right choice but I didn't know anything about America and GAC did manage to find us a few other gigs.

This was an era when arranging for UK groups to tour the States was far from easy. Very few English agents could do it. You needed Musicians' Union consent on both sides of the pond; for every UK musician working in the USA, an American musician had to be given work in the UK. The fact that we made this tour possible was just astonishing to every agent in London. They could not believe it and suddenly Ellis-Wright was regarded as a major threat to the status quo, as in the past the well-established Harold Davison agency had the musician exchange situation with the US all but sewn up.

A guy in Los Angeles called Lenny Poncher had a business providing support management for British acts coming over to America, booking the internal flights, hotels, and transportation and taking care of the logistics of the tour for 5% of the gross. The only problem now was I had to find the money for the airfares to California, which I did by signing a publishing deal for the band with a company called King Music.

King Music had an interesting history. Run by Dorothy Calvert, it had been launched by her late husband, Reginald, who owned Radio City, a pirate radio station on Shivering Sands Army Fort in the Thames Estuary, outside UK territorial waters. Pirate radio was pretty cut-throat in those days and Reg Calvert had fallen out with a Radio Caroline director, Oliver Smedley, over a merger deal that went wrong in June 1966. Calvert confronted Smedley who shot him dead, but was acquitted of murder on the grounds of self-defence. With pirate radio coming under increasing pressure from its detractors in the government and the BBC, this unsavoury incident helped give the impetus for the passing of the Maritime Broadcasting Offences Act, which outlawed pirate stations in August 1967. Dorothy Calvert had inherited the publishing company and Malcolm Forrester, who ran the company for her, came up with the £1,500 to cover Ten Years After's airfares to America.

We flew on Pan Am from London to Los Angeles. In the sixties, the planes could not always reach the West Coast in one go and we stopped to refuel in Winnipeg, Canada. Then there was a technical problem with the plane and we had to spend the night there, arriving in LA a day late.

The first Ten Years After US tour was an amazing, truly eye-opening experience for me. It's hard to explain the enormous impact that landing at Los Angeles International Airport had on this 23-year-old kid from Lincolnshire, especially when after we cleared customs we were picked up in a stretch limo and driven through Beverly Hills to the Sunset Marquis on Sunset Boulevard in Hollywood. It was experiencing a lifestyle that I could never have imagined, even in my wildest dreams.

Talk about culture shock. England was still scarred by the after effects of the last war, and London and Manchester were riddled with bomb sites. Los Angeles had palm trees. We had two TV channels that said goodnight with the national anthem at 11 p.m.; they had nearly 100, many of which broadcast 24 hours a day. America had drive-in restaurants and movies, and huge record stores that stayed open all night. Like so many Brits of my generation lucky enough to visit California in those days, I fell in love with the country immediately.

Major cultural differences in California, not least attitudes to sex, soon became apparent. The next day I stayed behind as Ten Years After did some promotion at a local radio station. They mentioned on air that they were hoping to meet some girls and announced where they were staying. Within minutes there was a knock at my hotel door. The girl waiting outside said that she had heard the interview and wanted immediate sex. I explained that the group would be back shortly and keyboard player Chick Churchill might be able to help her but this Californian girl was clearly up for it and decided that I would do just as well.

For whatever reason, I declined this kind offer and she waited impatiently until the more obliging Chick returned. I'm not sure if it went well, but the band never made a similar announcement again!

We played two dates at the Cheetah Club in Venice Beach before driving to Phoenix, Arizona, where we had been booked into a venue called the Star Theatre, supporting The Grateful Dead, who in the event were fairly displeased to find themselves upstaged by a group from England they had barely heard of.

The temperature in Phoenix hit 115°F and after the shows we made some new friends – and headed out to the desert to watch the stars. Alvin and I became particularly friendly with two girls, one called Andie and a girl of Native American extraction whom we christened Peaceful Waters. They said they would like to meet us again a few days later in San Francisco.

Returning to LA via the Grand Canyon, we then played the Whisky A Go Go on Sunset Boulevard, where the buzz about the band led to superstars like Eric Burdon of The Animals and Doors singer Jim Morrison coming down to watch them. We then flew up to San Francisco for 10 days.

We played the first weekend at the old Fillmore Auditorium in San Francisco, opening for Albert King and Canned Heat, and the band went down a storm. The reputation of the Fillmore was now so big that the venue had become too small, and Bill Graham was relocating it to a bigger place. We were due to open the new Fillmore West, in the old Carousel Ballroom, the following weekend.

At this point in the tour I decided it was time to reconsider my appearance. I had flown to the West Coast looking like Beatles manager Brian Epstein: a stiff-looking Englishman with short hair, a suit and a briefcase. The Fillmore was full of hippies sitting on the floor getting stoned. Everybody there was high, even the police officers, and they were all staring at me. I couldn't blame them. I stood out like a sore thumb.

Yet that was soon the least of my worries. Two nights later, I woke up in the early hours being violently ill. I was sharing a room with Ten Years After's bass player, Leo Lyons. I had been similarly ill once before in London and Terry Ellis had taken me to the Middlesex Hospital. I had thought I was going to die but they told me it was constipation and sent me home to my bedsit where I spent a lonely, painful weekend.

By contrast, in San Francisco they carted me off to the Children's Hospital where they diagnosed a huge attack of appendicitis. They operated on me straight away and took my appendix out. Afterwards, the doctors told me I had clearly had a previous attack and they were amazed I was still alive. Thank you, Middlesex Hospital! It was lucky I had arranged travel medical insurance before the trip: the hospital performed the operation on the understanding that it would be reimbursed.

As soon as I was discharged from hospital it was time for the show at the new Fillmore venue. I hadn't shaved for five days while I was under medical supervision so at least my image fitted in a little bit more and I looked less like a narcotics agent. The gig, again, was excellent. We shared the bill with Creedence Clearwater Revival and Steppenwolf, and Ten Years After formed a special bond with the San Francisco fans that was never broken.

My appendix operation had temporarily put an end to any romantic activity on the road for me but Alvin's new friend from Phoenix, Peaceful Waters, or PW, flew up to join him in SF. We then moved back to Los Angeles and spent 10 days in Huntington Beach playing a blues club called the Golden Bear, similar to the ones back home. That was a relaxed few days and a pretty idyllic time.

The last leg of our States jaunt saw us in New York to play the Fillmore East. After laid-back California, the Big Apple was a massive shock to the system. At the airport, we were met by Dee Anthony, the New York representative for our US tour arranger, Lenny Poncher. He had a little speedboat and he took us all the way around Manhattan Island. It was fabulous.

Ten Years After went on first at the newly opened Fillmore East before the Staple Singers. The headliner was Big Brother & The Holding Company, and Janis Joplin was unbelievable. Her band did two songs without her before she emerged from the wings clutching a bottle of Southern Comfort and singing 'Piece Of My Heart'. It was one of the greatest musical experiences of my life.

In the more than 40 years that have elapsed since then, I have never seen a better or more charismatic singer than Janis Joplin. We saw quite a lot of her in the two years she had left to live, and became quite friendly with her. She even had a fling with Tony Stevens, the bassist from Savoy Brown, another band I used to represent.

My first American trip was an incredible adventure I will never forget. Meanwhile, Terry Ellis had been left to hold the fort in the UK, dealing with Jethro Tull and a variety of different agency artists, and hadn't had an easy time of it while I'd been away. We had hardly communicated: we couldn't afford to make phone calls so we wrote letters, although I received hardly any of Terry's letters as I was always on the move. It would be an understatement to say that he was pleased to see me back.

Within weeks of my return, I was unrecognisable from the slightly balding, straight-back-and-sides businessman who had stood out at the Fillmore West. I grew my hair super-long and my beard was halfway down to my navel. I ditched the briefcase and instead carried a leather hippy shoulder bag with racoon tails hanging from it. I was now steeped in the rock counterculture.

By mid-1968, we were representing Jeff Beck, who was managed by the already intimidating Peter Grant, as well as Marc Bolan's Tyrannosaurus Rex and The Nice featuring keyboard wizard Keith Emerson. Amazingly, from a standing start of less than 12 months ago, Ellis-Wright had become one of the foremost rock agencies in the UK.

However, the business still revolved around our university bookings and, during that summer of '68 while the colleges were out, we were pretty penniless. I managed to survive on my cut of the money from the Ten Years After tour of America, which was quite an achievement. There was no such thing as record company tour support in those days.

We lost one or two artists to rival agencies. It was a very dog-eat-dog world. Big agencies would always try to attract or steal those artists that looked like they were about to make it from the smaller players. The biggest hitters were the Robert Stigwood Organisation and the Rik Gunnell agency, which was known as a very difficult agency for artists to leave.

There were plenty of gangsters in our business. Even the Kray twins had an agency, the Kray Entertainment Agency, owned by their brother Charles. It booked the bands into the Speakeasy, for a while the most happening club in London.

Yet the most infamous agent was Don Arden, whose daughter Sharon, now Osbourne, would one day make as big a mark on the industry as her notorious father. Originally a vaudeville performer, Don Arden was banned from the circuit after beating up a promoter in Huddersfield. He once famously had his henchmen hold Robert Stigwood over the edge of a fourth-floor balcony on Cavendish Square with the gorillas saying "Shall we drop him yet boss?" and Don saying "No, I'll tell you when." Stigwood had apparently been trying to poach The Small Faces, one of Don's groups. When we were struggling to pay bills, the first we always managed to pay were from Don Arden or Rik Gunnell.

Unfortunately, one bill Terry hadn't paid was the one from the travel agency for Ten Years After's flight tickets to the US. Instead, he used the £1,500 earmarked for this from the Ten Years After publishing deal to put Jethro Tull in the studio and record *This Was*, their first album, even though we had no record deal in place for them. Deram's Mike Vernon only rated Mick Abrahams, the guitarist, and told us he would sign them only if they dropped the singer and flute prayer, which we were clearly not prepared to do.

Things began to get very hairy. We had representatives from big agencies turning up at the office demanding money for artists we had booked and the travel agency was suing us for non-payment of the airfares. Terry and I began making sure there was only ever one of us in the office, so we could use the excuse that both of us had to sign the cheques. We were on the brink of going out of business.

Fortunately, I was able to reclaim the cost of the appendix operation from the health insurance company and I used that money to pay off the travel agency, which was threatening to close us down. That bought us a few weeks grace. But by now, the Children's Hospital in San Francisco had realised it hadn't been paid for my surgery. I felt awful about delaying that because they had looked after me so well, but I just didn't have the money to pay them.

I was able to finally settle that account when the colleges came back and we had money coming in again. It had been like a house of cards: it all stayed upright, just. Amazingly, had it not been for the appendicitis attack the house of cards would have toppled, bringing an end to Elllis-Wright. Terry and I had both signed personal guarantees with the bank, so we would have been washing dishes for the next 20 years to pay back every penny.

In August 1968, Jethro Tull and Ten Years After appeared at the Eighth National Jazz & Blues Festival at Kempton Park racecourse, the forerunner of the Reading Festival. Ten Years After were greeted as conquering heroes and Jethro Tull played on the Sunday night and went down a storm in front of 50,000 people.

Suddenly, every record company wanted to sign Tull so we were able to sell the record Terry had made. We chose to do a deal with Chris Blackwell at Island Records for everywhere except America. It wasn't a big advance but we decided Island was the right company and founder and owner Chris Blackwell was a kindred spirit.

Because we had made *This Was* ourselves, with Terry producing, we decided also to become a production company. We thought we might as well start a music publishing company too. Thankfully, by now we had figured out what music publishing was.

Until now Terry and I had maintained our separate projects, our only joint responsible being Jethro Tull. It seemed time for a rethink. While I was in the States, Terry had written to me explaining his vision for the future, but we only began to talk properly about it now. Terry wanted to develop the company into a multi-faceted organisation in a way that hadn't been done in the UK before – a forerunner of the 360 degree deals that would be the talk of the music industry in the 21st Century.

Terry's inspiration was Berry Gordy Jr.'s Tamla Motown operation in Detroit, which combined record company, management and music publishing functions. So he and I agreed that, instead of being two separate operations working under the same umbrella, we would become partners in every respect. I could have said no, as I owned 100% of Ten Years After's management, and 50% of Jethro Tull's, but I didn't. The move made sense to me.

The Ellis-Wright agency became Chrysalis in September 1968. Terry employed a design company who came up with the concept of having the butterfly as the logo. The name Chrysalis Productions first appeared on 'A Song For Jeffrey', the Jethro Tull single released through Island the same month. Their debut album, *This Was*, came out at the end of October and made the Top 10 in the UK.

When we decided to spurn all the other offers for Jethro Tull in favour of Island, we had made it clear to Chris Blackwell that Island was signing a production agreement with Chrysalis Productions and not contracting the group direct. Chrysalis had already signed the group to a recording contract and paid for and made the album. We then told Blackwell that we had plans to make further records and that if we ever got to the point where we had had 10 records in the Top 10 in the UK, either in the albums or the singles charts, in the future all our records would be released on our own label, which we were, of course, going to call Chrysalis. Blackwell agreed, not expecting us to hit this audacious target.

Meanwhile, the second Ten Years After tour of the US in the autumn of 1968 enabled the band to consolidate the fanbase they had already built there and their second album, *Undead*, charted on both sides of the Atlantic.

In order to try and capture the thrill of their stage shows, I decided this second album would be recorded live. There were no mobile recording studios back then but the band often played a jazz and blues club called Klooks Kleek in the Railway Hotel, West Hampstead, next to the tube station. This happened to be within spitting distance of the Decca Records studio, so we were able to lay lines from Klooks Kleek into the studio and record what, to this day, remains a fantastic example of a British blues rock group at its live best. The album features 'I'm Going Home', the Alvin Lee number that would be included in the *Woodstock* film and cement the band's status as one of the most exciting live acts around.

Klooks Kleek was just one of a number of similar clubs that were dotted around London. Rhythm and blues acts like John Mayall, The Yardbirds, Chris Farlowe, Cream and Fleetwood Mac all got their start in these clubs, and though the mainstay was the Marquee I have very fond memories of Bluesville 68, run by a couple called Ron and Nanda Lesley at the Manor House near Tottenham, the Zodiac Club in Beckenham, the Wooden Bridge at Guildford and the Toby Jug Blues Club in Tolworth, Surrey.

All the groups represented by the Chrysalis agency performed regularly at these venues, with John Mayall's Bluesbreakers and Peter Green's Fleetwood Mac providing the main competition to Ten Years After. But all the big acts developed through this route: Cream, The Yardbirds, Jeff Beck and even Led Zeppelin. It was such a vibrant scene.

Quite why a whole generation of English youth was so attracted by a diet of American Delta Blues performed by British groups is a question that has puzzled rock historians for years. It all seems to have originated with Alexis Korner, the godfather of British blues, and man to whom many owe a profound debt. Sadly as the groups grew in popularity they graduated to the big concert halls and these clubs closed one by one.

As Terry and I were moving more into management and hoping to develop a record company, we decided we needed help in running the agency. For one thing, we wanted to avoid potential conflicts between the agency and our management company. We also needed to stop managers who brought their artists to us for agency representation worrying that we might end up taking over their management.

With this in mind, we came to an agreement with two other agents: Kenny Bell and Richard Cowley who were operating an agency called Universal Attractions. This was merged into Chrysalis and they effectively took over the running of the Chrysalis Agency. Within one year of starting a business with the Ellis-Wright agency, Chrysalis now encompassed most aspects of the music industry.

Through the Chrysalis agency, we took on the representation of The New Yardbirds with Jimmy Page and booked their first tour in Scandinavia and Germany. After that they realised they were so good there was no need to remind audiences that Jimmy had been in The Yardbirds, and they changed their name to Led Zeppelin.

Naturally, it wasn't all plain sailing for us. Soon after Jethro Tull became successful, problems started to emerge between Ian Anderson and Mick Abrahams over the direction the group should take. Were they going to be a guitar-based blues group or something different?

It is always difficult having two dominant personalities in the same group, especially if they come from different musical backgrounds. It was Terry's decision that Mick should leave. Mick, of course, went on to form Blodwyn Pig, who did well on both sides of the Atlantic. Their records, also produced by Chrysalis, helped achieve the 10 chart entries required by Island to let us have our own Chrysalis label, a mere six months after we had negotiated that contractual clause. Blodwyn Pig's career was only compromised by the fact that Mick refused to fly, although he did manage a couple of US tours by road.

In December 1968, Jethro Tull performed 'A Song For Jeffrey' on the now legendary *Rolling Stones Rock And Roll Circus* TV special, along with bluesman Taj Mahal, Marianne Faithfull, The Who and a supergroup billed as The Dirty Mac that comprised Eric Clapton, John Lennon, Keith Richards and Mitch Mitchell. It was the only time Tony Iommi, the guitarist from Black Sabbath and for a while the likely replacement for Mick Abrahams, appeared with Tull. Iommi decided to stay with Sabbath and Martin Barre joined instead.

We had been trying to get a record deal for Tull in America. Lenny Poncher and I had spoken to Warner Brothers whilst I was in California but Terry had been contacted separately by Ahmet Ertegun, the co-founder of Atlantic Records, which already had Cream and was about to sign Led Zeppelin. In fact, Ahmet thought he had a deal but Terry didn't want them to sign to Atlantic. We had a variety of other options and he wanted to take his time, but the bank was still anxious as to whether our increasing overdraft would ever get paid off.

Atlantic was about to sue us for non-fulfilment of contract, and it suddenly became a huge minefield. Warner Bros/Seven Arts had acquired Atlantic the previous year but left Ahmet and his brother Nesuhi Ertegun in charge. Around the same time, the Kinney National Company, a New York-based funeral parlour, car parking and limousine business, which was being run by the owner's son-in-law, the brilliant young entrepreneur Steve Ross, bought Warner anyway. They renamed the company Warner Communications, so the two companies fighting over the group ended up in the same ownership.

They kind of carved up the Jethro Tull deal between themselves, and Warner Brothers came up with a decent offer, which, if we accepted, would get Atlantic off our backs. Terry didn't like being steamrollered into a deal but the advance from Warner Brothers was $40,000, which was an absolute fortune to us at the time.

After a lot of soul searching, and plenty of persuasion from me, we signed Jethro Tull to Warner Brothers in the US. I believe that Ahmet never really forgave Terry for not choosing Atlantic, and their relationship would always remain frosty. When the cheque for $40,000 arrived and we could pay all of our bills, as well as our overdraft, it was an amazing day for us. It was an equally amazing day for Harry Wardell, the friendly bank manager in Welwyn Garden

City who'd been supporting us. He later confided that he'd feared his job was on the line for extending us so much credit.

Now we had a massive weight off our shoulders. Chrysalis was truly in business. It had been quite a year.

CHAPTER 5

I'm Going Home

I never like to admit it but I was not at Woodstock. Missing this momentous event is one of the great regrets of my life. At the time, before it happened, Woodstock was just another festival, another booking on Ten Years After's date sheet. It was, however, destined to become a hugely defining moment in their career.

The band and I had been on the road in the US for several weeks and we ended up back in New York City. We had about 10 days of gigs around the East Coast and New England, and I told our representative Dee Anthony, who was helping to look after the band and was based in New York, "You don't need me. I'll go back to London and deal with stuff there in the office."

I had a lot on my plate at the time. We were working towards the launch of Chrysalis Records as a stand-alone label and it seemed unfair to leave Terry to carry too much of the load alone.

In any case, this was Ten Years After's fourth American tour in 16 months. Sure, Woodstock was in the middle of it all but there were huge festivals going on all over the place. On the 4th of July weekend, 1969 they had appeared at the already world famous Newport Jazz Festival on Rhode Island together with Led Zeppelin and Jethro

Tull. Newport had originally been a purist jazz and folk festival, but all that changed when Bob Dylan famously plugged his guitar into an amplifier in 1965, horrifying the folk traditionalists.

The following weekend we played the Laurel Pop Festival in Maryland with quite a British contingent since Jethro Tull, The Savoy Brown Blues Band, The Jeff Beck Group and Led Zeppelin were also on the bill. Two weeks later, we did the Seattle Pop Festival, a three-day event attended by 50,000 people which was headlined by Led Zeppelin. A fortnight after Woodstock, Ten Years After appeared at the Texas International Pop Festival with Canned Heat, Janis Joplin, Santana, Sly & The Family Stone and Johnny Winter, all of whom had performed at Woodstock. An estimated 150,000 turned up there.

So there were plenty of US festivals that summer but it was all about Woodstock. No one talks about the others. There was only one Woodstock. Two things made Woodstock. One: it was in upstate New York. Two: it was filmed.

No one had any idea that Woodstock would become so momentous until they realised over 400,000 people were trekking up to Max Yasgur's farm. That's when the magnitude of the festival hit home. The logistical problems for the groups were enormous. Ten Years After were scheduled to appear at 8.15 p.m., immediately after Country Joe & The Fish and just before The Band, but it was not until the early hours of Sunday morning that they hit the stage. They had to be helicoptered in and out in order to get past the crowds. The music went on virtually all night, for all three days of the weekend. In fact the last act to perform was Jimi Hendrix who eventually went on stage at 8 a.m. on the Monday morning with only around 50,000 people left on the site.

However, it wasn't really until the Michael Wadleigh documentary came out in US cinemas in March 1970 and was screened at the Cannes Film Festival a few weeks later, that Woodstock achieved the prominence it did. People then started talking about the Woodstock generation.

The film supercharged the careers of a whole host of artists who performed and were included in the movie. If you weren't in the film, you weren't at Woodstock. Albert Grossman, who had always managed Dylan, couldn't cut a satisfactory deal and didn't allow the acts he managed, Janis Joplin, The Band and The Paul Butterfield Blues Band, to be in the film. Their careers suffered as a result. Dylan, incidentally, declined an offer to play Woodstock and instead spent the weekend on the Queen Mary sailing to England to perform at the Isle of Wight festival scheduled for a couple of weeks later.

You could argue that Ten Years After exemplified the 'Woodstock effect'. Already a great live group, the way their performance was filmed – and then shown on a screen split in three – simply lit the touch paper for fans and band alike. Alvin Lee's performance of 'I'm Going Home', his full-tilt solo played on his cherry red Gibson with its prominent peace symbol, turned him overnight into a guitar hero of world status.

Of course, Ten Years After were not the only band to enjoy a huge uplift after the release of the Woodstock movie: The Who, Joe Cocker and Santana also benefited, among others. But it took us to another level.

We began to realise this when we went back to America to tour in the spring of 1970. Ten Years After had gradually moved into larger venues: 5,000-seat theatres, some college halls holding up to 10,000 people and even some basketball or ice hockey stadiums where the capacity was just short of 20,000. On this tour we were also returning to venues that had been good to the group over the past couple of years, such as the Fillmores in San Francisco and New York, the Aragon Ballroom in Chicago, The Boston Tea Party and the Grande Ballroom in Detroit.

What we had not allowed for was the impact of the Woodstock film. The first date of the tour was a small college in New Jersey. A stage had been built in the middle of the room with a small passageway from the dressing room through the crowd for the group to get on and off. The venue probably held 7,000 people but there must have been twice that amount of fans there. It was chaos.

The police were called to try and control the situation. Undeterred, the group went on stage, but halfway through a long set it became clear that not only would they not be able to get off the stage to the dressing room and back on to do the encores, they may not be able to get off the stage at all. We had no alternative but to leave immediately after the last number, with no encores, with a police escort

This set the tone for the whole tour. Their popularity had sky-rocketed. I spent most of the shows sitting in the promoter's office counting copious amounts of dollar bills to collect the overage on the advances we had been given against a percentage of the door receipts. I was pretty sure that if we didn't get the money on the night, we might never get it.

By the time we reached San Francisco, I had four or five days' worth of overage in cash on my person, which I had somehow to pay into our account in New York. My normal attire by now was a capacious kaftan over a pair of jeans, accessorised with a raccoon-tailed hippy bag, clothes that attracted far less attention in San Francisco at that time. I managed to stuff $87,500 into my jeans pockets beneath the kaftan that I now routinely wore and walked about 12 blocks down Van Ness Avenue from the Continental Lodge, where most of the groups stayed, up to the first bank I saw.

I stood in line waiting for a teller. When my turn came, the poor chap was confronted by a dishevelled, unshaven, hippy-looking Englishman. I asked for a cashier's cheque, which I intended to mail to the office.

"How much for?" asked the teller.

"$87,500," I replied, lifting up my kaftan and starting to count out the money in front of him. His face went white. Two armed guards immediately appeared and stood either side of me. On my way out of the bank, I was intercepted by two opportunists trying to sell me taxation advice. You can't blame them: in today's money, I had just deposited about a million dollars.

As the money became more and more ridiculous, I had to take extra care. The music business was still in its infancy and populated by some unpleasant people. In fact, Terry Ellis was once held up at gunpoint at the Continental Hyatt House hotel in Los Angeles after a Jethro Tull concert at the Forum. Two masked guys barged into his hotel room. At first, he thought it was two members of the band playing a prank on him but it wasn't. He was pretty shaken up.

These days, when groups go on tour, there is an army of accountants, caterers and security men at their beck and call. Even when Ten Years After were at the height of their success, they had the tour manager, who doubled as a sound engineer, a roadie to help with the equipment and me. I drove one of the two cars, I counted the money, I got them on and off stage, decided on the number of encores, organised backstage interviews and meetings with the record company, got them back to the hotel, and then woke them up in the morning in time to catch the flight, or flights, to wherever the next gig was. Quite a task.

Mostly, being on the road is a combination of stress, boredom and fun. Places like San Francisco, Miami, Las Vegas or Vancouver were fun; Cleveland, Detroit and elsewhere in the Midwest could be less exciting. However, in the late sixties and early seventies, the Deep South was something else entirely. The backward world portrayed in *Easy Rider* lived on, and in redneck country, young white guys with long hair and beards were barely tolerated – if they were tolerated at all.

On one occasion, in the crazy period after Woodstock, the chief of the local police department paid me a visit before the show backstage. He told me that he had been informed by his counterpart in another city that Ten Years After encouraged the audience to get out of their seats and move down to the front of the stage. I was to ensure this did not happen. If it did, I would be arrested and thrown in jail.

It was impossible to prevent this happening. The audience reacted naturally to the music and the energy of the show. I had no control over any of it. We managed to leave the venue without me being arrested, but I was petrified during 'I'm Going Home' as the whole audience surged towards the stage.

Then there was the possibility of some kid sneaking in backstage and spiking the group's drinks with LSD. Sometimes, especially in San Francisco, fans would try and give musicians extra strong dope and try and put tabs of acid in whatever they were drinking. They felt it would make the band play better! It was very hard to protect against this. I didn't really think about it… until it happened to me.

It happened at the Fillmore West in March 1969. As usual, we were all drinking from plastic cups out of a big Coca-Cola bottle and I got spiked. What was it like? Utterly, utterly weird.

I ended up going back to my hotel with a girl I had met. This was unusual for me because I was normally too busy to end up with girls. Soon after we went to sleep, I started hallucinating like mad about the most amazing things. The next morning, I made a mental note never to drink anything unless it was out of a can that I had opened and that had never left my hands.

Incidentally, this was before the days of Diet Coke, when Coca-Cola was full of sugar, and constantly drinking the stuff out of a bottle totally rotted my front teeth. As a result, they eroded away, and I have had crowns on those teeth ever since. They're not The Real Thing, I suppose!

This was also the stage when watermelons entered our lives. Ten Years After's slot in the Woodstock film ends with a fan rolling one of these giant fruits on to the stage and Alvin picking it up and carting it off on his shoulder. After that, people were always trying to come on stage and give Ten Years After watermelons, like an offering to the gods. We were given several each night. Some people would also try and spike the watermelons with LSD using a syringe. We couldn't eat any because you never knew.

The night after my scary 1969 acid trip, I met a girl called Chelle, at the Sound Factory in Sacramento, the band's next gig. She was working part-time behind the bar and involved with the light show and we hit it off straight away. Ten Years After played three shows at the Sound Factory and Chelle spent three nights at my hotel. It could have been just one more on-the-road encounter – but, somehow, it didn't feel like it.

We kept in touch as the tour went on and a few weeks later, during a break in the schedule, I flew from LA where I had based myself, to Sacramento, hired a car, and Chelle and I drove around California together for a week, going out to Big Sur and up to Lake Tahoe. On one fantastic night in July 1969, we sat in a log cabin on Lake Tahoe and watched the moon landing.

We met up as often as possible, got very involved and serious. Chelle was great, easy-going, intelligent, a lot of fun. She had an interesting hobby: she was the only child of a father who had desperately wanted boys and so grew up doing lots of boyish things. This included driving racing cars around the western States, and her home was full of trophies that she had won.

Slowly but surely I realised a major relationship was developing. I guess maybe I was in the right frame of mind to import a bit more stability into my frequently chaotic life, and when I returned to London at the end of the summer, Chelle followed to come and live with me. What she found on her arrival was possibly not what she expected – or hoped for.

At the time, I was living in a rented flat on the King's Road above the Safeway supermarket, sharing with a *Melody Maker* writer named Tony Wilson. Chelle arrived to find that there was nothing in the flat other than a couple of bean-bags and an expensive stereo system, my most prized possession. The bed was a mattress on the floor. She took me out shopping to Heal's on Tottenham Court Road, twisting my arm to buy some furniture, a chair, a dining table and a proper bed. My place probably needed the feminine touch, and it got it.

Tony had been an interesting flatmate. After a long weekend, he would arrive home on Sunday night spectacularly drunk with three albums to review for *Melody Maker* for first thing the following morning. He would drop the needle of his Dansette on the first two minutes of the first track and the last two minutes of the last track and churn out his reviews, seemingly unhindered by his inebriation.

Tony was also having an affair with a married woman, the wife of a well-known movie producer, and using our flat for afternoon liaisons. Chelle's arrival cramped his style somewhat and he soon moved out.

Chelle had only been in London for a few weeks when I had to return to the States with Ten Years After. I felt very guilty that I had brought her over from California then immediately disappeared. I had only just turned 25, she was 22 and I left her to fend for herself in a strange country. I simply had no choice. That was what my life was like then.

We were always looking for ways to expand the Chrysalis business and in May 1969 we started promoting our own concerts for our own artists. We booked the Royal Albert Hall in London and put on Jethro Tull and Ten Years After as joint headliners and Clouds – who had been one of Terry's bands – as support. That was quite a statement for Chrysalis.

Our friend Dave Robson left the company to pursue a career of his own and we looked for a replacement. I suggested Doug D'Arcy, who had taken over from me as social secretary at Manchester University, and Terry suggested a guy called Nelson Bathurst who had been social sec at Birmingham University. We could not agree, so we hired them both. Nelson never turned up: apparently, he had found a job in Canada instead. Doug ended up staying with the company for 25 years.

I had known Doug well for a few years by this time. In Manchester, he had been the first man I had ever seen with long hair. Doug had always had a decidedly Bohemian attitude, but he was very intelligent. At first he was treated as the new boy at Chrysalis, with all that that entailed. Once, John 'Bonzo' Bonham from Led Zeppelin and Stan Webb from Chicken Shack took him down to Oxford Street and strapped him to a bollard in the middle of the road with gaffer tape. He spent the afternoon there, to the amusement of the passing shoppers and motorists.

We also brought into the company Harry Simmonds, who was managing a couple of British blues rock groups, The Savoy Brown Blues Band, with his brother Kim Simmonds on lead guitar, and Chicken Shack. The latter featured on keyboards and vocals one Christine Perfect, who later married John McVie of Fleetwood Mac and eventually joined that group.

Our existing offices off Regent Street soon became too small. There were seven people squeezed into a space meant for four, and we had to stagger our lunch breaks to fit everyone in. We soon took over a floor in the 155-157 Oxford Street building vacated by Chris Blackwell when Island Records moved out to West London.

This iconic building still housed Island Music, as well as Peter Grant, who managed Led Zeppelin and Jeff Beck, and pop guru Mickie Most who was involved in the careers of so many artists including Herman's Hermits, Lulu and Donovan. There was a lot going on there and it became our home for the next few years.

Peter Grant was a colourful character and became a great friend. He was also somewhat of a mentor, having been a successful manager for several years. Prodigiously built, he was once a stunt man for the English actor Robert Morley, and then the tour manager for US acts like Gene Vincent, Chuck Berry, Little Richard and the Everly Brothers. This gave him a great grounding at the sharp end of the business and a canny ability to grab the cash that flowed within it. Peter could somehow handle an often drunk Gene Vincent, who used to carry a gun with him, and took careful note when Chuck Berry demanded an additional fee in cash before he would perform an encore.

Peter's management career began when Mickie Most asked him to put together a group to take to America as the New Vaudeville Band, with whom Mickie had had a huge hit with the song 'Winchester Cathedral', on which he used only session musicians. After Peter passed this test, he and Mickie became partners. He had come a long way since then.

By June 1969, Ten Years After were working on *Ssssh*, their fourth album, which followed the slightly bizarre and appropriately named *Stonedhenge*, an album that was quite a departure for TYA. We were all blown away by how good *Ssssh* sounded in the studio and believed we had a monster on our hands. My excitement was somewhat tempered when I got a call from Peter Grant asking me to come up to his office.

"Colonel? Have you got a minute? I wanna play you something."

"Sure," I said.

I went up in the lift. Peter Grant and Mickie Most worked at separate ends of the same office with a PA outside looking after both of them. Mickie wasn't there that day. Peter proceeded to play me 'Whole Lotta Love', 'The Lemon Song' and several more cuts from the yet-to-be-released *Led Zeppelin II*.

The unique thing about great music is that you can always remember where you were when you first heard it, and the memories live forever. I was completely blown away and also in truth demoralised that Led Zeppelin had managed to produce something so extraordinary. *Ssssh* was successful and made the Top 20 on both sides of the Atlantic but there was no comparison with *Led Zeppelin II*, one of the greatest rock albums ever made.

I wanted to capitalise on the success of *Ssssh* and managed to extricate Ten Years After from their deal with London Records for North America. I arranged for them to sign to Columbia in a $1million four-album deal, the first big deal that Clive Davis signed after he became president of the company. Here I was, in my mid-twenties, negotiating a seven-figure deal. If I thought too hard about it, it was utterly surreal.

Ten Years After had arguably reached their peak, and there was some trepidation at Columbia about recouping. The first album under the deal was *A Space In Time* and Clive seized on one particular track, 'I'd Love To Change The World'. Alvin Lee considered it a throwaway track and hated it. It was certainly the most pop thing they had done.

Clive insisted it was released as a single and sensibly argued: "If they don't like the track, why did they put it on the album?" Eventually

I persuaded Alvin we would have to go along with Clive. It became their biggest hit, but Alvin still hated the track until the day he died.*

By this time, Led Zeppelin had left the Chrysalis agency, as Peter wasn't totally convinced by Richard and Kenny who were running it, but he and I remained good friends right until his death in 1995. We spent many a date together in the States with Ten Years After and also with Jethro Tull, who supported Led Zeppelin throughout a US tour in summer 1969.

It was Peter Grant who nicknamed me Colonel, after Colonel Sanders, the long-bearded, wispy-haired founder of the newly launched Kentucky Fried Chicken food franchise. Thankfully, this nickname didn't spread too far beyond my immediate circle and didn't last long.

Meanwhile, former Tull guitarist Mick Abrahams had recruited Jack Lancaster, a multi-instrumentalist who played the saxophone and flute, for his new band Blodwyn Pig. Live, Jack would blow into a tenor and a baritone sax at the same time *à la* Roland Kirk and give the group a unique sound. The Top 10 success of their debut album, *Ahead Rings Out*, in August 1969 certainly helped the emergence of the Chrysalis label. It was a wonderful album, almost verging on jazz at times with the highlight being the haunting 'Dear Jill'.

The title, *Ahead Rings Out*, obviously had drug connotations, made even more apparent by the sleeve concept, if that isn't too grand a word. I bought a pig's head from a butcher's in the West End, brought it back to the office and we put a pair of headphones and sunglasses on its head and a spliff in its mouth. The album deserved a better cover and I have no idea how we disposed of the pig's head after taking the photos.

Ten Years After, of course, were no strangers to drug references on their album sleeves. A later album, *Cricklewood Green* was even named after a particularly strong strain of cannabis that their tour manager

---

★ This is ironic, as even recently it generated more than half a million euros for him, as the writer, from its use in a telecom advertising campaign in the Balkans.

had procured in America and grown from seeds in his garden in Cricklewood. A photo of his two-metre-tall harvest adorned the back cover.

Unfortunately, as I mentioned earlier, Mick Abrahams had a phobia of flying, which became a real problem for Blodwyn Pig. On our way to Bremen in Germany to perform on the TV show *Beat-Club* – terribly important exposure in the late sixties – Mick did a runner just as the plane doors were closing, and never went near a jet again. We tried everything, including hypnotism, but nothing worked.

Via boats, buses and trains we managed to successfully complete a couple of tours of North America, but relations between Mick and the rest of the group frayed and Mick moved on to a solo career. This was a great shame since the group's second album, *Getting To This*, had been a respectable US hit, but Terry and I both felt it was a disaster because it did not reach the level of success achieved by Ten Years After and Jethro Tull.

Meanwhile, Ian Anderson's development as a songwriter and performer was simply astounding. Within a year, Jethro Tull scored four consecutive hit singles with 'Love Story', 'Living In The Past', 'Sweet Dream' and 'The Witch's Promise'. In August 1969, they topped the British album charts with *Stand Up*. The record came packaged in an amazing pop-up woodcut gatefold sleeve that cost a fortune to manufacture but reflected their Celtic, folk and classical influences.

American audiences took a while to catch on to what Jethro Tull was all about. Nevertheless, Ian's image and identity made him a one-off and the band went from strength to strength. They were totally embraced by the underground music community.

All in all, it was a fantastic time to be involved in music, an art form that was rapidly becoming the cornerstone of every young person's existence. It was unquestionably the most memorable period of my life.

It seems to me now that three different aspects coalesced to create what became the counterculture in the States. Firstly there was the proliferation of "underground" FM radio stations, all of them willing to play obscure tracks with no regard for the commercial nature of their content. The second was the enormous amount of illegal soft drugs, notably marijuana, which was smoked openly at all gigs, thereby enhancing the pleasure of listening to 10-minute extended guitar solos. And the third was the Vietnam War.

It is impossible to overstate the cultural resonance of Vietnam. Music and anti-war demonstrations were entwined. As much as Woodstock defined a generation, so did Kent State, when the National Guard opened fire on peacefully demonstrating students, killing four young adults. Who can forget the Crosby, Stills, Nash & Young song about the incident?

The Country Joe & The Fish anti-Vietnam anthem at Woodstock had been one of the highlights of the festival, its lyrics resonating not just with the half million who camped out at Max Yasgur's farm but with millions more across the USA who felt the war was unjust: "And it's one, two, three what are we fighting for? Don't ask me, I don't give a damn, next stop is Vietnam". And "Five, six, seven, open up the pearly gates, well there ain't no time to wonder why, Whoopee! We're all gonna die … Be the first ones on your block, to have your boy come home in a box".

Vietnam was the first war replayed each evening on national TV. Everyone could see the atrocities close up, and most young people could not understand why the US was there in the first place. Every male between the ages of 18 and 20 dreaded the draft papers that could arrive any day, sentencing them to fight and probably die. Some 56,000 young men came home in body bags, countless more returned both physically and mentally crippled.

At the height of the war over half a million Americans were in action in Vietnam. The war united everyone, and they found their release in music. Backstage at our concerts, we would meet traumatised kids who that very morning had received their draft papers. It would be three more years before they could legally drink a Budweiser. No wonder everyone was getting stoned.

Ten Years After were doing great but they had internal problems. There was always a degree of tension between Alvin Lee, the lead guitarist, singer and principal songwriter, and the rest of the group. Guitarists can be notoriously difficult and Alvin was no exception but he was a brilliant performer and an outstanding player.

Many criticised him for showboating his virtuosity. A technically brilliant blues guitarist, he was known as the fastest guitar in the West. It almost defied belief that he could perform at that pace. Just watch the clip of Alvin at Woodstock, it's amazing to behold.

Alvin was clearly the focal point of the group and many a time I had to step in and put out smouldering fires as they developed. The second number in the group's show was the old blues standard 'Good Morning Little Schoolgirl', first recorded by Sonny Boy Williamson. Ten Years After's version involved both Leo Lyons, the bassist, and Alvin playing solos to each other as keyboards and drums fell silent.

It usually coincided with a row between the two of them as to whose amplifier needed turning down. Alvin would walk over to the bass amp and turn the controls down, Leo would turn them back up again and so it went on. By the time they reached the middle of the song, it had gone beyond mere musical sparring.

As they stood face-to-face, I sometimes feared they were about to come to blows with their instruments. The crowd had no idea that the intensity of the playing came from their anger towards each other and thought it was absolutely brilliant. One night, while playing at the Montreux Jazz Festival in 1969, they actually did thump each other. The audience thought it was part of the show, and loved it.

Terry and I became particularly adroit at moving our groups' careers to the United States. This did not happen to the same extent with the acts signed to the Rik Gunnell Agency like Fleetwood Mac, despite the fact they had topped the UK singles charts with 'Albatross', and this modus operandi of ours helped to make our name.

By now we were getting plenty of requests to manage other bands but there were only so many hours in the day. Managing Ten Years After, Jethro Tull and Blodwyn Pig was pretty time consuming in its own right. Also, in my case with Alvin Lee and probably in Terry's case with Ian Anderson too, the relationship with the artist was intense and a lot closer than a normal artist-manager relationship.

After Steve Marriott left The Small Faces to form Humble Pie in 1969, the other three members, Kenney Jones, Ronnie Lane and Ian McLagan, came to see me to say that they were planning to team up with Rod Stewart and Ronnie Wood from The Jeff Beck Group to form The Faces. They wanted me to manage them but Alvin Lee took issue with this and regrettably I passed on the opportunity.

Working with Procol Harum, however, was too good to miss. I had first met their pianist, singer and composer, Gary Brooker, when he performed at Manchester University in 1965 with his first band, The Paramounts. I was to be reacquainted with him and introduced to Keith Reid, the group's lyricist, at a party in London in 1970.

Procol Harum had enjoyed a worldwide number one with their first single, 'A Whiter Shade Of Pale', a key song of 1967's Summer of Love. They'd had reasonable success with the follow-up, 'Homburg', but were in danger of becoming one-hit wonders.

At the time, they were managed by two Americans, Bennett Glotzer and Ronnie Lyons, but were disappointed with how their career was developing and wanted to change and add fresh impetus into their management. They asked me to take over and I readily accepted. Turning their fortunes around would prove a challenge and hopefully provide another example of our managerial nous.

When we came on board, Procol Harum had already made *Home*, their fourth studio album, full of rather morbid compositions like 'The Dead Man's Dream' and 'About To Die'. It was also their first without Matthew Fisher, the organist who had contributed so much to their signature sound and had helped produce them as well. Still, the musicianship of Brooker, guitarist Robin Trower and drummer BJ Wilson – who had played on Joe Cocker's tour de force version of 'With A Little Help From My Friends' and been considered by

Jimmy Page for the drum role in Led Zeppelin – were huge assets. We believed we could reinvigorate interest in the group and sent them regularly to the US where they were signed to A&M Records and had enjoyed steady album sales.

By the summer of 1970, when I found myself juggling US tour dates for Ten Years After, Procol Harum and Blodwyn Pig, I began to worry about my ability to cope with the workload. The bands weren't making it easy. Chick Churchill, the keyboard player in Ten Years After, was arrested with marijuana cigarettes at Toronto airport and thrown in jail. I had to fly to Canada and bail him out. Two days later, Procol Harum's BJ Wilson decided to go skinny-dipping in the middle of the night in a hotel pool in Baltimore, and was also arrested. I had to fly there and sort that out, too.

Furthermore, I was often trying to make three concerts in the same night. Some of those were outdoor festivals where the groups weren't going until four or five o'clock in the morning. I was burning the candle not only at both ends but also in the middle.

The end of August, bank holiday weekend 1970, we had Ten Years After, Procol Harum, Jethro Tull and Mick Abrahams all appearing at the Isle Of Wight festival, the biggest event of its kind held in the British Isles. It was the European equivalent of Woodstock and lasted five days.

We had booked several of the bands for Isle of Wight through our agency but hadn't received the money in advance of the weekend. We had to go to the bank manager after closing time, before we left London, and knock on the door to make sure that the money had been paid.

Our finance man Nick Blackburn, who had joined us after answering an ad for a 'groovy accountant' I had placed in the *Daily Telegraph*, found a country house to rent for the week on the Isle of Wight. We all went over. The owner of the house, a lady called Mrs Fyvie-Gould, had two single daughters, Suzanne and Mary Anne. Chick Churchill started dating Suzanne and eventually married her, and her sister dated Terry for a while.

Mrs Fyvie-Gould, who readily entered into the spirit of things, warned Chelle and I that our room had a ghost. We slept in two single beds pushed together, but to our amazement in the middle of the night some unseen force hurled them apart. It was terrifying.

Ten Years After, along with all of our artists, flew into the nearby aerodrome, and then to the festival site by helicopter. It was amazing to fly over the site, and see the masses of humanity underneath us.

On the Saturday night, Ten Years After followed Joni Mitchell, Tiny Tim and Miles Davis so the crowd were ready for a bit of rock'n'roll. It was dusk, a great time to go onstage. I stood on the side of the stage and looked. There were people as far as I could see. They estimated there were 600,000 people on the island that weekend.

Ten Years After were going tremendously but, because they were running late, the organisers wanted to cut the set short so Emerson, Lake & Palmer could get on. I told Nick Blackburn to make sure this didn't happen and Nick went up to the DJ, Jeff Dexter from the Roundhouse, grabbed him by the neck and stopped him putting any records on until Ten Years After finished their set.

On the Friday night, Chicago wouldn't go on stage without being paid upfront and there was no money to pay them. We had to pay Procol Harum so we drove around all the festival gates in a Morris Minor, collected the cash and put it in the boot. Backstage, once we had Procol Harum's money, we sat in a tent and watched Chicago's manager counting out their cash until he had enough to allow them to go on stage.

Filmmaker Murray Lerner shot the entire festival. I had often discussed releasing it as a film, but it was fraught with legal issues. It's a pity, as the footage is at times brilliant – and, of course, the Isle of Wight festival was rendered forever iconic by the fact that both Jimi Hendrix and Jim Morrison died soon after performing there.

Despite high points like the Isle of Wight, my working life continued to be extremely stressful and just before my 26th birthday I received a major wake-up call. On tour with our three main groups in the US, I branched off to New York for a series of meetings with agents and record companies.

I had always been an absurdly heavy smoker. In the days when you could smoke in offices, on planes, everywhere, I probably got through three packs of 20 a day – or more. As I worked through the day's meetings in Manhattan my legs were growing numb, and in the early evening I walked into a doctor's surgery beneath the company's New York apartment.

The doc diagnosed third degree nicotine poisoning: the worst kind. He told me my heart was experiencing severe problems and complications because of it. The next cigarette could easily kill me. He gave me some knock-out sleeping pills and told me not to get out of bed for the next three days, then to go to see him again to check if I was fit enough to go on a recuperation holiday.

Luckily, there was a break in the tour and Ten Years After were flying back to the UK for 10 days. After I came round from a few very groggy days in bed going through severe withdrawal symptoms, I flew to Bermuda with Chelle until the tour resumed. How did I cope? I just smoked even more herbal cigarettes.

Who knows how bad my nicotine poisoning really was, but that NY doctor did me a huge favour diagnosing my problem so early in my life. My chain-smoking may appear stupid looking back from an informed 21st century standpoint but back in 1970 nobody really had a clue that smoking was bad for you: it was just what everyone did. As a result, I haven't smoked a cigarette since that day, although unfortunately I spent the next 35 years of my life in smoke-filled rooms until the belated introduction of smoking bans.

My physical health may have been poor but my financial standing was getting way better. By anyone's standards, by late 1970 we were all making a fair amount of money. When we returned to the UK, Alvin Lee wanted to look for a house in the country, outside London, where he could move to and live a more peaceful life, away from the craziness of touring.

This was before the M4 out of London existed beyond junction seven. Anything past there was country, not suburbia. We drove out to near Wokingham. The first house we looked at, Locks Barn, was a modern house built onto a small period Tudor frame with a large Tudor thatched barn and a farmhouse at the entrance gate. The house itself probably belonged in Beverly Hills rather than the English countryside but it had 10 acres of gardens and ornamental plants.

Alvin immediately decided that it was far too ostentatious for him but Chelle and I liked it and I decided to buy the house. It cost me the princely sum of £36,000 for the main house and £10,000 for the farmhouse.

Alvin and I had agreed we should live close to each other and so we looked at a few other local houses until he found his dream place, a gorgeous replica of a beautiful Tudor house. He and his girlfriend, Lorraine, were very happy there for a couple of years but then, prompted by an offer from a developer of a quarter of a million pounds, a figure they could not refuse, moved on to an amazing manor house at Checkendon near Henley. Alvin built a recording studio there that was so state-of-the-art that it was later used by Pink Floyd. Trevor Horn was also to live there, decades later.

Locks Barn had six bedrooms, a swimming pool and was a wonderful place to entertain. My parents loved the house. In the first few years of my career, they would always ask me when I was going to get a proper job. They had sold their farm so I could go to university and felt I was wasting my life running around the world with rock'n'roll groups, dressed like a hippy. It was only when they came to Locks Barn that I was able to inform them that in a proper job I would not earn enough money to pay off the mortgage. That was when they realised that, actually, I was doing OK.

CHAPTER 6

Oh! You Pretty Things

In the music business, we all make mistakes. One major opportunity we missed was deciding not to sign David Bowie to Chrysalis Records.

Bowie had a deal with our embryonic publishing company. As I have indicated, publishing was not an area with which Terry and I were terribly familiar, so when we launched Chrysalis Music, we took on Bob Grace to run it. Bob was very well established: his father, Sydney, had been one of the most important theatrical agents of his time.

Bob was very keen to sign David Bowie, who had had a big hit with 'Space Oddity' in September 1969 but had not managed to follow up that success. We paid Bowie a £5,000 advance – an enormous amount of money at the time for an apparent one-hit wonder. That was against future royalties on 75 songs he would write and record over the next five years.

Soon after we made the deal, David Bowie's management was taken over by Tony Defries. At the time, he had no recording deal. That gives you an idea of the way Bowie was perceived. He was stone cold. On top of that, he was regarded as a pop artist, not an act with any longevity, although, of course, that was all about to change.

After he had signed to Chrysalis Music, Bowie was in our office in Oxford Street all the time, often pleading with us for money to go and make demos. He would come in with his wife, Angie, a dominant American who appeared to wear the trousers. Our receptionist would ring around and we would all pretend to be out. To his credit though, Bob Grace took a real interest in Bowie and worked with him closely.

Unofficially, since Defries was looking around for a new record deal, we also had the option to sign Bowie to Chrysalis Records. We also considered signing him to Chrysalis agency for his live work, but Kenny Bell, who ran that company, felt he would never make it as a live act.

Bowie made the *Hunky Dory* album at Trident Studios in London and Terry Ellis listened to it. I was in the States at the time. Terry called me and said the album was disappointing. He mentioned one or two songs he particularly disliked. I trusted Terry's judgement on something like that and thought no more of it. So we turned him down and Defries signed Bowie to RCA.

Yet when I eventually returned to the UK and heard *Hunky Dory*, I immediately felt we had made the wrong decision. The album was full of great songs like 'Changes' and 'Life On Mars?'. It included a wonderful composition called 'Oh! You Pretty Things' which Bob Grace placed with Mickie Most for Peter Noone, formerly of Herman's Hermits, who scored a solo hit with his Most-produced version in May 1971. That set the ball rolling and put us well on the way to recouping our investment, though *Hunky Dory* only belatedly made the charts the following year when Bowiemania exploded with *The Rise And Fall Of Ziggy Stardust And The Spiders From Mars*.

As it turned out, the publishing deal gave us the rights to the two albums Bowie had made for Mercury, *Space Oddity* and *The Man Who Sold The World*, as well as *Hunky Dory*, *Ziggy Stardust*, *Aladdin Sane*, *Diamond Dogs* and tracks that ended up on *Young Americans* and *Low*.

After Bowie's success I naturally tried to extend his publishing deal but when Tony Defries turned up two hours late to a lunch with our money man Nick Blackburn, we figured we weren't his main priority. We did renegotiate our existing deal when it ran out in 1975, and Chrysalis Music retained our 25% of David's publishing for the full period of copyright, which will be until 70 years after David's death.

So we missed out on signing one of the greatest recording artists of all time to Chrysalis Records, but he certainly helped our publishing wing get off to a brilliant start.

Chrysalis as a whole was doing great in Britain, beyond Terry's and my wildest dreams, but things were looking a little rocky in America. We had by now discontinued our relationship with Lenny Poncher and appointed Dee Anthony, Lenny's New York man, with whom we had developed a great relationship, as our sole US representative.

Dee's real name was Antonio D'Addario. He was short, quite stout, savvy, streetwise, a very tenacious, pugnacious Italian American. He was extremely friendly and Ten Years After, in particular, took to him. He helped to plan all the tours and had dealt brilliantly with the logistical nightmare of Woodstock.

On our first trip to the US in 1968, Dee had taken me to meet Frank Barsalona of Premier Talent. They were, at the time, a relatively small booking agency. Dee and Frank both came from southern Italian families and were good friends.

Dee proposed we make a long-term commitment with Frank for all the artists we managed, which I agreed to. So we left our first US agency, GAC, and Premier Talent booked the dates for Ten Years After and later became the US agent for Jethro Tull. He was certainly a good man to have on our side but, conversely, would have made a ferocious enemy.

Within a year or two Frank became the foremost booking agent in America, certainly in the area of the growing rock market, and he ended up representing all the major British artists and a great many of the Americans too. The promoters around the country with whom he worked were totally loyal to him, and being part of his organisation was tantamount to being a member of a very select club, whether artist, manager or promoter. But, fall out with Frank and your business could be finished. He was that powerful.

Every time I went to New York, I hung out with both Dee and Frank. I stayed at Dee's apartment on the Upper East Side, living almost like one of his family. His second wife, Valerie, was English. Her father had been involved with the ownership of *Record Mirror*. It was all really fascinating.

Dee had originally been a tour manager, a role that he performed for Tony Bennett who, like most crooners of his era, found himself mixed up with the racket guys in his early career. Through Dee, I met Tony Bennett's first wife, Sandy. The word was that Tony Bennett eventually bought himself out of his underworld contract.

After Dee's association with Tony Bennett was ended, he performed the same role for Buddy Greco, and then the actor and singer George Maharis, but by the time he joined up with Lenny Poncher and with us, he was kicking his heels.

He certainly still retained some connections from his tour management days. On one occasion in New York I was reading the book *The Valachi Papers,* about a gangster called Joseph Valachi, who had been part of the Mafia and had been caught, sent to jail, and then spilt the beans on the whole organisation. Dee was familiar with the story, and expressed zero sympathy for the Mafia informer. One character in the book was a major hit man for the Mafia: the next morning, to my astonishment, the very same guy turned up at Dee's apartment for a cup of coffee. I didn't dare tell him I'd been reading about him the night before!

Later on the same day, Dee and I were driving around the city. We stopped outside an Italian restaurant on the Lower East Side and Dee told me: "Stay in the car." He went in and I sat outside for an hour or more. Eventually Dee came out with a couple of other guys; there were huge smiles and celebrations. Apparently there had been a successful sit-down to resolve a major dispute on the termination terms when Dee had been replaced as manager of another singer. Around the same time, I was in New York when Vito Genovese, who was the *Capo di tutti Capi* – bosses of all bosses – died. Everyone seemed to be at the funeral.

The guys in the groups all liked Dee, Alvin Lee particularly, and things with him seemed to be working well. Dee then started looking after other British acts like Spencer Davis, Humble Pie and Joe Cocker.

I was happy with our relationship and thought nothing of it when Dee asked for a letter confirming our arrangement. I guess I was slightly out of my comfort zone and I said: "Sure, we'll give you 5% of our earnings in America." This was incredibly naïve of me, but on all of the Chrysalis letterheads it said 'No offer contained herein shall constitute a contract' so I assumed the letter had no real legal standing. I meant it as an informal agreement.

Dee Anthony had started his own company, Bandana Enterprises, with his brother Bill and their father. He continued to open doors for us. When Ten Years After played Detroit, we had problems getting hotel rooms because the World Series between the Detroit Tigers and the St. Louis Cardinals was taking place there. Dee made a few calls, got us all rooms and threw in World Series tickets to boot – my first experience of baseball.

Dee's brother Bill was a handsome, personable guy with a huge smile who could have been the maître d' at the Cipriani in Venice. On the road, if we were somewhere where the sun was shining, he would sit by the pool with a sun reflector to make sure his face was permanently tanned. He became our US tour manager and was the ultimate professional. Some nights I might party with the band, go to bed at 3 a.m. and still be bleary-eyed after the wake-up call. I'd go downstairs to breakfast and Bill Anthony would already have been up for an hour and greeting everyone with a huge smile on his face.

Dee started managing US groups too, like The J Geils Band, who he met with me at the Fillmore East. Frank Barsalona had set him up to manage them. Dee hadn't done his homework because he kept calling Peter Wolf, the singer, who was dating Faye Dunaway at the time, Giles. He initially assumed he was the main guy when John

Geils was actually the guitarist. But then anyone could have made the same mistake. When he was singing with The Jeff Beck Group, Rod Stewart got used to people coming up to him to say, "Jeff, you were great and your guitarist is pretty good too."

Dee was certainly at the opposite end of the music industry spectrum to the hippies of California. Before Ten Years After gigs, he would slip the compere $100 to whip up the stage announcements and say, "This is the greatest group in the world!" He was a hands-on talent coach. He would give the acts pep talks, drill stage moves into them, and other tricks to win audiences over.

By 1970, both Ten Years After and Jethro Tull were doing really well in the US. Dee was great at making them feel wonderful. Limousines and first-class travel and hotels were the order of the day. But, at the end of each tour, after he had taken his percentage, there wasn't any money left because it had all gone on expenses.

Dee wanted the groups to love him and they did. But it came at a cost, and when the tour failed to produce any take-home pay, it was Terry and I who got the blame. Terry Ellis saw the problem quite clearly and said: "We've got to get out of this situation and start our own company in the US as well. We can do it ourselves; we don't need Dee. If we don't, we're going to have a huge problem." I knew he was completely right.

Predictably, getting out of our so-called informal agreement proved to be more difficult than we thought. Was our contract with him legally binding? All that we had ever signed was my letter promising 5%. So in January 1970 we bit the bullet and announced the opening of our own US operation.

We hired Derek Sutton, an old friend of Terry's from Newcastle University who was working in Vancouver, to run our US arm. Terry was still smarting a little that it was my mate Doug D'Arcy from Manchester University who had joined us in London and he wanted to redress the balance. We flew Derek to New York, rented Chrysalis an apartment at 350 East 65th Street, hired a secretary and readied ourselves to go it alone.

The first call that Derek took in New York was from Dee Anthony. Dee told him: "You'd better get out of town or you'll be at the bottom of the Hudson River with concrete boots. Right?" Then he hung up. It was quite a baptism of fire for poor Derek, who at the time had no music business experience, and certainly none of dealing with mob-like threats of that nature.

We booked American tours for Ten Years After and Jethro Tull and Dee managed to secure an injunction to halt the tours. A major court case loomed and when Terry Ellis, Nick Blackburn and I flew into New York for the trial I confess I was feeling pretty scared. We were very careful about where we went at night and I knew if the verdict went against us, we could be finished in America.

On the first day of the trial, the judge took both sides aside in an anteroom and told us that we had to settle out of court. It took three days of tense and fraught negotiation to thrash out a deal and we finally settled on the courtroom steps. We agreed to pay Dee $186,000 and we had three years to pay it off. That was what it cost to extricate ourselves from the situation and start Chrysalis' own operation in the United States. It was a terribly painful learning curve, and a huge amount of money to find, but absolutely necessary.

I was concerned that Alvin Lee might react badly as of all the artists, he was the closest to Dee. Dee had always seen Alvin's potential, which did not always endear him to the other members of Ten Years After. But he was supportive of what we had done, and we were able to move on.

Terry Ellis had been the most prepared for battle and had been strong throughout the crisis. Maybe it was easier for him as he did not enjoy the same relationship with Dee as I had. Ian Anderson was another who wasn't taken in by Dee's bonhomie. We had certainly lost control of the situation, and we had to act fast or we would have been finished.

In truth, everybody seemed to fall out with Dee Anthony sooner or later: Steve Marriott and the guys from Humble Pie, even Peter Frampton. Dee did a great job with *Frampton Comes*

Alive! in the mid-seventies, and turned it into the biggest-selling live album of all time. Peter was a bit like a fresher faced, less heavy version of Alvin. Dee made him into a huge pop star, although he would probably have been more comfortable to be positioned as a skilled guitarist.

However, after the enormous success of *Frampton Comes Alive!*, Dee got him to star in the film based on the Beatles album *Sgt Pepper's Lonely Hearts Club Band* which was produced by Robert Stigwood. A monumental disaster, the film cut Peter's career stone dead. Not Stigwood's, though: he went on to do rather better a year or so later with *Saturday Night Fever* and then with *Grease*.

Dee Anthony had three rules for success. The first was 'always get the money', the second was 'don't forget to always get the money' and the third was 'don't forget that, whatever else you've done, to make sure you get the money'. He was one tough cookie.

But I try never to carry a grudge for too long and I made up with Dee a few years down the line. He died in October 2009, but his family's presence in the music industry continues: his daughter, Michele, is a very senior executive who spent many years as an Executive Vice President at Sony Records.

Dee was very good with the live side of things and I hope I was too. With Ten Years After, I would help write the set list, tell them to drop a number that wasn't working and would pick the encores according to the audience's reaction when they came off. I always told Alvin Lee: "They also hear what they see. If you're just standing there, they think it's dull. But if you move around and shake your head, they think 'Wow'". And Alvin, with his trademark blondish locks, white clogs, and his red Gibson guitar with the peace symbol, became a truly amazing performer.

Procol Harum were a different matter. Keith Reid, the lyricist, was an equal but non-performing member of the group and he went on the road with them. He really did not need to, as his lyrics were a fundamental component of what made the band so special, but I believe he felt the need to justify receiving his share of the concert income. Keith would make himself "useful" by preparing a set list, and insisting it was a different one every night.

It was crazy. It's not like doing a menu for a dinner party and saying, "Last night, we had lamb, so tonight we're going to have chicken." Last night, we were in Detroit, tonight we're in Chicago. Nobody at tonight's show saw last night. It worked really well, you don't need to change it, apart from dropping the odd number and putting something else in. And they always changed the encores too!

Procol Harum had so much potential. The first album they made for Chrysalis was *Broken Barricades* in 1971. Robin Trower, the lead guitarist, was trying to exert more influence on the group and the album had much more of a rock sound but he left at the end of that year and was replaced by Dave Ball.

In September 1970, following the Isle of Wight festival, Procol Harum and Ten Years After had played on the same bill as Jimi Hendrix at the Deutschlandhalle in Berlin. That was Jimi's penultimate gig before he died. Trower was exceptional and Hendrix said to him something along the lines of "I am passing my mantle on to you." When Jimi died in London two weeks later, Robin took it as his sign to set out on his own. However, he stayed with Chrysalis, both for management and recording.

One of the best things we did when we took over the management of Procol Harum was to have them re-record several of their classic tracks in a live setting with an orchestra. In November 1971, they were invited to perform with the Edmonton Symphony Orchestra in Canada, which provided the ideal opportunity for both a recording and a relaunch. Gary Brooker did the arrangements, writing out some of the charts for the orchestra on the flight out there.

Due to re-recording restrictions, we were unable to include 'A Whiter Shade Of Pale' and 'Homburg' but, at the insistence of Jerry Moss, they performed a wonderful version of 'Conquistador' which became a huge hit around the world and generated an enormous amount of interest in the *Procol Harum Live In Concert With The*

Edmonton Symphony Orchestra album. It remains their best-selling album and completely regenerated their career.

They had a huge cult following in the States. I remember once in New York, after the group had done about 10 encores at the Fillmore East, the entire audience refused to leave and eventually ended up doing the conga all the way down Second Avenue at two o'clock in the morning. On another occasion, at the Grande Ballroom in Detroit, the power went off halfway through 'A Whiter Shade Of Pale' and stayed off for a good 10 or 15 minutes. The entire audience sang the song in unison until the power returned and the band were able to join in again.

Procol Harum had their great moments but their bad times too. In Tokyo, they got so drunk on sake that they ended up performing 'Bringing Home The Bacon' three or four times in a row without realising it. Whenever I was asked who was the best group I worked with in a live situation, and who was the worst, my answer would always be the same: Procol Harum. They were incredible on a good night and incredibly bad on a bad night.

Grand Hotel, their 1973 album, was a great record, one of their classics, with a brilliant title track alongside 'Toujours L'Amour' and 'A Souvenir From London', the single that was banned by the BBC, inevitably perhaps because the lyrics were about a sexually transmitted disease. The album had a wonderful *fin de siècle* flavour. The atmospheric title track gave the writer Douglas Adams the idea for *The Restaurant At The End Of The Universe*, the second book of *The Hitchhiker's Guide To The Galaxy*.

With the group's contract with A&M at an end, in April 1973 *Grand Hotel* was the first album released on the Chrysalis label in America, with distribution through Warner Brothers. We had a big launch party for the album at the Plaza Hotel in New York with everyone, including the band, wearing long black formal coats, with white waistcoats and white bow ties, as they are dressed on the album cover. Carly Simon, James Taylor and Andy Warhol all attended.

The band's 1974 album *Exotic Birds And Fruit* also featured some wonderful material like 'Nothing But The Truth' and 'As Strong As Samson'. The song 'Butterfly Boys', about Terry and I, has a chorus that runs: "Those Butterfly Boys, at play with their toys." We suggested they change the lyrics and the title to 'Government Boys', but they quite rightly refused.

There are still people out there who know Procol Harum only for 'A Whiter Shade Of Pale'. They are missing out: they were a great and highly innovative group, with brilliant music and lyrics.

With the Dee Anthony court case resolved, the New York apartment at 350 East 65th Street became the base for all of our US operations. Derek Sutton lived there and Terry Ellis, myself and other members of the company would stay in the guest bedroom when in town. It served as an office, a hang-out, and a crash pad. The location was superb, right on First Avenue, and on the same block as Maxwell's Plum, at the time one of New York's hottest singles bars.

The US company we formed was called Chrysalis Artists Services Inc – or CASI, for short. Although it never occurred to us at the time, a few of our acquaintances found this acronym rather amusing.

Nick Blackburn, our 'groovy accountant', distinguished himself on his first trip to the States. From New York he spent a few days on the road. His first stop was Chicago, where he ended up with a *Playboy* centrefold model. He then returned to Manhattan. I called up from London the day after he arrived to speak to Bob Garcia, the press officer for A&M Records, to check on the progress of the Procol Harum album.

"I met your accountant last night," he informed me.

"How did you find him?" I inquired.

"Stoned, naked and with a prostitute," Bob replied.

Bob had been out to dinner with Derek Sutton, and when they returned to the apartment they had caught our money man in flagrante. Nick was to claim that he had met an important local madam, who was so impressed by him that she offered him her best girl for free. He still insists that is true, even today.

Nick's Big Apple experiences certainly showed him a different world, and soon after he left for a job at Decca Records. He later took over the Procol Harum management before running See Tickets, the UK's largest ticketing company. His marriage lasted many years. When his wife divorced him, on the discovery of an affair, Nick asked for 185 other counts of adultery to be taken into consideration.

My own love live was very happily starred at that time. Chelle spent quite a bit of time on the road with me. We generally had a no-girlfriends-on-the-road policy for bands and managements alike, but we relaxed it now and then when it suited us.

Yet her lack of a British passport caused her all sorts of problems with permits and visas and she often had a difficult time at the immigration desk. We were getting on really well so we decided to get married, and chose to do so on March 15, 1972, the 25th anniversary of her parents' wedding.

The ceremony took place at the Church of St Martin In The Fields at Trafalgar Square in London, and was conducted by the rector, the Reverend Williams, the father of Doug D'Arcy's future wife, Kate, who was also our bridesmaid.

After a reception at the Hurlingham Club Chelle and I had a very short break. That is all I had time for. I had bought an old Bentley Continental, which we drove down to the south-west of France for a long weekend. Then it was back to work. However, a few months later, both Ten Years After and Procol Harum went on tour to Japan, after which Chelle and I took off for a couple of weeks and had a well-earned delayed honeymoon.

We went to Hong Kong, Bangkok – both of which in those days were very different from how they are now. Our main mode of transport in Hong Kong was rickshaws, powered by coolies. In Bangkok, there was an old lady with a rickety boat who rowed you across the main Chao Phraya river. Nowadays of course, it is criss-crossed by a zillion freeways.

Chelle and I then flew to Kathmandu in Nepal, a major centre on the hippy trail, stayed there for a few days and went on to Delhi and

Agra in India. It was a wonderful time, and it was to change our lives more than we could ever imagine – our first son, Tim, was conceived during this idyllic trip.

The tour of Japan was Procol's first, but Ten Years After had already toured there the year before, and had gone down extremely well. The promoter, Mr Udo, expected them to do even better business second time round, but this did not happen, and he ended up losing money. The Japanese market in those days was relatively unsophisticated and a lot of people clearly decided, 'Oh, I've seen Ten Years After before – I don't need to see them again." As I wanted to protect the ability of both groups to return, I even refunded part of the fee.

Mr Udo is the most important promoter there and hugely important in the Japanese music industry. I met him recently on a trip to Tokyo. He told me I was the first person to ever do this for him, and also the last! The tour was also memorable for the fact that Procol managed to literally drink the plane dry on the flight from Honolulu to Tokyo.

We had to try to devise a career path for Robin Trower post-Procol Harum. I hadn't tried to talk him out of leaving the band. Hendrix's death had convinced him he had to make his own mark and there wasn't much we could do about it. In any case, from a business perspective, a split wasn't always a bad thing. We sometimes ended up with two groups for the price of one as had happened with Jethro Tull and Blodwyn Pig. Glenn Cornick, the original Jethro Tull bass player, had left after *Benefit* and formed Wild Turkey in 1971, and they too were reasonably successful.

At first we put Trower into a band called Jude with Frankie Miller, a singer from Scotland we always thought had a fabulous voice. Jude also featured Clive Bunker, also ex-Jethro Tull, on drums and Jimmy Dewar from Stone The Crows on bass. It was when supergroups were in vogue and I suppose we were thinking along those lines.

Jude rehearsed for a while but you never know when something is going to work and when it isn't. Their widely anticipated first date took place at St Albans Town Hall on a Saturday night. Nick and I were at the gig. We had driven up to Manchester to see City beat West Ham 3-1. It was the season City looked like becoming champions, until they signed Rodney Marsh from QPR, after which their season went pear-shaped. When we arrived at the venue, Jude, to our amazement, died a death. It just didn't work, which was a surprise to everyone, and the group broke up soon after.

Trower then formed a three-piece with Dewar, who took over vocal duties, and Reg Isidore, a black drummer from the Dutch Antilles. We didn't know what to expect. The first gig we booked them was in Kiel in Germany and I flew over for it. They were utterly brilliant and brought the house down. It was amazing that two similar groups could be so different. Jude, the one we thought had all the right ingredients, didn't work and the one that was just short of the right ingredients worked like magic.

The first Robin Trower album, *Twice Removed From Yesterday*, was released on the Chrysalis label worldwide, including America, in 1973, but my favourite is the next one, *Bridge Of Sighs*, one of the best records Chrysalis ever put out. The title song was incredibly atmospheric, but tracks like 'Day Of The Eagle' and 'Too Rolling Stoned' were iconic.

Unfortunately, to the immense dismay of Warners in the States, Terry, by now responsible for the US record company, was fixated on the fact that an act like Robin Trower should not release a single that early in their career, à la Led Zeppelin. I believe in hindsight that this was a mistake, and that the album would have been multi-platinum on the back of a hit single. Regardless it was still a gold record, and launched the group as a major concert attraction.

Chrysalis' growing success meant we were now able to attract other artists to the label, as well as the ones we managed. After an Irish folk duo, Tír na nÓg, the first significant non-management act that we signed was the electric folk group Steeleye Span in 1972. Their singer, Maddy Prior, had a hugely distinctive voice and they became very popular.

Steeleye Span were originally managed by Joe Lustig, a pugnacious New Yorker living in London who was very active on the UK folk scene. They then passed into the care of Tony Secunda, a larger-than-life figure who had achieved notoriety in 1967 when he distributed a cartoon postcard to promote a single by The Move. It defamed Prime Minister Harold Wilson, who sued, and the band were forced to pay all of the royalties from the song 'Flowers In The Rain' to charity.

Secunda continued his stunts with Steeleye Span – at one gig at the Hammersmith Apollo, he sprinkled around one thousand £5 notes over the audience from the roof of the venue during the show. The band were doing really well. They had a big hit at the end of 1973 with the Xmas carol 'Gaudete' and a Top 5 single in 1975 with another traditional song, 'All Around My Hat'. We had no idea that a variant of that number was an Irish republican anthem, but the Troubles blighting that country were about to impact on us in a very direct manner.

Ten Years After, however, remained one of our major artists. Although when I had extricated them from their London Records deal I had signed them to Columbia in the US, when the time came for them to leave Decca in the UK I arranged for them to join the Chrysalis label for all territories outside America.

The Woodstock effect had still not played out for them. Following the enormity of their sudden worldwide fame, Alvin Lee found it hard to cope with the attendant stress and had taken a decision to step back from the craziness. He told me that, as their manager, I had made them too successful and that he wanted to withdraw and not tour for a while. It may sound a strange decision now but it made sense then: after all, contemporaries and friends such as Jimi Hendrix, Janis Joplin and Jim Morrison had all lost control of their lives post-fame and died.

Alvin hooked up with a white American gospel singer called Mylon LeFevre and recorded an album, *On The Road To Freedom*, at George Harrison's home studio in Henley-on-Thames. It also featured contributions from Jim Capaldi and Steve Winwood from

Traffic, Ronnie Wood from The Faces and Mick Fleetwood from Fleetwood Mac, but even with all these famous names it was still a tough sell.

Luckily, Jethro Tull were going from strength to strength. The success of the classic *Aqualung* album worldwide propelled them to new heights, and by now only Led Zeppelin were out-grossing them in America. Things were moving away from pure blues-based rock groups, and progressive groups like Yes, King Crimson, Genesis and Pink Floyd, all doing more intricate and interesting things, were taking over. Jethro Tull became part of that progressive scene and soon surpassed the almost semi-retired Ten Years After as Chrysalis' biggest earners

As my 30th birthday neared, life seemed pretty good. I spent the days before it in the south of France with Ten Years After keyboard player Chick Churchill and his wife, Suzanne, the Isle of Wight landlady's daughter. I had recently been best man at their wedding. Chelle and I then marked my birthday in style, chartering a dilapidated old boat to cruise around Corsica, a trip I have repeated many times since.

November saw the arrival of a younger brother to Tim as Chelle gave birth to Thomas in November 1974. I nearly missed the birth. Chelle went into hospital to be induced and I was told to call in about three or four hours to learn what was happening. I had reason to call 30 minutes later to ask Chelle something and I was told she was already in labour. This necessitated a very speedy drive through London's streets. I arrived just in time for Thomas' arrival.

With my business and personal life both blooming, it was hard to see how things could get much better. But one terrifying evening in London, they found a way to get much, much worse.

By now, Chrysalis had moved further down Oxford Street to 388–396, closer to Marble Arch and next door to Selfridges department store. I had a corner office that overlooked one side of the department store, with Terry down the other end of the office. On December 19, 1974, I was working late with my secretary, Christine Ellis Jones, when I became aware of police sirens going off and officers clearing Oxford Street below us.

The police activity seemed to be centred on a car that was parked in the middle of a junction right below our office. This was in the years when the IRA was in the habit of mounting pre-Christmas bombing campaigns in London, and when I phoned Chelle to tell her I was stuck in the office and might be late home, she immediately said, "It could be a bomb: get out of the office!"

How prescient my wife was. Christine and I left the office, got as far as reception and were suddenly poleaxed by a ferocious explosion. It felt like someone had hit me on the back of the head with a sledgehammer. When we came round a few minutes later, we were surrounded by scenes of utter devastation.

The building looked like a war zone and my office had been destroyed beyond recognition. Every single pane of glass had been blown out, the furniture was upended, the stereo had been thrown from one side of the room to the other. Had I not heeded Chelle's advice, or had I even hesitated for a few seconds, there is no way I would have survived the blast.

It later emerged that Selfridges was the IRA's target and the bomb had been on a timer. The terrorists had phoned through three warnings just before the blast, enabling the police to evacuate the streets. The car that exploded ended up on the roof of an adjacent building: even Terry's office, at the far end of our building, was a wreck.

There was no question: as 1974 ended I might have felt on top of the world, but I had also been 30 seconds from meeting my maker. It was not an experience that I wanted ever to repeat. First my near-death from nicotine, and now this: I was beginning to wonder if somebody up there was looking after me.

CHAPTER 7

Over The Rainbow

The IRA attack had left our offices badly in need of redecoration. I decided I knew just the man for the job. I decided to get funky – or, to be precise, Funky Paul.

Paul Olsen was an artist from San Francisco, who designed amazing psychedelic posters and had moved to London in 1970. He had latched on to Procol Harum and created striking covers for three Robin Trower albums: *Twice Removed From Yesterday*, *Bridge Of Sighs* and *For Earth Below*. His paintings were optical illusions that misleadingly appeared to be three-dimensional but, of course, were actually not.

Funky Paul came up with the concept that every office door in Chrysalis – press, promotion, marketing, A&R, finance – would be painted with something related to that department. For weeks he came in at six in the evening and painted through the night, when no one else was around.

It was a labour of love for Paul and he was clearly possessed of an artistic temperament, because he flipped one day when Terry Ellis – who was not enthralled by the project, probably because it had been my idea – came in from an overnight flight from the States and rudely asked him, "Are you ever going to get this thing finished?"

Funky Paul didn't say anything then, but when we all arrived at work the next morning, he had painted every single door plain white. All of his gorgeous creations were destroyed. I was totally distraught, because his work was fantastic. Sadly, we hadn't even taken any photographs to remember it by.

It wasn't the first time that Terry's brusque and insensitive style had caused ructions in the office. At one point, peeved by the fact that some staff members were getting in late in the mornings, he wanted to install a factory-style clocking-in and clocking-out machine. Luckily, I managed to talk him out of that one.

Nevertheless, it was clear that problems were developing between Terry and myself. Terry had changed since I had met him six years earlier. He had moved from his flat, bizarrely and unknowingly above an upmarket brothel in Mayfair, to a mansion in north London, to which he had flown a young Danish architect from Copenhagen to make major renovations. He was dating Flick Colby, the glamorous choreographer of Pan's People, the female dance troupe from *Top Of The Pops*, and seemed to view himself as essentially an international jet-setter ready to leave grey England in his wake.

He was to get his chance. The miners' strike of 1973 had done for Edward Heath's Conservative government (personally, I had found the evenings by candlelight quite romantic, if admittedly inconvenient) and Labour returned to power under Harold Wilson in 1974. This dismayed many people around me, but my radical fires had not totally gone out and, initially, I was quietly pleased.

The new Chancellor, Denis Healey, announced his intention to "squeeze the rich until the pips squeaked" and introduced punitive rates of tax for top earners: 83% on earned income and 98% on investment income. Terry decided that he had to become a tax exile. I toyed with the idea myself but having a wife and a young family, as well as running Chrysalis, it didn't seem a viable option plus – strange as it may sound – I wasn't doing what I did just for the money. I was doing it because I loved it.

Terry, who in any case was spending vast swathes of time on the road, had no such compunction. He considered buying a house in Switzerland, before settling on a move to Tortola in the British Virgin Islands, where he built himself an exquisite cliff-top retreat.

He then turned his sights on me. With Ten Years After now touring less regularly than previously, Terry decided that, via the Jethro Tull management percentage, he was now generating far more income for the company than I was. This ignored the fact that we had decided that I would concentrate on building the record company, and that I had introduced Tull to Chrysalis in the first place.

Terry thus decided to start a new business without my involvement. Based in Tortola, he would run Friday Management together with Clive Walter, his original flatmate when we had first started the business. The logo was a footprint in the sand, representing Robinson Crusoe finding Friday on his island.

The first act managed by Friday was Gentle Giant, a progressive rock band formed in 1970 by the Shulman brothers who had previously been the core members of Simon Dupree & The Big Sound. They had supported Jethro Tull in 1972 and had by now made six albums. *Free Hand*, their first album for Chrysalis in 1975, reached the Top 50 in the US, but they never matched that with any of the five subsequent releases.

I was extremely upset by Terry's actions, but I didn't want to break up the partnership so I chose to ignore it and carried on looking after the British end of the operation. However, because Terry and I publicly appeared to be joined at the hip, everybody assumed I was involved with Friday Management too, and so Gentle Giant would call me if things went wrong.

We then had to incorporate Clive Walter into the overall Chrysalis management structure, which was completely unnecessary. Friday probably lasted for about a year and was a complete disaster. In fact the only good thing about the whole operation was the design of the logo, something that Terry was always particularly good at. The whole episode caused a great deal of resentment on my part, and to some extent, I never truly got over it.

Jethro Tull also became tax exiles. Having supplanted Ten Years After as Chrysalis' main act, they were by now very much Terry's group, which doubtless gave Terry his sense of entitlement. He had an impenetrably close relationship with Ian Anderson: Ian wrote a song about him, called 'The Teacher', and Terry dated a girl called Jennie Franks, who worked at Chrysalis, before she later became Ian's first wife.

Despite his outlandish hippy image, with the long coat, hair and beard, Ian Anderson was one of the straightest, brightest and most normal individuals you could ever wish to meet, and not at all the wild man of rock that audiences imagined. In fact, Jethro Tull as a band didn't go big on partying.

The fact that Ian cut such a distinctive figure as he played the flute on one leg undoubtedly helped Tull's status. He would reinvent the band at will, bringing in new players like John Evan (I believe he was born John Evans, but his performing name was Evan), the keyboard-player and the man the original band had been named after, and the arranger David Palmer, a seemingly extremely straight guy who was later to undergo a sex-change operation.

Under Ian's tutelage, Jethro Tull moved quickly away from the blues and forged a unique sound with bizarre time signatures. Their biggest album, *Aqualung,* felt like a concept album without quite being one and bore a cover image caricaturing Ian as an old man.

However, with the heavily conceptual albums *Thick As A Brick* and *A Passion Play*, Tull suffered a critical backlash in the UK even as they topped the charts in America. They became tax exiles, moved to Monte Carlo and made *Minstrel In The Gallery* in 1975. Becoming homesick, they returned to Britain, precipitating the collapse of their tax scheme.

When Jethro Tull released *Heavy Horses* in 1978 – a record loved by Tim Rice, who regards Ian Anderson as one of rock's all-time great lyricists – I made the point to Ian that his fanbase probably wasn't particularly interested in old English shire horses. However, he was adamant that he had to reflect his life's experiences: he had left behind his lonely Shepherd's Bush bedsit years, and couldn't write about them any more.

His lifestyle diversified even further when he started his salmon farm and smoked salmon factory in Scotland. Strathaird Salmon Ltd was soon supplying places like Harrods and Harvey Nichols – not to mention Concorde. Chances are, if you were flying supersonic on BA in the eighties or nineties, you were eating Ian Anderson's smoked salmon.

But this was all in the future. Back in the mid-seventies, Chrysalis was going through fraught times and I could do little except put my head down and get on with running the business. Having decided we no longer wanted to manage bands that weren't signed to the label, we set about trying to extricate Supertramp, who I had been looking after for a while, from their contract with A&M Records in London.

Having told the head of A&M, my good friend Derek Green, that their current contract was no longer valid as Supertramp had had so many line-up changes, I demanded so much money and so many stringent conditions in our favour that Derek would surely walk away. The plan was then to sign them to Chrysalis. I could have fallen off my chair when Derek called me back and agreed to all of my terms. It transpired that A&M's head of A&R, Dave Margereson, had fallen in love with Supertramp and persuaded Derek to break the bank to re-sign them.

Having decided I wouldn't manage non-Chrysalis artists, I therefore phoned up Supertramp to inform them that I had secured them a new contract beyond their wildest dreams and was also handing them back their management contract. Some time later Dave Margereson would leave A&M to become their manager and I looked on as Supertramp recorded *Crime Of The Century*, one of the best albums ever made, and became one of the seventies biggest bands. Looking back, it was not one of the smartest decisions of my life.

Yet for every missed opportunity, there was also a stroke of good fortune. One morning, on a train into London, I bumped into Alistair Rainsford, the financial adviser and accountant for George Martin's company Associated Independent Recording (AIR). I knew Alistair as he had married Dawn Ralston, Chrysalis' original Girl Friday.

I had just come back from a States trip and so was a little out of the loop, and Alistair looked surprised when I asked him how things were going.

"Haven't you heard?" he asked. "All hell broke loose yesterday. We were selling the company to Dick James, the music publisher. The deal was ready to be signed. We were all in the lawyer's office. George Martin was about to sign when he noticed that, as part of his deal, he had to carry on working for the company for three years and report to Dick James.

"George said: 'I'm not going to work for you, Dick.' Dick replied: 'That's part of the deal. I just want to have the privilege of knowing you're working for me for the next three years.' George blew up and stormed out of the meeting. The whole deal is off."

This didn't seem the end of the world to me, but Alistair explained that one or two of George's partners had already decided how they were going to spend the money. A light bulb came on over my head.

"Tell George," I said, "that, if he's interested, I'll give him exactly the same deal that he had with Dick James and there won't be a personal service clause in the contract. He doesn't have to work for me at all if he doesn't want to."

Did I think this would actually happen? Probably not, but I got a call later that day saying: "Let's talk." We agreed a £1m deal for AIR that was signed in less than two weeks. The whole transaction had been driven entirely by my gut instinct, which is a theme that has recurred throughout my business life.

My offer might have sounded altruistic but was actually decidedly canny. Dick James was a very smart operator and I knew he would never agree to a deal that was not tilted in his favour. Before he became a music publisher and formed DJM Records to launch Elton

John, he had been a singer, enjoying a big hit with the theme song to the TV series *The Adventures Of Robin Hood*.

When Beatles manager Brian Epstein was looking for a publisher for 'Please Please Me', George Martin recommended he see Dick James who was just starting out and was full of energy and motivation. George had basically handed The Beatles to Dick, who consequently co-founded Northern Songs to publish their catalogue and became extremely rich. In his mind, George had made Dick, and so the idea of working for him was anathema to him.

To the astonishment of the AIR partners, the first thing we did when we bought the company was to audit EMI over The Beatles' producer royalties. In doing this, we almost recouped the entire £1 million that the deal had cost. We also picked up the internationally renowned studios near Oxford Circus, a continuing percentage of George's Beatles income, and the royalties generated by the other producers, plus some music-publishing rights.

Overall, Chrysalis' original investment in AIR has been paid back countless times over. AIR also owned a music publishing company in Scandinavia and Air-Edel, a company producing advertising jingles and TV and film music. That was a joint venture between AIR and Herman Edel, a New Yorker who moved to Aspen in Colorado and served two terms as mayor there.

The other tremendous bonus of the deal was that I became great friends with George Martin and his wife, Judy. After the AIR acquisition, he accepted my offer of a place on the Chrysalis board and held it for more than 30 years. George is a man of huge integrity and has been extremely loyal to me over the many years we have been involved with each other. A total gentleman, he is worthy of every single accolade he has received.

Chrysalis by now had a very diverse portfolio. A few years earlier we had taken over the lease of an old movie house in north London called the Finsbury Park Astoria that had hosted big-name package shows, including shows by The Beatles, and Stax revues in the sixties. Terry and I had taken over the building, totally refurbished it, renamed it the Rainbow Theatre and tried to create a Fillmore-style operation in London.

For a while it lived up to its expectations. The first act we had promoted there was The Who, who played three nights, November 4-6, 1971, and were absolutely brilliant. A chorus line of dancing girls preceded The Who on to the stage after an opening address by the theatre's manager, John Morris, who'd been the stage manager at Woodstock. The light show had been imported for the occasion from the Fillmore East, a venue from which the Rainbow took much of its approach. "Thanks for coming," Pete Townshend told the audience. "I suppose you had to come really, 'cause there's nowhere else to go, is there?"

Infamously, in December 1971, Frank Zappa was badly injured when he fell into the orchestra pit after being pushed off stage by a man who was evidently jealous that his girlfriend preferred Frank to him. In February 1972 Pink Floyd played four consecutive nights, premiering *The Dark Side Of The Moon*.

David Bowie had rehearsed and opened the second leg of his Ziggy Stardust tour there in 1972, with Roxy Music as support. Procol Harum played there with The Royal Philarmonic Orchestra.

The Rainbow also hosted some amazing one-off events. There was an all-star version of The Who rock opera *Tommy* presented by Lou Reizner with the London Symphony Orchestra backing Roger Daltrey, Pete Townshend, Steve Winwood, Sandy Denny, Ringo Starr, Rod Stewart and Peter Sellers. Pete Townshend talked Eric Clapton into doing a comeback concert featuring Ronnie Wood, Winwood and Jim Capaldi from Traffic that became a famous live album: *Eric Clapton's Rainbow Concert*.

True to form, Chuck Berry had insisted he wanted cash before going on stage and we had to come up with the fee on the spot from the box-office takings and whatever cash the staff had on them. Deep Purple were declared the loudest band in the world after the *Guinness Book Of Records* measured the volume level of their performance at the Rainbow in February 1973.

After the Clapton album, several other acts had recorded at the Rainbow. *It's Too Late To Stop Now*, the classic set by Van Morrison and the Caledonia Soul Orchestra, drew on his concerts there. Alvin Lee recorded *In Flight* at the Rainbow. Kevin Ayers, John Cale, Nico and Eno gave a memorable concert captured on the live album *June 1, 1974*. Thanks to Terry's liaison with Flick Colby, we even had Pan's People on stage with Jethro Tull!

We hadn't just promoted concerts. Liza Minnelli and Charles Aznavour filmed a TV special and we also showed films and the big boxing fights like the Rumble In The Jungle, Muhammad Ali's 1974 clash with George Foreman, via a satellite link from Zaire. However, try as we might, the overheads at the Rainbow were too high unless we had something on every night, and in 1975 Terry and I reluctantly decided to close it down.

We bowed out in style with a farewell concert on March 16, 1975. It featured Sassafras and Procol Harum, who also backed Frankie Miller, as well as Hatfield and the North and Kevin Coyne, two of the original signings to Richard Branson's Virgin, and John Martyn and Richard and Linda Thompson. *Over The Rainbow: The Last Concert, Live!* remains a lovely time capsule. The Rainbow went dark until January 1977. In 1995, the building was taken over by its current owners, a branch of the Pentecostal church.

We had tried our best but, I suppose, learned an important business lesson – even when the heart is right behind a project, there are no guaranteed successes in the music industry.

CHAPTER 8

The Show Must Go On

Chrysalis might have begun as an eclectic label for blues rock or progressive rock groups – or folk, in the case of Steeleye Span – but it was the worldwide success of Leo Sayer that took us into a different area completely.

When we signed Leo in 1973, he was co-managed by former pop star and actor Adam Faith and songwriter David Courtney. Between the three of them, they had written all of Roger Daltrey's first solo album, including the hit single 'Giving It All Away'.

When Leo's own debut, *Silverbird*, arrived in 1974 he already had an extremely striking image and identity. He wore make-up and dressed as a clown, a Pierrot, after his hero, mime artist Marcel Marceau. He made an incredible impression singing the single 'The Show Must Go On' on *Top Of The Pops* and quickly exploded. Both the album and the single went to number two in the UK, and he supported Roxy Music on a European tour.

By the time of his follow-up album, *Just A Boy*, he had ditched the Pierrot image for a Gatsby look, and had hits with 'One Man Band' and 'Long Tall Glasses (I Can Dance)'. That second album really set him up but what we really wanted was to break him in America.

Leo was already signed to Warner Brothers in America, as his management took the view that our operation there was still too much in its infancy, but as Warner was the US distributor for Chrysalis we had a very good relationship with the company. Our LA lawyer, Abe Somer, was very friendly with Richard Perry, who had produced Harry Nilsson and Carly Simon and we persuaded Richard to produce *Endless Flight*, the fourth Leo album.

This album was a masterpiece and ended up spawning five huge hit singles. When it was delivered we had a playback at AIR studios and the whole company was blown away. I particularly liked the ballad 'When I Need You', written by Albert Hammond and Carole Bayer Sager.

We went back to the office to talk through the project. 'You Make Me Feel Like Dancing' was all set to be the first single but I put forward an alternative plan: "What's really going to sell this album is 'When I Need You'. If we have that out at Christmas, it will be number one worldwide and we will sell millions." A flabbergasted Adam Faith replied: "Really? Do you think so?" I said: "I'm absolutely bloody sure. That is a monster, that record will be huge."

Adam asked me if he could make a phone call and promptly got hold of Richard Perry in LA to ask if he could stop the factory pressing the single, as Warners had scheduled 'When I Need You' as the flip side to 'You Make Me Feel Like Dancing'. They had no idea what they were sitting on, and had we called a few minutes later, the track would have been buried as a B-side.

There was a great buzz on the record. We booked Leo into the Roxy on Sunset Strip in Los Angeles on the week of the US release in November, 1976, and 'When I Need You' was, as I predicted, a huge worldwide hit. Richard Perry had assembled an amazing cast of session musicians, who would also tour with Leo. On the album, the song didn't originally have the saxophone solo: the middle eight was just a little burst of keyboard and nothing else. But the live version with the sax worked so well that I decided to drop that on to the single.

102

'When I Need You' topped both the UK and the US charts in 1977, and – very excitingly for us - was Chrysalis' first number one single. Leo was both delighted and relieved, as three previous singles had peaked at number two in Britain.

The week at the Roxy was a real triumph. You could feel a star being born, and each night the vibe grew. By Saturday, it was party time for all of us. It was one of those nights when you wake up wondering how you ended up where you were. I left the party with a girl called Nancy, who was wearing a sailor suit outfit, and woke up on a mattress in Santa Monica!

Richard Perry also produced the next two albums, *Thunder In My Heart* and *Leo Sayer*, the one with 'I Can't Stop Loving You (Though I Try)' and 'Raining In My Heart'. Leo was a strong writer but he soon started to move away from his image as a credible singer-songwriter, and instead became a purely pop artist with, inevitably, a limited shelf life. I really believe that he could have become a David Bowie or a Cliff Richard figure, but on stage he would do odd things, such as impersonations of Frank Spencer. It's safe to say that you wouldn't catch Bowie doing that.

Adam Faith and I always worked very closely on Leo Sayer. Adam had, to put it mildly, a full social life. He had a few liaisons which his wife, Jackie, may have been aware of, and quite a few that she probably was not, including one with the US tennis icon Chris Evert that he told me about. They apparently made a pact to leave their respective partners, in Evert's case British tennis player John Loyd. Adam had agreed to meet her in Miami but he chickened out at the last minute, and didn't take his flight.

Adam's real name was Terry Nelhams-Wright and all his friends called him Terry or Tel. In turn, he usually called everyone "cock", however high or mighty they might be. At his insistence we learned to fly together and he nearly killed himself flying a helicopter. I was close to getting my own licence but quickly abandoned choppers.

Adam was certainly no stranger to scrapes. In 1973 he had almost died and nearly lost a leg after a horrific car crash in the early hours of the morning near his home in Sussex. He was so poorly in hospital that he asked me to look after Leo and take over the management. I declined, and told him to stay positive until he recovered, otherwise he would end up regretting it. Thankfully, Adam pulled through.

The truth was I didn't really want to manage anybody at the time, despite how big Leo had become. We were concentrating on being a record company and I just didn't want the responsibilities and the phone calls at three o'clock in the morning. But Adam never forgot that I had refused his offer to relieve him of his prized possession at a time he was most vulnerable, and we remained close friends ever after.

This became tricky after Adam and Leo fell out over irregularities in the way his business affairs had been handled. Leo engaged heavyweight theatrical lawyer Oscar Beuselinck, the father of performer Paul Nicholas, to represent him. Beuselinck met with us and told us that he would sue both Adam and his partner Colin Berlin for every penny they had. They went their separate ways, with Leo agreeing to a gagging order. Colin Berlin, who was a good friend of mine and a big horse racing fan, later disappeared off the face of the Earth.

Undeterred, Adam, who always had the prefix millionaire pop star before his name, developed a reputation as a financial guru, and formed a financial services company with Paul Killick, the stockbroker. He also wrote a weekly column in the financial section of the *Mail On Sunday*.

Adam sadly died in 2003. He had been a huge star in the UK, both as a pop singer and an actor. He starred in a long-running TV series as the lead in *Budgie* and died in bed next to a 22-year-old girl in a hotel in Stoke-on-Trent, whilst performing in repertory there. And he died virtually penniless, leaving his wife, Jackie, with very little means of providing for herself. Adam was, however, great fun to hang out with, a real character, and is sorely missed.

Chrysalis continued to expand our roster – and we seemed to have a knack of unearthing great guitarists. Our next was Irishman Rory Gallagher, who found fame with his trio, Taste, in the late sixties and had since fronted his own bands under his own name. Now managed by his brother Donal, Rory was a superb bottleneck player and a major live attraction whose unpretentious, workmanlike approach was much appreciated by fans. Sadly, we couldn't take Rory to the next level but anyone who listens closely to U2's The Edge will hear his influence.

Unfortunately, lead guitarists often seem to be bands' most troubled characters. UFO were a case in point. We had signed them just after they had recruited German guitarist Michael Schenker in 1974: he dovetailed well with lead singer Phil Mogg.

Ten Years After had just broken up, and their bass player, Leo Lyons, did a great job of producing UFO's first Chrysalis album, *Phenomenon*. He did the same for their next two records, including *Force It*, whose striking cover featured Genesis P. Orridge and Cosey Fanni Tutti from art-rock band Throbbing Gristle.

However, Michael Schenker always seemed to be on the verge of leaving. He quit UFO at the end of 1978, just as we were about to issue *Strangers In The Night*, the live album that turned out to be the most successful of their career. Michael went on to make several albums with his own group for Chrysalis. He often blamed problems on his bad English but, if a particularly attractive girl came backstage, he suddenly became very articulate.

Mind you, UFO's bass player, Pete Way, also had his foibles. Once he walked out of his house telling his wife he was going to buy a packet of cigarettes. She next heard from him three days later, when he called her to say he was in Tokyo.

Also in 1978, Chrysalis signed South African singer-songwriter and multi-instrumentalist Trevor Rabin. He was very talented but his three albums for us flopped, although he did go on to enjoy success in Yes, with whom he performed from 1982 to 1994, and for whom he co-wrote their US number one hit 'Owner Of A Lonely Heart'.

I was equally impressed by Trevor's manager, Clive Calder, a very bright and energetic South African who had just relocated to London and was clearly going places. I thought we should sign a deal for us to fund a joint venture with him. Terry Ellis was opposed and vetoed the idea, possibly feeling threatened by Clive.

If he was, he was right to be. Calder went on to form Jive Records and Zomba Music Publishing, moved to New York to catch the first wave of hip-hop, and shaped the pop success of Will Smith, Backstreet Boys and Britney Spears. Eventually, he sold out to BMG for a staggering $2.5 billion, making him the most financially successful executive in the history of the music industry. Unsurprisingly, he is now retired and lives in the Cayman Islands.

All human life was there at Chrysalis in the seventies. We signed Mary O'Hara, an Irish harpist and soprano singer of traditional songs, and a former nun, who would headline New York's Carnegie Hall. Lee Garrett from Mississippi was a blind protégé of Stevie Wonder who had a big hit in the UK with 'You're My Everything', which sounded similar to something Stevie might have written.

Terry Ellis took a shine to a band I had signed called The Babys, who were managed by a very strange man called Adrian Millar, who claimed to be in with big-time London gangsters like the Krays and the Richardsons. Terry worked them hard in the US, where they achieved minor fame, before the lead singer, John Waite, went on to have a successful solo career with hits such as 'Missing You'.

One of our more interesting seventies hits in Britain came when a man called David Dundas – the son of the third Marquess of Zetland – co-wrote a TV commercial for Brutus jeans for Air-Edel, our jingles company. We took the Brutus reference out, called it 'Blue Jeans', and it was huge in the US and across Europe.

With the constant travelling and seemingly perpetual jet-lag, I developed an unfortunate habit of falling asleep at inappropriate times. This may have proved costly and it probably cost us The Kinks. They were out of a deal and we were keen to sign them, so Terry and I flew to New Orleans for a meeting. Jet-lagged, I nodded off during their show. Ray Davies was not impressed, so that was probably why they signed with Clive Davis instead.

I did the same thing auditioning Vangelis in the front room of a large house in London's Holland Park; quite difficult when the whole room was taken up by his equipment. He went on to make a fabulous soundtrack for the film *Chariots Of Fire* but sadly not for Chrysalis.

Branching out even further, Chrysalis signed up German experimental classical composer Karlheinz Stockhausen and made an album with him called *Ceylon/Bird Of Passage*. We even had an official reception at the White House that both Terry and I attended in July 1976. Stockhausen might have come from classical music but he had a huge rock-star ego and attracted his fair share of groupies, though his music was obscure to say the least.

Throughout the seventies, a major drive for Chrysalis was trying to replicate the success of our British record label in the US. We had initially opened as a licensed label through Warner Bros, moved into offices in downtown Hollywood and employed Ron Goldstein to manage the operation. This generated an enormous amount of excitement.

In 1972 we switched from a licensing deal to a hybrid distribution arrangement, which was launched with huge fanfare. Warners provided its Gulfstream Five corporate jet for Terry Ellis, myself, Mo Ostin and Joe Smith of Reprise/Warners, and various other Warners head honchos to fly around America visiting all the distribution branches, making presentations. It was a fantastic week.

Mo is a music man of the calibre of Ahmet Ertegun, Jerry Moss and Clive Davis. Once when he was in London in the eighties, Chelle and I were due to have dinner with Mo and his wife, Evelyn, to celebrate her birthday, but George Harrison insisted we all went out to his house, Friar Park, in Henley to hear his new project. After dinner, we went up to his studio and listened to the Travelling Wilburys album. It was wonderful: as I said before, you never forget the first time you hear great music.

But our ultimate goal was to be a totally fully-fledged independent operator in America, and when our arrangement with

Warners came to an end, we took a deep breath and decided to do it. This created significant overheads because, suddenly, we were not relying on the Warners mothership to provide manufacturing, sales, promotion or marketing. It was quite a daunting prospect, and Terry Ellis moved from Tortola to Los Angeles to supervise the proceedings.

Relations between Terry and myself had remained frosty since the Friday Management debacle. We needed a rapprochement and luckily we got one. While in New York, I ran into Herman Edel, of AIR-Edel. He was flying home to Aspen the next day.

I knew Terry was renting a ski lodge in Aspen. He was staying there with Clive Walter and his assistant, Diane Baker, who usually travelled with Terry wherever he went. So I called him up out of the blue and said: "I'm coming out to Aspen to see you."

It was a major peace summit and Terry had a free room so I stayed with him. It soon became clear from our conversations that he was struggling with the launch of the US company, so we put our disagreements behind us and agreed to move on; Terry suggested I spend the summer in LA to help out.

It was then that I learned of a major development in Terry's life about which I was totally ignorant. When I woke up in his chalet in Aspen the next morning, to my amazement I heard 'On Top Of The World' by The Carpenters coming from his hi-fi.

Although Karen Carpenter had an incredible voice, The Carpenters were the antithesis of everything that Chrysalis stood for. We were involved in rock'n'roll, heavy rock and alternative rock. I would have expected Terry to play the new UFO album. Then, over breakfast, the mystery was solved. One of the party told me that Terry was dating Karen.

I was amazed. Karen was one of the biggest stars in the world. Terry had been introduced to her by Edie Lefler, who managed Van Halen, and his wife Frenda, and Paul Bloch, a PR agent at Rogers & Cowan, who worked for both The Carpenters and Chrysalis in the US. He thought they would be right for each other, and they were... for a while. Ultimately, though, there were just too many diametrically opposed aspects to their personalities.

Chelle and I hung out with Terry and Karen quite often but it soon became clear to us that Karen was a very different creature. She was a family-orientated girl who had moved to Downey, an ultra-conservative LA suburb in southern California, in her early teens and lived with her parents until she was 25. She had no European sophistication. She was not part of the rock music scene but had become used to living the life of a major star, like having to have coffee available wherever she was 24 hours a day, even before the days of huge, extravagant riders in the contracts.

In stark contrast, Terry was much more sophisticated. He particularly enjoyed travelling around France and eating at three Michelin star restaurants. Because of his tax-exile status, he could only spend so many days in the UK, so we would often meet in France for gastronomic weekends. Lunch would normally finish just as dinner was about to start. That was exactly how we managed the company for a while, often joined by managing director Doug D'Arcy and finance director Terry Connolly.

Michelin restaurants were not establishments that offered 24-hour room-service coffee machines so when Terry was with Karen, they had to arrange for coffee to be outside the room, even in the middle of the night. This could be quite tricky.

Karen also refused to eat dinner after six o'clock, and it is impossible to have dinner before six o'clock in France. Terry liked to have both a lunch and a dinner every day. The only way they could compromise on that one was by booking a table for the last sitting at lunch, for about 1.45 p.m., turning up at two and ordering just before the kitchen closed. They would stretch the meal out and still be there at six o'clock.

We had some good times with them, though. One gorgeous Californian afternoon, Terry and Karen acted as godparents when my youngest son, Tom, was baptised in the Episcopalian Church on Santa Monica Boulevard in LA. It was the same church that featured in the movie *10* with Bo Derek and Dudley Moore.

Nevertheless, the appearance of Terry Ellis in Karen's life must have been a nightmare for all the people around her at the time. I met Richard Carpenter, her brother, and he coped with it. But can you imagine being The Carpenters' manager, Sherwin Bash, or Jerry Moss, the chairman of A&M Records, or Gil Friesen – the president – and suddenly having Terry Ellis of Chrysalis Records as the boyfriend to your major artist?

Terry may have publicly said, "Well, I'm not managing her" but he doesn't know how not to be involved. He was not someone to stand aside and think: "The record company is releasing the wrong single from my girlfriend's album but what the hell has that got to do with me?" The whole situation became very fraught at times but a combination of the record company, the manager and Karen's brother managed to keep things vaguely on track.

Things took a marked turn for the worst when Karen became anorexic. We didn't understand anorexia nervosa at the time. I first became aware of it when we were with Karen and Terry in Europe, having dinner, and ordering various courses. Karen would say, "Have some of mine, it's fantastic!" The next thing you knew, you had all been cajoled into having something from her plate and she had eaten nothing. She was also visibly getting thinner and thinner.

I wasn't around them the whole time, so I did not fully understand the dynamics of their relationship, but they lived together in LA for a while. Apparently, Karen used to natter to her mum on the phone so much that Terry forbade her to talk to her after six in the evening. Eventually, it all disintegrated and they parted, but remained friends. Complications from the anorexia eventually killed Karen in 1983. By then, Terry was married to Danielle but it still hit him pretty hard.

After the trip to Aspen I stayed out in Los Angeles for the summer to help Terry out with the record company. Chelle, Tim, Tom and an au pair joined me. We rented a lovely house in Coldwater Canyon, which was referred to as the Julie Andrews home, although I suspect there were several houses in LA named as such. The trip was so successful that I then took out a one-year's rental on another house nearby, with the intention of spending half my time there, but on my return to the UK, I was so busy, I spent barely a few weeks there.

Terry had already hired Sal Licata, who had previously been with Blue Thumb, as president, but the company was far from the finished article. Terry had also hired a finance director who didn't work out. Terry suspected he was playing hooky in the afternoons and going off to the race track at Hollywood Park.

Terry became very concerned about it and we sent over Paul Hutchinson, our former London accountant, to stabilise the company. I also arranged for Roger Watson from the London A&R department to relocate there too. Roger was instrumental in signing Huey Lewis & The News and The Divinyls. Soon things were well on track.

Terry and I did find ourselves getting involved in some very strange projects. One was a concept album called *Flash Fearless Vs The Zorg Women Parts 5 & 6* that had echoes of both *The Rocky Horror Picture Show* and *Flash Gordon*. It was a really good album featuring John Entwistle of The Who, Justin Hayward of The Moody Blues, Alice Cooper, Elkie Brooks and Chrysalis' Frankie Miller and Maddy Prior, but this was long before Jeff Wayne turned *The War Of The Worlds* into a concept album. Unfortunately, it was just ahead of its time.

We licensed British folk/rock veteran Roy Harper for the US. He had a track called 'When An Old Cricketer Leaves The Crease' from the album *HQ* and we made it the title of the album in the States. When we gave away bags of cricket bats and kit to all the promotion people, I suspect they had no idea what we were talking about.

Frankie Miller was a problem for us. He had a soulful voice and was a really good writer but we couldn't find the right vehicle for him. While I was in LA, I arranged for him to record an album, *The Rock,* in San Francisco, with Henry McCulloch from Wings on bass and Elliot Mazer producing.

Elliot had a great story about Neil Young. He had co-produced *Harvest* in 1971 and whilst I was there, he played me some tracks they had cut right afterwards. They completely blew me away. I asked why they hadn't been released and he said: "Neil thought it was too good, that it would be the wrong thing to release after *Harvest* as it would expose him to a bigger and more pop audience." There are artists who just make decisions like that, and maybe such behaviour is one of the reasons why Neil Young has always managed to maintain his credibility and his sanity.

Listening to *The Rock*, you could almost smell the amount of drugs being smoked in the studio. The album suffered a little bit because of that but was nevertheless very good. The famous Alcatraz prison in the San Francisco Bay was visible from the studio, hence the title, and its title track had the great line: "I think of all the guys who couldn't conform to society, and I see myself standing on the rock." The record was clearly much more suitable for the American market than for Britain, and could probably be a huge hit for a country artist, but at that time Chrysalis US was ill-prepared to break an unknown Scottish singer.

Frankie Miller's greatest legacy was as a major influence on Bob Seger, who had a big hit with Frankie's composition 'Ain't Got No Money' on his *Stranger In Town* album in 1978.

We tried very hard to break Frankie in the UK. He never really made it until we teamed him up with a pop producer, Dave Mackay, in 1978. 'Darlin'' was a Top 10 single and Frankie appeared on *Top Of The Pops* looking dishevelled with his long straggly hair. When the public saw him, they didn't like what they saw. It wasn't what they expected from the singer of a Top 10 hit, so the record stalled and so did Frankie's career.

After that, the only place Frankie hit big was Norway, where the company there released a compilation entitled *Frankie Who? Frankie Fucking Miller That's Who!* It sold more than 100,000 copies. EMI used a politer version of that title for its box-set of *The Complete Chrysalis Recordings* (1973-1980).

Sadly Frankie Miller suffered a brain haemorrhage in New York in 1994, while writing material for a new band he had formed with Joe Walsh of The Eagles. He is now permanently in a wheelchair and unable to talk. His wife, Annette, does a wonderful job looking after him.

Chrysalis was becoming a major success and my lifestyle began to reflect this. As I was by now spending most of my time working out of the London office, commuting from Wokingham was no longer practical, so I bought a big house in Phillimore Gardens, Kensington and used the Wokingham house as a weekend property.

It was also around this time that I bought a huge Mercedes 600 limousine, and hired a chauffeur to drive it. Incredibly ostentatious, we called it the Iron Butterfly. In January 1975, we flew down to Midem, the music industry convention in Cannes, and arranged for the driver to drive the Iron Butterfly down to the French Riviera so he could shepherd us along the Croisette while we were staying at the Majestic Hotel. It was the days of excess in the music industry and I guess I was guilty – if it is a crime, that is – of playing along.

I also started taking an interest in, and buying, wine, a hobby I pursue to this day. This was instigated by Terry Ellis, something else I have him to thank for. He even wanted to make a record with the wine expert from Christie's and call it *The Auctioneers*. I stayed well away from this hare-brained scheme, which thankfully never materialised.

Life was frequently a whirl in those days. I made a trip to Paris to try to collect some money that our sub-publisher there, Francis Dreyfus, owed us. I was irritated when Francis persistently attempted to change the subject by offering me, instead of the cash, which he was struggling to locate, a share in a new artist he had just started working with called Jean-Michael Jarre. Becoming increasingly annoyed, I rejected the offer outright: again, not my finest moment.

It was not all travel, fine wines and glamour, though, and the stresses of staying on top of Chrysalis' ever-expanding business led me to develop septicaemia from a spot on my leg over Christmas 1976. I very nearly died: there was certainly no way that Chelle and I could go on the New Year holiday to Rio that we had planned.

I did get to Moscow, with Des Brown, our international director, and Doug D'Arcy, in early 1977. The Soviet Union was obviously still going strong and a peek behind the Iron Curtain could be a scary experience. The three of us were monitored the whole time; a very attractive female KGB agent refused to let us out of her sight for a second, and when I didn't eat my hard-boiled egg at breakfast, the hotel staff took it up to my room; apparently, it was too much of a delicacy to waste.

Oddly enough, back in London Des Brown had a meeting with a representative of a British trade delegation to the USSR. They wanted him to go back to Russia and produce reports for them. I think they saw an opportunity to use Des as a spy if he was planning to be spending more time there. I strongly advised him to have nothing to do with it.

Des deserves the credit – or, possibly, the blame – for one of the most bizarre signings we ever made. Blonde On Blonde were a couple of attractive topless models, blondes of course and more accustomed to seeing pictures of themselves on page three of the *Sun* than in the pop papers. Both Jilly Johnson and Nina Carter went on to have interesting lives: in fact, Nina was married to Rick Wakeman for a while. Although they did not have a hit in the UK, they became quite a sensation in Japan, where, of course, they were known as Bronde On Bronde.

Des was always a magnet for trouble. As our head of international for several years, he and I travelled the world incessantly. His scrapes usually involved women: an incorrigible flirt, he was also long-sighted and unable to see if a girl was attractive or plain, so he treated them all the same. He never seemed to mind rejection, so he would hit on several different girls before he found a willing partner, often leaving him with a lot of explaining to do when he got home to his wife.

One morning he woke up with a huge love bite on his neck in Hamburg and decided to say that he was so hungover he managed to badly cut himself shaving, thus explaining the large band aid strategically placed on his neck. After a night out in Barcelona that ended with some wild sex he woke up with lacerations all over his back. We had two hours on the plane home to devise a cover story.

We fabricated a tale that the local licensee had insisted on taking us to a beach restaurant outside Barcelona, where we proceeded to drink far too much wine. So much so that, despite our advice, Des insisted on trying to water ski, but went far too fast and crashed into the rocks on the side of the bay, almost requiring hospitalisation for the damage to his back.

When he span this yarn to Rebecca, his wife, she simply said, "Des, you are so stupid." Rebecca wasn't, however; she eventually divorced him, tired of his serial infidelities.

Des once won a £5 bet off me when he joined the mile-high club with an Asian girl who joined the first class section of a BA flight from Sydney to London at Kuala Lumpur. He had to work quickly as she was getting off at Mumbai, or Bombay as it was at the time. That was when the upper deck of a 747 was still a lounge bar, which did make introductions easier. Des eventually left to move to LA to work in the burgeoning music video industry. We threw a great goodbye party for him.

I was no Des but I was no saint when it came to extra-marital relationships, and for a while had an occasional thing with a girl that had popped out of Des' cake at his leaving bash. She had also been in the Adam & The Ants video for *Stand And Deliver*. However, relationships in London were mostly out of bounds, with one or two exceptions. A temporary secretary who came to work for Terry Ellis was speedily removed when Terry suspected something was going on between us.

A trip to Argentina nearly landed me in a scrape. It was the era of the military junta of General Galtieri, when everyone had to carry an ID card, and you had to be clean shaven in the photo. Sometimes, members of the unofficial opposition would grow a beard to avoid recognition. Therefore my long beard led to me being hauled out of the car driven by the representative of RCA, our licensee, at gunpoint, opposite the main railway station in Buenos Aires. I was spreadeagled against the car with a gun in my back while my case was discussed, and my pockets searched. I confess to being greatly relieved when I finally left town, although I now enjoy trips to that wonderful country.

Terry and I had now been running Chrysalis for 10 years and despite a few bumps and scrapes along the way, our hard work was well rewarded and we were enjoying the fruits and the lifestyle that had come our way.

My life was made even richer on November 23, 1978, when Chelle presented me with my first daughter, Chloe. I was thrilled: the two boys were great, but this time around I really wanted a little girl, and we were delighted to have one.

So everything was great on the domestic front and Chrysalis seemed to be going from strength to strength. Could it get even better? Yes: unknown to us, everything was just about to go up another notch.

CHAPTER 9

Picture This

Terry Ellis always loved working with female performers and this trait led us to sign arguably the most exciting act ever to record for Chrysalis, Blondie.

Our relationship with the band began in the summer of 1977 when Terry called me and said he wanted to spend half a million dollars buying Blondie's contract from Private Stock, the label which had released their debut album at the end of 1976. I said: "OK, it sounds good to me." I knew of the group and had seen the album, but I'd not yet heard it.

It is quite rare to buy up a contract, but RCA had done it for Elvis Presley with Sun Records in 1955, and in 1967 Clive Davis and Janis Joplin's manager, Albert Grossman, gave the small Mainstream label $250,000 to take over the five-year contract of Big Brother & The Holding Company and sign them to Columbia. I am therefore sure that at the time it was the largest "transfer fee" for an artist ever paid. It certainly worked out for us with Blondie. The group went on to sell 40 million albums and became part of the cultural zeitgeist, our biggest act between 1978 and 1982. Debbie Harry, who stills fronts the band today, and co-wrote many of their biggest hits, remains the most iconic star I have been associated with. Comparisons with Marilyn Monroe were no exaggeration.

Private Stock had been started by Larry Uttal, who had previously owned the Bell label. He was a good record man but his expertise lay in singles and bubblegum pop like David Cassidy and Tony Orlando & Dawn. Their big acts at the time were Frankie Valli from the Four Seasons and David Soul, who had several big hits while starring in the TV series *Starsky & Hutch*. So Blondie didn't quite fit in.

Debbie Harry and Chris Stein, who was then her partner as well as the group's co-founder and guitarist, had started Blondie in New York in 1974. Debbie was one of three girl singers in a band called The Stillettoes that used to play at Club 82, a famous downtown lesbian bar, and Chris played guitar in their backing band. When The Stillettoes split up, Debbie and Chris got together to become Blondie alongside original members Clem Burke, an Anglophile and a powerhouse of a drummer, who is still with Debbie and Chris today, keyboard-player Jimmy Destri and bassist Gary Valentine, who composed two of their early hits, 'X Offender' and '(I'm Always Touched by Your) Presence, Dear', but left before we came on board. By that time, they had added Nigel Harrison, a British bassist, and Frank Infante, another guitarist.

At first they played downtown New York venues like Max's Kansas City and CBGB's alongside Television, The Ramones and Talking Heads, and were part of the city's thriving mid-seventies new wave scene that attracted plenty of press interest though the major labels, fixated by big-selling AOR rock, seemed strangely reluctant to invest in them.

Their eponymous debut was a little power pop gem, produced by Richard Gottehrer who had been around since the sixties. He had been a Brill Building songwriter, coming up with 'My Boyfriend's Back' for The Angels, and also scored hits like 'I Want Candy' with The Strangeloves, a fictional group of which he was a member. He was a real mover and shaker, co-founding the Sire label with Seymour Stein. He also produced *Plastic Letters*, the second Blondie

family portrait with my mother, father and sister. This would have been taken in about 1950 when I was six years old.

king in the North Yorkshire Moors aged 15 — my first
day without the family.

field of study
étudiant en
estudiante de
studienfach

POLITICS /

year of study
anné d'étude
año de estudio
studienjahr

educational institution
établissement
establecimiento de enseñanza
art der hochschule

Manchester
university

address
situé à
dirección
hochschulort

Oxford Rd
Manchester 13

My international student card, with a picture of me aged 20.

Graduation day at Manchester University, 1965 aged 21. I got a second class honours degree in politics and modern history.

school trip as a 16 year old. I'm on the extreme left, next to a teacher.

Chrysalis football team at our first international meeting. The top row includes Nick Blackburn, Terry Ellis and myself. Terry nolly is in the middle of the second row, with Doug D'Arcy below him. On his right is Roy Eldridge, and on his left England 1966 ld Cup winner Alan Ball.

BILL GRAHAM

in San Francisco
FILLMORE AUDITORIUM
1805 GEARY BOULEVARD, Zip 94115
Phone (415) 922-3220

February 19, 1968

Mr. Chris Wright
Carrington House
130 Regent Street
London W.1, England

Dear Mr. Wright:

We are very interested in bringing "Ten Years After" to the
Fillmore for a Thursday, Friday, Saturday weekend. When you
make your plans to bring the group to the States, we would
appreciate price and availability for them. I might mention
that we are now booking into May.

We are also opening a Fillmore-type operation in New York City
that will be in full swing within a month. Please give us
price and availability for that city too.

Yours truly,

Bill Graham

B:mvg

The letter that dropped through the post in 1968, totally redefining our history. Bill Graham, America's top rock promoter, died in a helicopter crash in Vallejo, California, in 1991.

Years After signing a contract with a very happy Dee Anthony (far right) in 1968. That's drummer Rik Lee at the front with me, Chick Churchill, Leo Lyons and Alvin Lee at the back.

our in the States around 1970, when the limousine broke down. Nearest the camera is Lorraine, Alvin's girlfriend, then Chelle, lf, Leo, and Ric. Alvin was the photographer!

My wedding to Chelle, on March 15, 1971 at St Martin-in-the-Fields, Trafalgar Square. Terry Ellis, the best man, is next to Chelle's parents, and Kate D'Arcy, the Matron of Honour, next to mine. The bridesmaid was Chick Churchill's step daughter, Samantha.

Four generations of Wrights, with Tim about one year old. My grandfather was approaching 100.

th Gary Brooker of Procol Harum, collecting an award for the *Grand Hotel* album in Lisbon, Portugal, 1974.

as Student Social Secretary at work in my office at Manchester The posters were for an upcoming gig with The Small Faces, Mad Barron DJ.

At the opening of Air Studios in Lyndhurst Hall, before the performance of *Under Milk Wood*, with the Prince of Wales, Sir George Martin, Chelle and Sir Anthony Hopkins. RICHARD YOUNG

Celebrating the success of Jethro Tull's *Songs From The Wood* album with Ian Anderson, Terry Ellis and myself. On the left is Jo Lus who took over Tull's management from ourselves.

With Adam Faith at an industry function in the mid-seventies. In the middle is former Radio One chief, Doreen Davies.

album. Richard's production work had a real sixties, girl group, pop sensibility that suited them perfectly.

At Chrysalis, we all bought into the idea of Blondie. They had toured Europe opening for Television in May and June 1977 but little had happened after that. Private Stock had been too busy with David Soul. Blondie were an underground, alternative group; new wave before the expression was invented in order to make punk more palatable to US radio.

The first country where Blondie had a hit was Australia. Ian 'Molly' Meldrum, the presenter of the music TV programme *Countdown*, played 'In The Flesh', the B-side of 'X Offender', in his show instead of the A-side, and both the single and the album went Top 5 there. That laid the foundations for their international success.

In November 1977, we reissued and re-promoted the first album in the UK, putting out a three-track 12″ single with 'Rip Her To Shreds', 'In The Flesh' and 'X Offender'. The band made their first British TV appearance on *So It Goes*, the Granada show presented by Tony Wilson, who later started Factory Records. Their storming performance of 'Rip Her To Shreds', with Debbie in a black top and thigh high black boots, made quite an impression. They also did a short European headline tour. In February 1978, Debbie graced the covers of *New Musical Express*, *Sounds* and *Record Mirror*, three of the four British music weeklies, all on the same week. We released 'Denis' and they did *Top Of The Pops*. Talk about impact! The next day they played Sheffield University and there was a near-riot. It seemed everybody in the city who'd watched her on TV the previous night was desperate to see them.

The main reason for their success was obvious: Debbie Harry. She exuded star quality, the poster girl and style icon that all the girls wanted to be and all the boys simply wanted. She didn't need to dress up; she could just wear a big red shirt and red boots like she did on her mesmerising debut on *Top Of The Pops*. Blondie became *Top Of The Pops* regulars, performing '(I'm Always Touched By Your) Presence, Dear' and 'Picture This' on the show later on that year.

Debbie had a fantastic voice and, even if their breakthrough hit, 'Denis', was a cover, the group wrote most of their own material. They were the whole package. We were very conscious of how striking Debbie looked and our creative marketing made the most of it. Her face had looked amazing as the front cover of *Sounds* and we used the same photo, by Gus Stewart, on the 12″ single for '(I'm Always Touched By Your) Presence Dear'. By the end of the year, Debbie and Blondie were everywhere, from the cover of *Cosmopolitan* magazine to the newly launched teen bible *Smash Hits*.

For whatever reason, although the band's music and attitude had really connected with the British, European and the Australasian markets, America didn't seem quite ready for Blondie. They had toured with Iggy Pop and The Kinks but had made little headway into Middle America, remaining simply a cult act popular on the east and the west coasts. Terry poured his efforts into them and in the summer of 1978 he persuaded Mike Chapman to produce *Parallel Lines*. That proved a masterstroke: the album went on to sell 20 million copies.

Mike Chapman became an integral part of the success of both Blondie and Chrysalis. He had arrived in England from Australia in the late sixties and was working as a waiter at Tramps, the London members' club, when he met Nicky Chinn. Teaming up, they wrote hits for Sweet, Suzi Quatro and Mud. They were the glitter rock songwriters par excellence but they fell out, ostensibly as Mike felt, perhaps with some justification, that he was predominantly responsible for their success.

As a producer, Mike was to make fantastic records for Chrysalis with Pat Benatar, Nick Gilder and Toni Basil, amongst others, and his work on *Parallel Lines* was phenomenal. *Parallel Lines* included four major hit singles: 'Picture This', 'Hanging On The Telephone', 'Heart Of Glass' and 'Sunday Girl'. 'Heart Of Glass', a track they had first demoed in the mid–seventies, changed everything. Combining elements of disco with the electronic music of groups like Kraftwerk, it became a huge worldwide hit in 1979. It was also the company's first Transatlantic chart-topper since Leo Sayer's 'When I Need You' two years earlier. Blondie finally exploded in America and for a while became just the biggest pop act in the world. In June 1979, they were on the cover of *Rolling Stone* magazine. The cover line said it all: Platinum Blondie.

For a while, they were unstoppable. *Eat To The Beat* and *Autoamerican* were also both huge records as their fame grew. We were so sure of ourselves, we filmed a video for every single track on *Eat To The Beat*, not just the singles 'Dreaming', 'Union City Blue' and 'Atomic', effectively making it the first long-form video, two years before MTV was launched. David Mallet, who had worked with Bowie, directed them all.

Success did not come easy however. There was a bit of a reshuffle in the Blondie camp – they changed managers from Peter Leeds, who had been their manager from day one, to the highly experienced Shep Gordon, Alice Cooper's manager. Nevertheless, Blondie had trouble coping with the enormity of their success. There was dissent in the ranks when the media focused almost exclusively on Debbie – hence their famous, defiant T-shirt with the message BLONDIE IS A GROUP – which put more pressure on her. There was also too much excess on the road.

In 1981, Debbie recorded her first solo album, *KooKoo*, with Nile Rodgers of Chic, who had just produced a hit album for Diana Ross and went on to have great success with David Bowie, Duran Duran and Madonna. We had a lavish party to launch the album but it didn't live up to expectations. The artwork, by the Swiss artist H.R. Giger, was striking but also slightly grotesque. It certainly did not capture Debbie's sultry charms. I have a framed proof of the cover on one of my office walls. It's a reminder of how things can go wrong.

I wasn't even sure Debbie Harry needed to make a solo album. She was the iconic person in the group: despite what the T-shirts said, Debbie Harry and Blondie were synonymous, just as Ian Anderson effectively is Jethro Tull. She was already fantastic in that group context. Debbie also became an actress, putting herself on the line when she appeared in *Videodrome*, the disturbing sci-fi horror movie directed by David Cronenberg. She was great fun in *Hairspray*, the John Waters comedy that has since been turned into a musical.

Blondie regrouped but went off the rails with *The Hunter* album in 1982. Chris Stein fell ill during the subsequent tour. At the time, everybody assumed that it was drug-related, but it was actually a serious illness, eventually diagnosed as pemphigus vulgaris, a rare auto-immune disease of the skin. It almost stopped the group stone dead. They had some tax issues and they broke up at the end of that year. It was a great shame, although Debbie was to make three more fine solo albums for us, and Blondie eventually reunited and are still gigging today.

Blondie generated an enormous amount of income for Chrysalis, especially as they were also signed to the music publishing company. They wrote some exceptional songs that didn't just garner radio play and chart success but also featured on major TV commercials and movie soundtracks throughout the world.

Oddly enough – and this is quite surprising – Blondie's biggest grossing song wasn't one of the obvious ones like 'Heart Of Glass' or 'Call Me', but 'One Way Or Another', recently covered by One Direction. 'One Way Or Another' wasn't one of Blondie's biggest hits, it wasn't even a single in the UK, but it always seems to be cropping up on film soundtracks and was used in music video games like *Rock Band* and *Guitar Hero*. It was one of the songs Debbie performed when she guested on *The Muppet Show* in 1980, along with 'Call Me'.

As huge as they became, I sometimes wonder why Blondie weren't even more successful than they were. Debbie Harry had everything; she was beautiful, she was a style icon, she was a wonderful performer, she had a distinctive voice and she wrote and co-wrote wonderful songs. She was the forerunner for so many female artists: Madonna, Lady Gaga and many others in between. None of them can hold a candle to Debbie.

You have to ask yourself what went wrong. Could Chrysalis, as a company, have done more? Perhaps not. Events were conspiring against us, dealing with the enormity of their success, the difficulties they encountered touring and then issues with Chris Stein's health, the illness that nobody understood and put him out for a couple of years, crucially at the height of their fame.

Debbie was very loyal and nursed him through it. Because it coincided with the beginning of the AIDS epidemic we were concerned at the time that it might be an AIDS-related disease but thankfully it had nothing whatsoever to do with AIDS.

The early eighties was an era when a great many people in the music business were doing an awful lot of cocaine, including people connected with Blondie and people at Chrysalis involved with the Blondie project. The title *Parallel Lines* was a veiled reference to that. Maybe it all went off the rails a bit. There were some difficult times between Debbie and Chris and us, especially with Terry who had been fundamentally responsible for bringing Blondie in, and directing their career.

We even gave Chris Stein his own label, Animal Records, and he produced albums by Iggy Pop and The Gun Club and the soundtrack to *Wild Style*, the hip-hop film produced and directed by Charlie Ahearn. Debbie and Chris were not only a glamorous New York couple, they really had their finger on the pulse of the alternative scene, as they proved with the groundbreaking 'Rapture', the first US number one to feature rap.

When Blondie were inducted into the Rock And Roll Hall of Fame by Shirley Manson of Garbage in 2006, there was a definitive *froideur* from Debbie and Chris towards Nigel Harrison and Frank Infante. But both Terry and I were present and it meant a lot to us that Debbie and Chris were gracious to us and thanked us both for the contribution we had made to their career. I have an enormous amount of respect for them and Blondie will always form a huge part of the Chrysalis story.

As will Pat Benatar. Our first encounter with her came in 1978 when Terry Ellis and I were having dinner in New York. Since I was London-based and he was living in LA, this was a regular event. We ate at La Caravelle, the top French gastronomic restaurant in New York and, as usual, the dinner involved the full menu and a couple of bottles of the finest French wine.

We had got to the point where Terry wanted to order dessert and quite possibly a bottle of Chateau d'Yquem to go with it when I reminded him we had promised Jeff Aldrich, our A&R guy in the US, that we would go and see a girl sing at Tramps, a club in Greenwich Village. As important as music was to Terry, he loved his gourmet dinners, so I had to do a bit of cajoling to persuade him to skip dessert and head off to see Pat Benatar.

Pat had a great voice but she was singing like a bar singer. I knew nothing about her background in the theatre: I just thought she was all over the place stylistically. I said she was worth considering and we should arrange to see another show, but Terry was adamant we sign her without a second look.

Her manager was Rick Newman who owned Catch A Rising Star, a cabaret club where stand-up comedians like Robin Williams, Billy Crystal and Jerry Seinfeld had started out. Pat Benatar was slightly off-tangent for him. Terry got his way, we signed her, and a couple of months later, I was back in New York and Jeff Aldrich took me to see her somewhere out on Long Island. Pat was still all over the place.

I despairingly asked Jeff, "Who is responsible for her A&R?", and he sheepishly replied that he was. I suggested he should get her a role in a Broadway show, because that seemed to be where she was heading.

Meanwhile, the sessions for the first album were going nowhere. Eventually, Terry and Jeff arranged for her to go out to LA to record with Mike Chapman who was turning into the Chrysalis goose that laid the golden eggs.

Fresh from producing Blondie and The Knack, Mike helmed *In The Heat Of The Night*, Pat Benatar's debut, in 1979. Mike suggested she cut 'I Need A Lover', the John Cougar Mellencamp song that helped to establish her. He did four tracks and put his engineer, Pete

Coleman, in charge of the rest. Pete brought along Neil 'Spyder' Giraldo, who subsequently became the guitarist in her group, her confidant and her second husband.

Pat Benatar wore her hair long when we signed her. Women had to fight certain obstacles in the music industry in those days, and to this day she is upset that Billy Bass, the Chrysalis creative director, managed to airbrush nipples onto the album cover. But it made it an even more striking shot and the album – and Pat – quickly became huge.

Pat's second album, *Crimes Of Passion*, sold five million copies in the US and in August 1981, the video for her cover of the Young Rascals' 'You Better Run' was the second most played on MTV, after 'Video Killed The Radio Star' by Buggles. She soon became one of the stars of the MTV era.

Pat's relationship with Neil Giraldo naturally impacted on her career. He was a good, fun guy and his heart was in the right place but we inevitably found that we surrendered a degree of creative control over Pat's career to Neil because he was the husband. He became her producer and, although they had both written hits, most of her big songs like 'Hit Me With Your Best Shot', 'Shadows Of The Night' and 'We Belong' were penned by outside writers.

Billy Steinberg and Tom Kelly, who wrote 'Like A Virgin' for Madonna, came up with 'Sex As A Weapon'. We were getting great songs for her. Mike Chapman and Holly Knight wrote 'Love Is A Battlefield', her biggest international hit. But we got to the point where Pat would not record songs that Neil didn't like or often ones that he had not co-written.

We also had '(Simply) The Best', by Mike and Holly, on hold, and Neil and Pat refused to do it. Tina Turner ended up cutting it instead in 1989. What a missed opportunity!

There are songs that will give an artist a year on their career. There are songs that give an artist five years on their career. And, very very occasionally, you come across a song that will give an artist a career for life. '(Simply) The Best' would have been that song for Pat Benatar. She would have sung it brilliantly, it would have been her song for life and she would have been a global superstar.

Neil could sometimes be unpredictable. Once Jeff Aldrich and I flew Jim Vallance, who had been writing and working with Bryan Adams, from Vancouver to LA. We had lunch at the Beverly Hills Hotel with Pat and Neil and they hit it off great. Pat seemed to really gel with Jim and said: "Why don't you come back to our home studio and take a listen to what we have been working on?" At which point, Neil just said: "No." The whole lunch went flat and another chance was missed. It was so frustrating.

Ultimately, Pat and Neil had a very strange dynamic. He came from a Sicilian-Czech family, her background was Polish and Irish, and in a way they tried to create an old-fashioned European family. Pat would tell me: "I just want to be at home, go down to the supermarket and do the shopping in a pair of jeans and not be recognised! I want to be the good Italian wife at home with the pasta sauce always on the stove."

She would say that and I would smile, nod, and think to myself: "Ninety-nine per cent of the world do that. They dream of being you."

Mind you, Terry Ellis' Midas touch with female artists did sometimes desert him. In 1977, we signed Bonnie Tyler to Chrysalis for the US. We tried very hard to break 'Lost In France' which had been a big hit for RCA everywhere else, but, according to our promotion department there, US radio stations wouldn't play it because of the mandolin in the middle eight. So Terry insisted that we drop Bonnie.

I could see his reasoning but I would have given her one more shot. I met up with Dave Mackay, who was producing Bonnie's follow-up, and gave him our decision. Dave said, "You ought to listen to the next record first" – he thought he had a smash on his hands. I told him that Terry's mind was made up and there was nothing I could do. Bonnie signed to CBS and her next single, 'It's

A Heartache', topped the charts around the world and made the top three in America.

The success of Blondie and Pat Benatar in Australia and New Zealand helped cement a very productive working relationship Chrysalis had there with the Australian entrepreneur Michael Gudinksi. I had first met Michael at a *Billboard* magazine convention in Honolulu when he was barely out of his teens and had already launched the soon-to-be iconic Australian label Mushroom Records. Like Chrysalis, Mushroom was licensed to Festival records, a company owned at the time by Rupert Murdoch.

Festival licensed all the major international independent labels like A&M and Island in Australia. Alan Hely, who ran Festival, was the patriarch of the Australian music business and a bit of a father figure to me. On my first visit to Festival's HQ in Sydney, I watched Alan walk from his managing director's office into the factory where rows of women manually pressed 7- and 12-inch vinyl records on machines that were euphemistically called semi-automatic presses. Like a class of schoolchildren addressing their teacher, they all greeted him with, "Good morning, Mr Hely."

Alan always treated Michael Gudinski like a son. Michael was then at the start of an incredibly illustrious career both in Australia and internationally. As well as founding Mushroom – which took over from Festival as the largest independent record company in Australia until he sold it to James Murdoch in 1999 – he is also Australia's major independent music publisher and one of its largest concert promoters.

The first time that Michael and I did serious business together was in 1976 when he sent to the UK a group from New Zealand called Split Enz. They were an eccentric bunch with unusual, angular hairstyles, weird make-up and offbeat, arty clothes. Phil Judd and Tim Finn, the main writers, drew on a bizarre range of influences from music hall and pantomime to Expressionist cinema and modern art. They had supported Roxy Music down under in 1974, which seemed fitting – in fact, Roxy Music guitarist Phil Manzanera produced *Mental Notes*, Split Enz' first Chrysalis album.

Tim Finn's younger brother, Neil, joined them in 1977 after Phil Judd's departure. They were well on their way to developing a cult following in the UK and had Split Enz remained based in London, I believe they would have been very successful. However, each time, just when it seemed they were beginning to break the ice in the UK, they would be on a plane back to Australia and New Zealand to tour their home markets and generate the income they and their management needed. We never quite got there with them and we dropped the band, though they subsequently had several hits on A&M. Neil Finn went on to form the brilliant and far more successful Crowded House in the mid-eighties.

We were more successful with an Australian group called Icehouse, who were discovered by Jeff Aldrich, who had also found Pat Benatar. The group was originally called Flowers but, because there was a Scottish group of the same name, they changed it to Icehouse, which was the first track on their 1980 debut album.

Icehouse enjoyed success with us on both sides of the Atlantic, being often (erroneously, in my view) compared with Ultravox. Their main man was the classically trained singer and multi-instrumentalist Iva Davies, who made some fabulous records with Icehouse, particularly 'Great Southern Land' and 'Hey Little Girl', a worldwide hit in 1983, the year they supported David Bowie on tour, before going on to compose symphonies and write film soundtracks. He is a rare talent and even today I rarely visit Australia without seeing him,

Another Antipodean group, The Divinyls, didn't quite work for us. Their singer, Christina Amphlett, was quite shy and lacked confidence yet she developed an outlandish stage persona, often wearing schoolgirl uniforms. We paired them with Mike Chapman but even he couldn't engineer a breakthrough and when we let them go after three albums, they were unrecouped to the tune of $1m. We then looked on as they had a worldwide hit, the suggestive 'I Touch Myself', with Virgin.

Some you win, some you lose. By the late seventies, Chrysalis were winning more than we were losing, and we felt we knew exactly how the music industry worked – but, of course, that industry was about to be turned upside-down by a seismic explosion.

CHAPTER 10

Rebel Yell

I would love to be able to say that I saw punk rock coming and predicted the way it would rewrite the rules of the music industry. But I would be lying – because I was as surprised and shocked by it as everybody else.

By this stage in my life I had been through blues bands, the hippy movement and into the progressive era and the birth of heavy metal. The most important quality had always been musicianship. If the guitarist wasn't great or the rhythm section didn't gel properly, a band wouldn't get signed. Punk blew all that out of the water; being able to play didn't matter. Suddenly, what counted was anger, energy and, most of all, attitude.

Yet the punk explosion was exciting and Chrysalis tried to get involved right at the start. In the summer of 1976, I went with Doug D'Arcy and Roy Eldridge, the UK head of A&R, to see the Sex Pistols at the 100 Club in Oxford Street. It was my first experience of a punk gig and for an old hippy like me who was used to people sitting on the floor; the edge and air of violence was an eye-opener.

We decided we would try to sign them. I arranged a meeting about five o'clock one afternoon in the Chrysalis office with Malcolm

McLaren, the band's manager, and his lawyer Brian Carr. We negotiated the basics of a deal but we were £10,000 apart. Malcolm wanted £50,000 and we offered him £40,000.

Malcolm claimed he had a meeting with EMI later that day and said he would sign with us on the spot if I agreed to £50,000, but otherwise he would go on to see EMI. I called his bluff because I genuinely didn't think that the Sex Pistols would ever sign with EMI. They were such an alternative group so why would they sign with the most establishment and old-school of all the record companies? It did not make sense. So I stood my ground and told him that he could go and see EMI. We agreed he would call the next morning to let me know if he was going to accept the £40,000 that I was offering or sign to EMI.

I doubted Malcolm and his lawyer were going to EMI, which was around the corner from our office, in Manchester Square, so I arranged for Phil Cokell, our marketing manager, to trail them. The following morning Phil told me: "I followed them, they never went to EMI." So I called up Malcolm McLaren who assured me that he had been offered £50,000 by EMI but said if we could match it, they would still sign with us.

Confident that he was pulling a fast one, I didn't budge and the Sex Pistols signed to EMI. I was astonished. Either Phil had been watching the wrong door, or they had held their meeting elsewhere.

There again, I thought we might have had a lucky escape when the Pistols appeared on Thames Television's *Today* show with interviewer Bill Grundy in December 1976. Provoked by Grundy, the band called him a "dirty fucker" and a "fucking rotter" and a media storm erupted around them.

EMI's shareholders were so horrified by the Pistols that the chairman, Sir John Read, insisted they drop the group instantly. I then took a phone call from Leslie Hill, the EMI managing director, asking if we would take them off their hands, as Chrysalis was where the group really wanted to be. We reconsidered our position, and eventually decided we would pass.

Brilliantly manipulated by Malcolm McLaren, the Pistols bandwagon rolled on when they were signed to A&M by Jerry Moss and Derek Green in March 1977. The band celebrated by running amok in their offices, upsetting some of the female staff, and were kicked off the label after just one week. The Sex Pistols were back to square one and running out of labels and options.

We were still in two minds. So Roy Eldridge, Doug D'Arcy and I went to another Pistols gig, this time at the Screen On The Green in Islington in April 1977. Roy was a tall guy, a weekend rugby player and that night I was glad that he was there. We didn't look like punks, felt threatened by the intensely violent atmosphere and bailed out halfway through. I went home, thought hard and realised that I didn't want an act on the label that I couldn't take my wife and friends to go and see. So I turned down the Sex Pistols for the second time.

The Sex Pistols were very successful at Virgin, of course, becoming cultural icons as well as hitting number one with their *Never Mind The Bollocks* album before imploding at the end of 1978. Johnny Rotten's departure and Sid Vicious' death stopped McLaren generating any more cash from chaos, and watching the whole circus from the outside, I can't say I regretted not signing them.

We did have our own punk A-lister, of course, and his name was Billy Idol. I had first seen him with his band, Generation X, at Dingwalls in London in June 1977. They seemed very marketable, not as chaotic and dangerous as the Sex Pistols, and we snapped them up.

In contrast to Johnny Rotten, Billy Idol – or William Broad, as his parents knew him – was a middle-class boy. He had dropped out of Sussex University and became part of the Bromley contingent that followed the Sex Pistols around, along with Siouxsie Sioux. A face on the punk scene, Billy had dyed his hair peroxide blond, developed an Elvis sneer and formed Generation X with bassist and lyricist Tony James.

Generation X were one of the first punk bands to appear on *Top Of The Pops* with 'Your Generation' and had a great run of pop-punk singles including 'Ready Steady Go', 'King Rocker' and 'Valley Of The Dolls'. The latter was the title track of their second album which was produced by Ian Hunter, the former lead singer of Mott The Hoople who was also signed to Chrysalis as a solo artist at the end of 1978.

Generation X spent ages trying to finish their third album, *Kiss Me Deadly*, with different guitar players, including John McGeoch, of Magazine and Siouxsie & The Banshees, and Steve Jones of the Sex Pistols who played on 'Dancing With Myself'. Keith Forsey, an English producer who had worked with Giorgio Moroder in Germany, did the best he could under the circumstances. After Generation X broke up in 1981, Keith remixed 'Dancing With Myself' for Billy's debut solo EP, as well as a cover of Tommy James and the Shondells' 'Mony Mony'. This helped to launch Billy in the US.

I drafted in Kiss manager Bill Aucoin to mastermind Billy's career in America. Bill came over to the UK and went with Roy Eldridge to the Isle of Man where Billy was playing a festival. Bill was gay and had never heard of the Isle of Man but thought it was a real hoot that there was a place by that name. He was blown away by Billy and we moved him to America where Bill and Terry Ellis guided the next stage of his career. It worked like a dream.

Bill Aucoin teamed up Billy Idol and Keith Forsey with the New York guitarist Steve Stevens, with whom Billy still works today. That proved a potent combination on tracks like 'Hot In The City' and 'White Wedding'. His second album, *Rebel Yell*, was even better, with the title track, the sublime 'Eyes Without A Face' and 'Flesh For Fantasy'. Billy quickly became a mainstay of MTV. An artist made for those times, he became a superstar.

Yet inevitably, things started to go off the rails. Billy took three years to make *Whiplash Smile*, then broke up the successful songwriting partnership with Stevens and split from Aucoin as well at the end of 1986. We had to wait four years for the next album, *Charmed Life*. Every time I went to the studio, they would play me tracks and assure me the record was almost finished. I soon stopped believing them.

Billy's personal life was also falling apart. He was picked up in New York with a girl who was carrying cocaine, and became addicted to heroin and cocaine. In the late eighties, he moved to Los Angeles where he continued the same, dissolute lifestyle. He began dating a porn star, who would bring her friends to visit him in the studio. It's fair to say he wasn't getting a lot of work done. But he was one of our major artists and the endless delays were putting Chrysalis under severe financial stress.

Things got worse in February 1990 when, riding his motorbike home from the studio in Hollywood, he ran a red light and was hit by a car. It was a terrible crash. Billy came close to losing a leg and had to pull out of filming James Cameron's *Terminator 2: Judgment Day* with Arnold Schwarzenegger, which would have taken his career to another level and into another direction. The accident delayed the album even further. David Fincher (who later directed *Seven*) directed a video for the 'Cradle Of Love' single by only shooting Billy from the waist up. Billy even played a tour on crutches.

When *Charmed Life* finally appeared, Billy came over to the UK to promote it. We rented him an apartment in Mayfair, which he completely trashed. He was due to appear on Radio 1's Friday evening *Singled Out* record review show and he went there with Roy Eldridge. Halfway through the show, Roy phoned me in a panic and said Billy had been thrown off the programme.

"What for?" I asked.

"Three fucks and four c★★★s."

Some people thought Billy Idol was a plastic punk but let me tell you, he was the real deal. The stories of debauchery are endless, and more often than not his manager, Bill Aucoin, was an accomplice in his excesses (apart from the girls, of course, who were not Bill's thing). In 1982, for example, I was backstage at the Whisky A Go Go in Hollywood arranging for a photographer from *Billboard* to snap Terry Ellis and myself congratulating Billy on his show. Billy, however, was distracted – by a Hollywood soap actress pleasuring him orally without seeming to care who was watching. We asked the actress to curb her enthusiasm, but to no avail; she was intent on seeing through her mission. So our company publicist Toby Lubov said, "Let's just take the photo and we will only show the head and shoulders".★

This kind of thing was a pretty regular occurrence at Billy Idol gigs. Often, we would end up waiting an hour or more to pay him our respects while he "socialised" with not one, not two, but three or four young ladies in a row, one after the other. Billy loved the lifestyle and, before the lifestyle became the be-all and end-all, he wrote some great songs.

If Billy Idol was not taken totally seriously by cultural commentators and music critics, The Specials certainly were. They were probably the most politically and socially important group that Chrysalis ever signed.

In May 1979, on the day of the General Election that swept Margaret Thatcher to power, Roy Eldridge came into the office and said he'd seen a fantastic group the previous night. The Specials had a multi-racial line-up, came from Coventry and played a mix of ska and punk: in fact they were the first UK group to fuse both black and white British youth and music cultures.

The gig that Roy had attended, at the Moonlight Club in London, had blown everybody away and the whole industry wanted to sign them. The complication was that they had started their own record label called 2-Tone and wanted us to sign not just them but also their label. The case for the group was so compelling that we broke all the rules and gave them a label deal.

It exceeded our expectations as, within a few months, the ska revival became a nationwide phenomenon. In November 1979, we had three 2-Tone acts on the same edition of *Top Of The Pops*: The Specials performing 'A Message To You Rudy', Madness doing 'The Prince' and The Selecter singing 'On My Radio'.

★ The actress has since become a Hollywood A-lister but at the time she was clearly important enough to penetrate the backstage security.

Madness, of course, went on to join Stiff Records and became one of the biggest UK groups of the eighties. They are still around today. The Selecter, fronted by the striking Pauline Black, stayed with 2-Tone and then signed to Chrysalis. They scored a few hits though they were unlucky when the assassination of John Lennon scuppered the release of the 'Celebrate The Bullet' single at the end of 1980.

2-Tone was also to launch The Beat, another Midlands band who moved on to Arista after the success of their version of 'Tears Of A Clown', and The Bodysnatchers, who became the Belle Stars and signed to Stiff. Agreeing to take on the 2-Tone label had worked out brilliantly.

Yet 2-Tone's prime movers remained The Specials, led by songwriter and keyboard player Jerry Dammers. Their songs captured problems of inner-city life for both black and white kids in Britain and spoke authoritatively on so many of the social issues of the day. A track like 'Too Much Too Young', which topped the British charts in February 1980, tackled the problem of teenage pregnancies. 'Ghost Town', which reached number one in July 1981, talked about youth unemployment in Coventry.

Yet The Specials were always a volatile band and the original line-up splintered in 1981. Lead singer Terry Hall started Fun Boy Three with Lynval Golding and Neville Staple, enjoying a slew of hits before going on to form The Colourfield followed by the less successful Terry, Blair and Anouchka.

The Specials' legacy outlived them, however, and never more so than at the start of 1990 when 'Free Nelson Mandela' became an anthem that you heard back on news broadcasts from South Africa and, in fact, all over the world in the weeks leading up to Mandela's release from prison. I felt very proud to have been responsible for releasing it and would go as far as saying that it is the most important record Chrysalis has ever put out.

Of course, Chrysalis wasn't all about punk and new wave at the end of the seventies and our A&R department with Doug D'Arcy,

Roy Eldridge and Chris Briggs was normally pretty on the ball in all areas. However, even they occasionally dropped a few howlers.

When Dire Straits' eponymous debut album came out in 1978 on Phonogram's Vertigo Records imprint, prefaced by the 'Sultans of Swing' single, I thought as a dyed-in-the-wool guitar aficionado that it was fabulous. I would have loved it to have been on Chrysalis. I could not believe we had missed out on the band and I decided to conduct a post-mortem.

At a meeting with the A&R team, I demanded to know whether we had been offered Dire Straits and, if so, who was responsible for rejecting them. It transpired that I had been in the States while they had been considered, and I had never heard the demo, but Chris Briggs had been to see them and reported back that they were "very good, but very very boring". Chris went on to mastermind the recording careers of many successful artists including Robbie Williams.

Dire Straits were not even the only big fish who got away. We had also missed out on an opportunity to sign Def Leppard at the same time, following a trip Roy Eldridge had made to Sheffield. Roy had decided they were good, but not quite good enough for us.

Luckily, this kind of missed opportunity was the exception rather than the rule. From the mid-seventies through to the mid-eighties, both the British and the American companies were steaming ahead. For a while it seemed as if everything we touched turned to gold.

Chrysalis was probably the hottest record label around, almost the first port of call for any artist on both sides of the Atlantic. My days were incredibly busy, with little time for anything else, and at times I seemed to be spending the majority of my life at 35,000 feet. It was gruelling, demanding and, fairly often, extremely exciting, far removed from my life as a farmer's boy from Lincolnshire.

CHAPTER 11

Hot Hot Hot

As I worked at my career and continued to build the Chrysalis empire, I wasn't been big on holidays. There was never really time to take one. One exception, however, was when Chelle and I flew with Terry Ellis for a break in Jamaica, a country first introduced to us by Chris Blackwell, of Island fame.

Blackwell is one of the most charismatic, creative and successful people in the history of the music business. Born in London to a wealthy white plantation-owning Jamaican family, he spent most of his childhood in the Caribbean. His mother, Blanche Lindo, was of Portuguese-Jewish decent, while his father, Joseph Blackwell, was a dashing young Irish officer who ended up as aide-de-camp to the Governor General of Jamaica. Chris was thus readily able to be all things to all people: an erudite old Harrovian in England, a Jamaican in Jamaica, and even Jewish in New York thanks to his mother. The legendary music exec Ahmet Ertegun nicknamed Chris the baby-faced killer as he could be both ruthless and extremely personable at the same time.

Blackwell started his music business career in England by selling Jamaican records to the immigrant community from the boot of his car. He launched Island Records in 1961, initially to import Caribbean ska records into the UK, and opened an office in London the following year. His first hit, a number two in 1964, was 'My Boy Lollipop' by Millie Small, on the Fontana label, through which Island had a marketing arrangement. Blackwell then launched the career of Steve Winwood, the teenage prodigy of The Spencer Davis Group, who would later form Traffic and become one of Island's first signings in 1967 when it became the UK's first truly independent, creatively motivated rock label. Other early signings included Fairport Convention, Free and Cat Stevens, and they would go on to nurture world megastars U2 at the start of the eighties. But for all their success with white rock, Island and Chris Blackwell will probably always be best known for introducing reggae and Bob Marley to the world outside Jamaica.

Chris' mother was a long-time confidante of James Bond author Ian Fleming and Chris took over Goldeneye, the idyllic property that Fleming owned in Jamaica, and he developed it into one of the most exclusive holiday resorts in the world. Through the seventies, Jamaica became a regular port of call for me, either with Chelle or with exhausted artists who were winding down from long US tours.

Once Chelle and I flew to Haiti, where Papa Doc and his sinister secret police, the Tonton Macoutes, were still in power. We stayed at the hotel Oloffson, the infamous Hotel Trianon in Graham Greene's marvellous book *The Comedians*, which so accurately portrays Haitian society. I entered through customs with a copy of another Greene book, which led to some serious questioning. Everywhere we went we were shepherded by ominous looking large drivers with thick sunglasses. The character on whom Greene's Petit Pierre was based was a constant presence in the Oloffson bar.

In Jamaica, with our very long hair and long beards, we stood out like a sore thumb in the Jamaican community. The locals had never seen anyone like us and called us white rastas. After Bob Marley was shot in 1976 we stopped going to the island because it just became too violent. Indeed, I have been only once in the last 30 years, for a Jamaican New Year's Eve party in 1994 that was produced by Chrysalis TV for Channel 4.

Instead of Jamaica, Chelle and I started going to the eastern Caribbean. We would fly to Antigua in the Leeward Islands after New Year's Eve, and stay on little islands in places like Nevis, Saba, St Barts and Anguilla, before they became fashionable.

Soon after Terry Ellis moved to Tortola, I visited him and was sitting by a pool when I saw a seaplane taking off and wondered where it was going. So we chartered a plane and flew off to several different islands. The first we visited was Anguilla, which had declared its independence from Saint Kitts and Nevis only a couple of years earlier.

Anguilla was a forgotten outpost coloured red on the map, a reminder of the days when the British government controlled the bulk of the Caribbean. As the bigger Caribbean islands like Trinidad and Tobago, and Jamaica gained their independence, the British government was left with the smaller islands like Montserrat and Anguilla.

No doubt at some point Saint Kitts and nearby Nevis had wanted their independence and Anguilla, being 70 miles away and sticking out in the northern part of the eastern Caribbean, was completely overlooked. Someone in the Foreign or Colonial Office must have said let's put Anguilla with Saint Kitts and Nevis. It thus became Saint Kitts, Nevis and Anguilla, without the Anguillans having any say in the matter.

The only difference between Anguilla and every other island is that Anguilla is very dry and therefore never had a sugarcane industry. For this reason, it had no commercial infrastructure so no one ever went there. But it did have the most beautiful beaches, a natural paradise. Foreign aid clearly went no further than Saint Kitts, leaving Anguilla as an impoverished, inhabited speck of sand.

Nevertheless, Anguillans are very resourceful. They'd had enough and they rebelled. Saint Kitts sent a planeload of soldiers to quell the rebellion but they failed. So the British government sent in a contingent of Metropolitan police officers. What the Anguillans really wanted was a return to being governed by Britain and that is exactly what came about.

Chelle and I holidayed in Anguilla every year for several years until it became very ritzy and they started building big hotels. In the early days we could walk two to three miles, the length of the longest beach, and encounter nobody.

Caribbean holidays became our great indulgence, often with Gary and Frankie Brooker, George Martin and his wife, Judy, or Doug D'Arcy and his family. We would island-hop, and as the children got older and wanted more activity, we would stay in Antigua. Doug, Derek Green, New York lawyer Owen Epstein and I even bought and co-owned a villa there. Sadly, Owen was to die of a brain tumour in 1998, aged only 36.

As my family grew the villa became too small for us. We needed more space. Initially I rented Eric Clapton's old place, Babylon, at Galleon Beach. It was a lovely house but, when Eric decided to build Crossroads, a drug and alcohol rehab centre in Antigua, the local government allowed him to build a fabulous new house at Standfast Point, further down the coast. He ended up selling Babylon but I managed to buy from Eric another plot of land that he owned alongside where we subsequently built my house, Casablanca.

With a name like Casablanca it naturally had to be a white house and, equally naturally, we furnished it with a hint of Moroccan style. It is a wonderful retreat with gorgeous views overlooking the beach and all the boats entering the harbour, and with Montserrat on the horizon.

As well as numerous holidays, the Caribbean was also the location of a major new business venture. When we acquired the AIR group from George Martin and his partners, we had unwittingly bought an idea that George had proposed to his partners but was struggling to bring to fruition. He wanted to build a studio on a large boat and make it available for recording artists to use as a floating studio anywhere in the world.

Had it been a reasonable-sized boat operating only in the Mediterranean, the idea could have been a commercial success. But George's idea was far grander: it would be an ocean-going vessel that could pitch up anywhere in the world so if The Rolling Stones wanted to make their next album in Bali, the boat would sail across the ocean and dock there. The group would not be able to stay on the boat, but a state-of-the-art recording studio would be available to them.

George's partners were pretty horrified at the idea. We had thus inherited three guys – John Burgess, Ron Richards and Peter Sullivan – who were desperate to knock the initiative on the head and George who was equally keen to progress it. We managed to persuade George that it was a very expensive project, and that the likelihood of it ever making a profit was doubtful. The idea looked to have died.

However, in 1977 George returned from a trip to the Caribbean and announced a new scheme to build a studio on the island paradise of Montserrat. At the time Montserrat was incredibly obscure. I would not have heard of it were it not for my frequent Caribbean trips, but obviously Terry knew it from living on Tortola.

We were only slightly keener on this than we were on the boat scheme. Typically, Terry's first reaction was that the studio should be on Tortola where he was based, and where we had some form of infrastructure. He and George argued and I proposed Antigua, which at least had a certain logic behind it. Several flights a day from London and New York pass through Antigua and it has 365 white sand beaches and a booming tourist economy.

However, George and Judy had visited the Caribbean specifically to find the right location, pitched up in Montserrat, been greeted warmly by the governor and his wife and the Chief Minister and fallen in love with the island. They were adamant: this was where the studio was going to be. George bought 31 acres on Montserrat with a farmhouse for $70,000 as a base for the studio. He was specifically attracted by the fact that Montserrat was not at the end of a runway and believed the studio needed to be a little off the beaten track, something that artists preferred.

Montserrat is a strange island. It has no white sand beaches. Its black beaches were the result of a dormant volcano which still had open fissures that hadn't erupted for centuries and were not expected to do so ever again. Its main claim to fame as a tourist destination was that it had a very good nine-hole golf course, which pulled in an older, middle-class demographic – not really very rock'n'roll.

However, it is a very attractive, mountainous place, known as the Emerald Isle of the Caribbean because of its high rain levels. Originally populated by Roman Catholic settlers from St Kitts and Nevis who felt persecuted there under British rule, its logo is the shamrock.

It was also extremely difficult to access, with a very basic port and an airport suitable only for small planes. So when we did eventually agree to co-fund the project, we had to embark on what was a major logistical exercise. Everything had to be flown into Antigua and shipped to Montserrat. We knew that once the studio was operational, if the piano needed tuning, the piano tuner would have to fly in from Antigua. If artists wanted the recreational stimulants that are euphemistically called 'fruits and flowers', they would have to come in from Antigua too.

Once George had found the plot, we built the studio to withstand anything. It was hurricane-proof. There were back-up generators to ensure that the air conditioning would work at all times to protect the expensive equipment. We would provide all meals at the studio but artists would not live there: they would rent houses on the island.

I'm still incredibly proud that Chrysalis built a state-of-the-art recording studio on the remote island of Montserrat. We opened with a fanfare and a huge party in 1979 and over the next few years the crème da la crème of the recording world beat a path there: Elton John, The Police, Dire Straits, Duran Duran, Paul McCartney, Art Garfunkel, Eric Clapton & Phil Collins, James Taylor, Keith Richards, Luther Vandross, Simply Red, Sting and The Rolling Stones.

However, it was very difficult to generate an effective bottom line from the Montserrat studio and inevitably a point came when Terry Connolly, by now our MD, advised me to close it. This idea was anathema to George. He had a huge emotional commitment to the island and its people and saw the studio as a great success, at least from a creative standpoint.

We struck a deal which satisfied all parties. We gave George back Chrysalis' 50 per cent shareholding in the studio in return for him extending his producer's contract with us. The studio continued to operate under George's ownership for a while until Hurricane Hugo hit the island in September 1989 and destroyed its infrastructure.

One thing Hugo didn't demolish was the studio. It was hurricane-proof. But it did destroy a great many of the houses where the artists stayed. Faced with this problem, even George reluctantly decided that he had to close down the studio. Within a matter of days, I had a phone call from Jerry Moss in Los Angeles asking me if there was any way that he could buy the mixing desk from AIR Montserrat for A&M Studios on the old Charlie Chaplin film lot in Hollywood.

This was a compliment to the great reputation of the desk, which was a major part of the sound of the studio and it was duly shipped out to Los Angeles. George was thus able to recoup some money from the loss of the studio.

George had bought a six-bedroom hotel on Montserrat, Olveston House, which he continues to use as a family home. However, in 1995 disaster struck the island again when the Soufrière Hills volcano that had been dormant for many centuries erupted, shooting lava and boulders over two thirds of the island and destroying the whole of the capital city of Plymouth, which is now totally under ash like Pompeii after the eruption of Vesuvius in 79AD.

Following the eruption, the government created an exclusion zone. Technically speaking, Olveston House should have been inside it, but the authorities knew how important George was to Montserrat and so made an exception for him. Not everyone was so lucky. Midge Ure had built a home right in the middle of the affected area, which he obviously lost.

Most of the islanders had to leave. Some went to Antigua; some came to the UK. There are now only 4,000 people on the island, down from the previous 12,000. With typical generosity, George staged a benefit concert in 1997 at the Royal Albert Hall. McCartney, Clapton, Mark Knopfler, Sting and other superstars who had recorded at AIR Montserrat appeared. It was one of the best shows I have ever been to.

George has since raised money to build an arts and community centre in Montserrat's new capital, Little Bay. He and Judy are the saviours of Montserrat, effectively its king and queen – not that they would thank me for saying something so extravagant about them.

The Soufrière Hills volcano continues to erupt and I still watch it occasionally from my house in Antigua. A few years ago, George and Judy went to Montserrat for their Christmas holiday and had to be moved out of Olveston House as the ongoing eruption made it too dangerous to remain there. Thankfully the place is now back in operation.

Nevertheless, AIR Montserrat was an amazing success in many ways, even if it never quite took off commercially. Thankfully, I managed to claw back some of our losses after one Christmas holiday. Everywhere I went in Montserrat, I kept hearing the same soca song being blasted out from the bars. Then when I went to Anguilla for a few days, I heard the same catchy tune.

The song was 'Hot Hot Hot' by a Montserrat artist named Arrow. I signed it up to Chrysalis Music and over the years, it has generated millions of pounds via commercials, film soundtracks and cover versions. It was even revived for the 1986 World Cup in Mexico. I still hear it nearly every week, especially in the summer months, and it has been turned into a big football chant.

Every time I hear 'Hot Hot Hot', I think fondly of building that studio against all the odds, and of the beautiful idyll of Montserrat. Few places in the world hold such incredible memories for me.

CHAPTER 12

Gold

As the seventies turned into the eighties, Chrysalis was linked to the ska revival via our 2-Tone deal but that wasn't all that was going on. The New Romantic movement that followed punk and new wave saw bands begin to dress up and look like dandified pop stars again. We embraced two bands at the forefront of this showy, exciting new scene: Ultravox and Spandau Ballet.

Spandau Ballet were immensely important to Chrysalis even though my first reaction to them was that their name was pretty awful. They had come out of the Blitz club scene in London's Soho, they put on events at the Scala Cinema and on HMS Belfast, rather than doing traditional gigs, and there was a major buzz about the band.

It certainly helped that they were a good-looking bunch. Saxophone player (and original guitarist) Steve Norman was the band's heart-throb, alongside Gary Kemp, their songwriter and leader. However, Tony Hadley, the singer with the big presence and the stentorian voice, and Martin Kemp, Gary's bass-playing younger brother, had their fans too.

Our A&R man Stuart Slater was very keen on Spandau Ballet and a bidding war broke out over them that we won in the end.

Their manager, Steve Dagger, who was effectively part of the band, drove a hard bargain. We gave them the highest ever advance for a new British act − £200,000 − creative control, a clothing budget and their own label: Reformation. But it paid off immediately: their first single, 'To Cut A Long Story Short', did very well, as did *Journeys To Glory*, their debut album, and 'Chant No 1 (I Don't Need This Pressure On)' which reached number three in July, 1981.

Spandau Ballet quickly became very big in the UK and mainland Europe but like everyone else they wanted to break America. They were always considered to be in a fierce rivalry with Duran Duran and were as popular in Britain, but it wasn't the case in other parts of the world. At the end of 1982, we sent them to Compass Point Studios in Nassau, in the Bahamas, to be produced by Tony Swain and Steve Jolley, who had worked with the group Imagination.

I flew to Nassau to listen to a playback of what became *True*, and I was hugely impressed. They had made a wonderful blue-eyed soul pop album, notable not only in its superb title track − a UK number one in April 1983 − but also with 'Gold'. Unluckily for them, *True* came at a point when it was hard getting the American side of the company to work on groups signed in the UK.

This created a problem. I had promised the band that *True* would go gold in America and paid them a further advance to demonstrate that belief, but it was difficult to get Terry Ellis interested in them. When the record didn't go gold, they were very unhappy, despite the fact that it was hugely successful in countless territories around the world. I could see their point: the US arm of Chrysalis should have done better as the *True* album sold almost as many copies in Canada, close to half a million, as in the States, and normally Canada would account for just 10% of the US sales.

Spandau Ballet sued Chrysalis and the whole situation became very fractious. In December 1985 we sent the group a case of wine as a Christmas present but Steve Dagger sent it back to us with a rude message scribbled on it. After the next album, *Parade*, they wanted to leave the label and go elsewhere. It's the only time in my career that we ever lost a group in such regrettable circumstances.

The only remotely good thing about the fallout was that Spandau Ballet gave us an awful lot of money – around $2 million – to buy out the rest of their contract and sign to CBS. Yet apart from *Through The Barricades*, which was a good record, they didn't have as much success as they did with us after switching labels. They certainly didn't have any more hits in America. On the whole, in my experience it's very rare for a group to leave one record company and become more successful elsewhere.

I'm on very good terms with Steve Dagger nowadays and never took the conflict personally. He was just doing what he thought was right for his group at the time. In reality, it was no different from me taking Ten Years After away from Deram in 1971 – and arguably, they weren't necessarily any more successful when I moved them to CBS, either. Maybe Steve later came to realise that Spandau Ballet received the Rolls Royce treatment from Chrysalis; they were treated like superstars because, in terms of our record company, they were superstars. When they went to a major corporation like CBS with hundreds of acts, they were just another group.

I have seen this happen time and time again. Acts who have been treated well at independent labels think they'll get the same treatment with a major label but it doesn't happen because they get lost in the flood, and of course once they've signed to the big label they realise their mistake – but by then it's too late.

Towards the end of 1979, two old-school rock managers, Chris Morrison and Chris O'Donnell, who had previously managed Thin Lizzy, came to see me in my office. They played me a couple of new cuts by Ultravox: Midge Ure, who had been in the teenybop band Slik and the new wave group Rich Kids, had replaced John Foxx as their lead singer and guitarist. I thought it was right on the button as regards where music was heading, so I agreed a deal on the spot.

There was some internal company embarrassment to follow: when I told Doug D'Arcy, our managing director, and Roy Eldridge, the head of A&R, that I had signed Ultravox, they replied that they had turned them down two weeks before! Fortunately, another guy who worked in the A&R department, Steve "Archie" Andrews, really liked the group so I wasn't fighting a lone battle.

Ultravox began recording their first album for us. It was supposed to be titled *Torque Point* (which is now the name of one of their fan-sites). It had already been decided that the first single would be 'Sleepwalk', which went Top 30 in June 1980. But the tipping point came when I heard 'Vienna', which I just knew would be a monster hit. Everybody else at the label said it was too long, too slow, too weird, too depressing, but I knew it was the standout track on the record and insisted we retitle the album *Vienna*.

This wonderfully atmospheric song is the record most people associate with Ultravox today. It spent several weeks at number two but it never reached number one. After John Lennon was killed by a gun-toting lunatic at the end of 1980, three of his singles re-entered the charts and '(Just Like) Starting Over', 'Imagine' and 'Woman' all took it in turns to go to number one. We thus postponed the release of 'Vienna' to January 1981 and made a great video for it with Russell Mulcahy in London and in Vienna. It was a mini-movie, directed to resemble a scene from the famous film *The Third Man* and was pretty ground-breaking. How ironic, then, that it was kept off the top of the chart by the Australian Joe Dolce's novelty single 'Shaddap You Face', a strong contender for the worst number one in the history of the British charts. 'Vienna' was recently voted the best ever single not to make number one.

Ultravox then went into a bit of a dip in their career but hit big again with 'Dancing With Tears In My Eyes' in 1984. I had to fight with Midge Ure for six months to get it released as a single off the *Lament* album. He had been determined to go with a track called 'White China' instead. Luckily I prevailed and it hit number three.

As a consequence, their greatest hits album *The Collection* sold over a million copies. Midge, of course, went on to enjoy a good solo career and, with Bob Geldof, become one of the prime movers behind Band Aid. In my job, you get plenty of things wrong, but I am proud that I always seemed to call Ultravox right.

Huey Lewis & The News were another major act who hit big for Chrysalis. Huey and keyboard player Sean Hopper had first emerged in London-based Californian band Clover, who had backed Elvis Costello on his debut album, *My Aim Is True*. After going back to the States, they had regrouped and evolved into Huey Lewis & The American Express but when we signed them we figured the credit card company would probably object so we changed the name of the group to The News.

Their first album didn't get anywhere but on the second one, *Picture This*, they began recording material by other people alongside their own compositions. Their first hit, 'Do You Believe In Love?', was written by Robert John 'Mutt' Lange, who went on to work with AC/DC and Def Leppard, and marry Shania Twain.

When they delivered the 1983 album *Sports,* I was really impressed. We took five singles off the album: 'Heart And Soul', 'I Want A New Drug', 'The Heart Of Rock & Roll', 'If This Is It' and 'Walking On A Thin Line'. They all made the Top 20 in the US and *Sports* went on to top the album charts and sell 10 million copies. They were great live, especially when they added The Tower of Power horn section to the line-up. They toured extensively, and were very professional, with none of the traumas of some artists.

Huey's catchphrase on stage was always, "This is the first time we have played in [the town's name] but I promise you it will not be the last." He even said it when I saw them play in St John's, Newfoundland, one of the most remote places in North America. The entire population of the town, from aged seven to 70, seemed to be there.

In 1984, the band were approached to contribute to the soundtrack of *Ghostbusters*, the movie starring Bill Murray and Dan Aykroyd, but turned it down since they were already committed to doing two songs for *Back To The Future* with Michael J. Fox. Ray Parker Jr. did the *Ghostbusters* theme song but his composition borrowed heavily from 'I Want A New Drug' which had been out a few months prior. Huey and News guitarist Chris Hayes, the co-writers of 'I Want A New Drug', sued for copyright infringement and the matter was settled out of court in their favour.

The following year, *Back To The Future* was the hit movie of the summer and propelled 'The Power Of Love' to number one around the world. Huey also appeared in the film. 'The Power Of Love' established the group internationally and confirmed Chrysalis as a major player that could break US acts around the world – something that to date had eluded our arch-rivals Virgin and Island.

As Huey Lewis & The News' fame grew, they sang 'The Star-Spangled Banner' on an unforgettable night in Candlestick Park in November 1985, when the San Francisco 49ers took on the New York Giants. Doug D'Arcy and I watched the match from the players' bench but sadly the band's efforts were not enough to inspire the 49ers to victory.

On another memorable evening a year later, Bruce Springsteen and Bob Geldof both sang with Huey during the encores of a show in Paris. Afterwards I took them all out to dinner at Fouquet's on the Champs-Élysées, Huey and Bob were besieged by autograph hunters but nobody bothered Bruce Springsteen – in his jeans and T-shirt, he just looked too normal.

I don't have a bad word to say about Huey Lewis & The News, a great bunch of guys who deserve all the success they have achieved. I ran into Huey and fellow band member Johnny Colla in LA recently. They gave me a copy of their album of old soul songs, *Soulsville*. It's fantastic, but I guess their days of chart hits are behind them.

Luckily, I had a natural feel for, and empathy with, the grand sweep of Ultravox, the various musical styles – synth-pop, funk, soul, dance and rock – embraced by Spandau Ballet, and the melodic soft rock of Huey Lewis. I was less well versed in theatre but that didn't stop us investing in it every now and then, often very successfully.

In 1974 Chrysalis invested in the very first Monty Python film, *Monty Python And The Holy Grail*, along with Elton John, Led

Zeppelin and Pink Floyd. It was another gut instinct decision by Terry and myself, because it seemed a good idea and was a great film. Maybe, as Python would say, we were in the mood for Something Completely Different.

We had less success with *Only In America*, which I co-produced with Freddy Bienstock, an all-time great music publisher. Freddy had started out working as an office boy for his cousins at Chappell Music in New York and had spent much of his career working with both Elvis Presley and the legendary songwriting team of Jerry Leiber and Mike Stoller (who, incidentally, had produced the Procol Harum album *Procol's Ninth*). *Only In America*, written by Ned Sherrin and Caryl Brahms, was a musical based on the duo's songs.

We staged it at the Roundhouse with the American actress and singer Bertice Reading heading the cast. Personally I thought the show was marvellous but, because of a few technical hitches with some of the props on the opening night, it received mixed reviews. The show did not transfer to the West End or to New York but it was arguably the forerunner of all the jukebox musicals that have been so successful since.

Only In America was my only foray into attempting to produce a West End show, but in 1981 I had the opportunity to invest in *Cats*. Brian Brolly, a theatrical producer working for Andrew Lloyd Webber, came in to see me. They were in the final throes of putting together the financing for *Cats* but at the last minute they were short of a significant chunk of the budget for the show to open.

They were really struggling and in an attempt to bridge the shortfall they arranged for some board members from CBS Group in New York to fly over to attend a run-through with a view to investing in the show, but they passed. Brian Brolly wanted me to step into their shoes. The investment required was less than the cost of signing an unknown group.

I didn't really know Andrew Lloyd Webber at the time, although we have since become good friends, but back then, I was particularly friendly – as I still am – with Tim Rice. Tim ran Heartaches Cricket

Club and we played them regularly at Locks Barn, my house in Wokingham, throughout the seventies. With an oak tree in the middle, the pitch was not quite up to Test match standards but it was still a glorious setting for cricket.

Chrysalis had a pretty good side, including Nick Blackburn, Storm Thorgerson, the graphic designer from Hipgnosis who created so many striking album covers for Pink Floyd and some of our acts like UFO, and Tony Burrows, the session singer who once sung on three separate hits on the same edition of *Top Of The Pops*. The Heartaches were our most regular opponents.

Tim wasn't involved in *Cats* and I wasn't sure about investing in an Andrew Lloyd-Webber show without his famous partner's input: Andrew's previous show without Tim, *Jeeves*, had not been a success. So, for a combination of business and friendship reasons, I turned down the chance to invest in *Cats*. Even worse, I went along to the first night and during the interval was congratulating myself on how I had made the right decision.

I wasn't convinced by the show and the opening night wasn't helped by a bomb scare which meant Brian Blessed had to go on stage and ask everyone to evacuate the theatre. The reviews were very mixed: people either loved or hated it.

Of course, passing on the record-breaking, phenomenally successful *Cats* proved to be one of my very worst business decisions. It is safe to say musicals are not my strong point: I went to the opening night of *Mamma Mia*, the ABBA musical, in 1999 and also predicted failure. Nearly a decade and a half later, it is still running.

Back in the music industry that I knew, I became deputy chairman of the BPI Council, the trade association of the British record industry. The chairman, John Fruin, ran WEA in the UK, but had to resign after being accused of over-pressing quantities of hit albums specifically to sell as surplus stock (cut-outs, as they were known) to a company he owned privately.

After Fruin's departure, I became chairman of the BPI for the rest of that term and was then elected in my own right for a following term.

It was extremely time-consuming, but it showed how significant Chrysalis had become as a record company. I like to think that, during my time as chairman, I was at the forefront of several major innovations in how the industry was run.

Home-taping had first become a thorny issue within the record industry when the cassette player became a standard component of most stereo systems. When music cassettes became popular, hardware manufacturers started selling double-deck cassette recorders that allowed music fans to duplicate cassette copies of anything. I guess they were the forerunners of today's illegal downloads.

Throughout the early eighties, I was at the forefront of a campaign lobbying the government for a levy on blank tapes. We launched a campaign called 'Home taping is killing music' using a skull and crossbones logo to emphasise the fact that cassette copies were 'pirate' recordings.

We weren't helped by the fact that the record companies didn't present a united front on the matter. Island Records was selling an item called 'One Plus One', a chromium dioxide cassette which combined a pre-recorded album by an Island act on one side with the other side left blank for the consumer to use and tape whatever else they fancied. I had to persuade Chris Blackwell of the folly of this campaign.

However, my chairmanship of the BPI is probably best remembered because in 1982 I originated what was to become the BRIT Awards. Having attended the Grammy Awards in America several times, I felt we really needed something like that in Britain as a vehicle for promoting artists to a wider audience.

The only annual event at the time was the *Music Week* Awards and I thought they were too business related and disrespectful to some of the musicians. I met with a good deal of resistance from the other record companies because nobody wanted to upset *Music Week,* as they were dependent on their support for breaking artists, but I was adamant that we needed a regular event in the calendar.

The first BPI Awards, as it was then known, started as a BAFTA-like black-tie dinner at the Grosvenor House Hotel in Park Lane, with no live performers and no TV coverage. David Jacobs compered the event and it honoured Adam & The Ants, The Human League, Police and Soft Cell, among others. In 1983 it was renamed the British Record Industry Awards, hosted by Tim Rice, and Culture Club, Dexy's Midnight Runners, Dire Straits and Kim Wilde triumphed.

However, the event really took off with television coverage. In 1985, Prince made headlines when he appeared to collect his award with a bodyguard who towered over him. The next year, Phil Collins opened the show and Huey Lewis & The News won Best International Group and performed 'The Power Of Love'. In 1988, we moved to the Royal Albert Hall and from 1989, the event was renamed the BRITS.

In a similar vein, I also helped to instigate the Prince's Trust rock galas. I was first approached by Tony Stratton-Smith, the founder of Charisma Records, who introduced me to Peter Smith, who was close to the Prince of Wales and helped to run The Prince's Trust. Their idea was to start a more contemporary version of the Royal Command Performance.

Prince Charles wanted to involve music groups from under-privileged areas that the Trust had already helped, and give them a showcase in a major concert in the West End. I set up a committee including George Martin, and artists like Pete Townshend, to choose the bands from the Trust, and I set about putting together the rest of the show.

The first event in 1982 was at the Dominion Theatre in Tottenham Court Road, and as we had a short deadline to find the artists many of the performers were acts I personally knew: Jethro Tull, Madness, Joan Armatrading, Phil Collins, Kate Bush and Pete Townshend. With the public unsure as to what the event was all about, the show only sold out the day before.

The following year, I wisely involved Harvey Goldsmith in helping put together the show, and we were able to secure Duran Duran and

Dire Straits, both of whom were flying high at the time and had been widely acknowledged in the press as being Princess Diana's favourite groups. Our former finance director Nick Blackburn was handling the ticketing and when he mentioned this to Princess Diana on the night, she told him: "Oh no, they are not my favourite groups, Supertramp are. What has happened to them?"

Nick replied that they, as happens with most groups, had simply come to the end of the road. "It sounds just like a marriage," replied the Princess of Wales. Nick was flabbergasted.

The Dominion had been a nightmare from a security point of view, and the following year we moved it to the Royal Albert Hall. Princess Diana always really enjoyed the evenings and the Prince's Trust Rock Galas became an established event for many years.

Under my tenure, the BPI also began spending around £2 million a year producing official industry charts for sales of singles and albums. Up until 1969, there hadn't really been an official chart. *Music Week* had its own chart, as did magazines like *Melody Maker* and *New Musical Express*. Things had improved in the seventies with the British Market Research Bureau but we arranged for the BPI to join forces with the BBC and *Music Week* in 1983, and in order to have one official chart we broadened the number of shops surveyed.

The BBC and *Music Week* both helped to finance the chart, which didn't require much of a sample in order to get an accurate picture of which records were selling but needed one large enough to prevent record companies from manipulating the charts. Of all the innovations that I introduced during my time in charge at the BPI, this is the one of which I am most proud, an achievement for which I hope I will be long remembered.

As chairman of the BPI, I also joined the board of the international record company association, the IFPI. Meanwhile, Terry Ellis, through Chrysalis Records in America, had joined the board of the RIAA, the Recording Industry Association of America, and shortly after was also elected chairman. There was thus an amazing period when the two major record industry trade associations were chaired by Terry and myself.

It showed how big Chrysalis had become and how far Terry and I, as co-founders of a small British independent record company who began our careers by booking acts for our respective university unions, had progressed within the music industry on both sides of the Atlantic.

However, the accolade came at a price as it really did not make sense for both of us to be spending so much time on industry matters when we were both so important to the continued success of our own company.

In a way, it was maybe also a worrying sign that the friendly competitiveness that was so important to the dynamic between Terry and myself was beginning to get out of control. The line that divided us, that made us click, was very fragile. Was it about to snap?

CHAPTER 13

Crime Of Passion

Horses and horse racing have long been a passion of mine and my interest was initially triggered by an unlikely figure – Dave Robinson, the founder and owner of the renowned punk/new wave record label Stiff Records.

Halfway through a BPI board meeting I was chairing in 1981, Dave rose from his seat, made vague excuses and left. He called me the next day to apologise and I said, "That's OK, we all have things to do. I guess you had an important meeting to run off to?" Dave told me, no, I went to Doncaster to see a horse run. I have to admit that I was surprised.

He went on to tell me that his horse had won and he had picked up a pretty decent purse into the bargain. The prize money was £10,000 and he had bet £1,000 at 10-1. So while I was chairing a BPI council meeting, Dave had been swanning around a racecourse picking up £20,000 in cash. Jealous, I suggested that he should have told me before, as I would have had a bet on it.

Dave explained that he was in the process of putting together a consortium to buy a training yard in the famous Berkshire horse racing town of Lambourn, under trainer Ray Laing. Tony Stratton-

Smith, the founder of Charisma Records, Chris Blackwell of Island, Chris O'Donnell, who was co-managing Thin Lizzy and Ultravox, and Billy Gaff, who looked after Rod Stewart, were all involved. I decided I would join them and we got the training yard up and running. We owned 20% each, but it was not a success, certainly not from a financial standpoint, and it wasn't long before everybody abandoned that scheme.

However, Tony Stratton-Smith, or Strat as his friends called him, had always had horses. He sponsored the Charisma Gold Cup at Kempton Park for many years. I'd first met him in the late sixties when he used to frequent a music biz drinking club called La Chasse, a few doors up from the Marquee on Wardour Street. His normal line was "mine's a large one dear boy". He became a great mate.

Strat was a bon viveur and raconteur who managed The Creation, The Nice and The Bonzo Dog Doo Dah Band before starting The Famous Charisma Label – as its court jester logo used to claim – in 1969. Geordie folk-rockers Lindisfarne were their first notable success but Genesis proved to be more durable in the long term. In fact, Terry and I met with Genesis in an attempt to lure the group to Chrysalis. At one point I thought we were close to signing them but I decided to withdraw because of my friendship with Strat. It seemed unethical to me.

This was unusual in a dog-eat-dog world of rock where everybody was trying to steal everybody's artists all the time. Most label owners in my position would have had no compunction about nicking ours, but I just didn't think it was the right thing to do.

Strat had been the football writer for the northern edition of the now defunct *Daily Sketch* national newspaper. A great friend of legendary Manchester United manager Matt Busby, he was scheduled to fly on the plane that crashed at Munich in 1958, killing 23 including seven United players. The night before the flight to Belgrade, he was sent to Wrexham to cover a Wales under-23 international but got snowed in and couldn't get back to Manchester to make the flight.

When Strat eventually sold Charisma in 1983, he came to see me. At the time, Chrysalis and Virgin were the hottest independent companies in the country, and he was in negotiations with both of us, but Virgin offered him more money.

I made him what I thought was a very good offer before he went to see Richard Branson. Strat then called me from Richard's office, with Richard listening to the call, to tell me he had a bigger offer, and asked me to increase mine. I was tempted to figure out how I could rescue the deal, but I knew that Richard, having got him in his office, would not let him leave without an agreement. So, just to muddy the waters, I said, "Whatever Richard offers you, I will double it." I imagine Strat extracted a little more from Richard and that was that.

I was upset as it struck me that buying Charisma would have been the perfect solution to solve the problems that were developing between Terry Ellis and myself. One of us could have had Charisma and the other one could have had Chrysalis. I would have been equally happy with either. We should really have broken the bank to buy Charisma.

Strat moved to the Canary Islands for tax reasons, but died of pancreatic cancer in 1987. There was no TV coverage of British racing there, so he flew to the Channel Islands, which he was legally allowed to enter, specifically to watch the Cheltenham racing festival on TV. Tragically, he died the morning of the first day of the 1987 meeting, and his ashes were scattered over the last fence at Newbury racecourse. Or, at least that was the intention, but a combination of a strong wind and rather inebriated 'scatterers' saw the ashes deposited all over the clothing of those present. Maybe it's what he would have wanted. That day Strat's horse, Sergeant Smoke, romped home at 20-1!

Strat was responsible for starting the training career of Jenny Pitman, the first woman to train a Grand National winner. In the late seventies he and I had even owned a horse in a partnership but since then my interest had waned.

Strat left me a parting gift before his death. In 1981, after Dave Robinson had rekindled my interest in horse racing, Dave, Strat and I went with trainer Ray Laing to the Newmarket yearling sales. Strat pointed to a filly in the catalogue and told me he thought she would be perfect for me. I bought her for 12,000 guineas and named her Crime Of Passion after the very successful Pat Benatar album.

When I came back from the Christmas holidays in January 1982, I began hearing from both Dave Robinson and the trainer that Crime Of Passion could be quite useful. This came at a time when Terry Ellis had moved back to England and had bought a house in Newmarket, another training centre, where he spent weekends.

Terry was not involved with the training yard in Lambourn but he decided he wanted an involvement with racing. So he bought a horse and I bought half of it and he took half of Crime Of Passion. We would be partners in each other's horses.

We got off to a flyer. Crime Of Passion won her maiden race, at Kempton Park, and she won next time as well, at Newbury, in a more competitive race. That meant she had earned the right to run in the Queen Mary Stakes at Royal Ascot, the top race for two-year-old fillies at that stage of the season, giving us all a big day out in the process.

She ran a great race and came second which at the time I was very disappointed by. It shows how well she had been doing: in reality, coming second at Royal Ascot is something that happens once in a blue moon and we should have been thrilled about it. She was beaten by a filly owned by Sheikh Hamdam Al Maktoum, one of the Dubai brothers who were just beginning to make their presence felt in English racing.

The big day out was marred by an unfortunate incident. Terry and I had taken a box at Royal Ascot for the day and invited lots of friends. When we picked up the race cards, for some unknown reason, Terry's name had been omitted from the race card as being one of the two owners.

I had no idea why it had happened but was concerned that Terry might think I had done it on purpose. I thought maybe it was an error on the part of my trainer but the system doesn't work like that. The racing authorities take care of this kind of stuff. It was no one's fault but it was really embarrassing and it ruined the whole day because I was upset for Terry. Bizarrely, I have never known this mistake to happen again in 30 years of racing horses.

Anyway, having come second in the Queen Mary, the next big race for Crime Of Passion was a few weeks later in the Cherry Hinton Stakes at Newmarket, a similar kind of race, except one furlong – 200 metres – longer. A lot of the top two-year-old fillies were running, including the one that had beaten her at Royal Ascot, and that horse had to carry three pounds extra as a penalty for her win. This was the ideal natural progression for Crime Of Passion except for the fact that her pedigree and style of running suggested she would not be quite as effective over the longer distance.

For his part, Terry had by now decided he wasn't getting any fun out of co-owning Crime of Passion. He was still smarting over the Ascot race card omission. His trainer told him that she would have no chance of winning at Newmarket as she would be inconvenienced by having to run over a longer distance, and that her current resale value, by now about £50,000 or £60,000, would be affected if she ran badly.

Terry advised me not to run her but I refused, saying adamantly, "She is going to run." "Well, you can buy me out, then," he responded. We did a deal and I bought 100% of her while he got 100% of his own horse back. I gave him a pretty decent profit on his purchase price based on her then valuation.

Lo and behold, in an unbelievably exciting race at Newmarket, Crime Of Passion managed to hang on by a nose and win, beating her conqueror from Ascot. I now felt embarrassed once again because, at his insistence, I had bought out Terry before the race and the horse had done what no one expected and won. This obviously increased her value, but by how much I had no idea.

I immediately started receiving a number of phone calls from people trying to buy Crime Of Passion at a price way above the valuation Terry and I agreed when I sold him back his share. Philip Mitchell, who was representing the Dubai Maktoum family and now runs Prince Khalid Abdullah's British stud farm interests, asked if I would I be interested in selling Crime Of Passion. I declined as I felt I couldn't really sell her at a profit, having just bought her from Terry. He then offered me the staggering sum of £400,000 for her.

I said I would consider it but I still felt awkward, and said no. Philip Mitchell came back and relayed an offer of £450,000. I knew nothing about the economics of selling racehorses and at this point was well out of my depth. Philip said the potential buyers were very rich, and that there were two horses they were trying to buy. They had bought the other one and now they wanted to buy mine. He thought they would go up to £500,000.

I didn't quite understand the significance of what he was saying but I still felt I was in a very difficult situation. I didn't want to make the problem with Terry worse so I declined yet again. The next morning, I read in the *Racing Post* that Her Majesty the Queen had sold her top filly, Height Of Fashion. That was the other horse the Maktoum family had been trying to buy! So, I had said no and the Queen had said yes. I could only think: how stupid of me was that?

As it happens, the filly the Queen sold on that occasion became one of the greatest foundation brood mares of all time and has been responsible for Derby winners and a heritage of top horses. With hindsight, the Queen should not have sold her.

For my part, on purely economic grounds I should have sold Crime Of Passion. She never won another race, but I kept her and she became the foundation brood mare of my whole breeding operation. In fact her grandson, Bungle In The Jungle – named after a Jethro Tull song – won major races at Goodwood and Ascot as recently as summer 2012. The pleasure that Crime of Passion and her descendants has given me is beyond words.

Chelle and I also settled in horse-racing territory with the purchase of Glebe House in Gloucestershire in 1981. We had moved around, from Locks Barn via a couple of London residencies, to a country property in Buckinghamshire.

This place had originally been an inn called The Ship, which was renamed the Shakespeare House because Shakespeare used to stay there on his journeys to London. Chelle had fallen in love with it and it was full of history – including a monk's crawl, where Catholic priests would hide during the Reformation of the 16th century – and housed several ghosts, but it wasn't in an interesting part of England. After a couple of years, we decided that, if we were going to have a country house, it should be somewhere nice like the Cotswolds.

Chelle was quite friendly with the wife of Stephen Gottlieb, a long-standing record company executive in the UK who had been chairman of PolyGram. Her sister, Leslie, married to the artist Bill Jacklin, owned a house out near Chipping Norton that they were trying to sell. We went to see this house and agreed to buy it.

We got to the stage of going out to sort out the carpets and curtains. I had flown back from America, arrived on a Friday morning and was in bed trying to grab a couple of hours sleep before going to the office. Flicking through *The Times,* I saw an advert for a couple of houses in Gloucestershire that looked interesting. I thought perhaps we should go and look at them. There was nothing to lose since they were located near where we were going anyway.

We didn't like the first one but as soon as we got to the second house, Glebe House, I fell completely in love with it. Chelle did too but she was wary of the aggravation of changing our plans around. We then had to go to Bill Jacklin's house and we were very reticent about agreeing which curtains and carpets to buy from them because, once we did that, we would be committed. We were back-pedalling a little bit.

We then went back to our house in Buckinghamshire. It was Guy Fawkes Night 1981 and I decided on the spot that I wanted Glebe House. However, it was a Saturday night, I was leaving for Australia for 10 days two days later, and we had to have a second look. I couldn't decide from just one look so we had to go back.

We had no sales particulars, and could not remember the address. I re-looked up the advert in *The Times* and by some process of detective work we managed to get hold of the woman who owned the house. She said she had people coming to look at the house every hour on the hour that Sunday but in the end she agreed that if we came at 2.30 she could show us the house again while other prospective buyers were in the gardens. That visit was enough. We decided to buy it.

Since I was going to Australia, we were hoping to get it done quickly. The house was on the market for £150,000 at the time. So I offered them £140,000 and they said no. I then offered the asking price and they turned that down too.

Just as the plane was going to leave, I said I would make it £160,000 just to get the deal closed before I went away. When they came back to me, they explained they'd had so much interest that they were going to go to sealed bids in a week's time, in the middle of my Australian trip. I had to arrange for an estate agent to act on my behalf in my absence

The agent advised me that we could not rely on the selling agency keeping my bid confidential prior to the deadline and that the only way I would get it would be if my bid came in at one minute before the deadline. I arranged for my driver to go down with the bid and do exactly that. I worked out a bid of £183,310 by a process of trying to make sure that I was above everybody else. In fact, it was really no more than inspired guesswork, but I believe I was the highest bidder by £100 or something like that.

Incidentally, the Chipping Norton house that we nearly bought until dropping out in order to buy Glebe House was subsequently bought by David (now Lord) Sainsbury and his wife, Susie, who then sold it to Jeremy and Frances Clarkson. They still own it and have extended it extremely well.

Richard Branson was for many years my friendly nemesis and main rival in the music industry. Are we at all similar? Well, Richard was once famously described as a businessman pretending to be a music man while I was called a music man pretending to be a businessman. I guess it is pretty hard to argue with that.

Richard's rise to become one of the world's most successful entrepreneurs was not without a few hiccups along the way. Richard and his partners launched Virgin Records in 1972, and I first ran into him in Cannes in 1973. However, his first foray into the music business – the launch pad for all his other enterprises – nearly ended up with him having a very nasty shock to the system. Apparently the headmaster at his school, Stowe, was quite prophetic when he said Richard would end up either a multi-millionaire or in jail. For a while it looked a little touch and go as he was discovered by the customs and excise authorities to have been illegally selling records in the UK which had been granted export licenses, thus removing the requirement to pay purchase tax on their sales. It was only when his competitors began to question how he could undercut their prices to such an extent that the authorities twigged his scheme. I believe the Branson family home ended up being re-mortgaged to pay the legal fees to get him off the hook. But, as they say, the rest is history and he deserves enormous credit for the way in which he has achieved his success.

Having survived that setback, Richard had started Virgin Records and had tremendous success with Mike Oldfield's *Tubular Bells* before signing the Sex Pistols and new wave acts like Magazine and XTC. In the early eighties, as both labels enjoyed their halcyon periods, Virgin and Chrysalis were deadly rivals.

We had Spandau Ballet, Billy Idol, Pat Benatar and Huey Lewis & The News: they had Orchestral Manoeuvres In The Dark, The Human League, Simple Minds and Culture Club. For a while, we went toe to toe against each other. A&M and Island, who had been around longer than us, were the other two major independents back then, but we always seemed to be coming up against Virgin.

One Friday evening in 1985, I invited Richard over for a drink in Gloucestershire specifically to discuss the way the competition between the A&R departments at Chrysalis and Virgin was driving up the cost of signing new acts. It was crazy and the only people benefiting were the major labels. He arrived with his wife, Joan, their four-year-old daughter, Holly, and toddler son, Sam.

I told Richard, "We're not the competition: the majors are! We should be working together. The majors are rubbing their hands with glee seeing us go head to head over everything." Richard admitted that Virgin had identified Chrysalis as being its main competitor but said that there was nothing he could do about it.

Richard stood at the window of Glebe House as Holly made quite a good job of trying to trash all our antique furniture, and said: "Chris, that's a fantastic view. Do you own all the land?" I explained that I only owned the house and the gardens while the rest was owned by the church commissioners but was about to come onto the market. They were selling the farm and 420 acres.

"I suppose you're going to buy it," said Richard.

"No," I replied. "I'm not really interested. I grew up on a farm in Lincolnshire, I've spent too much of my life on a farm."

"Well, I will, then," said Richard.

"I was only joking!" I told him, as quick as a flash. "Of course I'm going to buy it."

Richard had been deadly serious. Unbeknown to me, he had recently tried unsuccessfully to buy an estate about three or four miles away. It was one thing to be in competition with Richard in the music business but I didn't fancy having my arch rival living next door to me at the weekend as well.

Had it not been for Richard Branson, I would not have purchased the farm. However, having bought it, I set about converting it into a stud farm. It is now one of the most renowned studs in England, and is building a worldwide reputation with the help of John Wall, who has worked for me from the very start.

In fact, had it not been for Richard's audacious offer, my whole life would have been vastly different. I would no longer be living in Glebe House or in the village, because I would eventually have wanted to own a stud farm and I would have moved somewhere else to get the land to do that. Unwittingly, he did me an enormous favour.

We also sold our large London property in Phillimore Gardens and bought an apartment in York House near Kensington Palace Gardens for when we needed to stay in the capital. It was all change in that particular area of my life − and unknown to me, there were plenty more radical alterations on the way.

CHAPTER 14

One Man Band

The drug culture in the Chrysalis Los Angeles office at the start of the eighties may not have been the worst in the industry but it was certainly a contender. The London office also had its moments but the problem was nowhere near the same.

We had hired Russ Shaw from Warners as VP of artist development, but his real role was to grease the wheels with the talent. His expenses were spectacular. Russ was great fun, gay, an enthusiastic and serial substance abuser, and died very young at the beginning of the AIDS epidemic.

With the London and LA offices thriving and artists from both sides of the pond regularly crossing the Atlantic, I spent a good deal of time in LA, and almost always enjoyed it. I would usually fly out for about a week or 10 days, taking the 10 a.m. Concorde to New York, and connecting on to the 9.30 American Airlines flight to LA, getting there in time for lunch – particularly useful on Sundays, when I could deliver the newspapers with the football results to the resident Brits in those pre-internet days.

Terry had decided in 1978 to move into a massive house in Pacific Palisades. It was so big that I suggested he might convert the drawing room into an indoor tennis court! It had originally been a ballroom for an even larger estate. Terry hired an English butler and bought a Rolls-Royce Corniche. Huge Hollywood parties were regularly held there. He was living the life of the Hollywood music tycoon.

The seventies and eighties were the good old days of the music business, but Terry was living a life of excess in more ways than one, as many people in Los Angeles were doing back then. It was also quite a dangerous period. Historically, drug culture in the music business had been pretty innocuous and mostly involved marijuana, but now it was all about drugs such as cocaine that were far more lethal.

On the whole I managed to avoid it. Silly as it may sound, I think it was the fact that I played tennis every morning. Having grown up playing table tennis in Lincolnshire, I had begun playing tennis far more regularly after building a tennis court at the Locks Barn house. It helped to keep me fit, and sane.

I was no puritan, or stranger to showy excess. When I visited LA, I usually stayed in a suite at the Beverly Hills Hotel, where I kept an open-top Mercedes with QPR registration plates. The hotel had two tennis courts run by the 1959 Wimbledon men's champion, the Peruvian Alex Olmedo, and in addition to him I also played with our lawyer, Abe Somer, at his beautiful house in the Hollywood Hills.

Terry had no such sporting interest or release. It became quite clear that he was suffering from the excesses of the life that he was leading in California. Unlike me, he had no wife or family to help keep his feet on the ground, and as the British wing of Chrysalis continued to prosper, he took to complaining that he had the worst end of the deal in being in LA. His behaviour became increasingly unpredictable: he even banned all employees in the LA office from wearing blue jeans, for no obvious reason. Quite difficult in the music business in California.

His romantic life was equally erratic. After Karen Carpenter, he dated a girl called Marilyn Grabowski who was photo editor for *Playboy* magazine. She was older than Terry and, with all due respect, never looked like the kind of calming influence he needed or a partner with whom he might start a family.

Things came to a head when our UK head of business affairs innocuously introduced him at a function in London as "Terry, who runs our American company". Terry took huge offence to this as he was my partner in Chrysalis and resented being portrayed as the chap who ran the satellite office in LA. So, after a good 10 years of shuttling between Tortola and Los Angeles, he declared that he was going to return to London.

Oh dear. We had been living apart for many years now. Would London be big enough to hold both of us?

Before he moved back to the UK, Terry attended a Chrysalis corporate get-together at Leeds Castle in Kent. He was not in great shape. To most people there, his behaviour looked pretty erratic: he seemed to be in a bit of a mess. I had my work cut out trying to get him to hold it together and not make phone calls at four in the morning.

I decided to take him away for a few days. Chelle and I had a house on Cap D'Antibes. Having bought a Porsche sports car in Switzerland and needing to get it down to the South of France, I thought it might be a nice idea to fly to Geneva with Terry and drive the car down to Cap D'Antibes. Terry loved his gastronomic trips so I suggested staying at places down the Rhône Valley for a couple of nights on the way to the French Riviera. He and I stayed in some wonderful hotels and had a good time, but his behaviour remained erratic and the middle-of-the-night phone calls continued. I realised his problems ran way too deep to be cured by a few days away – and his determination to return to live and work in London was absolute.

Yet Terry's profile remained very high in the US and in 1982 he was invited to make the keynote speech at the National Association of Record Merchandisers (NARM) Convention in LA. This was a huge event in the record industry calendar and although it was essentially an independent distributor conference, it attracted the full complement of senior executives from the majors.

Terry made a controversial speech that went down like a lead balloon. He began by stating that if he were a 25-year-old entrepreneur, the record business would have little to attract him and furthermore, if he had a son, he would advise him to seek another career path. He highlighted the problems the industry would face from video players and software and cable TV, pointed out that increased opportunities for consumer entertainment spending would cut heavily into industry profits, and foresaw a sophisticated cable music network that could eventually lead to a world of music without records, which meant that the record business as we knew it was in danger of extinction.

In hindsight, Terry's speech was incredibly prophetic, although it was typical of him that it was the right speech but very definitely at the wrong time and in the wrong environment. With 3,000 executives in the audience whose careers and prosperity were totally connected to the success of the record business, it was not a keynote address they wanted to hear.

The speech received muted applause and not the usual obligatory standing ovation and afterwards, many record executives and merchandisers did their best to counter the message of his keynote address. Jerry Moss was quoted as saying "the music business is as good a place to be now as it was 20 years ago". One speaker who didn't mention Terry by name made a slighting comment about those who knocked the industry yet drove Rolls Royces parked outside.

In the event, following the recession of 1981, the industry remained extremely healthy for a decade or so, not least because the introduction of CDs enabled labels to resell records to consumers who had previously bought the same music on vinyl. However, in today's era of digital piracy and illegal downloading, Terry's comments appear more prescient than ever.

With Terry's return to London imminent, it became clear that major structural changes to the company would be necessary. It would be impossible for him to remain in hands-on control of our American operation with the eight-hour time difference to Los Angeles. We therefore took a decision to relocate the US operation to New York, which would make communication easier.

At the same time, we decided to end our relationship with the network of independents who had distributed our records in the USA and do a deal instead with CBS. This was fraught with problems. With records in the States all supplied on a sale or return basis, we were bound to endure a deluge of returns as the indies flushed out all the stagnant product from the system.

We knew it would create a cash-flow nightmare that would severely affect the company and were not sure if we could withstand it. We even considered selling 50% of the US company to CBS, and dispatched two of our top men, Terry Connolly and Nigel Butterfield, to New York to commence negotiations on this last-resort option, which we codenamed Project Elephant. Thankfully, we didn't need to as we managed to secure loans to see us through the tough period.

Moving to New York was a major logistical undertaking. We had to find offices plus hire new staff, as some of the LA staff declined to relocate to the East Coast. We took a lease on a floor of offices at 645 Madison Avenue and, at CBS' insistence, hired a music business veteran, Jack Craigo, to run the New York-based company. Jack had worked for CBS, so we felt he would help smooth the transition.

Our US president, Sal Licata, did not relocate – and was not given the opportunity. Terry held the view that Sal was so close to the independent distributors that his heart would not be into making the change, and that a new start with someone keyed in to the CBS system would be a positive. Sal was most unhappy as he had kept the company stable in a difficult situation.

Thankfully, most of the other key staff did relocate. Our head of A&R, Jeff Aldrich, had originally come from New York and was happy to go back east, which was lucky as he was closely involved with Pat Benatar, Billy Idol and Blondie. Our VP of promotion, Billy Bass, a very cool operator, also made the move.

Billy was the epitome of a high maintenance US promotion man with all that entails, especially in the field of expenses. On one occasion a group of us flew up from New York to Toronto for the evening to see a band perform. We all arrived at La Guardia airport with small overnight bags, except Billy who pitched up with two large suitcases. Somewhat perplexed, we thought nothing further of it until Jack Craigo later checked his expenses and found that Billy had taken three months' supply of dry cleaning with him to have it attended to and paid for as part of the hotel bill!

A&R and radio promotion were the only two important functions in the US in those days. It was a simple formula; you signed the right acts, you made the right records and you got them played on radio. So, those two guys were your key people. It was a little different in the UK, where weekly pop papers like *New Musical Express* and *Melody Maker* and the *Top Of The Pops* TV show were influential in helping to create artists.

America didn't even have an equivalent to *Top Of The Pops* which was why, when MTV launched in 1981, only English acts were familiar with the concept of video, and MTV was full of their clips, triggering a new British invasion of acts like Duran Duran and Billy Idol. Of course the US acts soon caught up and began spending hundreds of thousands of dollars on their videos.

One Chrysalis executive who stayed in LA was Cathy Nelson, who had been hired as head of A&R administration and then later took up a position with Chrysalis Music. She left and went to MCA, under Irving Azoff, and built a stellar reputation as the top movie soundtrack compilation consultant in the industry. Most hit soundtracks bear her hallmark.

With Concorde our office in New York was only three and a half hours' flight time away, so it became possible for Terry to keep on top of things from London and communication became easier for all of us. We did, however, keep some of our space in 9255 Sunset Boulevard for the music publishing company, which would remain there, along with a West Coast support office for the record company.

One of Terry's last acts before returning from the US was to persuade me that we should invest in a US TV production company with a woman called Linda Yellen. Chrysalis Yellen was to make programmes for the networks and sell them overseas. The business model was, you secured a commission from a network for a show and they would pay you, say, $1 million to produce the programme. You would make the show, own international distribution rights and, hopefully, make your profit from overseas sales. You might even spend more on the show than the network paid you – which was known as deficit financing – if you were confident of securing excellent international deals.

Linda Yellen had some form. Before Chrysalis came along, in 1980 she had produced the film *Playing For Time*, starring Vanessa Redgrave as Fania Fénelon, a Jewish woman sent to the Auschwitz concentration camp who joined an orchestra playing classical music for her captors. It won four Emmy Awards.

Chrysalis Yellen made two more films for television. They were both real-life stories. *Jacobo Timerman: Prisoner Without A Name, Cell Without A Number* with Roy Scheider and Liv Ullman, was the story of an Argentinian man who disappeared without trace.

However, the most high-profile project was *The Royal Romance Of Charles And Diana*, a 1982 made-for-TV movie based on the love story between the Prince of Wales and Lady Diana Spencer, with Christopher Baines and Catherine Oxenberg. Olivia de Havilland was the Queen Mother, Dana Wynter the Queen and Stewart Granger Prince Philip. It was a long way from anything we'd done before and, to a degree, an embarrassment for the company to be associated with at the time.

However, I had to admit I found it was very amusing. There was a funny breakfast scene between the Queen and Prince Philip with the Queen checking the form in the *Racing Post*, obviously a cameo introduced by Terry because of his knowledge of the Queen's interest in horse racing, something which would not normally have appeared in an American film about the Royal Family.

(Incidentally, Linda Yellen clearly figures if it's not broke, don't fix it: she recently produced a similar film about the Duke and Duchess of Cambridge called – wait for it – *William & Catherine: A Royal Romance*.)

Chrysalis Yellen was struggling financially. Linda herself was guaranteed significant production fees by the business regardless of whether it made a profit. We were paying more money in deficit financing in the US than we were getting back in international deals. The company was destined to lose a considerable amount of money and it didn't help my fragile relationship with Terry because I felt this was not what we should be doing at that point in time. It was an unnecessary distraction.

At the same time, Terry did create a London office for Beryl Vertue who had worked for Robert Stigwood on the television distribution side, having previously been an agent for Tony Hancock and Frankie Howerd. She was a bit of a lost soul in the office, but if we had structured a situation where Beryl had been fully integrated into the company in the UK, we could have created something worthwhile. She has since been very successful with her company, Hartswood Films, producing many big shows such as *Men Behaving Badly* and *Sherlock*. She was also awarded an OBE for her services to television.

Having arrived back in London fairly disoriented from his adventures in Los Angeles, Terry was understandably keen to put down some roots and get his life moving again. Chelle and I unwittingly helped him on this path by finding him a wife.

My eldest son, Tim, was attending Hill House in Mayfair where his best friend was Frederic Moeller, whose mother, Danielle, was divorced from his father, a successful art dealer called Achim Moeller. Danielle's father worked in the French diplomatic service.

Chelle and I used to throw big dinner parties and charitable events at that time. At a cocktail party we held to raise funds for one particular charity, Chelle arranged for Danielle to be Terry's blind date. There didn't appear to be any chemistry at all and Chelle and I later agreed that the date appeared to have been a disaster.

How wrong we were. Terry and Danielle became an item and before too long were living together, with Danielle's two kids from her marriage to Achim. They then announced that they would marry in Tortola, where Terry still had his home, in April 1980 – and Terry asked me to be his best man.

I flew out to Tortola a week early with my family and we chartered a sailing boat and sailed around the Virgin Islands for a week. Arriving in Tortola for the wedding, I realised I had not brought a white suit, which Terry felt was a prerequisite for my best man role. I was about to be relieved of the job when, at the very last minute, a friend of Terry's who lived on the island stepped in and lent me one.

Back in London, Terry Connolly had made a deal with Nigel Thomas, who managed Joe Cocker, for us to provide the finance for a new company to be called Records To Read which would publish glossy biographies of artists in the shape of a 12-inch LP, which could be stocked in record stores in the LP racks. After providing over a million pounds of capital, it became apparent that no Records To Read would ever be delivered. Nigel Thomas had simply pocketed the cash.

Terry, coincidentally, had also agreed to buy Nigel's apartment near the Royal Albert Hall as his London home. Somehow, I ended up having to write off the whole loss on the deal, and at the same time arrange payment to Nigel, at Terry's request, for the purchase of the flat.

Terry's lifestyle had now altered completely. He was ensconced in London, with a wife, two stepchildren and eventually children of his own. He also bought a country home in Newmarket, where he joined the local hunt, and rode with the hounds.

Nevertheless, his newly found relative personal stability didn't seem to make our relationship any easier. We were beginning to fall out over everything and nothing, even the ownership of a race horse! As difficult as it was for me it was equally a problem for Chelle who now had to cope for the first time with another queen bee in the hive.

On opposite sides of the planet, Terry and I could work well together. In close proximity, it soon became clear that we just could not rub along any more. I resented him encroaching on my space, as I saw it, and suspected that the Chrysalis Yellen TV business had been a way of carving out an area of activity for himself whose management I wasn't involved in.

It would be wrong for me to claim that everything was Terry's fault. There were faults on both sides. I could certainly have been more gracious in welcoming him back to London, but as we struggled on, treading on each other's toes and arguing, the staff were finding it increasingly difficult having two bosses giving them conflicting requests and orders. Chris and Ellis were at loggerheads and Chrysalis was becoming unmanageable.

There could not have been a worse time for me to fall ill, so that was precisely what I did. In the autumn of 1982, I flew to Nassau to listen to Spandau Ballet's third album, *True*. When I returned to London, I started getting back pains that were so severe that they were frightening.

A series of tests produced a diagnosis of kidney stones. This was not in itself terribly serious. The stones were a result of having been in a hot climate and not replacing fluid lost from dehydration. However, a routine X-ray showed that, apart from kidney stones, I also had a very large gallstone in a delicate position in my gall bladder. Although it had given me no pain, my doctor was aware that I spent a great deal of time travelling, on occasion to very remote locations, and strongly recommended elective surgery to remove the gallstone.

Unfortunately, this was just before the days of keyhole surgery and I had to undergo a complicated and difficult procedure requiring 12 days in hospital and a three-month recuperation period. It was a wearying and debilitating process that hit me for six, both physically and mentally. I entered the hospital as an extremely fit and healthy person and left very much the worse for wear.

My protracted absence gave Terry an opportunity to step back into running the UK company in my absence. This further aggravated the problems that existed both between him and me, and between him and the senior members of the UK staff.

Yet the straw that broke the camel's back came from a most unexpected direction. As part of the TV business, Terry went to the 1984 Cannes Film Festival, where he ran into Alexander Salkind and his son Ilya. They were big independent producers who were producing a film with Dudley Moore called *Santa Claus: The Movie*.

Dudley had, of course, starred in *Arthur* and *10*, but had been in a few flops since then. Undeterred, Terry agreed a deal to give them £4 million in return for Chrysalis having the rights to compile and release a soundtrack album for the film and to receive a small percentage of the box office take for the film in the UK market.

This really put the cat amongst the pigeons. The rest of the company, especially Terry Connolly and Doug D'Arcy, thought that Terry had finally flipped. They knew it was a crazy deal. I instinctively knew that we shouldn't be doing it but I tried to be rational. I read the script several times, analysed the numbers, and tried hard to make sense of everything from a professional standpoint.

I didn't particularly like the script and I didn't think the film would be very successful. After a few days I said I was going to stop this deal and war broke out. Terry made it very clear that, if I didn't support this deal, our partnership was over. On the other hand, I knew that if I allowed the deal to happen, I would have triggered a major walkout of the senior staff in London, because they thought it was close to commercial suicide. I stood my ground.

"We are not going ahead with this deal," I told Terry.

"Right, well that is it, either you support me or we should dissolve our partnership," he said.

Dissolving the partnership was going to be a logistical nightmare. Terry and I initially decided that he would own Chrysalis in North America, including all the acts that were signed to the American record and publishing companies. I would have Chrysalis outside of America and all of those acts, and we would have cross-licensing across the two businesses.

With hindsight, this crazy plan would never have worked. It would have been a nigh on impossible structure to assemble, not to mention the problem of finding motivation to work on each other's acts. The artists would also certainly not have been happy to be caught in the middle of two warring ex-partners. We just weren't seeing things clearly at the time.

We both had to appoint lawyers and advisers to get the whole thing sorted out. I assumed that I would be represented by Abe Somer, who had been Chrysalis' lawyer in America for many years, but was never particularly close to Terry. Abe and I were great buddies. He stayed with me in London and Gloucestershire most summers and we had watched tennis at Wimbledon, cruised Corsica and skied in Aspen together. We had even considered buying a winery in the Napa Valley together (and what an investment that would have been, in hindsight).

Despite our closeness, Abe decided quite correctly that it was not possible for him to act for me because he represented the company in America and it would create a conflict of interest. This upset me as I had assumed the personal relationship would come first. Our friendship suffered for a while, although thankfully those problems are now behind us.

Instead, I contacted Allen Grubman, who was to go on to be the most important lawyer in the music business, but at that point had only a few select clients such as Tommy Mottola, the manager of Hall & Oates who became the president of CBS and then Sony Records and later married Mariah Carey, Village People manager Henri Belolo, TK Records owner Henry Stone, and the K-Tel compilations company.

Grubman, a very street savvy and larger-than-life character, flew to meet me in Cap d'Antibes and we hit it off straight away. He had a colossal appetite. At one point he became hungry and went looking for food, at which point he found a whole chicken in the fridge ready for the children's dinner. He devoured the lot.

It would not be inaccurate to say that Allen eventually ran the music industry when it came to legal business. When he was married for the second time, to Debbie at New York Public Library in 1991, his guests (all of them clients) included Madonna, Robert De Niro, David Geffen and Mariah Carey – but at the point that he took on my representation, I was one of his more significant clients. Terry was represented by a London Lawyer, Michael Loup, the senior partner at Boodle Hatfield, a very establishment, conservative practice.

The situation was that I had to come up with a price that Terry would pay for my half of the American company, and he had to come up with what he wanted me to pay for half the British company. Both sides set about working out the numbers. Naturally, I put a really high figure on the value of the American company for Terry to buy me out and he did the same for the value of the UK company.

The horse trading and posturing continued until we were ready to sit down to negotiate. Allen flew into London to meet with Loup. It must have been quite a contrast. I suspect the very proper Englishman was taken aback by the very brusque New Yorker. Then Allen called me to say that there had been a major change in tack.

"Terry has changed his mind," he told me. "He will take your offer on your valuations for both companies. On your valuation for the US company, you can buy him out, and on your valuation for the British company, you can buy him out too."

The lawyers had come up with a ballpark figure of around £17 million for me to own the entire company. I was staggered by this dramatic turn of events.

What was the whole business really worth at that time? It was difficult to say. It was probably between £20 million and £25 million maximum. So I would be paying, not 50% but at least 75% of the value of the whole thing. But immediately I said yes and ended up paying £17.3 million, including costs, to own 100% of a company that was worth around £20-£25 million. It left me having to borrow a lot of money, but at least I would have an ongoing business to run.

We had very little time to find the money. Terry Connolly and Nigel Butterfield were very helpful. We did not have to go to the banks but borrowed US$12 million from CBS, our distributor in

America, and renegotiated our European licensing agreements with BMG for a significant advance. The interest rate was favourable compared to what we would have got from UK merchant banks.

We also had at least two or three million pounds in the bank, which allowed us to fund the balance of the consideration from cash flow. We also had a £1 million working capital overdraft facility from NatWest – but did not use it at the time. The master plan was to pay back the borrowings from trading and future record sales, expectations for which were on a high at that time with our heavily anticipated release schedule.

It seemed totally out of character for Terry Ellis to sell the whole company to me. I suspected until the very final minute that he would change his mind, or that maybe he thought I would change mine. But we both held firm. I arranged for UK head of business affairs Peter Caisley to drive up to Newmarket to secure his signature, and we were all to some extent shocked when Peter called to say he had it in his hand.

For all of our recent fallouts and disagreements, this was a highly emotional and poignant moment for me. Terry and I had been together for 17 years and built Chrysalis from scratch. On completion of the deal Terry seemed to disappear for a few weeks. Where he went I do not know.

Perhaps the best result would have been if we had put all of our problems behind us and agreed to pass on the Alexander Salkind deal over *Santa Claus: The Movie*. However, I suspect Terry did not want to lose face with the Salkinds after being the big guy down at the Cannes film festival splashing the cash around, only to find that, in the end, he couldn't deliver on a commitment, albeit one he should never have made. *Santa Claus: The Movie* was a minor hit and does occasionally get re-played on TV over the festive season. But it would have recouped only a very small amount of our investment.

Nevertheless, I will never underestimate the value of the early, successful years of our partnership. When Terry and I worked well together we were a formidable combination. Without him, the record and publishing companies may never have started. He was a great manager for Jethro Tull. I am not sure I would have resolved the Dee Anthony issue without him, which was crucial to the development of the US company, and of course, the signing of Blondie was a momentous moment in our history. Terry's relationship with Mike Chapman, who produced so many great records for us, was also paramount.

How would Chrysalis' history had differed if we had both backed off over *Santa Claus* and kept the partnership together? It's difficult to say. The company was certainly to develop in a completely different way over the next stage of its existence, moving into areas in which Terry might not have been comfortable. Maybe as a partnership we had run our course and this outcome, however painful, was best for both of us. One will never know for sure.

I did not impose a non-competition clause on Terry when I bought him out. A couple of years later, he started Imago Records in New York. He had a degree of success with Baby Animals, an Australian band with a female vocalist, as well as the singer-songwriters Aimee Mann and Paula Cole and also Henry Rollins from the US punk band Black Flag, who was starting to make a name for himself as an actor and a spoken word performer as well as a musician.

Imago was a joint venture with BMG, but, like most start-ups, it was losing significant money and quite possibly maintaining an overhead more in keeping with a larger company. As a result BMG pulled the plug in 1994, otherwise he could well have made it work. Terry usually had good ideas and great instincts but he was not always terribly practical about putting them together. After Imago, he started Tiger Star, a record company aiming to embrace the dynamics of the newly emerging South East Asian market. It was a great idea in theory but not so easy in practice to operate. Like Imago, it failed to last the course.

I'm delighted to say that Terry has since put his all of his personal difficulties behind him. He attributes most of his problems in the late seventies and mid-eighties to abuse of alcohol. He certainly helped create a tremendous legacy which still stands as a testament to his personality, creativity and drive.

As for me? I was in a very different situation. I now had a worldwide company to run, and a huge debt to repay. It would necessitate seismic changes.

CHAPTER 15

Dancing With Myself

In 1985, just a few months after I bought out Terry Ellis' stake, Chrysalis became a publicly listed company on the London Stock Exchange.

This naturally affected the way we conducted our business in many ways. It enabled us to raise capital for further acquisitions and to start moving away from our core music activities, something that was to become increasingly more important. It also necessitated an adjustment on my part since I now had to deal with a different management structure and the vagaries of the stock market, not to mention fund managers and investment analysts.

The rules of the game had changed. We now had a public forum to whom we had to report our results, and of course we were now open to scrutiny in the financial pages of the newspapers. Unfortunately, this transition did not come with a how-to-do book, and we made more than a few mistakes along the way.

Before Terry's exit we had been talking to Bill Smith, who was chief executive of Management Agency & Music (MAM) PLC. Gordon Mills, the manager behind Tom Jones, Engelbert Humperdinck and Gilbert O'Sullivan, had started the company in 1970. Bill – Gordon's right-hand man – was about to undergo heart surgery and would not necessarily be in a position to continue running the company.

Gordon, like his protégé Tom Jones, was a Welshman. He had started off as a member of the Morton Fraser Harmonica Gang, who somewhat resembled my old temporary charges Dr Crock & His Crackpots, who provided me with my first official paid employment. Gordon had managed the careers of Tom, Engelbert and Gilbert from UK dives to Las Vegas showrooms, and he was especially close to Tom, his first client.

Eventually, Gordon fell out with Gilbert O'Sullivan who felt he had been given an unjust deal. The case went to court and Gilbert was awarded the return of his copyrights. The whole affair seemed to cause Gordon a great deal of grief, and could well have contributed to his wish to sell MAM.

MAM was looking for an exit. Bill and Gordon liked Chrysalis and they thought merging the two businesses would be sensible. At the time, MAM consisted of a small music publishing company which owned the rights to Paul Anka material in North America★, a concert promotion business run by Barry Clayman, some recording rights with Tom Jones and Engelbert Humperdinck, a hotel division of about half a dozen small hotels and a fruit machine and jukebox company. On paper at least the merger kind of worked.

Terry Connolly was keen on the idea, in part because his area of expertise was not specifically music-related. I was in two minds. Terry Ellis had been dead against it. However, now he had gone, we renewed our conversations with Bill Smith and Gordon Mills.

It became clear that merging MAM and Chrysalis into one company and simultaneously reducing my 100% stake down to 50% – as it had been when Terry was my equal partner – would enable us to pay back the debts we'd shouldered to buy him out.

★ This included 'My Way' for which Paul wrote the words specifically for Frank Sinatra. It was originally a French song, 'Comme d'Habitude', by Claude François. The song made millions for Chrysalis over the years.

This stratagem certainly wasn't what we had in mind when I bought Terry out but, having done that deal, it seemed to make a lot of sense. In effect, what I was doing was swapping Terry Ellis for institutional shareholders in a public company and, at the same time, picking up some publishing and record rights, and some additional businesses.

The MAM deal was announced on April 22, 1985. Gordon Mills was to join the board at Chrysalis but sadly he fell victim to pancreatic cancer and died soon afterwards. It was a sad loss of a good man and I regret not having been able to develop a real working relationship with him.

The industry in general felt the Chrysalis/MAM merger was a very smart move and, to all intents and purposes, it was. However, it meant we now found ourselves involved in some businesses we didn't know a great deal about. We were still tight for cash and had significant loans and debts from the buyout, but we raised £8.6 million from the proceeds of the sale of new shares and a further £10 million by selling off Kingsmead Hotels, the hotel division which did not fit in with the shape of a music and media group, at the end of 1986.

So, we had paid down the borrowing and reduced my shareholding back down to 50%, but what were we to do with these other businesses? The music publishing side could easily be merged into Chrysalis Music and the record rights into Chrysalis Records. The Tom and Engelbert records were licensed to PolyGram at the time, and we chose to continue this arrangement, as their repertoire would not have sat well in a hip alternative music label. It was still a business we understood. The concert promotion business soon disappeared, as Barry Clayman was not prepared to work for Chrysalis.

Peter Hazelrigg ran the fruit machine and jukebox business, which was was based at Theale, near Reading. Unfortunately, one part of this venture was facing a downturn. The period of our takeover coincided with CDs replacing vinyl records, and the decline of the 7″ single. Traditionally, jukeboxes contained the Top 40 singles at a cost of 50p per disc. You could fill a jukebox for £20.

When CD jukeboxes came in, they would hold 50 CD albums costing £10 each, meaning you were now spending £500 rather than £20. Plus people just seemed to have moved on. The whole concept of a jukebox was starting to look a little old-fashioned.

After the MAM merger, Chrysalis had five divisions under Terry Connolly as group managing director. Doug D'Arcy became worldwide managing director of our main business, the record label and music publishing company. George Martin headed the facilities division, which looked after the recording studios: AIR and Wessex Sound Studios, and Air-Edel, which produced jingles and made film soundtracks. There was the jukebox and fruit machine division, and a musical instruments and distribution company in the UK and Ireland. We had the Chrysalis agency representing artists including Culture Club and Bryan Ferry.

Then, in 1985, we bought Lasgo Exports, a wholesale distributor run by Peter Lassman, which would remain part of the Chrysalis group for the next 25 years. Lasgo, or as it was then known, Lasgo Exports, had been set up by Peter Lassman and Mark Ballabon, who left after our purchase. Peter stayed on to run Lasgo as part of Chrysalis and be a main board director of the group. In a different format, our business partnership continues to this day.

Lasgo is a trading company. It operates as an independent distributor and exporter, originally of CDs but more recently also of DVDs, 12-inch vinyl albums and books. It operates from a large warehouse in Willesden and has clients all over the world, especially in markets like Japan. It fulfils a great service to the industry, as it is able to supply record stores overseas with newly released British product very effectively, allowing these stores to be ahead of the game when it comes to offering cutting-edge material to their customers.

In many ways, Lasgo is a dream business. It has never required any investment, its staff are committed to the business, many have been there for several years, and it has always thrown off a very healthy bottom line profit.

With so many changes and so much upheaval behind the scenes, it was vital that Chrysalis Records did not lose sight of its main business of selling records. Luckily, our established stars Pat Benatar, Billy Idol and Huey Lewis & The News were all batting well for us, but we also made two crucial new signings in Go West and Paul Hardcastle.

Go West came to Chrysalis via Ron Fair, who had joined the company in America as director of A&R and who had more eclectic tastes than most people (he was to go on to be responsible for the careers of Christina Aguilera, The Black Eyed Peas and Pussycat Dolls). Ron had received a tape from Peter Cox and Richard Drummie, two British musicians who went by the name of Go West. The demo sounded great and we signed them up. It's a testament to Go West's expertise that it took us several attempts in the studio to match the sound quality of the demo they had recorded in a home studio.

Go West hit the ground running in Britain as their debut single, 'We Close Our Eyes', went Top 5 in February 1985. Following Terry's departure, I now had much more control over the priorities in America and we were able to really push them there. We put out 'Call Me', their second UK single, as the debut single in America, paving the way for 'We Close Our Eyes', which we considered the stronger track.

It immediately hit hard in the US. Thanks to our excellent promotion department, headed by Daniel Glass, who is now so successfully maintaining the Chrysalis ethos with his label Glass Note, in the first week of release, it received 40 adds at Top 40 radio, then the same number again the second and the third weeks. You needed about 130 adds on Top 40 stations to guarantee a huge hit and we were getting there. The record started steaming up the charts.

Throughout this period, the American record industry was dominated by the use of 'independent promoters', ie radio pluggers, though it would be an understatement to say they used different methods from their British counterparts. They were all supposed to be independent from each other, yet they seemed to work together as a cabal.

The main players were Freddie DiSipio, based in Philadelphia, Joe Isgro in California, and Jeff McClusky in the Midwest. Record labels paid these independent promoters to get their records played, then paid them on performance as well. Quite what they did with the money you gave them was none of your business but substantial amounts were involved and the system was open to abuse.

Initially, a little bit of money might grease the wheels, but soon everyone was indulging in this practice and so to have a hit you had to grease the wheels a lot more than your rivals. There was no point in giving the independent promotion men $50,000 a week to get your record played if another label was giving them $75,000. As a consequence, the cost of doing business in America escalated.

It's well documented that the independent record promoters had links to organised crime. The truth is, in the US, in the entertainment industry, one never quite knows where organised crime becomes involved and where legitimate business becomes illegitimate. There is a very thin dividing line and it all goes right back to the forties and Frank Sinatra and his entourage.

The Go West single appeared to be absolutely flying. I had to attend a CBS international conference in Honolulu, and the first person I ran into when I arrived was Joe Isgro. I had been on a long flight from Tokyo and so had not seen the new US chart, so I asked Joe what had happened to the Go West single.

"Oh, it went backwards," Joe told me.

I was flabbergasted. 'We Close Our Eyes' had reached number 41 the previous week and looked poised to go much higher: at least into the Top 20. I asked Joe what had gone wrong.

"Craigo took us off the record," he explained. "This was the week he should have double-paid us."

Once again, I was speechless. Jack Craigo, the president of Chrysalis US, had decided in his wisdom that 'We Close Our Eyes' was already such a guaranteed huge hit that he had told the independent promoters he wasn't paying them that week. And the pluggers had killed the record stone dead.

What could have been a Top 5 record in the US had just dropped like a stone. It just showed the incredible power the independent promoters had at that point in time: not just to create hits, but also to stop records becoming hits.

The following year, on the eve of the Grammies, NBC News did a huge exposé of independent promoters that left the record industry in a quandary. As much as people wanted to eliminate the independent promoters, they still had a huge amount of power in the industry. It was effectively a form of payola, although not as blatant as in the fifties.

There were companies, especially CBS (now Sony), headed by Walter Yetnikoff, who did not want to cut the pluggers loose for fear of what damage they could do to the business and their records. The NBC programme had showed Philadelphia-based plugger Freddie DiSipio in conversations with known mobsters, and Yetnikoff made a point of publicly feting DiSipio when he bumped into him at the Grammies the next day.

There was certainly no love lost between CBS Group chairman Thomas Wyman, a very conservative, preppy individual, and Walter Yetnikoff, who headed CBS Records and was the polar opposite. Wyman had to deal with regulatory issues emanating out of their successful broadcasting network that were difficult to rationalise alongside the maverick, freewheeling Yetnikoff.

Incidentally, Go West eventually scored a Top 10 hit in the US with 'King Of Wishful Thinking', from the *Pretty Woman* soundtrack. Ironically, this was one of the most played tracks on US radio in 1990, but I sometimes wonder what would have happened if we had managed to break the duo in the States five years earlier, as we should have done.

The Honolulu CBS conference was also memorable because the company was celebrating the unprecedented success of the Michael Jackson album *Thriller*, which Yetnikoff was taking full credit for and basking in reflected glory. Friends and foes would agree that he was a highly intelligent man who wielded his power ruthlessly.

The convention also marked the end of Maurice Oberstein's reign running CBS Records in the UK. Maurice, or 'Obie' as he was affectionately known, was a colourful New Yorker who became a hugely powerful figure in the British music industry. Obie was a true eccentric; he took his dogs – Charlie, the red setter, and later Eric, the English setter – to work, and supposedly played them demo tapes in order to decide whether to sign a group.

There had always been a little bit of antagonism between Obie and I, dating from the time when John Fruin, the managing director of WEA in the UK, had to resign as chairman of the BPI and I was elected in his place. Obie coveted the role and had stood against me for election as vice-chairman. In its wisdom, the BPI Council appointed me.

Obie was not a good man to have as an enemy. In fact, I would say he was the epitome of the proverb that you should keep your friends close and your enemies even closer.

We did, however, have one thing in common: a female chauffeur, which in those days was particularly rare in the UK. At all of the major industry functions, there would be Bentleys and Rolls Royces and only two female chauffeurs: Annie Simpson, who worked for me for more than 20 years, and Obie's driver, Shirley.

During that CBS convention in Honolulu, there was a power struggle between Obie and the CBS New York head honchos. Obie seemed to be intimating that he should be running CBS Records across Europe, not just in the UK, and no doubt threatening to resign unless he got the much bigger role with an enhanced salary package.

They were high stakes and CBS did not blink. On the second morning of the convention, as everyone sat down for the start of proceedings, Walter Yetnikoff got up on stage and said: "It is with great regret that we announce the resignation of Maurice Oberstein who has headed CBS records in the UK for so many years."

You could have heard a pin drop and the most surprised person in the room was patently Obie. He had no idea it was coming. Clearly he had threatened to resign the night before in a smoke-filled room, and the next morning they had called his bluff and simply announced his resignation in front of three or four thousand CBS people from around the world. Obie was pole-axed.

He wasn't out of work for too long but I imagine it must have felt like an eternity to him. When we returned to London, he invited me out to lunch and intimated that I might give him a role at Chrysalis. He said that although we had had a lot of problems in the past, he was sure we could work well together.

I didn't have a job for him, but a few months later he was appointed chairman of PolyGram in the UK where he went on to have a very successful second career. He eventually also became chairman of the BPI, before retiring to Miami, where he died in August 2001. He was also a big racing fan and apparently asked for his ashes to be scattered at Cheltenham Race Course and at Loftus Road, the home of QPR.

Besides Go West, Chrysalis' other major success in 1985 was '19' by Paul Hardcastle. The single topped the charts in virtually every country in the world. The A&R executive who signed Paul Hardcastle for us was a young man who had just been recruited straight out of university called Simon Fuller, who began to work incredibly closely with Paul.

Paul had two flop musical projects behind him in Direct Drive and First Light but '19' was clearly something special. An infectious dance record, it concerned itself with the fact that the average age of US combat soldiers in the Vietnam War was 19 and opened with a sample of newsreader commentary. The video used excerpts from an ABC television documentary entitled *Vietnam Requiem*.

I don't know how many people at Chrysalis thought '19' would be such a huge hit but it blew me away as soon as I heard it. In truth, the very talented Paul Hardcastle did not have a lot of charisma, but the record was so strong that it hardly mattered.

We were very intrigued to see how Paul would follow up this mega-hit and the answer was… more of the same. His second single, 'Just For Money', aped the format of '19', featuring the voices of Laurence Olivier and Bob Hoskins and was based on the 1963 Great Train Robbery.

This concerned me somewhat. While everybody in the world was aware of the situation in Vietnam, the Great Train Robbery remained a very parochial British affair and an unknown quantity in the rest of the world. This was three years before Phil Collins starred in *Buster*, a film based on the life story of one of the gang members; the movie was not successful internationally.

Simon Fuller regarded my misgivings as typical of what he saw as negativity on the part of the company towards his protégé. Although we threw a fair amount of money at promoting 'Just For Money', it peaked – funnily enough – at number 19 in the UK and barely made a dent on the charts anywhere else in the world.

The single simply didn't have the special buzz of '19', but Simon didn't see things that way. He was so incensed at its lack of success that he picked up his toys in the form of Paul Hardcastle, resigned from Chrysalis and set up a company to manage Paul, calling it 19 Management after the major hit that had announced their arrival.

The rest is history. Simon went on to manage Annie Lennox, be the Svengali behind the Spice Girls and make David Beckham the most famous footballer of his generation. He then launched *Pop Idol* and *American Idol* and is now one of the most successful and richest people in the history of the industry. He also now represents tennis star Andy Murray. He has come a long way since Chrysalis, Paul Hardcastle and a record about Vietnam soldiers. His company is still called 19 Management.

'19' was a hit on a specialist Chrysalis imprint called Cooltempo, which we had launched specifically to release dance music and hip-hop in 1984. It was nice little niche, a boutique venture headed by Peter Edge, who later moved to America and worked for Clive Davis and was responsible for the careers of both Dido and Alicia Keys. It really came into its own with rap acts like Doug E Fresh & The Get Fresh Crew, The Real Roxanne, Eric B. & Rakim and the early house music of Adeva, a black girl from Patterson, New Jersey who was very successful in England.

Unfortunately, Cooltempo was also the label that we used when we licensed the first four Milli Vanilli singles – 'Girl You Know It's True', 'Baby Don't Forget My Number', 'Blame It On The Rain' and 'Girl I'm Gonna Miss You' – from the German company Hansa, and Frank Farian, the German producer who had put the project together. When they became embroiled in a lip-syncing controversy and it was established that neither Fab Morvan nor Rob Pilatus had sung on the Milli Vanilli records, they had to return their 1990 Grammy for Best New Artist.

I was furious at this embarrassment as I knew nothing about what had gone on behind the scenes. Maybe, given the fact that Frank Farian had previously masterminded Boney M and Eruption, I should not have been as surprised as I was. It was certainly an unwanted and unpleasant episode that did not fit well with the Chrysalis philosophy.

Cooltempo was not the only specialist imprint launched by Chrysalis in the mid-eighties. We also formed a label called Blue Guitar which issued records by indie guitar bands The Mighty Lemon Drops and The Shop Assistants. They were well loved by the journalists and readers of *NME* and *Melody Maker* but this never really translated into record sales.

The same period saw us heavily involved with a slick and attitudinal computer-generated TV reporter. Max Headroom was picked up by Peter Wagg, whom we had brought into the company in 1985 specifically to oversee the development of the increasingly important video department.

Peter took on board a project that had been presented to him by a forward-looking pair named Annabel Jankel and Rocky Morton. They had come up with Max Headroom, who was supposed to be the post-death alter ago of Edison Carter, a fictional TV reporter who had his head chopped off driving out of a car park when the exit barrier came down on his car.

The reliably edgy Channel 4 picked up on Max Headroom but his fame exploded after Coca-Cola used him to front a major advertising campaign. The result was 15 one-hour shows funded by Channel 4 and, in America, by ABC. Max became an unlikely talk-show host on the American cable channel Cinemax with *The Original Max Talking Headroom Show* and there was even talk of a feature film. The project did not have a particularly long shelf life, however, and the public lost interest. Peter Wagg later left us to work for Cirque du Soleil.

Max Headroom's disembodied voice also featured on 'Paranoimia', a 1986 hit single by Art Of Noise, the conceptual group comprising Anne Dudley, Gary Langan and J.J. Jeczalik, who had been part of the team around Trevor Horn and Frankie Goes To Hollywood but had left Horn's ZTT operation to sign to China Records.

A good friend of mine, Derek Green, had founded China in 1984, having run A&M Records in the UK very successfully, signing Supertramp, The Police, Squeeze and Joe Jackson. Chrysalis marketed and distributed China in 1986 and 1987 and had a huge hit and won a Grammy for Best Rock Instrumental Performance with the Art of Noise featuring Duane Eddy doing 'Peter Gunn', a modern update of Duane Eddy's 1958 signature track featuring his distinctive twangy guitar.

Another China act was the British singer-songwriter Labi Siffre who had had a few hits in the early seventies, including 'It Must Be Love', a song published by Chrysalis via our MAM deal, later covered by Madness. He wrote the anti-apartheid anthem '(Something Inside) So Strong' which became a Top 5 single in 1987 and won an Ivor Novello Award – another milestone record that Chrysalis was involved in and one I'm extremely proud to have been associated with.

In 1998, Eminem sampled 'I Got The', an obscure song from Labi Siffre's 1975 *Remember My Song* album, for what would turn out to be his breakthrough hit, 'My Name Is'. He and Dr. Dre, his producer, failed to obtain clearance from us on it until the record was pressed and the campaign was well under way. Catherine Lascelles, who worked in our legal department, played the song and the lyrics to Labi who was upset by the homophobic content.

We had become Labi Siffre's music publisher as a result of the MAM deal and were determined to protect his interests. I had a panicked phone call from Jimmy Iovine, the record producer who had founded Interscope, Eminem's label. We had never heard of the artist but we were in a strong position to negotiate the right outcome for Labi. We asked Eminem to make some changes to the lyrics, which he agreed to do. Eminem and Dr. Dre also gave Labi Siffre a full songwriting credit, which was only fair as 'My Name Is' relied so much on the distinctive riff from Labi's track.

Chrysalis also enjoyed a licensing arrangement for a while with Go! Discs, the independent record company founded by Andy MacDonald, who remains a close friend. Go!'s biggest act was The Housemartins, a group from Hull University who came across as northern working class kids but were led by Paul Heaton, who had grown up in the Surrey stockbroker belt, and later added Norman Cook, now better known as the DJ and producer Fatboy Slim. Their first album, *London 0 Hull 4*, was a huge record and they had a couple of enormous hits, 'Happy Hour' and the Christmas single 'Caravan Of Love', in 1986.

Ultimately, however, a licensing deal with Chrysalis was well below Andy's expectations. He moved the label to PolyGram where success continued as The Housemartins evolved into The Beautiful South. In 1996, Andy sold Go! Discs to PolyGram, and started Independiente which has operated very successfully for the last 15 years or so with artists such as Travis and Tinariwen.

At the height of their mid-eighties success, The Housemartins toured with The Proclaimers, aka bespectacled Scottish twins Charlie and Craig Reid, whom we signed. The following year, they had a Top 3 hit in the UK with 'Letter From America', a particularly interesting song about how American corporations were buying up Scottish industries and later closing them down. The single was produced by the great Scottish singer-songwriter Gerry Rafferty, who had taken a liking to them, but The Proclaimers' biggest record was a brilliantly idiosyncratic track called '500 Miles'.

Around the same time, we also got involved with another very talented Scot but of a very different hue – Mike Scott of The Waterboys.

Doug D'Arcy and I went to a Waterboys gig at Hammersmith Palais in May 1986 and I was blown away by Mike Scott; one of the most charismatic performers I had ever seen. 'The Whole Of The Moon' was their big song but I also loved 'Red Army Blues' and was enraptured when he sat down at the piano to play 'The Thrill Is Gone', a poignant song about the disintegration of a relationship.

Doug and I just had to have The Waterboys even though they were still contracted to Ensign Records. Ensign was founded by Nigel Grainge (hence the name, N sign), a music industry major player who had signed Thin Lizzy and 10cc to Phonogram before launching Ensign in 1977 with his partner, Chris Hill, signing The Boomtown Rats and taking the imprint from Phonogram to first RCA and then Island. Today, Nigel's younger brother Lucian is the CEO and chairman of Universal Music Group worldwide, and thus probably the most important person in the music industry.

Doug and I were determined to sign The Waterboys either directly to Chrysalis or by acquiring Ensign. Island and Virgin were also in the running but we came out on top by giving Nigel Grainge and Chris Hill a lot of money to buy their label, and keeping them on to run it.

Yet the commercial success we confidently expected for The Waterboys never materialised. They took three years to make their first album for us, *Fisherman's Blues,* and it was nothing like what we expected. Mike Scott had abandoned The Waterboys' epic 'Big Music', decamped to the west coast of Ireland and made a record heavily influenced by traditional Irish music, with fiddle and accordion.

The title track was great and the album went gold but this was not the potentially messianic figure I had glimpsed in Hammersmith three years earlier. The groundwork was all done for them to explode and be massive – and they gave us an album of Irish jigs. Unsurprisingly, it under-performed badly.

One reason for the change in musical direction was that Waterboys co-founder Karl Wallinger had left the group. Karl contributed a lot to the band and made them sound contemporary, and his talent was evident when Chrysalis released *Private Revolution*, the brilliant debut album by his new band, World Party, in 1986.

I thought *Private Revolution* was one of the best albums Chrysalis ever released. The title track sounded like a lost Stones classic and 'Ship Of Fools' charted on both sides of the Atlantic, although the US company was initially lukewarm towards it. World Party's touring band also featured Guy Chambers, who became Robbie Williams' chief songwriter and wrote classics like 'Angels'.

I was a lone flag-waver for World Party in Chrysalis for a while until I convinced a few colleagues of their brilliance and I still think that if Mike Scott and Karl Wallinger had carried on together in The Waterboys, they could have been world-beaters.

However, our biggest success with Ensign had little to do with The Waterboys. Soon after we bought the label, Nigel Grainge and Chris Hill took me to a rehearsal room in Shepherd's Bush in London to see a dark haired Irish singer-songwriter they had signed called Sinéad O'Connor. She was wonderful. We put out her debut album, *The Lion And The Cobra*, and 'Mandinka' became a Top 20 hit in Britain and became a US college radio favourite. *The Lion And The Cobra* was considered an alternative rock album at the time of its release, but it went on to sell two-and-a-half million copies.

Our next multi-platinum superstar was about to emerge. It was just as well, and the timing was fortuitous as Chrysalis was about to enter some choppy waters, as indeed was my personal life.

CHAPTER 16

Too Much Pressure

Each summer, Chelle and I, together with Tim, Tom and Chloe, were in the habit of relocating to our house in the south of France, usually from the third week in July to the end of August. We would play tennis at the local club, take our boat out and generally just chill out. Occasionally I would commute back and forth to London and elsewhere.

Sadly, our holiday of August 1987 was marked by tragedy. Phone calls in the middle of the night are rarely good news and when I picked up the phone at 4am and Chelle heard the voice of her father, Lloyd Nelson, on the line, she started screaming. Sadly, her worst fears were realised: her mother, Lucille, had died. Lloyd had come home at seven in the evening from Lake Tahoe, where he worked building houses, to find Lucille dead in a chair. She had suffered an aneurism, and probably passed away instantly.

Losing a parent is a traumatic rite of passage for anybody but the shock is worsened when the parent is only 59 and seemingly in good health, as Lucille had been. Her parents were very young when Chelle was born and, as an only child, she had always been hugely close to them.

Obviously I had to get us all to California as quickly as I could, and certainly by the end of the day. It was the middle of summer. Most of the flights were full, and it was too early for the London office to help me.

I called up all the different airlines and I managed to find a 7 a.m. flight to Paris and a connection on to San Francisco. It only had four seats available so I decided that Chelle, Tim, Tom and myself would go and leave Chloe, who was eight, behind. We woke the boys up with the sad news – they were both very close to their grandmother – and jumped in the car for the airport. We left Chloe with the cook and an au pair. We didn't even wake her up.

With hindsight, this was thoughtless and insensitive. I should have taken Chloe with us and the fact that we didn't still rankles with her to this day. I can only say that when you have been woken up with devastating news, and you have to move quickly, you don't always make the most rational decisions.

It was a hideous, deeply upsetting experience, as these things always are. Lloyd had always left domestic administration to Lucille, had no idea where anything was and was obviously in shock, so I found myself sorting out the funeral arrangements, life insurance and other legal issues.

Chelle took the loss very, very hard. Feeling hugely responsible for her father as an only child, she felt that either we should move to California, or bring her father over to Gloucestershire. The first option was impossible for my business and would have meant uprooting the kids from schools where they were happy, and the second idea seemed impractical to me. Lloyd was in his sixties and his life was in northern California – what on earth would he do with himself in the Cotswolds?

Chelle felt that Lloyd wasn't really capable of looking after himself but almost immediately he started another relationship and remarried within a few months, which solved his problems but possibly made Chelle feel rather guilty.

The loss of Lucille also impacted hard on our relationship. Blaming herself severely, Chelle's way of coping was to look for something to take her mind off things. She took on an Open University Arts foundation course that became all-absorbing, opted out of our very busy social life and stopped doing many of the things she had always done with me. She seemed to be cutting herself off from our normal routine.

Like every marriage, ours had had its ups and downs. I can't claim always to have been totally faithful. I'd had a few flings and affairs, one of which was quite long-lasting. Eventually I'd met a real Glenn Close in *Fatal Attraction*-style bunny-boiler who started sending erotic drawings to my house. Unsurprisingly, Chelle's suspicions soon became aroused.

Chelle began questioning a few of the trips I was making. She called a few girls up to ask them exactly how they knew me. I had very little to say in my defence and naturally our relationship floundered for a while. However at the time of Lucille's death, our relationship was very strong again.

Since I had bought out Terry, the biggest change to my workload was that I was now also running the American side of the record company. Being involved in all aspects of the company was immensely time-consuming and I was travelling non-stop. Every second week, I would be in New York, and every fourth week, I would be in LA. Often I would fly to New York for a lunch or a dinner and be on a flight home the same day. This was in addition to trips within Europe and elsewhere.

I always seemed to be on a plane. I doubt many people, apart from David Frost when he was presenting chat shows on both sides of the Atlantic, took more Concorde flights to and from New York than me in those days. In fact, when British Airways introduced its Elite Premier Club it made me a founder and lifetime member.

In the American record business, if you are the boss, no one wants to speak to anyone else. If God exists, no one wants to speak to Jesus Christ, it's as simple as that. The workload and constant travelling were beginning to get on top of me.

In the midst of all this, the company started developing serious cash-flow problems. We were operating a huge infrastructure in America. As a frontline record company, we employed something like 70 or 80 people there and considered this the minimum staffing we needed to do an effective job in a market that size, even with the input of the CBS distribution network. In order to sustain that level of staffing and overheads, we needed a pretty solid throughput of product and we were relying on major artists like Billy Idol and Huey Lewis coming up with big records.

Fore! by Huey Lewis & The News had sold seven million units since its release at the end of 1986, and had spawned two major hits for the group, 'Stuck With You' and 'Hip To Be Square'. By early 1988, they were making a new album in San Francisco. In May, along with several UK executives I flew out to the Bay Area to hear the playback of the record.

Although *Small World* was a pretty decent album, it clearly wasn't anywhere near as commercial as the previous two. It significantly underperformed and, apart from 'Perfect World', none of the singles made any impact on the charts. To be blunt, we all knew that the record should not have come out when it did, and we should have asked the group to record a couple of extra tracks to make sure we had a decent hit lined up, but as a public company we had to make our numbers for the City and we had a company year-end coming up.

We even moved our company financial year back by two months from June 30 to August 31 on some pretext, simply to accommodate the record and have the sales registered in that financial year. This meant we had to get it out by June and therefore we had no chance other than to accept what the band had given us.

Meanwhile, Billy Idol had a serious drug problem that seemed to hamper any kind of progress on his next studio album, which was being produced by Keith Forsey. It was always ready to be delivered in a couple of weeks' time and it never looked like it would get delivered. Every time I went to America, I would go to the studio to hear what they had done and it didn't sound an awful lot different to what I'd heard a few weeks before.

In order to maintain some momentum, in 1988 we issued a compilation called *Idol Songs* but we were only marking time. What we – and by that I mean the Chrysalis bottom line – really needed was a new Billy album.

So we soldiered on trying to generate sales where we could. We made some interesting signings, including Paul Carrack, a singer and keyboard-player with a great pedigree. He had been a member of Ace, had written and sung their major hit 'How Long' in 1975, had joined Squeeze for a while and was one of the two lead vocalists in Mike & The Mechanics, the side project of Genesis guitarist Mike Rutherford. Carrack scored three US hits but he was never going to be a major star, even if he did co-write 'Love Will Keep Us Alive' for The Eagles.

John 'Jellybean' Benitez was a New York-born DJ, remixer and producer. For a while, he had been Madonna's boyfriend and had remixed several tracks on her debut album and produced 'Holiday', her debut hit, in 1983. We gave him a production deal and he recorded a series of dance hits with different vocalists.

Also in 1987, the British blue-eyed soul trio Living In A Box had a worldwide hit with a song of the same name. It was such a crossover R&B/dance hit in the US that the R&B singer Bobby Womack covered it. They had a few more UK hits including 'Blow The House Down', which featured Queen guitarist Brian May, but they too were short of superstar potential.

The American company, by contrast, had no significant releases and made a $7 million loss in 1987/88. Doug and I decided to part company with US president Jack Craigo and appoint Mike Bone in his place. We were intending to make the announcement immediately after a CBS Convention in Vancouver that we both flew in to attend. We decided we would tell Craigo in Vancouver but the news broke that Bone was joining us at the same time that

Craigo was making his presentation, and while we were still on the plane. It was all very embarrassing.

So the cost of the Terry Ellis buyout and the lacklustre US release schedule were having a major effect on overall cash flow. Finance director Nigel Butterfield repeatedly advised me through the spring of 1988 that he was worried we were running out of money. I discussed this with Terry Connolly and Doug D'Arcy, who both advised me that Nigel was just panicking, and everything was fine.

I suppose I believed what I wanted to believe until the Monday of the second week of Wimbledon. I was at Glebe House on Monday morning, more interested in watching the tennis than anything else, when Nigel Butterfield called me at 10.30 and said: "Chris, I cannot pay the wages this week. We do not have enough money to pay the staff salaries on Friday."

What? How could this be?

The alarm bells started ringing like mad. The next day, I arranged an all-day meeting in the private room at Motcombes in Belgravia and we went through everything to get to the bottom of the problem. We had to figure out how we could save the company.

To address the cash-flow issue, we had to reduce unessential expenditure immediately. On Doug's initiative, we had been planning to sign Sheffield electro group ABC, who had had major success a few years earlier. The deal was £1 million but we cancelled it – a good decision, as they never had another big hit.

It also became clear that mistakes had been made over certain royalty payments, specifically with Jethro Tull which shocked me to the core. There were legal interpretation issues rather than anything untoward, but Ian Anderson of Jethro Tull had been in at the start of both the record and music publishing companies and the thought that we might have short-changed him was abhorrent to me.

We had to find ways of raising money quickly. We got extra advances in from licensees, went cap in hand to the bank and tried everything we could think of. It was difficult as we were still in hock to people from the Terry Ellis buyout. Terry Connolly was prepared to take full responsibility and handed me a hand-written letter tendering his resignation, although he did say that he would stick around until we had sorted out the mess. Perhaps surprisingly I didn't try to persuade him to stay. I think maybe he had thought that I would.

We had not been keeping the stock exchange abreast of our trading situation. This was not deliberate: firstly, I was unaware that we had any problem with our trading numbers, and secondly, I was not experienced enough in dealing with the City to know that if it appears unlikely that a company is going to make the profit numbers that they are expecting you to make, you have to tell them immediately. I thought you told them at the time you reported your results.

We were a long way short of the numbers they were expecting and I feared this would make the share price crash. At the time, we were trading at about £1 a share, but nobody would know the full extent of the problems until the announcement appeared on the stock exchange screen at 8 a.m.

Terry Connolly, who had a significant shareholding in the company, used to commute in from Surbiton in Surrey. These were pre-mobile phone days, so before he got on his train, he called his stockbroker and told him: "As soon as the Chrysalis announcement comes out, sell all my shares, at any price: sell the lot." He was expecting the share price would collapse to 10 or 15p a share.

Our stock exchange announcement came out and when Terry got off his train at Victoria he called up the stockbroker to ask how he'd got on. He was completely flabbergasted to be told that he'd sold the lot at a pound a share. The price had not dropped at all!

How could this be? It transpired that, unknown to any of us, David Geffen, the American founder of Asylum and Geffen Records, and now a principal partner in Dream Works, had decided that he wanted to launch a bid for the company and the best way of doing that would be for him to start acquiring shares. He had given orders to a

London stockbroker to buy all the Chrysalis shares he could at about £1 per share.

Terry Connolly, along with everyone else desperate to dump their shares in a company that appeared to be about to go out of business, ended up getting the full price for all of his shares. For his part, David Geffen acquired about 15 per cent of the company in one fell swoop. I believe the strategy is called a 'dawn raid'. It was a bizarre situation.

Having quit as managing director, Terry Connolly agreed to stay on as a board member for 12 months to help us through the crisis. Replacing Terry was never going to be easy as he had played a key role in running the company for many years, and had been incredibly helpful on both the Terry Ellis buyout and the reverse takeover of MAM. It was Terry who had turned us into a public company and moved us away from merely being a record company.

Doug D'Arcy was still the managing director of the record company, but the corporate side of things was not his forte and, anyway, he had his hands full. With both Terrys now departed, I was really on my own. I did not want to sell the company and needed help from somebody with a good business brain. We had saved the business from going down the drain but we needed restructuring.

In those days I played tennis regularly with Michael Levy. He had owned a record label, Magnet, that released bubblegum pop artists such as Alvin Stardust, Guys 'n' Dolls, Darts and Bad Manners, plus Chris Rea, who would probably have sat more comfortably on Chrysalis. Michael had recently sold Magnet to Warner Brothers for around £10 million, and was doing nothing.

I thought he could be my salvation. I didn't need him to work on the creative side of the company, which I considered not to be his strong suit, but I valued his smart business brain and accounting ability. I asked him if he would be interested in joining me on a short-term consultancy to help me sort things out.

Michael was intrigued and suggested we met together with his lawyer Tony Russell. I was being assisted by Dennis Robertson, who was employed by Stoy Hayward, our auditors. Unfortunately Dennis developed cancer and died soon afterwards.

Michael undoubtedly saw the advantages of a relationship between himself and Chrysalis. Gradually we evolved into a situation where Michael would join the company as an important junior partner with significant shares and stock options and a very active role in day-to-day management. The negotiations moved towards this so gradually that I didn't immediately realise what was happening.

During summer 1988, I went to Venice to spend some time with Michael and his family, who were on holiday there. On our return to London in early September, the negotiations continued apace until we got to the point where all we had to do was dot the i's and cross the t's.

Michael visited the offices incognito on a Thursday night to figure out where he would sit. He reasoned that I had a large office so he should have the same. He suggested that we knock down the wall between George Martin's office and his assistant, John Burgess, to make a space for Michael there and relocate George and John elsewhere. The next morning, we met and shook hands on the deal.

On the Friday afternoon, I drove down to Gloucestershire feeling more and more uneasy. By the time I arrived, I really felt that I had made a mistake. From looking for a short-term consultancy, I felt as if I had allowed myself to be positioned into a situation where I was virtually partners with Michael.

I telephoned a couple of friends for advice. Allen Grubman, in New York, canvassed opinions from a couple of his major contacts who were both less than enthusiastic about the concept of Michael joining. I also spoke to Derek Green, who had run A&M and China Records and was a very good friend of mine. He thought it was an interesting idea that could well work, which somewhat surprised me.

I was really torn, yet this was not a decision anybody else was going to make for me. I had shaken hands on it and, as far as I am concerned, when I shake hands on a deal, I am committed.

Nevertheless, I felt uneasy about it and wondered if I could allow the deal to derail during the paperwork process by discovering things to fall out over in the small print. But I was uncomfortable about taking that line which in any event would have been even more unfair to Michael.

Normally when I agree something I am committed to it but in this particular case, I had made a decision that I was beginning to wish I hadn't made and I didn't know what to do about it. After a near-sleepless weekend, I woke up on the Monday morning and decided that I had no alternative but to call up Michael and say the whole thing was a mistake and we should call it off.

Unbeknownst to me that Monday was Rosh Hashanah, the Jewish New Year. Michael Levy is a very devout Jew and I could not get hold of him. Even his assistant could not speak to him. Eventually, at my insistence, she managed to contact him.

Apparently Michael's rabbi had by now given him permission to speak to me, and later that afternoon he called me back. I had the unpleasant task of telling him that it had all been a huge mistake and we should call the deal off. He was furious, as he should have been. I was hugely embarrassed, as I should have been. We had both incurred significant legal costs. The whole episode is something that I am not terribly proud of to this day.

Michael Levy subsequently met Tony Blair on the tennis court and became his special adviser on Middle Eastern affairs, and head of fundraising for the Labour Party. In fact, I would go so far as to say that, without Michael Levy, there may not have been a New Labour. Tony Blair was able to pursue a right-wing Labour policy and instigate the many things he wanted to do – including joining George W Bush in the war on Iraq – partly because he no longer required the trade union funding on which the Labour Party has always relied. Instead, thanks to Michael Levy, the party was now able to generate funds from the commercial sector. The entire political history of the country could have been different without Michael. His efforts for the Labour Party earned him a peerage and he is now Lord Levy, a member of the House of Lords.

Nevertheless, having devoted three months to try to complete the deal with Michael, I was now back to square one in terms of finding a replacement for Terry Connolly. I contacted Jorgen Larsen who had just retired from head of international at CBS Records and also had time on his hands. Jorgen wasn't interested in a role with Chrysalis but pulled out a CV from his desk drawer and plonked it in front of me, saying: "What about Joe Kiener?"

I knew Joe. He was a German guy who had had a senior position with Ariola Records, which became BMG, in Munich. He joined them just as they were buying Arista, the company founded by Clive Davis. I had always thought he was very smart and presented himself well. After Ariola, he had been headhunted to be the CEO of Adidas in North America, which showed how highly he was regarded generally, but it hadn't worked out. He was currently between jobs.

I called him up and, having first arranged for Allen Grubman to give Joe the once-over, jumped on a plane with Doug D'Arcy to meet him at his home in New York. I offered him a position in the company. Joe wanted to stay based in the States as his family lived there. This was not ideal but I hired him anyway. So the new management structure would be Doug D'Arcy with Nigel Butterfield in London, and Joe Kiener as vice-chairman of Chrysalis US in New York. Joe also joined the main board.

Joe's view was that the record company continued to be in danger of haemorrhaging cash if we kept operating such a large infrastructure. Chrysalis had got to the point where we were too big to be an independent and were running at fully-fledged major record company levels. This was especially true in the UK and the USA but also in France, Germany, Holland and Scandinavia.

However, our main problem lay in America, so often a graveyard for foreign companies, because the cost of doing business there is so high. However if you get it right, there is certainly a huge pot of gold at the end of the rainbow.

I was reluctant to exit from the US market or even to significantly downsize, specifically because it was so soon after I had taken over the company from Terry Ellis. Of course, it's quite likely we would have faced the same problems had Terry still been around – after all the industry was changing, but responsibility for Chrysalis was now mine and mine alone and I would have regarded it as a personal failure. So somehow or other I felt committed to retaining the American operation more or less in its current form, albeit with a reduced infrastructure.

By now I was acquainted with James Harmon, who ran the Wertheim Schroder merchant bank. James had a good input into Warner Communication through his relationship with CEO Bob Morgado.★

Through James I discussed a deal with Warner executives that would see me selling the record company to them and staying on to run it. Chrysalis would have become the label they would have used for their overseas operations. However they insisted I sell them the music publishing company as well, which I was reluctant to do. There was also the issue of what to do with the rest of the company, including the businesses we had bought with MAM. However, a deal with Warner had some attraction; at least it would have got the predatory David Geffen off my back, as he was still circling with his increased shareholding. David was affiliated with Warner, and sorting out his position was part of the package.

Yet none of the options seemed particularly appealing. That New Year, Joe Kiener, who was visiting his in-laws in Guadeloupe, came to Antigua with his family to spend a few days with Chelle and I.

★ James was later to become head of the US import export bank during the Clinton regime, and was heavily tipped to become Treasury Secretary had Al Gore defeated George W Bush in 2000.

Whilst we were there David Geffen insisted on sending the Warner jet, the Gulfstream Five, to bring us to New York to meet up.

As it happened, I was happy to go to New York. There was someone else there that I was very keen to see.

CHAPTER 17

Nothing Compares 2 U

By the end of 1988, running Chrysalis was beginning to become pretty stressful. The constant meetings and transatlantic flights, allied with the ongoing cash-flow problems, were beginning to make me feel that my life was overloaded with problems with little time for pleasure. And, as ever, nothing crystallises things so much as Christmas.

Among my major annual Yuletide duties was attending all three Chrysalis Christmas parties, in New York, LA and London. They were big events looked forward to not only by staff members but the wider music industry as a whole. And while flying across the world to attend parties might not sound too onerous, the hours in the air and consequent jet lag could take their toll. Thank God for Concorde.

I was on the hunt for potential financial partners for Chrysalis and on December 12, 1988, at the instigation of Allen Grubman, I had lunch in New York with Jim Fifield, who had just taken over as President and CEO of EMI. Grubman had continued to represent us after the split with Terry Ellis and had been approached by Fifield about the possibility of doing a deal for Chrysalis.

I wasn't interested. I believed we had other options, not least trying to reduce overheads in line with what was now a very inconsistent release schedule. From New York, I flew to LA for the Christmas party and also met up with Tony Dimitriades, who was now managing Billy Idol, to inquire on the progress of the studio album we had been expecting for well over two years. Little did I know it would be another 15 months before he delivered *Cradle Of Love*.

After the Christmas party in LA, as normal I arranged a dinner for some of the writers and other business associates. The next morning, I caught a plane to New York to attend the party there. Mike Bone, the Chrysalis US president, was a colourful southern guy who had an independent creative background and wasn't afraid to take chances. He famously told Sinéad O'Connor that if *The Lion And The Cobra*, her debut album, sold more than 50,000 copies in the US he would shave his head. After it reached the 200,000 mark, he was game enough to let Sinéad perform the task personally. That party went on into the early hours of the morning.

The following day, Saturday December 17, 1988, I got on the 9.30 a.m. Concorde from JFK to fly home for the weekend before Christmas. The regular customers always got the front row seats and I was seated in 1A. In those days, I seemed to know all of the crew as I was on Concorde so often. However, this time round there was a young and attractive crew member I had not met before, which cheered me up a little.

As the plane took off, it became clear to me that something had gone wrong. When Concorde took off from JFK, it had to bank steeply to avoid the houses in Jamaica Bay and then navigate around a US air force bombing range off the coast of Long Island before going supersonic and heading out across the Atlantic. On Saturdays, the bombing range wasn't operational so the Concorde could go straight up to Mach 2.

After about 10 minutes I realised that we were still circling around at about Mach point 45 – less than the speed of a normal plane – so I called a crew member over. It happened to be the new stewardess who had caught my eye earlier.

I asked her what had gone wrong.

She said: "What do you mean?"

I told her that I flew Concorde a lot and I knew when something was wrong. She replied that she also flew regularly on Concorde, and there was nothing wrong. I said she was incorrect and asked her to check it out.

Having asked the captain, she returned to assure me there was no problem. I told her bluntly that the captain was lying since we were still circling around Long Island and going nowhere. In an attempt to reassure me, she made a return visit to the captain, who then came on the PA and announced: "Those of you who travel with us regularly will have noticed that we have a problem."

The plane had lost its hydraulic system on take-off, and with it the ability to go supersonic. The captain had been circling around New York considering his options and decided that, if we landed back at JFK we would be there all day. However, the tailwinds were so strong that day that, if we flew at 25,000 feet, which was very low for any jet, never mind Concorde, we could make it to Shannon in Ireland, refuel and get to London that evening.

Naturally, I had plenty of banter with the stewardess over her misinformation and me knowing more about what was going on than she did. I asked her how long she'd been flying Concorde, and she said about 18 months. The technical problems naturally meant that the flight took five hours rather than the usual three-and-a-half and we also hung out together as we refuelled in Shannon, meaning that I spent the whole day talking to her.

Her name was Janice Toseland, and I made sure I got her phone number, telling her that I would get some concert tickets for her and the other crew members in London. Meeting her had undoubtedly lifted my mood and my various preoccupations faded into the background during this slower than usual but very enjoyable Concorde flight.

As it happens, Janice was the only young crew member in the Concorde fleet. The rest were very senior staff, and although there was no rule against younger members applying for Concorde they were all told their chances of success were remote so they tended not to try. Despite being only 26, Janice had been an exception and, to her great surprise, had found herself selected.

The following Monday, I called her up to tell her that there were no gigs she might like before Christmas, and offered to take her out for lunch instead. She agreed, but even that meeting nearly didn't happen, as she turned up about 30 minutes late, just as I was about to leave, having broken a heel of her shoe on an escalator.

We had an enjoyable lunch and I suggested we might meet again after the holidays. David Geffen sending his jet to Antigua after Christmas to bring me to New York was thus very timely, as it gave us the chance to meet up again during one of her weekly stopovers in the Big Apple.

Obviously I had to meet with Geffen first, but our meeting achieved little. Despite the shareholding he had acquired in Chrysalis, he had no real leverage, which he did not entirely appear to understand. And even though a deal with him may not have been such a bad idea, I hate to be in the position of being forced into something against my will.

However, I knew if I were to antagonise him, David Geffen would be a formidable opponent. He was famously the most dedicated and driven person in the music business. Even from his home in Malibu, he was still many New Yorkers' first phone call of the day as he was up so early. Most people were in awe of him, including his peers in Warner Communications. So he and I agreed to keep our channels open, and I headed off for a rather more relaxed dinner with Janice.

This set the pattern for the following weeks and months as I criss-crossed the Atlantic for a series of meetings with key New York-based industry executives, ensuring they all coincided with Janice being in Manhattan. Of course, I was still married – but nevertheless, our relationship was developing and deepening.

Thankfully, things were picking up again on a business level. Jethro Tull's commercial peak appeared to be well behind them, so we were flabbergasted in February 1989 when they unexpectedly won a Grammy for the *Crest Of A Knave* album.

Tull were nominated in a new category named Best Hard Rock/ Metal Performance Vocal or Instrumental and were up against Metallica, Iggy Pop, Jane's Addiction and AC/DC. I wasn't at the ceremony and nor was Ian Anderson, who had been specifically told by Chrysalis US president Mike Bone not to attend as he had absolutely no chance of winning.

There was a palpable sense of amazement when Jethro Tull were announced as the winners – and, of course, there was nobody there to collect the award. The presenter, Alice Cooper, made an embarrassing joke, and handed the award to himself.

The following week we took an advert in US music-industry trade publication *Billboard*. Next to a picture of a flute, Ian's trademark instrument, and some iron bars, was the line "The flute is a heavy, metal instrument." Metallica went on to win six metal Grammies, to date, and when they won in 1992 they had the good grace to thank Jethro Tull for not releasing an album that year.

Chrysalis' other early signing, Ten Years After, also reformed and in 1989 released an excellent new studio album entitled *About Time*. Although it was probably their most commercial and accessible album ever, I had a hard time convincing some of the staff to do their best by the band. The four guys came to Glebe House for a photo session, which was fun, but it proved impossible to relive the good old days.

The continued success of Jethro Tull and the return of Ten Years After put in perspective how far I had come in the last two decades but also reminded me of the obstacles that lay ahead. However, I had more pressing matters close to home.

Our daughter Chloe's school called Chelle and I to tell us that Chloe was having trouble reading the blackboard and might need glasses.

At the time, we didn't think this was any great problem. It is perfectly normal for children of that age to need specs, although we had started calling her Clumsy Clogs because she had a dreadful habit of running into trees and other things.

Once, during a family holiday in the South of France, she had put her foot through the plastic top of the swimming pool filter, causing a deep cut to her leg which required her to spend the summer with her leg in a bandage and visit the local hospital every couple of days to check it out. On a skiing holiday in Zermatt, I also had to scream at the top of my voice to prevent her heading over a precipitous, unprotected drop.

Nevertheless, we didn't imagine there was any great problem, even when two or three different opticians all told us the same story. They couldn't find any lenses that made her eyes work and even questioned that she might be faking the whole thing and there was nothing wrong with her eyes at all.

This was far from the case. The horrible truth emerged when we sent Chloe for a brain scan. The results revealed that she had an ultra-rare condition: a malignant tumour on the chiasm of her optic nerve. She was devastated, as were we.

The worst news was that there is no treatment for this condition. It is impossible to operate because the optic nerve is so infinitesimally small, and it's impregnated into the brain in such a position that any attempt to target it could result in causing other problems within the brain. Desperate, we had the scan sent to every possible doctor we could find anywhere in the world we thought might be able to help: Switzerland, New York, Los Angeles, Sydney.

Yet we knew that the doctors that were dealing with Chloe in England knew exactly what they were talking about and nobody had a magic formula to cure things. We learned that the tumour develops very slowly: it grows, shrinks, moves a little from one side to the other. It could remain benign. The doctors told us that as few as 40 people in the UK suffer from this condition,

I talked to Tony Martell, who was vice president of marketing at CBS records when his son TJ died of leukaemia in his late teens. Tony had started the TJ Martell Foundation in New York with an eminent physician called Dr James Holland. It was a major American music industry charitable foundation to raise money for kids with cancer and especially leukaemia. Chrysalis became a big supporter of the charity, and in 1982, Terry Ellis and I had even been the recipients of the annual TJ Martell humanitarian award, which was an enormous honour. It normally went to a really senior person in the US recording industry.

Personally, I was very surprised to be included in the list of honourees because Terry was at that time responsible for the US company but the foundation wanted to honour me at the same time and I was delighted to be able to accept. Pat Benatar sang 'The Star-Spangled Banner' at the event and Leo Sayer flew in and sang 'Land Of Hope And Glory', although I would have preferred 'Jerusalem'.

Chloe took her affliction particularly hard. As she realised her life could never be totally normal, she developed an eating disorder in her early teens. This was particularly poignant to me, of course, having lived through the terrible period when Karen Carpenter had died from anorexia.

Anorexia is a terrible ailment and difficult to comprehend. The immediate reaction when a member of your family develops anorexia is simply to tell them to eat, but it doesn't work like that. The more you tell them to eat, the less they do. It may be classed as an eating disorder but it's really a psychological condition that manifests itself as an eating disorder.

A psychologist would surely diagnose that, afflicted by her brain tumour, Chloe probably developed anorexia as one way, at least, to be in control of her body. Unfortunately, meal times, which should be pleasant shared family experiences, turned into a battle zone. When she, Chelle and I visited Florida for a short break to watch my horse Culture Vulture run in the Breeders' Cup Distaff, Chloe was effectively living on half a grapefruit a day.

It was a hugely upsetting and stressful period, but Chloe has long since learned to live with her tumour and eventually, thankfully, made a full recovery from the anorexia. She has never been able to drive or to play ball games but is an accomplished skier, has run marathons in London and New York, and after reading law at Oxford is now head of the music department at prestigious London lawyers Harbottle & Lewis. She should be an inspiration for any family with a daughter with a disability. I could not be more proud of her.

As ever, business matters distracted me from these domestic traumas to a certain extent. More and more people were making overtures to Chrysalis about buying the company. In June 1988, Berry Gordy, Jr. had sold Tamla Motown to MCA Records and Boston Ventures for $61 million. This set a benchmark for the financial value of an iconic music label and its catalogue of recordings, though I also noted that Gordy held on to Jobete Music, the music publishing company through which Motown's songs were administered.

Jim Fifield and EMI had already approached us but, as a German national, Joe Kiener was keen that we should speak to BMG and consider selling to that company. Meanwhile, David Geffen was still attempting to exert his influence on the proceedings, although the reality was that his 15% shareholding still gave him no real control over anything. My position was clear: I was only interested in doing a deal for Chrysalis Records and always intended to hold on to the publishing company, Chrysalis Music.

The spring of 1989 saw me still a fixture on Concorde, often with Doug D'Arcy or Joe Kiener, as we talked to BMG. I had a history with the company going back to the days when Ariola had been our licensee partner in central Europe. Eventually it was decided that we would go to Munich to meet with Michael Dornemann, the CEO of BMG Music.

Dornemann had proposed that he would pay $45 million for 50 per cent of Chrysalis Records to enter into a joint venture for 10 years. We would continue to run the company and, in 10 years' time, BMG would have an option to buy the rest of it on a pre-agreed formula.

On March 16, 1989, Allen Grubman flew into London with Joe Kiener and the nexy day joined Doug D'Arcy, Nigel Butterfield and me to go on to Munich for a day of meetings to close the BMG deal. The meeting appeared to be going well and we were almost there:

most of the business points were resolved. However, Allen Grubman was palpably uncomfortable. His heart was not really in the deal, which was very much Joe's initiative.

Doug too was far from happy. He felt that we had not fully explored the cost-cutting idea of closing down our US operation entirely and reverting to a licence deal there. The main stumbling block to this idea was that Huey Lewis, who was still our biggest artist at the time, had a clause in his agreement that were we not to operate a full-size structure in the USA, he would be able to leave Chrysalis.

With most of the major points agreed with BMG, we got down to discussing the smaller issues. One thing I wanted to stipulate was that every artist whose records had appeared on the Chrysalis label would continue to be on the label in perpetuity: Jethro Tull, Ten Years After, Procol Harum, Blondie, Spandau Ballet, Billy Idol and the rest of the roster.

In these days of digital downloads, record labels can be almost an irrelevance. Things were different back in 1989, when artists would sign to a record company like Island or Chrysalis because of the particular vibe and identity of the label.

I thought that this would be a request that BMG would readily agree to, but to my surprise Dornemann said no. I asked him why.

"Well we don't know how you're going to operate the label," he replied. "Maybe in five years' time, you'll start making pornographic records and devalue the label."

"That is ridiculous," I told him. "Of course I am not going to do that!"

"But I have no control over it," he insisted. "Maybe you will."

We argued back and forth until, frustrated, I told him: "Michael, it is a deal-breaker."

"Well, it is a deal-breaker, then," said Dornemann, and walked out.

It was by then about 4.30 in the afternoon. We sat there and by five o'clock Allen Grubman had itchy feet. By 5.30 there was still no sign of Dornemann returning and Grubman proposed going back to our hotel and calling Fifield at EMI. By 5.45, it was getting beyond a joke. We asked Dornemann's secretary if he was coming back and she clearly had no idea. So I went along with Grubman's plan.

At the time, I had not really considered making a deal with EMI. We had no real history of being involved with it and no relationship with Jim Fifield. I knew he had been the chief executive of CBS/Fox Video but he was new to the music business and I didn't really know him. BMG had always been my preferred choice.

Nevertheless, in my room at the hotel, Grubman got Fifield on the phone.

"We are in Munich, about to close with BMG but we will give you one last shot," he told him. "Here's the structure of the deal: 50% of the record company. Out in 10 years' time, $75 million, and a formula for the second half. If you get on Concorde this afternoon, we will fly back from Munich, meet you in London at eight tomorrow morning for breakfast, and see if we can close the deal."

I didn't hear what Fifield said on the other end of the line but the gist of it was clearly that he had meetings in New York and there was no way he could drop everything and get on that afternoon's Concorde to London to be with us. Grubman's response was uncompromising.

"Listen, schmuck, you wanna be back selling ladies' underwear in Poughkeepsie?" he asked him. "If not, get on the fucking Concorde!" At which point he slammed the phone down.

This unorthodox technique proved incredibly effective. A few minutes later we got a call back confirming the meeting would take place. Jim Fifield had his finance director work on the numbers all night and, having factored in what they would make in terms of the manufacturing and the distribution in addition to the 50% ownership of the company, they were very comfortable with our price.

We checked out of the hotel and jumped on the plane to London. The next morning we met with Fifield at the offices of EMI's merchant bankers. By the end of the day we had closed the deal, and we announced it that evening.

Michael Dornemann was shocked by this development. He called Fifield and asked him: "How could you pay so much?"

He then phoned to tell me he had only been bluffing about refusing my request regarding the artistes staying on the label in perpetuity.

"How did I know that?" I replied. "You said it was a deal-breaker, and then you left the meeting and didn't return."

At first glance, the price EMI was paying seemed exceptionally high, but its finance director, Philip Rowley, had done his sums well and in truth it was completely justified. It also set a trend. The other majors moved quickly to make their own acquisitions, and one by one Virgin, A&M and Island were snapped up on similar or even enhanced valuations.

Having agreed the EMI deal, we set out to complete the due diligence, which took two weeks of round the clock meetings, especially for Nigel and his finance team. Grubman Indursky, Allen's law firm, helped to complete the paperwork for it alongside our UK corporate lawyers, Clifford Chance.

Over the last 25 years, Allen Grubman has matured into the most important entertainment business lawyer in America. It is rumoured he is dyslexic and never reads contracts. That could well be true, but he doesn't always have to. In the case of Chrysalis, he earned his very large fee by the simple act of advising the worldwide CEO of EMI that if he did not drop everything to fly to London to meet with us, he would find himself back selling ladies' underwear in a small town in upstate New York. To this day I have no idea if Jim Fifield has any connection whatsoever with Poughkeepsie or whether he was ever engaged in selling ladies underwear.

CHAPTER 18

The One And Only

Dealing with our new partners at EMI was a whole new ball game for me. I had never really worked for anybody before: I had certainly never been part of a large company and I had never needed to play a game of corporate politics. Frankly, I went into our new venture like a babe in the woods.

There was very definitely a well-structured pecking order within EMI, with Jim Fifield at the apex, and I was quite confused myself as to exactly where I would fit into the scheme of things. After all the Chrysalis label was to be a joint venture between EMI and the Chrysalis group, of which I was still the executive chairman and responsible for the other businesses that it encompassed.

It was a while before I realised that for most people within the company their personal relationship with Jim was paramount to their continued existence and their career progress.

After we had announced the deal, late on a Friday evening at the Chrysalis offices in London, Jim Fifield suggested we ought to go out and celebrate. I said: "Absolutely. Where shall we go?" Jim doubted we could get a reservation in a good restaurant at this late stage.

"What about Harry's Bar?" I suggested.

Jim was somewhat surprised by the very idea that I would be able to secure a reservation at a few minutes' notice for dinner at the hottest restaurant in London. Harry's Bar was – and still is – a very upmarket members' club in Mayfair. I picked up the phone, booked a table for six and said we'd be around immediately.

I was also able to arrange Jim's membership to the club, which he had been waiting on for a couple of years or so. Although Jim was delighted I think he may well have been taken aback by my show of bravado and one-upmanship.

Perhaps in my own imitable way I was declining Jim's offer of friendship and camaraderie. He and his then wife, Betsy, are avid skiers, and a few months later in 1989 they invited Chelle and I to go skiing in Chile with them that August. I declined because that month was always our family holiday in the South of France, and I didn't really fancy spending my summer holiday skiing in Chile. Jim seemed very surprised, and only later did I realise no one ever turned down his invitations; on the contrary, they were desperately sought after.

The deal also brought other problems. As soon as it was announced, Bob Brown, the manager of Huey Lewis, went on the warpath. He and I had always been close and he was particularly supportive of me during my negotiations with Terry Ellis. He was therefore incensed that I had not kept him abreast of the negotiations between myself and EMI and even informed him of the deal before it was announced. He started calling Fifield at home late at night, threatening to sue to get Huey Lewis & The News out of their contract.

Bob demanded that the group be transferred to another label in the EMI Group, and that he be given back the songwriting rights, which were signed to Chrysalis Music, which was not part of the EMI deal. Under intense pressure from him, I caved in and acceded to his demands, giving away something that I had not sold to EMI and which was part of the continuing Chrysalis Group.

Having agreed this, I then felt morally obliged to offer Ian Anderson of Jethro Tull the same concession and to return to him his music publishing rights, although I imagine I would have done this anyway, following the sale of the label.

Maybe I should have realised that I was not a natural at working in a large corporation. Mike Allen, our head of international, and I did a quick trip around the world visiting all of the EMI affiliates, by whom we would now be represented. We had dinner with Peter Snell, who ran EMI Australia, and as we sat down, he informed me: "I could tell within five minutes of meeting you that you are totally unemployable." I wasn't sure whether to take this as an insult or a compliment.

I was not gelling within the EMI environment but some of those working for me, who were more adept at corporate manoeuvrings, were flourishing. Joe Kiener in particular had experience of this kind of politics, having worked in larger corporations, and was much more adroit at dealing with the EMI management.

I was also about to lose a major long-time ally. After the EMI deal, Doug D'Arcy decided that the time had come for him to move on. We went right back to university years and he had been part of the fabric of Chrysalis since 1968: this was a major blow.

It also left me needing to find a new head for the UK record company. I chose Paul Conroy, who was then number two to Rob Dickins at Warner Brothers in London. Crucially, Paul had independent record company experience, having worked closely with Dave Robinson at Stiff, so I was sure he would be suitable for the role.

Nevertheless, Dave Robinson's wife, Rosie, a friend of Chelle, fired a warning shot across my bows. She called up Chelle and suggested that hiring Paul might not be the best idea. Maybe I should have paid more attention to female intuition.

Paul Conroy joined the company in the autumn of 1989 and the first thing he did was suggest we move offices out of the West End and into a refurbished old brewery in Bramley Road, near Shepherd's Bush. The Chrysalis HQ thus relocated to a strange downbeat area with a new age traveller camp next door, but in the two decades since the move the area has become extremely hip and trendy, especially with media types. Bizarrely, a few years previously, a group of squatters around there had declared themselves to be the republic of Frestonia, attempted to secede from Britain and even set up a border with passport check points!

The new offices were very plush and at one point more than 300 people were working there. I even created a massage room, so that staff could arrange relaxing massages when they arrived back on overnight flights from the States. Yet we bought the building at the height of the 1989 London property boom: within months the market had crashed, and it was nearly 20 years before the property returned to the value that we had paid for it.

There were other management changes besides the arrival of Paul. Joe Kiener remained on the main board running the US company and worked with EMI in America to integrate the label there. I hired Nick Watkins, who had been managing director of Rank Video Services in the UK, as deputy managing director of Chrysalis to run our non-music activities – mainly the new communication division which emerged out of a ragbag of television production and television facilities businesses that we had bought. It was a fresh start from the Terry Connolly/Doug D'Arcy era of our golden years.

Although Island, A&M and Virgin all followed our lead in selling out to majors, I still occasionally wonder if we could have played things differently. As I suggested once to Chris Blackwell at Island and Jerry Moss at A&M, had the four big independent labels joined forces in some way, we could have been an absolute powerhouse as large as any of the other companies around.

At the time, everyone was too caught up in their own labels to get it together, but it would have been an amazing initiative. Between us we had some of the biggest artists in the world and had we joined forces, we would have become the biggest record company around.

Proof that the EMI deal had come at the right time came when the Chrysalis Group reported a loss before tax of £11.5 million in 1989, almost all of it derived from trading losses in the United States. So many English companies end up in the same situation and ultimately many of them choose to exit the market. It's hard to do that in the record business, especially when we had so many major US based acts signed to the label for the world.

Nevertheless, with the EMI deal in place, we regenerated immediately, with increased sales and profitability right across the board. In fact the year following the transaction was by far the biggest ever in the history of the record company.

This was partly down to Sinead O'Connor. Towards the end of the year she delivered *I Do Not Want What I Haven't Got*, the follow-up to her hit debut album, *The Lion And The Cobra*. She had composed and produced most of the album herself but her management team of Fachtna O'Kelly and Steve Fargnoli had suggrsted she cover 'Nothing Compares 2 U', a little known song Prince had written in 1985 for The Family, one of his many side projects.

Chrysalis used to stage biannual A&R get-togethers in Europe or the States for staff to unveil the projects they were working on, and in November 1989 we took over 17 rooms of an 18-room hotel in Martha's Vineyard. The other room had been booked by a couple on honeymoon. They were in for a surprise.

When Nigel Grainge played us Sinéad's version of 'Nothing Compares 2 U', the reaction was amazing. The now-famous video John Maybury had shot with her in Paris was simplicity itself, yet one of the most compelling ever put together for a piece of music. He framed her face and let the emotions show through. Suddenly, she wasn't this threatening-looking singer with the shaved head any more: she came across as vulnerable (which, indeed, she was).

As can so often happen Sinéad found fame hard to cope with. Things started to go off the rails when, during a US tour in August 1990, she insisted she would not go on stage if the American national anthem was played at the Garden State fairground in New Jersey. This created a huge uproar and some American radio stations banned her records. Her management handled the resulting furore very badly.

In truth, although playing the 'Star Spangled Banner' before rock gigs was a little bizarre, it was a well-established tradition in America. I know Peter Grant, the manager of Led Zeppelin, would always tell the organisers to play the anthem before the support band, not before Zeppelin, which meant it never became an issue with Robert Plant or Jimmy Page.

We then made a mistake as a label. She had a song called 'Black Boys On Mopeds' about how black kids in the UK were subjected to more harassment from the police than white kids. It could have pulled Sinéad back from the pop star she had become to the serious social commentary type artist she wanted to be: she had sung it over an acoustic guitar for *MTV Unplugged* and been mesmerising.

Against my better judgement, I allowed Paul Conroy to overrule me and instead we released a pop song, 'The Emperor's New Clothes', that Radio One liked. It's never a good idea to allow a radio station to dictate your artist's development, and the record was not a hit. When we had heard the original demos in Martha's Vinyard, we all felt that a third track, 'Three Babies', was potentially every bit as strong as 'Nothing Compares 2 You', and we specifically held back this track to come out as a Christmas single. But despite the huge success of 'Nothing Compares', by the time 'Three Babies' was released the gloss had gone off the project and that track did not even make the Top 40.

Sinéad's second album was one of the most exciting projects I have ever worked on even though I ultimately felt that we dropped the ball, albeit a very slippery one. Her career then went into a tailspin. In February 1991, even though she was nominated for four Grammy Awards and actually won Best Alternative Music Performance for *I Do Not Want What I Haven't Got*, she decided not to attend the ceremony.

She compounded this, and then some, in October 1992 when she tore up a picture of Pope John Paul II on the American TV comedy show *Saturday Night Live*. When, two weeks later, she appeared at the Bob Dylan 30th Anniversary Concert Celebration at Madison Square

Garden, she was booed off. Sinéad's career never really recovered. It is often the case that the best artists are the most troublesome and in Sinéad's case it is hard to argue: but it is the role of the record company to support, nurture and direct these difficult creative talents.

It wasn't all disaster after disaster for Sinéad, and in 1990 she had been one of two Chrysalis artists, alongside Debbie Harry, to star on *Red Hot + Blue*, a charity album instigated by New York lawyer John Carlin to raise money for AIDS charities. Chrysalis released the album and sold over a million copies, with 80% of the profits going to charity. Again, it is something I am very proud of.

Being linked to EMI increased the glamour quotient in my life. As a small independent company, Chrysalis had never been able to throw our own high profile parties at events like the Grammys and the MTV Awards. EMI could and did. In 1991 the Grammys temporarily moved from Los Angeles to Radio City Music Hall in New York and EMI invited me to its tie-in extravaganza.

I arrived unescorted as Chelle had chosen not to come and the event was too high-profile for me to risk taking Janice. However, there was quite a high quotient of supermodels there and I spent a large part of the evening talking to a particularly attractive tall blonde girl called Stacey, whose professional name was Donatella and occasionally spent weekends as part of a group helicoptering to Camp David with George H Bush and his retinue.

I also chatted to a beautiful black English girl from Streatham who had her own limousine waiting for her after the party and kindly offered me a lift back to my hotel. Her name was Naomi. I had never heard of her at the time but the next morning I was besieged by phone calls from people asking me how on Earth I had managed to leave a party with Naomi Campbell.

Back in London, in 1991 our lease on AIR Studios on the corner of Oxford Street and Regent Street ran out. We had to either rebuild the whole studio elsewhere or abandon the project, and should probably have done the latter. Despite the success of the first Go West record that was basically a home demo, we didn't realise the extent to which recordings could now be made in bedrooms rather than big studios.

Looking for a new base, George Martin came across Lyndhurst Hall, a big old Methodist church hall in north London, not far from Swiss Cottage. It resembled a miniature version of the Royal Albert Hall. We were in two minds about going ahead but managed to find a partner in Japanese electronics manufacturer Pioneer, which wanted to come in and joint-finance the whole project.

Lyndhurst Hall had the potential to be a brilliant spacious studio like Abbey Road, where George Martin had obviously done such fantastic work for EMI and with The Beatles. It was a fantastic opportunity, and with Pioneer on board we decided to go ahead and convert this Grade II listed building into a state-of-the-art studio. It was a major statement for the group to make, albeit with the benefit of hindsight not the right one.

We launched the studio with a performance of Dylan Thomas' *Under Milk Wood,* produced by George Martin and starring Sir Anthony Hopkins, Tom Jones, Jonathan Pryce, Harry Secombe and Catherine Zeta Jones and attended by the Prince of Wales. After the show we had a party, with the stars and Prince Charles belting out Welsh anthems with glorious abandon. (Charles' sister, Princess Anne, was equally vocal when she attended a charity Christmas gala that I organised, complete with carols, at the studio.)

AIR Lyndhurst was a great success for Chrysalis, creatively if not financially. The roll call of artists who made records there shows how highly the complex was thought of: Coldplay, George Michael, Paul McCartney, Elton John, Dire Straits, John Williams and Mary Chapin Carpenter.

Chrysalis was never particularly good at developing teen-pop stars but in 1991 we had our own teen idol in Chesney Hawkes, a good-looking kid who enjoyed a number one with 'The One And Only'. Chesney was the son of Len 'Chip' Hawkes, the bassist in The Tremeloes in the sixties, and it was fun for a while to have the office besieged night and day by screaming girls hoping for a glimpse of their idol, the only time in my career I ever remember this happening. Sadly, the song title proved to be rather prophetic when it came to Chesney's career.

The launch of Cooltempo had gained us some kudos in the rap world and in 1990, Duff Marlowe, our A&R director and a former DJ and hip-hop writer, signed two significant acts: Gang Starr, from New York, and Arrested Development, from Atlanta, Georgia.

Gang Starr consisted of the rapper Guru and the producer DJ Premier and they were pioneering an interesting fusion of jazz and hip-hop. In January 1991, they released *Step In The Arena*, their first album for us. Guru had a middle-class upbringing and his father had been the first black judge in the Boston municipal courts.

DJ Premier, however, was more the streetwise type and felt he had to live up to the image. In June 1991, he showed up at the New York offices of Chrysalis with a posse and had an acrimonious meeting with Ed Strickland, our 'black music' chief, about how much of a priority act they were, during which one of his entourage pulled a gun.

It was more for show than anything else but it shook everyone up. There was talk of kicking Gang Starr off the label but, eventually, they came in and apologised to everyone, we banned them from the premises for a couple of weeks, and it blew over.

By contrast, Arrested Development were a breath of fresh air and the antithesis of gangsta rap. They were led by Speech, a thoughtful, inspirational figure who composed their three crossover hits, 'Tennessee', 'People Everyday' and 'Mr. Wendal'. However, it took so long for their first album to appear that they named it *3 Years, 5 Months & 2 Days In The Life Of . . .* EMI took all the credit for their success in 1993 but they were arguably the last great Chrysalis signing.

Despite the deal with EMI, in the financial year 1990/91 the Chrysalis group made losses of nearly £8 million, of which almost £6 million was our share of the loss in the new joint-venture record company. A further £1 million was lost in two audacious but failed bids to operate ITV TV franchises, one in Yorkshire and the other in Wales and the West Country. We missed out on one for creative reasons, and the other because we were outbid.

But the main reason that we were haemorrhaging money so rapidly was that the record company was still carrying the same level of overheads in America. We had never cured the problem of running too big an infrastructure for the size of our release schedule; we had simply put a bandage on it and got someone else to pay half of the costs.

EMI, however, was doing fine out of the arrangement, as it had the manufacturing and distribution income, but we knew that we couldn't carry on like that. Furthermore, any changes to the operating base of the record company needed EMI's agreement and it was not prepared to countenance any. It seemed as if EMI was almost attempting to force us into a corner and the way the deal was structured seemed to be playing into its hands.

I had gone into the agreement with EMI believing that a 10-year deal meant what it said on the tin and I would be running Chrysalis Records for the next decade. I had also felt confident the Chrysalis Group would achieve a substantial pay-out based on the long-term success of the record company.

However, this was becoming less likely as each year went by. Our finance director, Nigel Butterfield, was now advising me that if things continued the way they were, at the end of the 10-year term we would receive no payment whatsoever for the sale of the second half of the company. He advised me that it would be in my best interests to listen to offers from EMI to buy out the rest of the company as soon as possible.

I would not countenance this. I was completely focused on continuing to build and develop Chrysalis Records, even if I was feeling decidedly isolated within the overall EMI organisation.

Meanwhile, EMI was faced with its own problems. It was operating three separate labels in New York: the EMI label, Chrysalis, and SBK, a label formed by Stephen Swid, Martin

Bandier and Charles Koppelman, who had bought CBS Songs, the publishing company the CBS group had chosen to sell prior to Sony acquiring CBS Records. They flipped their acquisition at a huge profit, selling it to EMI and in return getting the opportunity to start a record company.

For the EMI Group running three labels clearly didn't make sense, especially as it also had the jazz label Blue Note, not to mention Capitol Records in LA. An opportunity to merge any two of EMI, Chrysalis or SBK would make strategic sense. Strategically, the best merger would have been between Chrysalis and the EMI label but that couldn't be instigated while Chrysalis Group still owned 50% of Chrysalis label.

Furthermore, political issues did not just affect Chrysalis but were prevalent throughout the entire EMI music organisation. Jim Fifield was a highly competent executive but running an operation full of egos, both from the artists and the executives, is different from a normal commercial enterprise.

Both Charles Koppelman and Martin Bandier were staking a claim for their own territory. I remember one year just before Midem, Martin kindly offered me a ride to Cannes from New York on his EMI private jet. I said I knew when his plane was leaving and it did not fit in with my schedule, but he explained that I was confusing his plane with Koppelman's. They both had their own EMI jet!

Charles Koppelman was extremely adroit at working the system. He would fly into London, and then turn up at the corporate headquarters in a huge limo, wearing a posh suit and smoking a big cigar. Sir Colin Southgate, the chairman, loved it, and was really taken in by him. It was just what he expected from a music mogul, rather than someone in jeans and a sweater like me.

It was a similar situation to when Virgin Atlantic took on British Airways in a huge law suit and won. Lord King, the BA chairman, admitted after their defeat that he had totally underestimated Richard Branson: "If he had been wearing a suit I would have taken him seriously, but how could I when he was dressed like that, in jeans and a sweater?"

There again, Jim Fifield had entered the music business looking like an FBI agent in a suit, Brooks Brothers shirts and square-shaped glasses, but soon morphed into a music mogul, dressing casually and playing air guitar in his office.

EMI would hold six-monthly strategy sessions for all the key executives in various different exotic locations. The first such meeting I attended was in Taormina in Sicily. Another was in Antigua, at the St James Club.

Yet even if the location was attractive, these meetings showcased a ruthless corporate culture. Failure was not an option, and at each meeting some unlucky soul would well and truly have his feet held against the fire. I sense this is now much more prevalent in the music industry than it was, but at the time it was quite foreign to me. I suspect the rationale was *"Pour encourager les autres"*. I would always feel huge sympathy for the selected victim.

In addition, there were also six-monthly Chrysalis Records board meetings, usually held in London, New York or LA. These were more sedate affairs, but I was fighting hard to maintain our unique culture within the rapidly involving change that was overtaking the industry.

The political machinations were ratcheted up a notch in summer 1991 when Paul Conroy came in to see me. He was two years into a three year contract. He wanted a new deal and asked me for what I considered to be an outrageous sum of money.

Personally, I always got on well with Paul and it was always going to be a difficult task taking over from Doug D'Arcy, who had been with the company for over 20 years. He also deserves thanks for arranging – without my knowledge – for me to be the recipient of the prestigious Strat Award, named after our mutual friend Tony Stratton-Smith. Like me, Paul began his career in the music business as a university social secretary, but Strat gave him his first real job, booking acts for the Charisma agency, and we both held him in high regard. The Strat award is presented each year to an individual for exemplary service to the music industry, and Terry Ellis and I were joint recipients in 1989.

I was not receptive to his demands as I felt the company had not progressed sufficiently under him in the way I had expected. I felt we had dropped the ball on Sinéad O'Connor and Chesney Hawkes and allowed The Waterboys to carry on in their merry raggle-taggle-gypsy, un-commercial Irish-infused folk way. We had not used the EMI opportunity to rebuild the company in the way that I would have liked.

Although Paul was a very good marketing guy, he possibly lacked an overview in terms of certain other functions of a record company. Chrysalis had always been fundamentally focused on the area of artist development, and over the years we had excelled in this. While all record labels want and need hits, I had always regarded our function as being more inclined towards developing long-term careers for our artists, and it is a testament to this philosophy that so many of the acts on the label are still around today. We commenced negotiations but I was in no mood to cave in to all of his demands.

In August we all went off to Dallas for an EMI convention (sadly, my family month in Cap d'Antibes was no longer sacrosanct). I stopped off in New York on the way, met Jim Fifield and told him that Paul Conroy wanted an enormous new deal, I was not remotely bothered about losing him, and that if we could not agree terms I would find somebody else.

Fifield was fairly concerned about this stand-off and for the first time I began to suspect that EMI was questioning my role in the company, especially as there were plenty of people who were clearly gunning for me. I felt I was in the middle of a political maelstrom.

I certainly was, as became clear a few weeks later at the beginning of September when I was back in the States for a Chrysalis Records board meeting in LA. Although I was still negotiating with Paul Conroy, I had pretty much decided that I was going to let him leave, and that I would need to look for a new head of the international record company.

On the first of the two days of meetings, when we broke for lunch, both Jim Fifield and Paul Conroy separately excused themselves and claimed they each had lunch meetings that they couldn't get out of and slipped away. I thought this was strange, not so much in Fifield's case but certainly for Conroy, who I would have expected to have been present throughout the day.

When we reconvened in the afternoon, the meeting started with Paul Conroy making a speech about how it was impossible to run the company properly because he was having to work for, and answer to, two different bosses, and he was getting mixed messages from me and from EMI.

At which point, Jim Fifield immediately said: "There is only one solution. We will have to take over the rest of the company."

I was absolutely flabbergasted because I hadn't seen it coming. I suspect Paul Conroy had realised that he wasn't going to get the deal he wanted from me and decided he would try and get it from Jim Fifield. In turn, Fifield must have decided that he could more easily afford to lose me than lose Conroy.

I was so shocked by the events of that afternoon that when the meeting ended, I drove out of the St. James Club car park to go back to the Beverly Hills Hotel and, attempting to turn left out of the hotel onto Sunset Boulevard, almost had the most spectacular car crash. I was inches away from my death. It was a sign of my emotional state, combined with the jet-lag: I was a complete and utter mess.

I did not need to accept this, I had a contractual agreement with EMI that I would run the business for 10 years – but I felt as if there was nothing I could do about the decision. I felt totally backed into a corner and pressured. This had not been on my agenda, although Nigel Butterfield had been advising me that it would be the right commercial course of action anyway.

Fifield's plan was to merge EMI and Chrysalis in New York and have it run by Deane Cameron, who had been pretty successful at

EMI Canada in Toronto. However, his wife refused to move to the States so they were stuck. At which point SBK co-founder Charles Koppelman offered to run all three labels if they merged EMI and Chrysalis with SBK, which was probably something that had been in his mind for a while.

I tried to play hardball over the final negotiations and I remember being in my office until the early hours of the morning of the day that we were intending to complete. Although it was the Chrysalis group that was selling the second 50%, not me personally, I was trying as hard as possible to get the best possible deal for us. For its part, EMI was desperate to get it signed to announce it at the company's annual results meeting the following morning.

We were still tying up loose ends at 2.30 in the morning when Guy Marriott, the head of EMI Music Business Affairs, frustratingly asked me, "Chris, what will it take you to sign this deal?"

"I rather like the new Honda Accura sports car," I told him. "The one that looks like a Ferrari."

Without checking with any of his superiors, in an attempt to get the deal closed so we could all go to bed, Marriott agreed to give me a Honda sports car as a going-away present. "Thank you very much," I said, and finally signed the deal.

Marriott got into terrible trouble with EMI for having agreed to it and I got into a spot of bother with my people who felt (probably correctly, with hindsight) that it was not ethically correct for me to personally benefit from the sale of a division of a PLC. However, I was able to use that agreement over the Honda sports car to force EMI to pay part of our legal expenses with Allen Grubman and his firm in New York, so my procrastinations were not completely in vain, although a part of me regrets that I never got to drive the car!

EMI paid approximately $30 million to buy the second half of the company and took on $25 million of inter-company debt that had built up during the time of the joint venture. Chrysalis would receive a limited override on the worldwide sales of Chrysalis product for five years to December 31, 1996.

I felt that the decision to merge the EMI, Chrysalis and SBK record labels was a mistake. It may have made financial sense but the cultures of the labels were very different. SBK, in particular, was essentially a pop label with no distinctive identity. In the end EMI ended up destroying, especially in North America, a heritage that had been developed and nurtured over almost 25 years.

Paul Conroy got his big new deal to run Chrysalis in the UK, but soon after that he was poached by Virgin. EMI was outraged by this and put him on gardening leave for six months before he could take up his new job there.

To summarise his next few months: Conroy also received a bonus when the second half of Chrysalis was sold to EMI. He then took a more lucrative post with Virgin, and when EMI bought Virgin a year later in 1992, he got another huge disposal bonus and went to work for EMI again. He made four killings in the space of about nine months. All from EMI! Nice work if you can get it!

For my part, I had to start the process of dismantling the company, especially all the overseas operations, and personally telling my staff all over Europe, some of whom had worked for me for some 20 years, that Chrysalis Records was being absorbed into EMI and most of them were going to be out of work. It was a very difficult and emotional time.

I also took stock of our prospects. Crucially, we had not sold the music-publishing company. We still had the rump of Chrysalis Group including the export company, and the burgeoning TV company, and we were building AIR Studios at Lyndhurst Hall.

We had a strategic review of the group and decided that following the disposal of the record company we would expand our television production business and our music publishing interests and, in due course, once the two-year non-compete restrictions had expired, we would return to the record business.

However, for six months after the sale had been completed, I had nightmares about the whole thing. The thought of being out of the record business, even only for two years, left me distraught, even though the storm clouds that were gathering over the record industry actually made it look like a very smart move in hindsight.

Nevertheless, I knew I had work to do. I had to rebuild the company and create a new Chrysalis. And at the same time, I had to sort out my personal life – which by now had become complicated, to say the least.

CHAPTER 19

Love Is A Battlefield

In many respects ending the EMI joint venture prematurely was a good thing. If ultimately Chrysalis Group was to receive very little in terms of a payment for the second 50% of the company it would have been quite debilitating to continue being involved with an operation without the prospect of any ultimate financial reward. Also, I think I would have found it difficult to continue to motivate the staff, both those who were working for the joint venture and those who were part of the ongoing Chrysalis Group. In hindsight the whole concept of a 10-year earn-out makes little sense and it is not something that I would entertain doing again in the future.

It also, having cleared the decks, allowed me to concentrate on rebuilding Chrysalis, the ongoing Group, with a blank sheet of paper and with the opportunity to move into whatever areas I felt would give us the greatest chance of re-creating a vibrant and exciting company.

Clearly I needed to revamp the executive and advisory structure and my first move in that respect was to prove fundamental to the hugely exciting new company we were able to create. It was at this point that Charles Levison re-entered my life and he was to play a pivotal role in everything that I would do for the next 15 years.

I had known Charles since 1970, soon after we had started Chrysalis. He was a Cambridge graduate who had an excellent reputation and was a lawyer, a partner and head of the music department at Harbottle & Lewis (the position now held by my daughter Chloe). Charles had represented several music industry luminaries in the early seventies, but I had never personally worked with him, although Harbottle & Lewis had represented me.

Charles had helped to launch Richard Branson's career in the music business before going to work for Chris Blackwell at Island. For a while, he was based in Nassau where Blackwell had a centre of operations, and after that in New York, where he was running Island's US operation. So, he had worked for both of my two greatest friendly rivals.

On returning to England Charles had become managing director of the newly established Arista Records and later worked for another great friend of mine, Nesuhi Ertegun, as managing director of Warner Records in the UK. I had recommended Charles to Nesuhi during one of our many tennis matches in the South of France. Nesuhi was usually in the shadow of his more flamboyant brother, Ahmet, but he was a true music man. It was Nesuhi who gave Seymour Stein the money to sign Madonna, when others in the company had turned her down.

Charles had then worked for Branson again at the very early stage of Virgin's foray into media with the launch of British Satellite Broadcasting – BSB – an initiative that Virgin was involved with prior to Rupert Murdoch buying out BSB and combining it under the umbrella of British Sky Broadcasting.

It was Charles Levison's knowledge of satellite television, and the huge potential it represented for our TV production business, that particularly appealed to me, alongside his music business experience. With Chrysalis about to re-create itself as a multi-faceted media operation, I asked him to join the board as a non-executive director, and soon after as deputy chairman, a role tailor-made for him.

I invited Charles to join me on our annual Easter family ski holiday in Aspen. It was there in the spring of 1992 that we re-devised the company, much of it at his prompting. Every ski-lift journey was an opportunity to consider all the options, and to create the best structure for the future. And this was to be the framework for the next two decades.

On returning to the UK, together we set about creating what was to be the new Chrysalis. It was to be just as exciting and as successful as the original incarnation. Which is hard to believe as it all happened during what was, at times, a chaotic period in my personal and social life.

I had now been seeing Janice for a year. Obviously our relationship had to be secret as I was still with Chelle, but our marriage was far from what it had been. With Chelle seemingly still in shock and demoralised from the death of her mother, we were drifting ever further apart. She was probably oblivious to what was going on in my life.

By contrast, Janice and I initially had all the ingredients of an exciting, carefree relationship. Meeting in London, although not impossible, was difficult, but I was still travelling extensively all over the world, especially to the States, Janice was flying regularly to New York on Concorde and there were plenty of occasions for us to spend time together.

It was a lot of fun and we became very emotionally entangled with each other. We had a brief hiccup in the August of 1989, our first summer, when I was away with my family in France, but we then picked up as if we had never left off – with renewed vigour, in fact.

With Chelle hardly leaving Gloucestershire, Janice and I started spending even more time together. In a strange way, this became a routine, and having Janice around had certainly helped me cope with the stress of the whole EMI shenanigans.

In the spring of 1991 I made a trip to Australia for an IFPI board meeting and Janice joined me for a few days after that, although we returned home by different routes and at different times. I returned via a NARM convention in San Francisco, and the SXSW festival in Texas. Not long after we arrived back in England, she dropped a bombshell: she was pregnant. I was going to be a father again, but this time in very different circumstances.

Clearly, this was not planned, as many pregnancies are not. Initially I was pretty freaked out by the news, as would any married man be when his lover tells him she is expecting his child. I knew I loved Janice, but I also knew this was going to be a very challenging new development. Luckily, the news did not disrupt our relationship; if anything, after the initial shock, it brought us closer together. I was just as responsible as she was, and I had to accept that responsibility.

It was obvious that the baby would be born smack bang in the middle of the Christmas period. This was far from ideal, as it meant I would be tied up with family commitments, including the traditional post-Christmas Antigua family vacation. However, the festive season at least gave us one gift. Janice and I decided that, if we had a daughter, we would call her Holly.

I was on the beach in Antigua on December 29 when I got the news of Holly's birth. Ultravox manager Chris O'Donnell, who was staying at another hotel on the island, was in on my secret and gave me the glad tidings. However, it was not until over a week later, when I was back in London, that I was able to see my new daughter, with her very happy mother.

Naturally, with Janice now being effectively a single mother, our relationship and its dynamics changed. When she returned to work, she decided that she would leave Concorde to be able to spend more time in the UK. We couldn't travel together as we always had, and although we bought a house near Barnes for Janice and Holly to live in, our times together took on a different tenor.

I seriously considered telling Chelle about my secret life and moving out to live with the two of them, but Janice was still only 29, and I was not sure at that time that she could cope with the intricacies of my life. Furthermore, at home Chloe was struggling to come to terms with the disability resulting from her brain tumour and her anorexia was worsening. So there was no choice: I carried on living my double life.

It was at this difficult personal and professional juncture in my life that I began working closely with Charles Levison. It is no exaggeration to say that he was to play a pivotal role in everything I would do for the next 15 years.

Sometimes when your life is particularly stressful, you can take solace from engaging in charitable initiatives. With my interest in racing, it was always likely that I would become involved in the Nordoff-Robbins music industry charity's attempt to start a race day to raise funds.

Nordoff-Robbins has been the British music industry's chosen charity for more than 25 years. Essentially, it operates a network of some 100 or so therapists throughout the UK who work from purpose-built centres with severely autistic children to help them express themselves and their emotions through the use of musical instruments.

Over the years the charity has raised well over £10 million to fund its work, all of which has come from the music industry. Two of the leading lights in the Nordoff-Robbins music therapy were Willie Robertson, the insurance broker who had pioneered the introduction of insurance cover for performers, and concert promoter Andrew Miller. They were both involved in fundraising for the charity from the very beginning (and sadly, both passed away recently within a few months of each other).

It was Willie who first spoke to me about trying to start a Nordoff-Robbins race day. Using my knowledge of race meetings, we decided that Newbury would be the most appropriate location. A Nordoff-Robbins team of Willie Robertson, fundraising chief Audrey Hoare and myself headed off to the racecourse to discuss the idea with the chief executive.

Willie was the kind of eccentric figure that bridged the establishment and the music industry. Usually dressed in a pinstripe suit and very prominent glasses, he was an English-eccentric gent whose lunch started with a glass of rosé wine at 9 a.m. and normally didn't finish until 12 hours later. He was also a great racing enthusiast and had several horses. For her part, Audrey is a member of the famous Hoare banking family with an ancestral home at Stourhead in Wiltshire.

Arriving at Newbury, I told the receptionist: "We are the party from Nordoff-Robbins music therapy. We have a meeting with Mr Pank."

"You mean Brigadier-General Pank," she replied brusquely.

Suitably admonished, we were ushered into the chief executive's office. The chain-smoking Willie Robertson politely asked General Pank if he could smoke. This was in the days before the smoking ban.

"Yes, of course," replied the Brigadier-General with a totally straight face. "As long as it is not hashish."

Having been told he was meeting people from the music business, Brigadier Pank clearly expected a bunch of long-haired hippies spaced out on drugs. Instead he was in a meeting with an Old Harrovian insurance broker, a scion of one of the country's greatest banking families, and myself.

After this false start, the meeting went well and the first Nordoff-Robbins race day was held at Newbury racecourse in 1991. It moved to Sandown Park in 1997, and has been held there ever since, apart from 2011 when we moved for one year to Ascot.

Sadly that year was Willie's last race day as it coincided with him being in the final stages of pancreatic cancer. At Sandown the following year we held the Willie Robertson Memorial race, a very fitting tribute to someone whose larger-than-life persona helped raise so much money for severely disabled children. The entire music industry appeared to be at St Luke's & Christ Church in Chelsea for his memorial service on October 5, 2011.

The 2011 race day, the first under my chairmanship, happily broke all records for the charity and raised nearly £100,000. A similar

e road in the States in 1970, at the hight of the hippy era. That is how I looked when I walked into a bank in San Francisco with
00 in cash in my pockets!

At my son Tom's christening at the Episcopalian church in Beverly Hills, with Karen Carpenter and Terry Ellis, who were the godparents.

The head honchos of the British record industry in the 1980s, all former chairmen of the BPI. Back row: John Fruin, Maurice (O Oberstein, long term BPI director general John Deacon, and Rob Dickens; front row: Rupert Perry, Len (LG) Wood, and myself.

and I with the Prince of Wales, and Diana, Princess of Wales, at the second Princes Trust Rock Concert at the Royal Albert Hall.

Chrysalis Records management team in the late eighties, left to right: Roy Eldridge, Mike Bone, myself, Jeff Aldrich and
D'Arcy.

Doug and I in the mid-seventies with the group UFO, a very underrated band for whom TYA's Leo Lyons and George Martin produced some excellent albums. PAUL COX

With a diminutive Pat Benatar and her husband Neil Geraldo in the mid-eighties. On my right is Charlie Prevost, and on Neil's le⟨t⟩ are Jeff Aldrich and Jack Craigo. JEFFREY MAYER

h Chelle and old friend Nesuhi Ertegun, co-founder of Atlantic Records, at the IFPI board meeting in Istanbul in 1988.

e and I at La Colombe d'Or in St Paul de Vence with Terry and Karen in the late seventies. In the foreground are Chick Churchill YA and his wife Suzanne.

With Huey Lewis and Monty Luftner of Ariola BMG, after a News concert in Munich. GUNTHER REISP

With Chesney Hawkes at the height of his fame. Who manager Bill Curbishley is on my right, and Paul Conroy on the extreme lef

signing of the deal when Chrysalis Records was sold to EMI, left to right: Guy Marriot, EMI head of Business Affairs, EMI ⟩ Jim Fifield, Joe Keiner, myself and Doug D'Arcy. BARRY PLUMMER

with the re-formed Ten Years After, at Glebe House in 1988 when they re-signed with the label. They made a great record, but time appeared to have passed. BARRY PLUMMER

Presenting a gold album to Leo Sayer for *Endless Flight*.

With Jim Fifield, and mega music business attorney Alan Grubman in my London office, having just closed the EMI

Presenting a gold single to Blondie. Chris Stein is on my right, and Doug D'Arcy second from the right. BRIAN COOKE

result was achieved in 2012 when I secured a unique manuscript of *Someone Like You*, executed by our writer, Dan Wilson and co-signed by Adele for the auction. The race day has now raised well over £1 million for autistic children since its inception.

Horse racing brought me another wonderful moment in 2012 when I won a major European classic race with a filly I'd bought in Kentucky named Culture Vulture. She was clearly a promising horse: she had been voted European Champion Two-Year-Old Filly in the inaugural Cartier Racing Awards in 1991 after winning two championship group one races at the end of the season, the Fillies' Mile at Ascot and the Prix Marcel Boussac at Longchamp.

Although Culture Vulture had been training for the English 1000 Guineas at Newmarket in April 1992, she had only finished fifth. Paul Cole, my friend and her trainer, insisted that she was better than that, and was adamant she should run in the French equivalent, the Poule D'Essai Des Pouliches, at Longchamp on May 17.

As I awaited this exciting event, tragedy struck. My father, who was by now 79, had fallen ill and been admitted to hospital. Having smoked for much of his life, he suffered from emphysema. I barely remembered him smoking cigarettes, but he did for many years smoke a pipe, and would occasionally go to sleep with it in his mouth, sitting by the fire in front of the television.

He seemed to be recovering well in hospital and was due to come home on May 17 – the same day as the French Guineas. As it was such a major event, we had booked a private plane from Oxford airport to fly my whole family, Paul Cole and his wife, Vanessa, the jockey Richard Quinn and Chris O'Donnell. As we were walking out the door to leave, the telephone rang. It was the hospital telling me that my father had passed away.

I immediately forgot all thoughts of going to Paris, although the non-family members of the party took the plane. Chelle, the kids and I jumped in the car and drove straight to Lincolnshire to be with my mum.

When my phone rang in the middle of the afternoon and the voice at the other end said, "Mr Wright, it's Di from the yard," in my shocked state I assumed it was someone calling about funeral arrangements. When Paul Cole's secretary said "She won!" I had no idea what she was talking about.

Di-from-the-yard had to explain several times why she was calling me before it sank in to my confused head that she was telling me Culture Vulture had won the Poule D'Essai Des Pouliches. She was the first ever English-trained filly to have triumphed in that race. Chris O'Donnell fittingly collected the trophy in my absence.

Unfortunately, the greatest ever win of my career as a racehorse owner took place at a time of great personal sadness. Bizarrely, as a result of the filly's victory, my father's death was reported on the sports pages of every national newspaper in the country the following morning. Having been such a massive sports fan throughout his life, he would have had a huge chuckle if he had been able to read them.

Culture Vulture's triumph was a nice boost as I struggled with feelings of loss over my father and worry about Chloe's anorexia – and at the same time, of course, I was trying to rebuild Chrysalis according to the master plan Charles and I had devised in Aspen.

Under the terms of the EMI agreement, we were banned from starting a front-line record company for two years. However, we were permitted to operate in the fields of record compilations and spoken-word product. This allowed us to launch a label called The Hit Label, which was run by the Cokell brothers, John and Phil, who were also shareholders in the label.

The first album release on The Hit Label in 1992 was a Tom Jones compilation album entitled *The Complete Tom Jones,* which we were able to do principally because when we sold the Chrysalis label to EMI we did not sell the rights to the material we had bought through MAM. To our delight, the compilation duly went gold in 1992.

Later that year, when EMI bought Virgin Records, Steve Lewis, who had been with Virgin for his entire career, found himself without a job. Richard Branson suggested I hire him to head Chrysalis' music division, with a brief to re-enter the mainstream record business when our time restrictions came to an end.

I did not know Steve, but he came highly recommended, especially by John Kennedy, the leading music lawyer who was to go on to head Polygram in the UK, and then become chairman of the IFPI. When we came to discuss his contract, Steve dropped a real howler.

Steve and I were discussing the terms of his bonus provision. Realising we were in the process of re-signing the group Wet Wet Wet to a publishing deal, he insisted that their deal would not impact on his profit share, being sceptical that they would achieve any further success.

Steve was not to know that the group had just cut a cover version of an old song written years ago by Reg Presley, the lead singer of sixties group The Troggs. The record 'Love Is All Around' was the lead track in the film *Four Weddings And A Funeral* and was the biggest hit of the year by far. On the back of it, Wet Wet Wet's record company released a greatest hits album that sold over a million copies in the UK, generating huge income for the group. I guess Steve was just unlucky as it would have been hard to have expected this windfall, and to be fair Wet Wet Wet did not have any further major hits.

However, Steve was to come up trumps with a contact that was to give a huge boost to the new Chrysalis. Richard Branson had created Virgin Records with the help of a significant investment from Japanese record company Pony Canyon, a division of multimedia corporation Fujisankei. It had always remained a substantial shareholder in Virgin, and Steve knew Harry Kaneko, the head of international at the company.

Pony Canyon was disappointed that it was no longer involved in the international business following the sale of Virgin. We suggested to the company that it may want to be involved in our new, as yet unnamed label, and made an approach suggesting it invest $20 million in return for a significant stake in the new company. Its people asked for time to consider the proposal but we heard nothing. I assumed the idea had bit the dust.

Steve set about reorganising the music division's management structure, bringing in an old Virgin colleague, Jeremy Lascelles, to run the publishing company. Jeremy was to eventually take over the division from Steve, and ended up staying with us for nearly 20 years.

At the same time, I was looking for someone to head our television activities. I was aware of a smallish listed company, SelecTV, which was effectively an independent production company. It made the long-running comedy *Birds Of A Feather*. We suggested that we took over SelecTV in an all-share merger, with a cash alternative for any shareholders that would prefer it.

SelecTV's principal shareholder was Allan McKeown, and had he agreed terms with us the merger would have gone ahead. However he was not at all interested but I did manage to poach his managing director, Mick Pilsworth, to join us to run Chrysalis Television. Together we developed the strategy of acquiring production companies in different TV genres and keeping their names and independence, much in the way that record companies have imprints for different kinds of music.

Incidentally, Allan McKeown eventually sold SelecTV for £52 million in 1996 to Pearson, the owner of the *Financial Times*, which was keen to develop its television interests. Allan was married to comedienne Tracy Ullman, and they left to live in LA, where Tracy secured her own show on American television with the Fox network. On one of Tracy's early programmes, they gave a slot to a new cartoon show to give them some exposure, in return for a percentage of the cartoon's earnings in perpetuity were it ever to take off. This fledgling show was called... *The Simpsons*!

Despite the fact that I was currently barely still in the record business, I had retained my position on the board of the IFPI. In hindsight, I cannot really understand why this international trade body had kept me on, although it did allow me to continue to sit at the top table of the industry, together with all the leaders of the major companies. The IFPI spring board meeting for 1993 was to be held in Miami.

This was convenient for me as by now my son Tim was studying at the University of Miami, something we were able to organise for him on the basis that he was along with the other children technically qualified as a Native American. Chelle's maternal grandmother had actually grown up on an Indian reservation in Arizona. I would quite often fly back from US business trips via Miami and spend a couple of days there with Tim. It was a trip I was looking forward to – but it was ruined by a terrible tragedy.

Arriving in Miami on a Thursday evening, in time for an all-day meeting on the Friday, I phoned Tim and made arrangements to meet up with him on Saturday morning. However that morning I couldn't get hold of him. I eventually was put through to someone in his hall of residence who passed me to one of the teachers. He had exceedingly bad news.

Tim's best friend had been having some problems academically and felt under pressure. His problems became overbearing, resulting in him taking Tim to the top of their hall of residence building from where he killed himself by jumping off the roof as Tim looked on in horror.

How do you cope with something like that? Tim was understandably in pieces and I was desperate to do all I could to help and support him. Despite being so distraught, Tim was determined to make his friend's funeral in New York – but this was to prove harder than it sounded.

The day of the suicide, the entire eastern seaboard of the United States was hit by the largest storm for over 100 years. It became known as the Superstorm '93. Airports all over the region were closed and the snow made the roads north of Florida impassable, even into Georgia. Travel in and out of Miami was virtually non-existent.

Tim's friends' parents called me to pressure Tim to make the funeral, but I said there was no way Tim could make it, either emotionally or logistically. In the event, somehow he managed to get on a plane when the storm lifted.

However, not long after that Tim decided he could no longer stay in Miami, and left university to come back to the UK. He didn't even stay to finish his degree course – a sign of the devastation that this terrible incident had wreaked upon his psyche. I'm sure he is still affected by it today.

I was also undergoing personal turmoil. Since Holly's birth, Janice and I had continued to see each other but it became less frequent and slightly less carefree, as Janice raised Holly alone and I struggled to relaunch my business. I was always supportive of them, but we began to realise we could not go on as we were. It was not fair to anyone, least of all Janice and Holly.

A beautiful and vivacious woman, Janice had never been short of romantic offers, including from rich and famous passengers on her Concorde trips. Yet when she began seeing somebody else, it was a pilot – George Stinnes, who also had a senior management job with her airline. I was horrified, but who could blame her? George was in a position to offer her what I could not – a normal relationship.

I may not have been surprised by this development logically, but emotionally I was shattered. Janice and I had now been together – or, rather, not strictly together but seeing each other – for three-and-a-half years. Plus, of course, she was the mother of my child. I had always known this could happen, but had hoped against hope that it would not.

Confused and disoriented, I contemplated coming clean to Chelle and seeing if this honesty would help us rebuild our broken marriage, but quickly decided against it. I figured she would probably be totally unforgiving after being deceived for so long, and in all honesty this was not the relationship that I wanted to mend. I very much doubted it was recoverable and I wanted Janice back.

I knew I needed friends to talk to and turned to Chris O'Donnell and Nick Blackburn. They were both supportive but Chris had the bizarre suggestion that I should go to see a clairvoyant. I was highly sceptical but so miserable that I was prepared to try anything.

Chris knew of a woman called Josephine who read tarot cards, and I went along to her semi-detached house in Brondesbury Park. Josephine was a totally normal-looking middle-aged housewife and her home also looked very ordinary: there were no astrology charts or crystal balls lying around.

Josephine dealt the cards and started talking. She made no mention of my emotional state or my relationship with Janice, but instead told me as her opening gambit that I was about to take a long flight and she could see a lot of money involved.

Profoundly unimpressed, I replied that I regularly made long plane flights, but was not planning on making one for a few weeks. Josephine was adamant I would be flying in the next few days but I thought that was impossible, as I knew my schedule, and had nothing planned.

As for her "lot of money involved", I very much suspected that she had seen me pull up outside her house in a Bentley. In any case, what would be "a lot of money" to Josephine?

"How much money?" I asked her. "£100,000?"

"No, much more than that," she replied, to my surprise.

"A million pounds?"

"No, much more," she insisted, "I mean a lot of money."

I was thoroughly perplexed by all this. What was she on about? It made no sense. However, my main feeling was disappointment that she had not a word to say on the subject that I was most interested in: my future, or lack of it, with Janice. I left feeling the visit had been a complete waste of time.

Back in the office, Steve Lewis was anxiously waiting to see me – and had major news. "Guess what's just happened?" he asked me.

Steve had just received a phone call from Harry Kaneko in Tokyo. The board of Fujisankei had concluded a meeting and given approval for Pony Canyon to invest $20 million in our new record company. They wanted to meet at the beginning of the following week in LA, a convenient location for both sides, with respective lawyers to conclude the deal.

A long flight? A lot of money? I was so totally astounded you could have knocked me over with a feather.

CHAPTER 20

'Golaccio'
(I'm Stronger Now)

A Chrysalis involvement in British television had started as long
ago as 1980. Up until that time no British television stations
operated in the early morning. As a frequent traveller to America, I
had often wondered why we had no equivalent in Britain of the long-
established and thriving institution of breakfast television. When the
government invited tenders to operate a Breakfast Television franchise
on the ITV network we decided to get involved.

We had submitted what I thought was a pretty strong bid, backed
by high-profile City people, an experienced chairman in Sir Peter
Thornton and excellent talent such as Ned Sherrin and presenter
Julian Pettifer. However, the government awarded the franchise
to TV-AM and its "famous five" presenters: David Frost, Michael
Parkinson, Angela Rippon, Robert Kee and my old university friend,
Anna Ford.

We hadn't gone the celebrity route because my view is that,
when you launch any creative business, you start with producers and
directors and executives; you can always hire in the talent later. It

seemed the Independent Broadcasting Authority didn't understand that and was blinded by the array of talent that was already on board in this competing bid. Despite that, TV-AM was not initially successful and only turned things around when Greg Dyke arrived and introduced Roland Rat.

I guess the Chrysalis television business really got going in 1987 when at the suggestion of our corporate development director, Richard Huntingford, we acquired a Nottingham outside-broadcast and facilities company, Recording and Production Services Ltd. We renamed the company Chrysalis Television Mobiles.

Thanks to my connections in horse racing, the first contract it secured was for the live transmission of all races from British racecourses into betting shops in the UK. Up until that point, the betting shops could not broadcast pictures of horse racing, simply audio commentaries. The addition of live pictures revolutionised the sport and it was great to see our OB trucks on every racecourse in the country.

Via the MAM deal we had also inherited a post-production television facility in north London called Research Recordings, which we renamed Air TV Facilities and then later Chrysalis Television Facilities. This had some of the most state-of-the-art equipment in the country, including the facility to upload programmes onto satellite, a delivery system which was still in its infancy.

When MTV Europe launched in Europe in 1987, as a joint venture between Viacom, British Telecom and Robert Maxwell, we won the contract to provide its facilities. It was an adjunct to what we were already doing through the recording studios and our outside broadcast facilities business. It was something we had the skill and expertise to do and I became very close friends with Bill Roedy, who was responsible for launching MTV internationally.

Robert Maxwell was a maverick figure to deal with. When we won the MTV Europe contract, he contacted me on a skiing holiday in Zermatt to tell me that he personally wanted a substantial percentage of shares in Chrysalis in return. I had to explain to him that I couldn't just give him a load of shares as a thank-you. We were a public company with a wide shareholder base. It was impossible – but I am not sure he understood this.

Meanwhile, Chrysalis Television Mobiles had a large infrastructure of outside broadcast trucks and equipment. Aside from the horse-racing contract, we were short of work and needed to generate more business for the company. David Dein, then the principal shareholder and vice-chairman at Arsenal, was a leading light in Division One – now the Premier League – and wanted to expand its live football coverage to overseas markets.

I had known David for quite a while. We both had American wives and often saw each other socially. He also shares my birthday, although he is one year older. So when the Football League began looking for someone to supply live matches to countries outside the UK, I was fortunate enough to have Chrysalis Television Mobiles and be able to tender.

The tendering process was quite lengthy but we were granted the contract, provided we could do a successful dummy transmission. The event chosen for this was the Sherpa Van Trophy, the competition restricted to teams from the two lower divisions, which in 1988 was between Wolves and Burnley at Wembley.

We had to devise the show's production style, supply the presenters and introduce innovative ideas. Martin Tyler did our commentary, Wolves won 2-0 and we did an excellent job, satisfying the Football League that we could do this effectively on a regular basis.

Football thus became a mainstay of Chrysalis Television Mobiles for many years. Although we had only entered the process to obtain more work for our OB facilities we ended up with an entirely new business, and sports production was to become a key element of Chrysalis' future business.

David Dein also gave us the contract to supply live coverage of the Arsenal matches on the big screens at Highbury. It was the first time this had ever been done in any football stadium in the world. We also screened the occasional Arsenal away game on the screens at Highbury. These developments proved we had clearly moved on from just being a facilities supplier to being a production company, and we needed to hire someone with the right kind of skills to run the division.

In 1988, Mark Sharman came in to run what became Chrysalis Television News and Sport. Mark brought in Neil Duncanson, a former reporter, as his number two in 1990, and both men were to contribute greatly towards our fortunes in the TV field.

In December 1990, we also started the process of building up our television-drama production side by buying 50% of a company called Red Rooster Film & Television, which was owned by Linda James and Stephen Bayly. They had a great reputation as an independent production company and went on to make *The Life And Times Of Henry Pratt*, their first highly acclaimed mini-series for the ITV network, in 1992.

We also started a company called Chrysalis Multimedia, which operated at the leading edge of technology in CDI software. We continued to produce home videos on the Chrysalis home video label and launched a company called Chrysalis In-Flight Entertainment to service the increasing demand for in-flight entertainment on airlines. It was a success, albeit not enough to guarantee its long-term future.

Having retired hurt from bidding for national broadcast franchises after the 1980 breakfast TV disappointment, we returned for another go in the early nineties, when the government decided to reorganise the entire commercial television network in the UK. We got involved in bids to replace Yorkshire Television and HTV in Wales and the West Country, but once again were unsuccessful.

However, we were about to happen on a very successful and, to a degree, game-changing venture. One spring afternoon in 1992, Neil Duncanson walked into my office and asked me what I thought about bidding for the rights to show Italian football in the UK.

This might have been an odd idea if not for one element: the Gazza factor. Having become a superstar during England's 1990 World Cup campaign in Italy, Paul Gascoigne had torn his anterior cruciate knee ligament playing for Spurs in the 1991 FA Cup Final before being transferred to Lazio in Italy.

Chrysalis Television had produced a documentary entitled *Gascoigne – The Fightback* about the aftermath of his knee injury. Ken McGill, the director, got amazing access, filming the player on the surgeon's table and capturing his determination to regain fitness and return to football. The documentary had been networked on ITV and repeated on Channel 4.

Gazza had mentioned to Neil Duncanson that it was a shame British people wouldn't be able to see him play in Italy, which gave Neil the idea for us to buy not just the UK rights to Lazio games but the UK rights for the whole Italian league. He explained it would cost us quite a lot of money but, with Gazza's appeal he thought there would be a market.

Up until that point, the Sports Channel on BSB and then Sky Sports had shown games from Italy. Many of the world's best footballers plied their trade in Italy, which had the best league in the world at the time. However, in 1992 Sky Sports had captured exclusive rights to live games from the newly formed English Premier League, with the BBC's *Match Of The Day* only able to show highlights. Come the new season, there would be a dearth of top flight games on UK live terrestrial television.

This sounded like a good idea to me. "How long have we got to decide?" I asked Neil. He explained that we would be entering the bidding at the very last minute as the contract was about to be awarded. In fact, bids had to be in by six that afternoon.

"Do you mean six UK time or Central European Time?" I asked him.

Neil gulped. "Six Central European Time."

I looked at my watch. It was 4.45. I had 15 minutes to make a decision. I asked Neil who we could resell Italian football to, and he replied with complete honesty: "I don't know. Maybe Channel 4: maybe Sky?"

We obviously had no time to try to sell the idea to either of them before we bid for the rights, so on the spur of the moment I said: "Let's take a flyer – let's go for it." Neil made a call to Rome there and then and put the bid in.

We acquired the UK rights to Serie A football for £1.5 million. Channel 4 proved very keen, and we were able to sell them not just a live game every Sunday afternoon but also a Saturday morning programme called *Gazzetta Football Italia*. In my opinion, this was one of the most thought-provoking football programmes ever produced. Presenter James Richardson added so much local colour, history and culture, alongside interviews, not just with Gazza but also fellow ex-pats David Platt and Paul Ince, that it became virtually a must-see show for anybody interested in football, or in Italy.

Italian football on Channel 4 duly became one of the biggest success stories in British televised sport. We launched *Football Italia* in September 1992 with a 3-3 draw between Sampdoria and Lazio watched by three million viewers, a fantastic figure for a delighted Channel 4. Gascoigne finally got over his injury and made his Lazio debut three weeks later.

Football Italia lasted a decade on Channel 4, changed the tired old way that football was presented on British television, and arguably influenced the way the game was played here. One of its plus points was that it wasn't afraid to be quirky: James Richardson even got Attilio Lombardo to do the lambada!

Football Italia also helped put Chrysalis Television on the map and helped us form a great relationship with Channel 4. Ken McGill made two more fine documentaries, *Gazza's Coming Home* and *Gazza*.

Keeping our eye on the televisual big picture, in 1993 we renamed our hotchpotch of different companies Chrysalis Visual Entertainment, with a mission to establish ourselves as a leading player in television production and visual entertainment. It was at this point that I hired Mick Pilsworth to help conceptualise and structure the business.

In our first meeting, Mick and I sat down in my office and came up with the idea that Chrysalis Television would be an umbrella organisation like a record company with a variety of different labels, each specialising in a certain style of repertoire, pop, dance, jazz, classical, as Chrysalis Records had done with 2-Tone and Cooltempo.

To make this vision a reality, the first thing Mick did was buy the 50% of Red Rooster that we didn't already own and make it a direct subsidiary. This would give us a direct involvement with all future productions (although I was unaware at the time that Mick was quite friendly with Sue Birbeck, one of the executives at Red Rooster).

Chrysalis Television Mobiles was also appointed to cover the European Formula One Grand Prix series for Fuji Television of Japan. I am sure that was helpful when Chrysalis Sport successfully bid for the rights to produce Formula One for ITV in 1993.

This was not only a very big deal for us but also the most high-profile sports-production contract ever awarded. Neil Duncanson and his team brought a series of innovations to how the sport was covered, and received many accolades in the process.

The first time we produced the Monaco Grand Prix, we rented space on a boat in the harbour. The port there is not very protected, and with the swell, our presenters Jim Rosenthal, Simon Taylor and Tony Jardine all got seasick. Fortunately, Murray Walker, who was the main race commentator on the actual race, was elsewhere and unaffected, but Taylor was too ill to make the broadcast.

I watched the Grand Prix from atop the outside-broadcast truck. I am not an expert on motor racing, but for the duration of our contract, I was constantly inundated wherever I went with people asking me about the intricacies of the sport. At times my ignorance could be embarrassing.

The following year, 1994, saw an enormous expansion in our TV activities. Red Rooster made several successful shows including *Wycliffe*, a detective drama series for ITV, and *Crocodile Shoes*, a major BBC series starring Geordie actor Jimmy Nail as a factory worker who becomes a country singer.

We also did a deal to bring into the company Cactus TV, headed by Jonathan Ross' brother Simon and his wife, Amanda. Cactus eventually poached Richard Madeley and Judy Finnegan from ITV to present a daily general entertainment late-afternoon show for Channel Four, which was a great success. Emanating out of this was the Richard and Judy book club, which had such an impact on the British book publishing industry.

We also linked up with Watchmaker Productions, founded by critic and broadcaster Clive James. Clive presented a weekly talk show for Carlton and ITV, and a series of other programmes. Watchmaker also produced a weekly talk show for the BBC hosted by Jeremy Clarkson and produced by Elaine Bedell.

We had no involvement in the BBC's *Top Gear*, but when its contract was up for renewal we came up with an amazing offer for Jeremy Clarkson to instead present what became *Fifth Gear* for Channel Five. It's a measure of the size of the fee that we offered Jeremy that the deal included giving him an airfield. However, although tempted, he decided to stay with the BBC.

For her part, Elaine Bedell became managing director of Chrysalis Entertainment, running all our drama production, before leaving for the Royal Shakespeare Company. After a spell with the BBC, she is now Director of Entertainment and Comedy at ITV.

However, one company we looked at but chose not to buy was the independent producer Kudos. The reason was simple: I had a fling with Debbie Mason, a Marilyn Monroe lookalike who was one of the two partners in the company, and although Mick was keen to bring Kudos into the fold it was something I refused to countenance. The potential conflict of interest made it too difficult.

As well as producing shows for the networks, Debbie Mason was also involved in the production of music videos, including those for U2. Once when she was supervising a shoot for Counting Crows we drove out from LA in the early hours to a huge multi-location movie set in the Mohave desert. The sun was beating down and yet it was bitterly cold with tumbleweed bouncing all over. Kudos was eventually snapped up by Elizabeth Murdoch's Shine Productions.

Chrysalis also bought 50% of a big independent television production group in the Netherlands called IDtv from its founder, Harry de Winter. Harry was involved with all facets of the industry, and great fun to hang out with. We also bought a 30% stake in South Pacific Pictures, the leading New Zealand production company.

However, I feel that by far our greatest accomplishment was bringing Brian True-May into the company. An old colleague of Mick's at SelecTV, Brian's experience was in developing and producing long-running serial dramas.

After a couple of false starts for us, Brian came up with the idea of a murder mystery series set in sleepy English villages, based on an original book by Caroline Graham. The series was named *Midsomer Murders*, and starred John Nettles as Inspector Barnaby. ITV commissioned *Midsomer Murders*, which was immediately a huge hit and has since been sold into almost every country in the world. It is fair to call it one of the greatest success stories in British television.

Of course, not everything was such a spectacular success. In the late nineties, we had a potentially interesting sitcom called *Babes In The Wood,* about three young girls sharing a flat in St John's Wood, starring Denise Van Outen and Samantha Janus. It could have been a more glamorous take on *Birds Of A Feather*, but the scripts were disappointing and the show didn't last.

Our most remarkable failure, however, was *Breakers*, an Australian soap set in a café on Bondi Beach in Sydney which we hoped would follow on from the success of *Neighbours* and *Home And Away*. We launched it in conjunction with Screentime, a production company in Sydney run by Des Monaghan and Bob Campbell and financed by a leading independent investor in Australian media, Charles Curran. We thought *Breakers* had all of the elements that viewers would want in a successful Australian soap and when we saw the first few episodes, towards the end of 1997, we were thrilled.

But we made a cardinal mistake. In our eagerness to own the show outright so as to maximise our long-term income potential, we had failed to secure a foundation broadcaster – ie, one in Australia – before production started. We believed that, once the show was in the can, we could conduct an auction. But, in order to sell *Breakers*, the international buyers wanted to see how successful the series was in its domestic market.

The first thing we needed was to find an Australian broadcaster and we had trouble because, of course, we were in competition with both *Neighbours* and *Home And Away*. The best we could achieve was an 11 p.m. slot on Network Ten, the third-rated commercial broadcaster in Australia at the time. It was completely the wrong time slot and it struggled to find an audience.

We did manage to sell *Breakers* to the BBC to show on BBC1 in the UK but, soon after the deal, the commissioning editor who had bought the programme moved on. Her replacement moved it to BBC2 and it was then shunted off to BBC Choice and eventually cancelled.

We were now left with about 150 episodes of an Aussie soap, costing us several million pounds and all paid for and produced. We struggled to find a market for them, and ended up losing an enormous amount of money on the project.

A couple of years later, when I was at the MIP TV market in Cannes with Mick Pilsworth, he said we had a meeting scheduled with Des Monaghan and Bob Campbell to talk to us about their new show.

"That's a bit of a laugh, isn't it?" I asked, possibly a tad bitterly. "We lost all that money on *Breakers*. They're hardly in the best position to get us to buy their new show."

Mick reasoned that we should at least listen to what they'd got to say. "They have bought a format that started in New Zealand called *Popstars*," he explained. "It's a singing competition with judges where the public vote on which artists they like."

This was a red rag to a bull. "What, like Hughie Green's *Opportunity Knocks* or *New Faces*?" I asked, sarcastically. "You must be joking twice, then! I'm not remotely interested in the kind of garbage you get on shows like that – and we've already lost a lot of money with Bob and Des."

So I cancelled the meeting, the show went elsewhere, and I had another entry on the list of my most appalling business decisions. This little New Zealand show called *Popstars* was to be the forerunner of *Pop Idol* and other reality television shows like *American Idol* and *The X Factor*.

One individual who was rather more clued in to that particular idea was former Chrysalis A&R man Simon Fuller. Simon bought the rights and, of course, went on to literally make hundreds of millions of pounds out of the format.

At the time, Chrysalis was the only music company that was actively involved in television production and so would have been in a superb position to monetise that format. The so-called talent that emerges from those shows would not have been the right fit for the Chrysalis record division: as a music company, we had always been involved with cutting-edge and left-field artists. Nevertheless, it was a huge opportunity missed, and I still occasionally wonder what would have happened had *Breakers* not been such a disaster, or had Bob and Des brought the *Popstars* idea to us before *Breakers*.

Nevertheless, having been steeped in the record and music business for over 20 years, from the start I enjoyed moving into television, which I felt did play to my creative strengths. With television, you can write a script, take a chance, produce the show to make it work and then keep your fingers crossed and hope for good ratings. If it doesn't work with the audience, that's it. In that respect it is similar to the record business, and as I was becoming a little less of the young music junkie I had been as I headed into middle age, I had relished this opportunity to work in a similar vibrant industry.

Having successfully established ourselves as a leading player in TV, the next challenge on the horizon was the film business.

Initially, we bought a 50% interest in Scala Productions, the company established by Nick Powell and Stephen Woolley, who had been successful with tremendous British films such as *The Crying Game*. Nick, in particular, came with quite a pedigree: he had been the childhood friend of Richard Branson, and they had formed Virgin together.

Chrysalis was about to enter an even bigger league.

CHAPTER 21

The Tunnel Of Love

A long flight and a lot of money is what Josephine the clairvoyant had told me to expect and true to her word the very next weekend Steve Lewis, Richard Huntingford and myself flew out to LA, along with the leading UK lawyer Tony Russell, to meet with Harry Kaneko and the representatives of Pony Canyon to thrash out a deal for their investment in our new record label.

Three days of intense negotiations yielded an agreement where they would totally fund the new project to the tune of $17.5 million in return for 25% of the equity. It was a staggering deal.

We decided to name the new label Echo; it had a certain resonance, and also reminded me somewhat of Chrysalis especially as the two middle letters C and H were the letters at the start of our former imprint.

Pony Canyon was a subsidiary of the giant Fujisankei Corporation which also owned one of Japan's major national newspapers and one of the major television networks in the country. It also owned Pacific Music, which was run separately from its recording activities and which was one of the largest music publishers in the country. I've always got on well with the Japanese and made an immediate connection with the high profile senior executives in the Fujisankei Corporation who were clearly among the most important people in Japan.

Board meetings were to alternate between London and Tokyo and for the next few years we would pay frequent visits to Japan where we were always entertained in the most hospitable manner possible.

Yet if my business fortunes were picking up considerably, my personal life was still mired in confusion. Janice was by now ensconced with George Stinnes in Cookham in Berkshire. Holly was now a toddler and I would see her for a couple of hours every week or two, but everything about the situation felt wrong.

Clutching at straws, I decided that Josephine the clairvoyant was clearly a prescient genius, because how else could she have predicted so clearly the Pony Canyon deal? Yet despite repeat visits to her, she never came up with a similar pearl of wisdom and never once gave me any indication as to what the future would hold and how the complications in my personal life would resolve themselves. I was in a very downbeat frame of mind as I headed off with Chelle and the kids for our traditional summer month in the South of France.

Back in London at the beginning of September things were no better, except I was able to throw myself into the business where matters were really hotting up. I was still spending most of my time alone in London, perhaps even more so than previously. One evening I was out with Nick Blackburn and Chris O'Donnell at a Kensington bar restaurant, 190 Queensgate. Standing with a group of friends was a tall, very attractive girl with long blonde hair. She caught my eye, and although I was too embarrassed to do so myself, Nick called her over to meet me.

Her name was Jane, she worked as a fashion-accessories buyer and we seemed to get on well. We made arrangements to meet up. I was leaving the next day to go to the States. On my return, I took Jane to see the new studios at AIR Lyndhurst, which was near her apartment, and afterwards we had dinner together.

267

Looking back, I was in danger of falling into a very deep depression after Janice and I went separate ways, and Jane saved me from my malaise. It took a while for our relationship to develop, and I have to confess that where I had always been honest with Janice about my married status, I was less so with Jane. By this time I was spending so much time by myself in London that it was easy to convince even myself that I was no longer married. I am sure to this day that if Jane had known about my convoluted personal life, she would never have become involved with me in the first place.

I was still on the IFPI board, and the next meeting was due to be held in both Hong Kong and Beijing. I used the opportunity to schedule a few days off in Bangkok and Vietnam, arranging for Jane to accompany me.

At this time, virtually no Westerners had visited Vietnam, and it was a truly eye-opening experience. The only place to stay with adequate creature comforts was an old converted cruise ship which had been towed into the harbour in Saigon and was being used as a floating hotel. It was a fascinating trip as the country still bore many of the hallmarks of the war that claimed the lives of so many young Americans.

We were taken down a network of tunnels that the Vietcong had used as a base and a hideout when they were fighting what were referred to as the American invaders. Wherever I visit I always attempt to integrate myself into the local society and I was able to do this by talking to the older people in French: a hangover from the French Indochina days.

Although Jane had visited Hong Kong before as part of her business I was able to show her a very different side to the Hong Kong she already knew. We went to the traditional Wednesday evening races at Happy Valley and took a moonlit cruise on a junk to have dinner in one of the offshore islands.

It was at the Hong Kong IFPI meeting that the subject of the internet and its potential threat to the music industry was first considered. I regret to say that very few of those around the table, including myself, understood the issues or took the conversation seriously. In hindsight, it occurs to me now that because none of the heads of the major record companies could grasp the long-term threat that the internet posed meant this was a pivotal meeting in the history of the record industry.

After Hong Kong, the IFPI board members flew up to Beijing. Chelle was flying to meet me in Beijing and there was obviously no way I could avoid telling Jane about this. She was terribly upset. I cannot believe that I had ever thought she would not be. That deceit is not something of which I am particularly proud.

In Beijing, the Chinese government feted the IFPI heads as if it were a state visit. It was the first trip to China for most of us, and we had a fascinating time. We saw a good deal of the country and also drove out of town to see the Great Wall. The official banquets took place in the People's Palace. We had been 'officially' warned to be on our guard about some of the food we might be offered at these state occasions. At the opening banquet the first dish worried me. I enquired of our hosts, who barely spoke English, what we were eating, and eventually deciphered his reply: cow stomach. As somebody who had managed to avoid eating tripe during five years in Manchester, I was not about to do so in Beijing!

It was at these meetings that I met a feisty young female executive called Lisa Gordon who the IFPI secretariat had recently hired. She had originally worked in the financial community and had an excellent overview on where the music industry was heading.

Lisa undoubtedly ruffled a few feathers, holding her ground against the likes of Jim Fifield, who was aghast that someone so young would disagree with him so intensely. Lisa's honesty about industry trends won her few friends at the IFPI, but I was so impressed with her that, when she left the organisation, I took the opportunity to hire her at Chrysalis, and gave her a position on the main board.

After Beijing, Chelle flew home, and I went on to Tokyo to meet up with Steve Lewis and Richard Huntingford for the first of our regular Echo board meetings. Nights out in Roppongi were always fun. There are many Westerners living there, but it is impossible to truly integrate with Japanese society, which is why there are bars employing European girls just to chat to visiting businessmen. The trendy disco at the time was Lexington Queen, and it was frequented by Western models working in Tokyo, who were also happy to meet international visitors like ourselves.

On one such occasion we ran into a beautiful Icelandic model called Begga, with whom I spent several enjoyable hours talking. However, as regards anything more than talk, this particular Begga disproved the old saying that beggars can't be choosers. Begga was able to choose, and she chose not to!

We also hung out on that trip with Simple Minds frontman Jim Kerr and Charlie Burchill, the band's guitarist, who were in Tokyo for a few days on a promotional trip and staying in our hotel. They, or more especially Jim, were accompanied by Nancy Berry, the wife of Ken Berry, the former Virgin executive who had taken a key role in EMI following the EMI takeover. Nancy too had become an important member of the EMI staff, but I was somewhat surprised to see her in such a hands-on role.

Returning to England, my workload increased as activity in the company became as intense as the pace of our development. But I was now back to my old self, really happy, and throwing myself into everything. Jane and I seemed to have settled into a comfortable relationship and we were able to be together most nights during the week, and even occasionally at weekends.

Maybe I was just kidding myself. No matter how close Jane and I had become, the fact that I was still married to Chelle ran like a fault line through our relationship. At the BRIT Awards after-show party in 1994, a chance remark to us from Nick Blackburn, along the lines of "Enjoy it while you can, because it can't last!" really upset Jane. She backed off from our relationship for a while, before I managed to talk her round.

Shortly after this came a morning that crystallised exactly how chaotic my complicated personal life had become. One Friday at breakfast time, Janice paid an unexpected visit to my Kensington flat. She was not alone. Neither was I – Jane was there too, preparing to leave for work.

Janice had brought Holly with her. The next surprise was her stated intention to spend the weekend away, in Cornwall, without Holly. It was about time I looked after our daughter, she said. Playing for time, I suggested I make her a coffee while we talked about it, and ducked into the kitchen. Moments later I returned to find Holly alone. I rushed into the bedroom.

"Where is she?" I asked Jane, assuming Janice had gone there.

"Who?" she replied.

"Janice."

I dashed back into the living room and through the window saw Janice driving out of the car park.

By now it was 8.00 a.m. and I was due on the tennis court at Queen's Club in 30 minutes. Annie, my driver, would arrive at any minute to take me there. After tennis I had a series of meetings at the office before I had to head off to Newbury Racecourse where I was due to meet Chelle and host a lunch.

So this was it. My fragile house of cards was finally about to collapse around me. What was I to do?

It was a crisis of the highest order, but luckily I thrive on crises. It was time to take a risk. When Annie drove up I called her in. She had worked for me for several years, and knew my every move, but she didn't know Holly even existed.

"You know all about babies, don't you, Annie?" I asked her.

Annie confirmed that she did, and in one fell swoop became Holly's 'Granny Annie'. She completely took control of the situation, allowing me to start rescheduling my day. Thoughtfully, Jane had remained in the bedroom until the immediate crisis was over but when she did emerge I had some explaining to do.

In the event Janice returned before too long but – as she hoped – she had given me cause to reconsider my behaviour. She had certainly given me a solid reality check.

And, incidentally, Annie relished her new role, and remained Holly's new grannie for years to come.

Understandably, this extraordinary domestic melodrama demonstrated to Jane yet again just how complicated my affairs were. Although she was aware of the situation, it did bring home to her the fact that a normal life with me was far from imminent, and once again our relationship became fragile.

But life is full of swings and roundabouts and after this episode I began to see a lot more of Janice and Holly. It seemed to me now that Janice was less committed to her relationship with George, and we seriously discussed the possibility of getting back together on a more permanent basis. She even considered moving back to the house I had bought for her in Barnes, which had been rented out, but it would take a while to vacate the tenants.

First, however, she had a three-week vacation planned with George in Canada, where he had a family home. We decided to think hard about things during this hiatus and meet on her return. When we did meet up she seemed to be glowing and in great form. However, much to her surprise, a couple of weeks later she found out she was pregnant again – with George's child.

We both knew that the decision was made right there. Here was our reality check. We were deluding ourselves to believe that we could have a future together, and with a second child on the way, Janice needed the stability that I simply could not provide. She and George would get married as soon as the arrangements could be made.

With Janice now out of the picture, Jane and I became close once again, and I decided it was time for me to get my personal life resolved once and for all. It was clear to me that my marriage was over in all but name, and it was down to me, finally, to summon up the courage to tell Chelle that it was time we went our separate ways.

I tried to broach the topic numerous times but didn't get very far as Chelle seemed immune to what I was trying to tell her. Perhaps the truth was that she didn't want to hear it, or perhaps I simply had difficulty expressing myself. On our next annual summer holiday, we spent very little time in each other's company and this seemed to register with her in a way that my words did not.

When we returned to London, Chelle interrogated most of our mutual friends and slowly pieced together glimpses of my years of serial deceit and the complications it caused. She probably always suspected something was going on, but she was distraught at exactly how ignorant she was of the full picture.

On my 40th birthday, Chelle and I had celebrated with a huge all-day party at Glebe House, with fire-eaters, stilt-walkers and more than 100 friends. On my 50th, we had dinner *a deux* at Raymond Blanc's Manoir aux Quat' Saisons restaurant at Great Milton in Oxfordshire. Over a two-star Michelin meal I confessed my many sins and deceptions. It was, to say the least, not an easy encounter. Shortly afterwards, on the day that Janice married George, Chris O'Donnell and I went to Doncaster racecourse to watch the St Leger, desperately trying and failing to enjoy the racing.

I suppose a part of me was quietly relieved that my complex double – or, rather, triple – life of intrigue had finally collapsed around me, and the pressure was finally relieved. But that was only a small part. Most of me was hurting like mad, and I felt truly remorseful about the way I had treated these women I cared for, all three of whom had deserved better.

Then, on the day after my 50th birthday, September 8, 1994, as all this emotion was tearing me apart, one of the most important events in the history of Chrysalis took place 80 miles away in Birmingham.

CHAPTER 22

The Heart Of Rock'n'Roll

Radio has always been an important part of my life. As a teenager back in Lincolnshire, in the evening I would be glued to a small transistor radio under the pillow listening to Radio Luxembourg broadcasting on 208 on the medium wave, at that time the only station playing pop music for the British public. Pirate radio arrived in England in the mid-sixties via ships like Radio Caroline or stations like Radio City which broadcast from a fort in the Thames estuary. It was not until 1967 that the BBC launched Radio One and changed the British radio landscape forever.

I had always been fascinated by American radio and its many different formats, including, when the market evolved from AM to FM, the early days of free-form underground radio when DJs might play one whole side of a vinyl album without a break. This trend had greatly benefited some of our acts, particularly Ten Years After and Jethro Tull. It was amazing to realise that in America a city might have upwards of 20 different popular music stations all playing entirely different styles of music and catering for entirely different listenerships.

I always felt radio in the UK had lagged behind the rest of Europe, never mind the US. Commercial independent local radio didn't get started in Britain until October 1973 with the news and talk network LBC and the pop station Capital, both in London.

Although over the next 15 years several further licences were issued by the radio authority, it was not until around 1990 that the pace of this increased and the authority was finally taking positive steps towards making commercial radio a valid competitor to the BBC. We were very keen for Chrysalis to become involved.

This wasn't our first incursion into the world of commercial radio. In 1989 we had bought a minority stake in Metro Radio, the company that controlled most of the commercial stations in the North East of England and was in the process of merging with the Yorkshire Radio Network, which operated commercial stations in Sheffield, Leeds and Hull. As a result, we ended up with a 20% stake and a seat on the board of Metro Radio Group for Richard Huntingford. He used this to develop his – and our – knowledge of the radio business.

We felt quite confident a couple of years later as we put together, at some considerable expense, our bid for a franchise to operate a station based in Manchester and covering the whole of the north west. We decided to go with a format that was widespread in America but hadn't yet transferred to the UK: soft adult contemporary, aimed at the 25-45 demographic and featuring, at the time, lots of Phil Collins, Lionel Richie and Tina Turner.

We needed local partners to give a local flavour so I arranged for Greenall Whitley, the north west brewery, to join the bid as I knew members of the family through my racing connections. Unfortunately, our application was not successful, and we lost out to the Guardian Media Group owned Century Station, which was hugely disappointing at the time.

When the Radio Authority advertised a similar licence for a station based in Birmingham and covering the West Midlands, we were wary of putting in another application because the Manchester one had been so costly. We therefore cut corners by lodging exactly the same application as for Manchester, obviously without the Greenall Whitley component.

We thought no more about it and assumed we would be disappointed again. At the start of October 1993 I was in my house in Cap D'Antibes for the MIPCOM TV market and when I saw a fax with a Radio Authority heading lying by my fax machine, I initially assumed it was a leftover from the failed north west bid of a few months earlier. I had to read it three times before the penny dropped. It was Richard Huntingford telling me we had actually won the Birmingham franchise.

The station was due to start broadcasting the following September. We decided to call it Heart FM, reflecting the fact that Birmingham was in the heart of England.

We had to find premises and hire staff, DJs and producers, studios and transmission facilities. We hired Phil Riley, an experienced radio operator, to mastermind the launch, an inspired appointment as he was to prove a superb executive for the company. Along with Richard, Phil was at the forefront of all the developments at the Chrysalis radio division.

Our launch party in Birmingham was a lavish affair with a stellar guest list of local dignitaries and artistes, and friends from London such as George and Judy Martin. As this coincided with the implosion of all the various aspects of my personal life, I doubt I personally was in much of a mood for partying.

We clearly made more than a decent fist of running Heart in Birmingham because two years later we were awarded the licence to launch a similar station in London. The announcement came as I was in Mexico City for an IFPI board meeting. With the time difference, I was woken up in the middle of the night to hear the amazing news.

Originally, the London station was to be called Crystal FM, but with the success of the Birmingham station, we decided to use the Heart brand in the capital as well. We launched it in September 1995 with a huge party at AIR Studios Lyndhurst Hall. Michael Bolton pushed the button to play the highly appropriate first record: 'Something Got Me Started' by Simply Red.

Heart London broadcast out of the Chrysalis head office in Bramley Road and it was an enormous success right from the word go. Since we now intended to concentrate on developing our own radio stations, we sold our interest in Metro Radio, and the whole of the Metro Radio Group was bought by EMAP, another very large UK radio company.

In 1995 we also bought Galaxy radio from the GWR group. This was a dance-music station targeted at a young audience and covering the Bristol, West Country and South Wales area. We now had three major radio stations: our portfolio was growing.

A couple of years later, in 1997, we acquired Faze FM, the company which had recently been granted a licence to operate regional dance stations in Manchester and Yorkshire. Both were trading under the Kiss banner and we renamed them Galaxy. We then added to this with a similar format covering the entire north east and based in Newcastle.

While Chrysalis diversifying into television had, I felt, played to my creative strengths, managing radio stations was rather different. Initially, when we launched Heart FM in Birmingham I felt I could have a major influence on programming. I would listen to the output and make personal observations about which records I felt worked and did not work as part of the playlist.

Very early on, we had played an Olivia Newton-John song from the *Grease* soundtrack album. I had nothing against Olivia personally but I intuitively felt that it didn't fit in to the format of what we were trying to do and the record was taken off the playlist.

However, as our radio business expanded, my ability to influence the programming diminished. Commercial radio tends to be a research-driven media with very little room for any independent and creative thought on the part of the producers or the DJs. It's a field where focus groups rule the roost.

As the working day ended teams of housewives from the suburbs would troop into meetings in the Chrysalis building to act as one of these focus groups. They would vote and decide which records should be added to the list. I found this bizarre, not least as we were paying huge salaries to programme directors to do exactly that. I questioned the logic but was told there was a requirement for both, and if in doubt the focus group's opinion would take precedence.

This never sat well with me. I've always felt that media industry professionals, whether in radio, print media or A&R roles within record companies, should lead the public in their acceptance of content rather than the other way around. By and large, most people tend to prefer the familiar, and dismiss new stuff they don't know. I would frequently ask why we weren't playing a certain record, only to be told it hadn't gone down well in the focus group meeting.

Invariably, I would find out three weeks later that the record had been added because it was now a hit and was being played extensively by other stations, and our focus group had now decided they liked the record after all. As a creatively minded executive, I would have preferred to have gone with my instinctive belief that the song was bound to be a huge hit.

The same syndrome worked in reverse. Sometimes – because the focus group liked it – we would still be playing a record that was plummeting down the charts. Maybe they did, but the record-buying public clearly didn't as the next week it would drop out of the Top 40 altogether, and, a week later, disappear from the Heart playlist.

Focus groups are equally endemic – and pernicious – in the movie industry. In the worst instances, film companies will show movies to groups that get to choose the ending. Is this really a good idea? I'm pretty sure that if the climax to *Casablanca* had been left to a gang of housewives from Iowa, they wouldn't have chosen the ending which saw Humphrey Bogart and Claude Rains walk off down the tarmac while Ingrid Bergman got on the plane with Paul Henreid. Bogart and Bergman would have wafted off, arm-in-arm, to live happily ever after.

On any music radio station the breakfast show is the most important programme, and Heart in London was no exception.

At the 1995 launch we scored a coup by luring Kara Noble, who had risen from traffic and weather girl to become Chris Tarrant's sidekick on Capital's breakfast show, to defect to us. This got us a good deal of publicity, especially when Kara made disparaging remarks about Tarrant.

Unfortunately, in May 1999 Kara landed herself in hot water by selling a topless picture of Sophie Rhys-Jones to *The Sun*. This was just prior to Sophie's marriage to Prince Edward, which made her the Countess of Wessex. Before her marriage to Edward, Sophie had been in the PR industry and had previously worked for Capital Radio and, indeed, Chrysalis Radio. She always came across as a good fun-loving girl.

On a 1988 Capital Radio junket to Malaga in Spain, Sophie and Kara had been larking about with Chris Tarrant and a few others. Tarrant pulled Sophie's bikini top up and Kara took a snap. This photo and others were pinned to a notice board in Kara's office at Capital Radio for years. Later, she took them down but she obviously hung on to them and tried to cash in.

This wasn't particularly embarrassing for Sophie as it had happened 10 years earlier and was old news, but the timing of the publication slightly took the gloss off the Royal wedding. We felt we had no alternative but to let Kara go and she vanished off the radar completely, in disgrace. I believe she emigrated to Canada.

On a selfish note, the scandal was also annoying for us as a few weeks earlier we had launched a bus, taxi and poster advertising campaign for the breakfast show. Kara was pictured in bed in a nightie with her co-presenter Jono Coleman and the tagline: 'Get up to mischief with Jono and Kara'. Thankfully the poster campaign had run its course and we only had to remove the advertising from the taxis.

The larger-than-life (in every way) Jono took it all in his stride and continued to present the Heart Breakfast show, with Harriet Scott as his new sidekick from 2002. Jono is a naturally funny guy, great in any social situation, and was at the helm when Heart knocked Capital Radio off its number one perch in London. This was quite a feat when you consider that Capital Radio had been around since the very beginning of commercial radio in the UK more than two decades earlier.

Happily, the Chrysalis stations were all successful. Heart 100.7 in the Midlands became perhaps the most successful station in the country in terms of overall market share in its area, beating its long-established competitor BRMB into second place.

Despite this, we seemed to hit the wall whenever we applied for other radio franchises. Our luck appeared to have run out until the end of 2000, when the government presented a White Paper entitled *A New Future For Communications* which paved the way for a relaxation of the radio ownership rules.

For the first time British radio stations could now be sold to American companies. The government was hoping to transform the UK radio market and turn it into one of the most dynamic in the world. However, the process quickly became a land grab.

Richard Huntingford and I to flew to San Antonio to meet Lowry Mays, the founder of Clear Channel Communication, to explore the possibility of a tie-up between Chrysalis and Clear Channel. It also owned thousands of billboards and outdoor advertising displays.

I was horrified to learn from Mays that he felt that a radio station and an outdoor billboard were essentially different variants of the same thing. Commuters drive in their cars; they listen to radio ads; they look at ads on billboards. There was no great difference between them. They performed the same function. This view was close to sacrilege to someone like me who felt that radio was an entertainment medium, and a station had to be nurtured accordingly, with significant creative input. Our talks went no further.

Around this time, an unfortunate lack of communication in the office caused me significant embarrassment. Richard Huntingford was keen to expand the radio business further, and there were radio stations coming on the market that we were interested in acquiring. One of these was LBC. But Richard hadn't told me of his plans in that direction.

Daily Express proprietor Richard Desmond had invited me over to his office at the newspaper for lunch. Unfortunately my PA had not realised that his office was right on the other side of town to Chrysalis, and the traffic ensured I got there very late. By the time I arrived, Desmond was so hungry that he had not only started lunch alone but finished it too.

I was deeply apologetic but we proceeded to have a good chat. He was keen to ask my advice: LBC was on the market, and he wanted to know if I thought Express Newspapers should bid for it. I discussed the pros and cons with him in a very impartial manner, went back to the office and told Richard Huntingford.

"That's a bit of a problem," said Richard. "We are already in the process of formulating a bid and it's a station I think we should buy."

It was left to me to make a very embarrassing phone call to Richard Desmond, explaining the situation to him. To this day, I'm not sure if he actually believed me or if he felt that our interest in LBC stemmed from him discussing the subject with me at the lunch we didn't eat together.

Nevertheless, in September 2002, we went ahead and bought LBC, a station that was losing £3 million a year, for the sum of £23.5 million. We hired presenters such as Henry Kelly, Caroline Feraday, Penny Smith and Sandi Toksvig. We had big plans and hoped to return its listenership to the heady days of the seventies, when one million people used to tune in.

One reason why LBC was making such huge losses was that it was actually running two 24-hour news radio stations, one on FM and one on the AM frequency. Compared to a music radio station where you simply have to pay the disc jockeys and the Performing Rights Society for the music, the costs of running a news network are immense. Skilled journalists have to be on the ball and topical, and that comes at a heavy price.

Commercial news talk radio is a successful format in many other markets of the world, especially in the US. However, in the

UK such stations are in permanent competition with the BBC, and its extensive international news-gathering facilities. BBC Radio 4 and Radio 5 Live have immense resources and huge marketing budgets.

Indeed, the biggest problem in general facing commercial radio in the UK is competing with the BBC. It seems to me ridiculous that you can scan through your FM receiver and find three or four of the strongest frequencies given over to Radio 3, a classical station with a very select listenership.

Not only is BBC Radio 4 still the most listened to station in Greater London, ahead of commercial stations like Heart, Capital or Magic and even Radio 1 or Radio 2, but there is also enormous cross-promotion between BBC television and radio. The free TV advertising that BBC radio stations receive would be worth tens of millions of pounds to commercial radio broadcasters.

Every morning, as BBC *Breakfast* ends on television, viewers are encouraged to tune into local BBC radio stations. This all means that, apart from major stations like Heart, Capital, Magic, Kiss and Classic FM, many of the other regional and local commercial stations struggle to make a profit of any description.

Furthermore, the demographic of news and talk radio is much older than that of music radio. Advertisers who are focused on attracting 28 to 35-year-old housewives are unlikely to advertise on talk radio stations with a mostly male listenership whose average age is in the fifties or sixties. At LBC we inherited a whole slew of advertisers pushing relatively geriatric products. We never managed to turn the station around and as hard as we tried it carried on losing us close to £3 million per year.

As a sideline, I enjoyed making the occasional appearance on LBC, particularly with Dr. Pam Spurr, our agony aunt and self-help guru. She was always looking for people to appear on her show at 8 p.m. and, had I chosen to unburden my private life on the airwaves, I would certainly have had lots to talk about! I occasionally dropped into her studio as I was leaving the office and joined in discussions but the Radio Authority complained – apparently, owners of radio stations should not be broadcasting themselves.

I always enjoyed a bit of banter with LBC's Nick Ferrari, an excellent and challenging broadcaster, although we had run-ins over topics such as the Iraq war (he was pro, I was anti). Prominent government officials also beat a path to the Chrysalis office.

At their height our radio stations made the Chrysalis building a magnet for politicians and personalities of every persuasion. The reception area was full of famous people from all walks of life and the whole building retained a huge buzz as a result of it. During his terms as Prime Minister Tony Blair paid several visits, and on one occasion even ended up hosting a show on LBC.

Overall, our involvement with the radio business was a huge positive for the company and made us an enormous amount of money. It was a great business to be in and I believe it still is. I enjoyed working with many of the people involved in the radio stations and on my visits to Australia, where he now lives, still enjoy catching up with Jono Coleman.

As one gets older, one's listening habits change and you turn more to talk radio. If I am in the car myself, I would be just as likely to have Radio Five Live on as a music station. Although the migration to digital radio has not been at the pace the industry would have wished, digital is an immense benefit, both for the improved sound quality and for the ability to continue listening without regularly retuning the dial.

I am sure of one thing – television, social media and the internet will all continue to grow, but whatever happens in the future, radio will be with us forever. It has always been, and always will be, a great medium.

CHAPTER 23

(Something Inside) So Strong

The nineties were possibly the most paradoxical decade of my life to date. My professional life appeared to be going from strength to strength as I rebuilt Chrysalis and many inspired ventures came off. Fifty had always sounded old to me, but actually it is a great age: you are old enough to know what to do, and still young enough to be able to do it.

My personal life, of course, remained rather less plain sailing. Most women confronted with their husband confessing many years of intermittent infidelities would be straight on the phone to a divorce lawyer, and Chelle did engage the services of the celebrated divorce specialist Raymond Tooth. Despite being hugely heartbroken, she initially thought there might be something to salvage and was determined to try and save our marriage.

This was never likely to happen, primarily because my heart was not in it but also because she laid down terms that I was unable to accept. Nevertheless, Chelle and I somehow remained on cordial terms. At her suggestion, we went to Bali for a few days to talk things over, and decided that we would stay together for the sake of the family and be together at weekends, but live separately in London during the week.

We sold the large apartment we owned in York House Square, and, in an attempt to make a clean start, bought a big studio in Holland Park, and two separate one-bedroom flats in Kensington and Barons Court. This meant that I ended up every Monday to Friday in my own very attractive Kensington flat, with a large terrace overlooking a private garden. I bought it from Nigel Havers. I never really liked the Holland Park studio and spent very little time there. We eventually sold it to Julian Lennon.

This all sounds very civilised but in truth the arrangement probably suited no one and we should have grasped the nettle and ended the marriage. It prevented me from moving on, and was unfair not just to Chelle, but to everyone else with whom I was involved.

Initially this was Jane, and though my relationship with her continued I was still unable to fully commit to her. After a further year or so of this stop-start emotional roller coaster, we both felt that the road was too rocky to make the journey worthwhile. It is a source of great regret that the relationship never really had a chance, but we had had wonderful times together.

Jane deserved someone who was able to devote his life to her, and as I understand she is now happily married, it appears she has found that person. I am delighted for her; she is another to whom I owe a huge debt.

Jane's departure from my life brought a sort of semi-freedom and for a couple of years I embarked on a series of relationships, but I still felt a huge emotional attachment to Janice, which inhibited me from truly committing to anyone else. Bizarrely, the fact that I was still officially married allowed me to continue my life of bachelorhood unabated.

For some strange reason I seemed to be able to take all the crises in my personal life in my stride, and concentrate on building the business. We were, by now, a three-legged stool: music, radio and television, with each leg as important as the others. Soon we would gain a fourth leg, movies, but this was to prove a very fragile element of the structure.

I was Chrysalis executive chairman and chief executive, combining the two roles with all the key personnel reporting to me. As we were a public company, I also was responsible for relations with the financial community. Charles Levison assisted me, and together we decided to strengthen the main board. The only surviving non-executive director from the days of the old Chrysalis company was Sir George Martin.

We decided to approach Oscar-winning movie producer Sir David – now Lord – Puttnam. We felt that his creative-industry experience would be an asset to our developing visual entertainment and TV side. We also approached an independent merchant banker, Tom Chandos (also a Lord), to add weight on the corporate side. However, these two additions substantially changed the dynamics of the board and made the management of the group difficult for me.

Hitherto, the final decision on matters had always rested with me. However, the new mantra of corporate governance was increasingly coming into play. Suddenly, I had two board members who chose to flex their muscles, and make their presence felt. Puttnam and Chandos both felt that the roles of chairman and chief executive should be split, but I thought that as a company we were not big enough to make this practical.

I should also have paid more attention to the saying 'once bitten, twice shy'. Given what had happened when Terry Ellis had wanted Chrysalis to diversify into films in the eighties, I should have known better than to have another tilt at the movie business.

We'd had the odd film success in the past: bankrolling *Monty Python And The Holy Grail* and also a 1980 movie, *Babylon*, directed by Franco Rosso. An accurate and valuable document of the West Indian community experience in London in the seventies, it has been revived at the BFI and was screened on BBC4 as part of the *Reggae Britannia* strand of programmes in 2011.

Our ongoing television successes and our 50% interest in Scala Productions made a return to films fairly inevitable for Chrysalis. Nevertheless, it was to prove a major mistake.

When the original announcement of Chrysalis moving into films was made in the trade press, one of the movie world's most larger-than-life figures, Michael Winner, contacted me and suggested we have lunch. We decided to go to Clarke's in Kensington, and Michael agreed to make the reservation. He then called back to say that he had been unable to do so, so I arranged it instead. I then got a call from the owner, Sally Clarke, asking if I was planning to meet Michael. It turned out he was banned from the restaurant. We went to Cibo instead.

I had first met Michael through an American music industry friend, Bob Summer, who had been president of RCA Records in New York and had also worked in a senior executive capacity at CBS. In fact Bob and his wife, Susan, together with Chelle and myself, all happened to be in the company of Michael and his then girlfriend, Jenny Seagrove, on the fateful night in 1993 that his career as a restaurant critic began.

We were eating at Le Pont De La Tour, the Terence Conran-owned restaurant by London's Tower Bridge. Michael decided that the service was poor and, more specifically, that his fish was not fresh.

The service had indeed been a little haphazard. Everybody's food did not arrive at the same time and the French staff were being particularly French about it all. Michael was thus already in a bit of a state when his Dover sole arrived.

"This fish isn't fresh," he told the waiter.

"I can assure you that it is," the waiter replied.

Michael asked to speak to the manager and repeated his complaint: "This fish is not fresh."

The very French manager rolled his eyes, stormed off to the kitchen and returned waving the bill from Billingsgate.

"Look here, look here, Monsieur!" he asserted. "Here: 75 Dover soles and today's date! This fish is fresh."

"This fish is not fresh!" insisted Michael. "Take it away. I want one of the fresh ones."

The slanging match went on for a full 10 minutes. Working for a Conran restaurant, and faced with a high-profile customer, the manager should clearly have given way and said, "I'm sorry sir, I'll go and get another Dover sole." Yet he continued to refuse to do so.

An aggrieved Michael wrote up the details of the evening and sent them in a letter to the *Sunday Times*. The newspaper printed it which caused quite a furore with Conran. The *Sunday Times* then contacted Michael and asked him to write a regular column for it reviewing restaurants. The resulting feature, Winner's Dinners, continued for almost 20 years until Michael's death in 2013.

Years later, Michael gave me a copy of his book, *Winner's Dinners: The Good, The Bad And The Unspeakable*. He wrote a nice inscription inside the front: 'To Chris, who was there at the very beginning.'

In his movie career, Michael worked with some of the biggest names in cinema – Oliver Reed, Marlon Brando, Burt Lancaster, Robert Mitchum, Sophia Loren, Lauren Bacall, Michael Caine and Roger Moore – but has never been a critics' favourite. Nevertheless, he knew a lot about the pitfalls of the film industry.

I assumed Michael wanted to go for lunch because he wanted Chrysalis to invest in one of his projects so I was rather taken aback when I realised that he was concerned about my involvement in film in general. He strongly advised me, in no uncertain terms, to rethink and to get out of my commitment to the film business as quickly as I could. I wish I had taken his advice.

Mick Pilsworth was the driving force behind our decision to re-enter the movie world, but little did he know what kind of ride was in store for us with David Puttnam on the board.

David Puttnam had been involved in some of the finest films of the seventies and eighties, most notably the multi-Oscar-winning *Chariots Of Fire*, whose success helped revitalise the UK film industry. He had gone on to produce *Local Hero*, directed by Bill Forsyth, as well as *The Killing Fields* and *The Mission*, directed by Roland Joffé. He seemed to have a knack for working with maverick filmmakers.

In 1986, he became Chief Executive Officer at Columbia Pictures but didn't last very long in Hollywood and returned to independent production in 1988. We felt David's creative industry experience, and his reputation as an industry icon, would be an asset to the visual entertainment and TV side.

However, one of the disadvantages of having a non-executive director who is an expert in a particular field is that the executive directors in that field can always be second-guessed on how they are running that particular side of the business. Ideally, a non-executive director should be there to give an overview – not act as an expert on the specific business that he directs at the main board level.

Chrysalis was structured, as is usual business practice, around regular management meetings for each division, and for the subdivisions within each division. I would attend the divisional meetings but not usually the subdivisional meetings. In theory, the film division was a subdivision of the visual entertainment division but it began taking on a profile greater than even the main board meetings.

David Puttnam would attend each meeting, which meant that the other non-executive directors wanted to attend, which meant that I attended as well. Some of the conversations around the film division table became extremely fraught. David understandably knew a lot more about the film business than did Mick Pilsworth, despite the fact that Mick had been hired to manage it on a day-to-day basis.

David persuaded us to recruit a lady who had worked for him at Columbia Pictures called Lyndsey Posner as managing director of the film division. Lyndsey had a business affairs background but no production experience, and right from the word go, I always felt we were never quite sure what our role in the film business was and how best to set out to achieve it.

Chrysalis Films quickly morphed into being primarily an independent distribution company, whereas in our television activities we were primarily a production company. Lindsey hired a head of sales as her number two and set about trying to find films to sell. At the time of starting the film business, we were under the impression that there was a gap in the market for a well-funded independent film distributor but we quickly realised that whoever had provided the funding for a movie, usually a studio company, ended up with the sales distribution rights.

We then made an umbrella deal with a New York-based producer that I met in Greenwich Village with Lindsey. I am not quite sure what we got out of that. We ended up with the infrastructure of a sales and distribution company and very little to sell. The whole thing was badly thought out to start with, and seemed to be going nowhere fast.

As the relationship between David Puttnam and Mick Pilsworth got ever worse, one volatile board meeting found Mick calling David a fucking nutter and David calling Mick a fuckwit, or was it the other way round? I insisted that Mick apologise, and when he refused, David set out to sue him, so it looked like the dispute was going to court. We even got as far as having counsel's opinion on which was the worst insult: a fuckwit or a fucking nutter. I believe the baffling conclusion was that a fuckwit was the greater insult. To bring the matter to a close I eventually brokered a deal between the warring parties, but Mick's intransigence in handling this issue to some extent contributed to his ultimate departure from the company.

On another occasion, David unfortunately had to leave a Chrysalis strategy meeting being held in East Anglia early because his wife's father had suddenly been taken very ill. He had been kept up most of the night attempting to sort out a problem on a movie set in Mexico and running up a phone bill in excess of £600 in the process which he was responsible for paying himself. As he left another row broke out between him and Mick, apparently over his request that an acquaintance of his be hired as a production assistant, although this time no one on the board was safe from a barrage of criticisms.

My own relationship with David was also challenging. He continued to insist that I could not be both chairman and CEO and that I should appoint a non-executive chairman. I disagreed and was comfortable that we had strong divisional chief executives in Steve Lewis, Mick Pilsworth, Richard Huntingford and Peter Lassman, although I should note that given the way corporate governance has evolved, by today's standards, David was 100% right. Public companies are do not normally have the same person as chairman and chief executive.

Eventually I half-conceded the point and engaged the services of Milena Djurdjevic, probably the most prominent media headhunter in the country. Milena, who had been involved in the recruitment of a series of major appointments, including that of Greg Dyke as Director General of the BBC, was a superb professional whose good judgement I came to rely on.

I interviewed several possible candidates for a senior position at Chrysalis. I was close to hiring someone on a couple of occasions, but was never certain we had the right person. On one occasion I offered the job to Julian Mounter, the New Zealand-based British chief executive of TVNZ, and agreed terms with him. He promptly returned home and never came back.

I was aware that the wrong hiring could have done untold damage to the dynamics of the company, which was performing beyond all expectations, so the change in the management structure that David was insisting on did not materialise.

Nevertheless, a few weeks later I received a CV from Milena which caught my eye. Philip McDanell had been chief finance officer at MTV Europe and was looking for a senior role in a creative company. I met with Philip who seemed a very competent chap and was able to get an immediate reference for him from my good friend Bill Roedy, the chairman of MTV Europe. Bill gave him a 100% thumbs up in every respect apart though he did mention that Philip was very boring.

Knowing Bill and his energy, I suspected that the worst thing Philip had done was leave a club before dawn one night after an MTV launch party. On that basis, I hired him to join the company not as chief executive but as group managing director, with all the

291

divisional heads reporting to him, and with Philip working in the next office to mine.

This was not a big enough sop for David Puttnam who, having enlisted the support of the other non-executive directors, including even Charles Levison, launched a fresh tirade. For his part, Philip was not totally embraced by the divisional heads, although to be fair, he was more likely to be the last to leave a party rather than the first. His big problem was an inability to make a speech sound interesting, and even though he had coaching on this particular skill it met with limited success.

David Puttnam was an enigma to me. He was so hard to figure out that I even read two books about him, both by Andrew Yule, the first called *Fast Fade: David Puttnam, Columbia Pictures, And The Battle For Hollywood*, and a biography entitled *Enigma: David Puttnam, The Story So Far*. By the end I was none the wiser, and I suspected that his biographer wasn't either.

Despite the backstage turmoil, we managed to invest in a few films. *I Love You, I Love You Not* was a romantic drama directed by Billy Hopkins and starring Jude Law, Claire Danes and the French screen legend Jeanne Moreau. The French TV channel and subscription broadcaster Canal+ also backed it but it sank without trace.

We had high hopes for *Stiff Upper Lips,* written and directed by Gary Sinyor, who had won several awards for his 1993 feature film debut, *Leon The Pig Farmer. Stiff Upper Lips* was a spoof on the Merchant-Ivory period dramas, with knowing references to *A Room With A View, Howards End, The Remains Of The Day* and even *Chariots Of Fire*. The cast included Peter Ustinov as well as Prunella Scales and her son Samuel West, who had both been in *Howards End*, and enjoyed sending themselves up tremendously. However, it received mixed reviews and didn't recoup its budget.

By this time, the losses in the film division were escalating at a pace; I could not see how we could change this around and Michael Winner's words were ringing in my ears. During August, 1996, on holiday, I read every conceivable book I could find on the film business, including *The Egos Have Landed, The Rise And Fall Of Palace Pictures* by Angus Finney, *My Indecision Is Final, The Rise And Fall Of Goldcrest Films* by Jake Eberts, and *One Hundred Films And A Funeral, The Life And Death Of PolyGram Films,* by Michael Kuhn. Reading these books led me to make a dramatic decision: to close down the film division at the earliest possible opportunity. The first thing I did when I returned to the office was to call a management meeting to discuss the situation and advise the other key executives of this decision. The announcement was made instantly. I decided not to tell David or his fellow non-executive director, Tom Chandos, in advance. Charles Levison however was fully in the picture.

When Puttnam found out, he hit the ceiling. For him this was the final straw. He decided to resign, and spent the following weekend working on a resignation speech to set out to the world at large the unacceptable, and dictatorial, management issues at Chrysalis. Fortunately, his letter of resignation did not generate the level of interest he had expected, our share price was unaffected, and things moved on.

Despite this acrimonious parting, David Puttnam turned up at my office soon afterwards with a gift for me: an old statue of a footballer, which still sits in my office. As much as we had challenging times in his period at the company, I still have the highest amount of regard for him. He remains a man of enormous ability, charisma and energy.

Away from work, the tenuous arrangement that Chelle and I had agreed upon – really, neither one thing nor the other – was always likely to prove fragile, and it understandably dissolved when Chelle met someone else that she decided she wanted to be with. We talked over her plans when we went on the French family holiday at the end of July 1996 and although the end had been a long time coming, the final decision to go our separate ways was very emotional and upsetting for both of us

Remarkably, Janice had also reappeared on my radar. We were obviously still in contact because of Holly, and when I left the French family holiday for a few days to work in the office, I invited Janice to Goodwood races for the day.

What happened next beggared belief. Despite running a high-profile entertainment company, I had never been a celebrity in the way that, say, Richard Branson enjoys being, but for some reason the *Daily Mail* decided that I was worthy of its scrutiny. It decided not only to send a photographer to tail me, but to have one in a helicopter hovering over the boat on which Chelle was sailing with family and friends in the South of France.

I was in blissful ignorance about all this until a call the following day from PR agent Brian McClaurin, telling me the *Mail* had pictures of Janice and I at Goodwood, including some showing my arm around Janice. I told him truthfully that I wouldn't walk around any race course with my arm around somebody, but the *Mail* had managed to procure a snap of me with my arm apparently around Janice as I ushered her through a gate.

I went a whiter shade of pale! Despite us agreeing to split, Chelle would be broken-hearted if she thought I was still lying to her, and there was no way Janice's husband could know about this. I spent a fortune buying the photographs from the copyright owner to keep them out of the papers.

I was clearly being naïve. Brian phoned again and told me the *Mail* would probably have a reporter and photographer at Janice's house too. I called her up to alert her to what was happening. When she didn't believe me, I told her to look out of the window. Right outside her gate stood a journalist and photographer.

With Brian on my other line, we discussed what to do, and decided the best thing was for her to put on something smart, leave the house, have her picture taken, then do some shopping, which is exactly what she did. The *Mail* ran a two-page story on my, Chelle and Janice's love triangle, but at least they didn't have the Goodwood pictures.

There was no way of keeping this from Chelle, and Brian advised her that she would be tailed when she returned to England. The press took an unconscionable interest in my affairs for a few days.

I just kept a low profile. Chelle had agreed to appear on breakfast television, but I managed to persuade her to cancel.

It was probably a relief for both Chelle and I to agree to go separate ways but there was also a very real sadness. For the most part we had had a good life and a good relationship together. We were also obviously very concerned about the children. Tom was away on a gap year in the Far East and was not contactable but he was upset when we eventually told him, as were Tim and Chloe. Chelle and I had clearly put on a very good front: they hadn't seen this coming at all, and they hated it. It was a difficult and painful time.

I suppose I had half-heartedly imagined I would revert to my middle-aged bachelor life but without the attendant guilt, but Nick Blackburn set me straight on that one. From his own experience, he explained, you are always far happier with the comfort of a permanent relationship. In my heart, I knew he was right.

What did I really want? I wanted Janice.

She was unhappy in her marriage, and over a series of clandestine meetings and phone calls, during the summer of 1997 she and I discussed the possibility of us getting together again. I knew one thing: if there was any chance at all, I didn't want to risk missing out as had I done over four years ago.

Janice was willing to try again. She knew that it would take a while to end her marriage to George, especially with Holly and their daughter, Tina, involved, but we immediately began to plan our exciting new life together.

Janice looked for a property for us to live in and found a very nice house in the village of Hurley, near Henley on Thames. Malthouse Cottage, next door to the Ye Olde Belle hotel, was not a mansion like Glebe House, but it would prove to be a very happy home for us.

As we awaited completion on the property, I made a quick trip to LA on music business, followed by a visit to New Zealand and Australia for the TV company and an Echo board meeting in Tokyo. Just another week in the life. When I returned, Malthouse Cottage was ready and we moved in. Chelle and I had agreed that neither of us would live at Glebe House until the divorce was resolved, so Hurley became my full-time home, with a Holland Park flat as my London base.

We announced our arrival in Hurley with a huge firework party on the night before Guy Fawkes Day. Janice obviously brought Holly and Tina to Malthouse Cottage with her, and so it was that I had to reacquaint myself with being woken up at six o'clock in the morning by two young children crawling over me in bed, an experience that had last happened to me over a decade ago.

It was almost nine years since Janice and I had first met on Concorde, that fateful flight when the plane's faulty hydraulics threw us together. The intervening years had been difficult, exciting and at times unbearable, but I suppose all this had to happen before we could finally be together, so happy and at peace.

In truth, I suspect that had we made the big move and partnered up nine years earlier, our relationship would not have strengthened and blossomed as it did – and, I'm glad to say, as it still does to this day. As we settled into Malthouse Cottage, I knew that finally my personal life was as it should be.

CHAPTER 24

Hit Me With Your Best Shot

My very first foray into the ownership of a sports team was as long ago as 1978, when soccer, as it is known in America, was beginning to take off. I had known Brian Lane, then the manager of Yes, for many years. In fact, I first met him outside Bryan Morrison's office in 1967, when, under his original name of Harvey Freed, he was notoriously employed to go around the country buying up records to influence the charts. He changed his name on his marriage, at the request of his wife, Elaine. Brian was responsible for the early career of Welsh diva Katherine Jenkins.

Brian had decided to put together a consortium to apply for a newly advertised franchise for a NASL soccer team in Philadelphia, which we named the Philadelphia Fury. In addition to Terry and I the other partners included Paul Simon and his business manager, Frank Barsalona from Premier Talent, and Peter Rudge whose New York-based company SIR Productions looked after the US affairs of The Who and The Rolling Stones and also managed Lynyrd Skynyrd.

Sadly, the Philadelphia Fury was an unmitigated disaster. We sent out several British players and an English manager, Richard Dinnis, a former school sports master, who had briefly managed Newcastle

United and who was eventually replaced by Alan Ball who became player manager. Our star striker was the ex-Chelsea hero Peter Osgood, who managed to score one goal in 23 matches.

Some players had been very good in their time but we also recruited some young kids who had never been out of the UK before, and they found it very difficult to adapt. I remember one young Irish apprentice player filling out his immigration form and, under the title occupation, writing down bricklayer. He was promptly thrown out of the country and sent back to England until we could sort it out.

Philadelphia was a great city for sport with the Philadelphia Flyers in ice hockey, the Phillies baseball team, and the Eagles in the NFL. However, the soccer team was never very good, never had a winning season, and as a result failed to draw big crowds.

We tried all kinds of marketing initiatives to draw people in. One showed a picture of a seven-feet-tall basketball player and a 250lbs American football player with a little footballer between them. The slogan ran "You don't have to be 150lbs, 5 foot 8 to be a soccer player but it does help". The idea was to demonstrate to Americans that only freak-sized professionals excelled at basketball and grid iron football but in soccer anyone of any size could play.

The Americans weren't convinced. They were desperate to have more goals to "make the game more exciting". They wanted to make the goal much bigger. Another idea was to allow the centre forward to catch the ball and throw it into the net. The whole thing was a debacle and eventually we decided to cut our losses. The team moved to Canada to become the Montreal Manic.

Aside from horse-racing, my next commercial involvement with a sport had been in 1993 when I sponsored the British tennis player Chris Bailey. I happened to be watching Wimbledon on television one night when Bailey was playing Goran Ivanisevic and lost the fifth and final set 9-7 in an absolute cliff-hanger of a match.

The next morning, I phoned up Bailey's agent, Clifford Bloxham, and offered to sponsor him. Sadly, this relationship wasn't as successful at it might have been, through no fault of either of us. Chris injured his anterior crucial ligament and never fulfilled the potential he showed that day. In fact, after several knee operations, he retired in September 1994 and became a TV commentator.

Also in 1993, Chrysalis Television was asked to tender for the contract to produce British basketball for Sky Sports. I knew very little about British basketball but I had watched a lot of it in the States, especially in Los Angeles where Tom Sturges, the then president of Chrysalis Music, was a huge fan of the LA Lakers. My regular ski trips to Aspen at Easter often coincided with the excitement of the Final Four, the conclusion of the college basketball season.

Having met with officials from the British basketball league, I was contacted by Yuri Matischen, an Englishman of Ukrainian descent, who was involved with basketball in Sheffield. At the time, Sheffield did not have a professional team, but the city had hosted the World Student Games in 1991 and thus had some excellent facilities. These included the Sheffield Arena and Ponds Forge, a leisure complex with a sports hall built specifically for weightlifting and judo that would be a suitable venue for basketball.

Yuri Matischen suggested that, with Chrysalis becoming involved in television coverage of the sport in the UK, we might also want to take over the amateur Sheffield Forgers, who were due to replace the Guildford Kings in the British Basketball League.

The conversation might have gone no further had it not been for the fact that the same evening I happened to be having dinner with my old friend Michael Gudinski. When the subject cropped up, Michael jumped out of his chair and started explaining how basketball had become the fastest growing sport in Australia. He was very excited at the opportunity of getting involved with a basketball team in the UK and asked to join me as a partner.

Spurred on by Michael's involvement, we decided to start a professional basketball team in Sheffield, to be managed by Matischen. We had to recruit a coach, players, start planning schedules for the season: it was all very exciting.

The thrill was heightened by the fact that, at the same time, Harvey Goldsmith and Ed Simons started a team at the Docklands Arena called The London Leopards, and concert promoter Barrie Marshall invested in The London Towers, who played at Wembley. We had the basis of some very good friendly music-business rivalry.

I had loads of fun with the Sheffield Sharks. In our first season, we won the BBL League Championship and National Cup. We did the double again in 1999, and won the Cup again in 2000, our fifth final in six years. I travelled all over the country to watch them play, especially at weekends. Despite the fact that the team were based in Sheffield, I got to many of the home games, as well as most of the away games in the south of England.

Often on a Sunday afternoon we would finish lunch in Gloucestershire at three o'clock, jump in the car and be in Sheffield three hours later for a 6.30 p.m. tip-off. I even managed to sell the sport inside the company and many of the Chrysalis staff regularly turned up for games, especially against the two London teams.

Unfortunately, British basketball has never taken off on a commercial basis. Television coverage is almost non-existent now whereas in the nineties we had regular coverage on Sky and with major events on the BBC.

We tried to move the Sharks from Ponds Forge to the Sheffield Arena but it proved too high a jump. Nevertheless, it was not a total financial disaster simply because the investment was relatively low compared to other sports. We finally relinquished our majority stake in 2001.

Had my involvement with professional sports gone no further than the Sharks, it might not have been a bad thing. It would have certainly saved me an enormous amount of money. However, throughout the winter of 1995/96, I had been talking to Nick Blackburn about buying a football club. Nick, a lifelong West Ham fan, normally watches well over 100 games a season.

With the Premier League going from strength to strength in the mid-nineties, the perception was growing in financial circles that football could become a commercially viable business on a serious level.

Nick and I looked at a few clubs that might be worth investing in, although none seemed quite right. He held meetings on my behalf with Portsmouth and approaches were made from Watford, but I was reticent to take things further.

At the same time, out of the blue, I was approached by Alex Finch, a club member, about Wasps, one of the top rugby union clubs in a sport that was still amateur but about to turn professional. Initially, wrongly as it turned out, I thought Alex was an important member of the committee. His concern was that the existing powers may have had difficulties taking the club into the professional era.

I knew little about club rugby. A few months earlier, I had had an exploratory meeting with Will Carling, the Harlequins centre and England rugby team captain who was rumoured to be having an affair with Princess Diana, to discuss the possibility of commercial involvement with club rugby. The conversation went no further but it was my first enlightenment as to how the club structure worked in England.

My lunch with Carling had slightly whetted my appetite for the sport but my experience ended at going to internationals at Twickenham where Chrysalis had debenture seats. One Monday morning, on my drive in from Gloucestershire, Alex Finch took me to see the ground at Sudbury in Middlesex, where Wasps played their games

I arranged to meet Alex at Hillingdon tube station and take a look at the facilities (it certainly was not a stadium). It was located in a residential area, at the end of a street of semi-detached houses, and was no more than a playing field with a dilapidated clubhouse at one end and a covered stand for perhaps 100 people on one side.

"How on earth can you expect to operate a professional sport from here?" I asked.

"You should see it during the season when we have the temporary stands up," Alex replied. "It looks fantastic."

I was nonplussed. Investing in Wasps sounded like a good idea but the infrastructure was just not there to accommodate a professional team. That was a pity because I was aware that Wasps were one of the leading clubs in the country, with a great reputation. Rugby union had established a league system and structure in 1987, and since then only three teams had ever won the championship: Bath, Leicester and Wasps.

I got back into my car to drive into London and within 10 minutes was on the A40. On my right I passed Loftus Road, where Queens Park Rangers, the team I supported, played. A light bulb came on over my head.

Maybe I could solve all of Wasps' problems by relocating their matches to Loftus Road and combining the rugby union team with QPR, the football team? Surely two clubs sharing facilities would provide a benefit of scale that would justify the purchase of both teams? I discussed my plan with Nick Blackburn and he shared my enthusiasm.

Queens Park Rangers had just been relegated from the Premier League and the owners, the Thompson family, were very keen to sell the club. The owners had become very unpopular with the fans – which, as I was to discover for myself, always happens when a team is doing badly. The way forward seemed wide open and Nick and I decided that I should go for it.

I began negotiating with Wasps' representatives for an involvement with the club which would necessitate me injecting sufficient money – around £4 million – to give them the commercial wherewithal to embrace professional rugby. At the same time, I negotiated with the Thompson family for the acquisition of 100% of the shareholding in Queens Park Rangers.

The negotiations on behalf of the Thompsons were handled by Clive Berlin, who had been a chief executive at QPR and then later at Millwall before he returned to QPR. He did a pretty effective job of trying to extract the best possible price from us. Clive claimed there were competitive offers, including one from Ernest Saunders, the former chief executive of Guinness PLC who in 1990 had been jailed for falsely manipulating the share price.

At one point, Ernest Saunders contacted me to suggest that, if I made him a consultant to Chrysalis on a retainer of £200,000 a year, he would withdraw his offer to buy QPR, leaving me a free run. I explained to him that I was buying QPR privately, and that it would be fraudulent to engage him and give him funds from a publicly traded company to assist me with a private enterprise.

Clive Berlin and I agreed that I would buy QPR for £10.5 million. Although I was borrowing most of the money to fund the purchase, we were hoping to partially fund it by floating off a minority stake in the combined entity on the Alternative Investment Market (AIM).

First, I had to complete the Wasps side of the deal. This entailed the club holding a full Members' Meeting in the Great Hall at Harrow School, where I addressed the audience before retiring to an ante-room while the members discussed my proposal. After an hour or so, I was told they had voted in my favour. I was to pay £4 million for a 51% stake to fund the club's professional future.

Given the newfound interest in sport in the City, we were successful in our attempt to float the newly merged company, to be called Loftus Road PLC, on the AIM. This would at least partially help pay back some of my exposure. With the remaining 49% of Wasps owned by the Wasps committee, on the flotation of the company we exchanged their shareholding for £3.5 million worth of shares in the overall umbrella company.

So when the 1996/97 season started, I now had a basketball team, a football team and a rugby team. If running Chrysalis and my convoluted personal life wasn't sufficient to fill my days before, it certainly was now, especially my weekends. I regularly found myself flitting from the Sheffield Arena to Wasps matches to QPR games all over the country.

I was anxious that running this multi-sports business would not have a detrimental effect on my ability to oversee Chrysalis, so we set out to form a board of many talents to manage Loftus Road PLC.

Along with Charles Levison, Nigel Butterfield, Nick Blackburn and Neil Duncanson, the Head of Chrysalis Sports TV, I appointed David Hudd, an old friend who had been chairman of public companies in the media and leisure sectors.

Wasps selected two board representatives: Bob Collier and Mark Rigby. I also asked an old university friend of mine, Lord [Terry] Burns to join, but he had to decline for political reasons. Terry was a die-hard QPR fan and did attend board meetings as an observer.

We instituted regular board meetings for Wasps and for QPR separately, and for Loftus Road PLC. Although I was the chairman of the holding company and of QPR, I initially chose to appoint Bob Collier as Wasps chairman.

After taking over Wasps, I was asked to attend some internal committee meetings which I thought were bizarre throwbacks from another era. The fixtures committee would meet, but I had no idea why, as the fixtures were all set by the sport's governing body. There was also a selection committee, despite the fact that the director of rugby, Nigel Melville, picked the team. Clearly the modernisation of the sport had left a few members of the "blazer brigade" behind.

Things were very different at QPR. There is something very exciting and intoxicating about owning a football team, especially one that you have supported for many years. My success with the Sheffield Sharks did not remotely prepare me for what lay in store at QPR.

From an emotional standpoint, it is impossible to prepare yourself for running a football club. When you walk out on the pitch – the scene of so many great and exciting moments in your life that you witnessed from the stands – and realise this is now something that you actually own, the feeling of exhilaration is quite overwhelming. It is also pretty humbling.

One consequence was that suddenly my profile in the UK changed beyond recognition. Despite having handled the careers of several international superstars, been a reasonably important figure in racing and run a PLC in a sexy industry, nothing compares to owning one of London's leading football clubs. Newspapers ran articles on me, my name was in the press all the time and every cabbie in London recognised me the minute I sat down. I even started appearing regularly on programmes on Radio Five Live and even on TV.

When I created Loftus Road PLC, I was clearly very busy in my role as executive chairman of Chrysalis. I had attempted to set up Loftus Road PLC, QPR and Wasps as an organisational structure in much the same way as you would set up a normal business. However, when it comes to football, all similarities to normal business disappear out of the window completely.

Initially, the fans were overjoyed that I had taken over the club as they knew I was a fan. The Thompsons had always balanced the books by regularly selling their best players, and had sold iconic striker Les Ferdinand to Newcastle United for £6 million the previous summer, replacing him with the less proficient Mark Hateley. This policy had led to the club sinking from the top half of the Premier League to being relegated with one of the lowest points totals that any Premier League side had ever amassed. The bar was thus set pretty low for me to make a good impression.

With QPR, we made mistakes right from the start. The first stupid mistake I made was to complain about the quality of the public address system, which was so bad as to be unlistenable. I spent about £250,000 – God knows where the money went – on a new PA system. It was hardly a top priority.

I inherited Clive Berlin, whom I made chief executive, and Alan Hedges, his assistant, whom I named stadium manager. Before selling the club Richard Thompson, at the time the youngest chairman in the football league, had for some strange reason promoted Berlin to chairman and Hedges to chief executive. So I appeared to be demoting them, which was clearly not a great tactical move.

QPR's player-manager was Ray Wilkins, someone for whom I have enormous respect. He was a great player in his day for Chelsea, Manchester United and England, but he was coming to the end of his playing career, and I wasn't sure that the concept of a player-manager would work with a team that had Premier League aspirations.

I made this point to Clive Berlin, who told me that Ray would only accept being player-manager, and indeed the main reason that he wanted to be manager was so that he could pick himself to play. I kind of accepted this, but after the first board meeting and no more than a couple of weeks into our first season, to my astonishment and with no inkling of it coming Wilkins resigned, leaving us without a manager.

Nick Blackburn and I set about trying to find a replacement. We approached Alan Curbishley, who was doing a very good job with Charlton Athletic, and we agreed a deal with him, but it all fell apart when Charlton found out that we were talking to Curbishley, and refused to let him leave.

Charlton gave Curbishley an improved contract, which was clearly the right decision for them as he went on to take them into the Premier League and keep them there for many years. He was a very good manager, and I think our whole history with QPR could have been different had we secured Alan Curbishley as a manager. (Alan's brother Bill, incidentally, has managed The Who since 1975, and also manages Robert Plant – another music business connection.)

Our second choice was Stewart Houston, who had been the assistant manager to Bruce Rioch at Arsenal. Houston had done a pretty good job at the Gunners as caretaker manager when Rioch was fired in August 1996, before Arsenal decided to bring in an unknown Frenchman named Arsène Wenger.

Houston obviously had experience of coaching players at the top level so Nick and I agreed a contract with him. Clive Berlin visited his home to get the contract signed on his way home from the office. The next morning, I noticed that the signed contract was for a significantly higher salary than the one we had agreed. I found this very strange. I questioned Berlin as to why, and he assured us that Houston had said he wouldn't sign it unless the salary was increased. He gave no explanation as to why he had not first consulted me. This was my first experience of the murky world of football finances.

With hindsight, it was clearly a major mistake on my part not to make a huge fuss about this and demand to know why I had not been called to discuss it. My acquiescence without comment almost seemed to condone a type of behaviour which I would never have permitted in a normal business. But this was football, I didn't understand it fully and I guess I assumed that was just how things worked.

We gave Stewart Houston permission to hire his own assistant and to our surprise he appointed Bruce Rioch, who had been his boss at Arsenal. This felt very odd because Bruce had been the dominant personality in their relationship and this appeared to continue at QPR. He was a disciplinarian of the old school, and his arguably old-fashioned attempts to whip the players into line caused more than a few grumbles.

I had naively expected that I personally would have some sort of role in helping to motivate the players, as I did the staff at Chrysalis, but the players seemed to be on a completely different level. They were not used to having any communication with owners or chairman, they didn't expect it and didn't know how to react to it. And certainly the managers didn't appear to welcome it.

This meant that I was left in a position at QPR where I felt it was very difficult for me to do anything other than just let the management get on with it. I suppose that is how things should operate, but I was unprepared for such an inactive role.

Having, as a fan, seen QPR sell their best players too many times, I wanted to reverse this policy and made it known that none of the star players who had been in our Premier League team the previous season would be allowed to leave. That was another big mistake because I had the feeling that some players felt that playing in a lower league was unappealing. I should have cashed in on those players. I think Trevor Sinclair may have been the only one on our books who would have commanded a large fee, and had I sold him I could have recruited others that would have been happy at the club.

We made a reasonable start to the season, but it was clear we needed to add to the squad, especially after our main striker, Kevin Gallen, collected a cruciate knee ligament injury in the second game of the season. However, Stewart and Bruce were not identifying players they wanted to sign.

I was getting so frustrated by this that at one point, during an Echo Board meeting in Tokyo, I told Nick Blackburn: "Tell Stewart Houston that if he doesn't sign somebody quickly, I will go out and sign somebody myself." Looking back, again, this was a pretty stupid thing for me to do.

We did eventually make some signings, notably Scottish striker John Spencer for £2,350,000 and Gavin Peacock for £800,000, both from near neighbours and local rivals Chelsea. We were certainly turning around the perception of the club as QPR went from being a club that always sold their best players to one splashing the cash out.

The performances improved, but as the end of the season approached, it became clear that we would fall short of automatic promotion back to the Premier League. We were in with a chance of making the play-offs until the penultimate game of the season, at home to Tranmere Rovers, a game we won 2-0. We were depending on other results going our way, and they didn't.

That game took place on the same day that the rugby season ended. I went to Northampton to watch Wasps clinch the championship in a 2.15 p.m. kick-off, and left before the end – while the game was still in the balance – to see the last half-hour of the QPR match. I had probably been at a Sheffield Sharks game the night before!

At the time I bought QPR, club owners were being presented with a whole new set of problems. The European Court had found in favour of a journeyman Belgian player called Jean-Marc Bosman, who had sued his club, Liege, for not allowing him a transfer to Dunkerque in the French league.

The resulting so-called Bosman ruling ended the practice that out-of-contract players could not leave the football club they were signed to without compensation being paid by the club to whom they were signing. The previous situation, unique to football, was an anomaly – why should compensation be paid, as the player no longer had a contract with the original club anyway?

However, it did introduce a whole new set of ground rules. Pre-Bosman, transfer fees had been the main source of income for clubs outside of the top tier of football. Now, clubs had to ensure that their players were on long-term contracts – otherwise, if the contract ended, they had nothing to sell. It thus became the norm to offer half-decent players three or four-year contracts, which also meant having to commit to hefty annual salaries.

The drawback to this was that some players sitting pretty on long-term contracts guaranteeing them six-figure incomes were not as motivated as they might be. At QPR, we ended up with a lot of players on long-term contracts on big wages to protect the value of our assets. Clive Berlin had negotiated all the contracts, and many were in my view generous.

Since Bosman, the balance of power had shifted and football contracts were now to the advantage of the player. Football has become the only business I know where the employer is totally committed but the player feels that, even when he has a contract with the club, he has no commitment whatsoever

If a club wants to sign a star player to a five-year contract for £250,000 a week, they are committed to paying him £250,000 a week for the next five years to play football for them whether he plays well, plays badly, scores goals, doesn't score goals or gets injured. And in many cases players can get injured for a very long period of time. Yet the player himself apparently feels no responsibility whatsoever to uphold his side of the bargain and expects to be able to leave if he can get more money elsewhere or doesn't want to play for the club any more.

We had a similar situation at QPR with John Spencer. He had a hugely successful first season after joining from Chelsea, was our top goalscorer and was voted player of the year by the fans. However, despite the fact that he had a contract for about £400,000 a year, at the start of the following season, he decided that he wanted to go elsewhere. The chief executive told me that we would have to let him go.

"That is ridiculous," I said. "That is not how we do things. He is our best player and he is staying here."

After that, Spencer's performances on the pitch appeared to deteriorate. This was not so evident at home matches, because players in general like to ensure that they stay in favour with the home fans, but certainly his away performances fell below the standard of the previous season. The travelling fans are so completely devoted to their football team that a player can play poorly and get away with it. The home fans are the ones that can get on a player's case if he doesn't perform.

So I reluctantly agreed to sell John Spencer. Everton were willing to pay £1.5 million for him, which meant we had made a loss of £850,000, and he was getting an increase in salary to go there. However, when the deal was on the point of completion, Spencer announced that he wanted a £500,000 pay-off or he wouldn't go.

I was flabbergasted. I had never heard anything like it. How did we resolve this situation? In the end, we split the half a million pounds, Everton paid half and we paid half, and he duly went off to Goodison to have his medical. He was ready to sign when Everton found that he had a medical problem and they wanted to pull out of the deal. At this point, I hit the roof. The last thing I wanted now was the player back. I called the Everton chairman at the time, Peter Johnson, we managed to thrash out an arrangement, and Spencer left.

Spencer's centre-forward role should have gone to Mike Sheron, whom we had signed from Stoke City for £2.75 million, probably in real terms still the largest transfer fee QPR have ever paid. However, either Sheron was injured when we signed him or soon afterwards: he didn't appear at all for the first third of the season and, when he finally did, he contributed very little for a player of that value.

In the meantime, the performances on the pitch had suffered and the crowd started baying for the blood of Stewart Houston, who I considered a decent bloke trying to do an honest job. I must confess that I was influenced by the supporters' constant chanting and I panicked and dismissed Stewart Houston at the end of 1997. He may or may not have been the right appointment in the first place, but I realise now I should have given him longer to try and make things work.

After Houston, I turned again to Alan Curbishley, but once again was unable to persuade Charlton to release him, even after he and I had agreed terms. Instead, at Clive Berlin's insistence, we appointed Ray Harford who had previously been assistant manager to Kenny Dalglish at Blackburn Rovers when they had won the Premier League in 1995.

Harford had struggled to replicate that success when he took over as the manager of Blackburn and had resigned in October 1996. However, he had got off to a good start managing West Bromwich Albion in the First Division after joining them in February 1997. In truth, I was mystified as to why Harford was so keen to leave WBA, a club of some significance and tradition, who were leading the First Division table at the time.

Clive Berlin, who had recommended Harford, told me that Ray was tired of commuting from Berkshire to the West Midlands and wanted to return to London. Clive and Ray enjoyed a very close working relationship during Ray's 10 months at the club, and always insisted on handling the transfer negotiations themselves. It often seemed to me that we were selling good players and replacing them with less skilled ones.

It was difficult to understand the rationale behind many of the transfer dealings. We were paying large fees for mediocre players often for no apparent reason. Sometimes the new signings were of a lesser standard than the players they had replaced. One player, Richard Orr, was signed from Sunderland for £600,000 and clearly had a career-threatening injury at the time as he never once kicked a ball in the blue and white hoops. Another player that never turned out for QPR was a Nigerian goalkeeper called Bankole who we signed from Crewe Alexandra.

It soon became apparent that we were highly unlikely to be promoted to the Premier League after our second season in the First Division. This presented us with major problems. Clubs that are relegated from the Premier League receive two years' worth of "parachute payments" of 50% of the income they would have had if they had stayed in the top league. When the 1997-1998 season came to an end, we would lose this income in all future years. We had spent a good deal of money and in order to remain competitive, we would need to budget to lose a lot more than we were already losing.

Although Loftus Road PLC was a public company listed on the AIM market, it was impossible to ask shareholders for more cash. QPR were only able to continue to operate through my personally guaranteeing the bank loan that was already creeping up into several million pounds.

The more that success eluded us, the more time-consuming and stressful the whole business became. I was trying to balance running QPR with my day job as executive chairman of Chrysalis, not to mention my responsibilities to Wasps and Sheffield Sharks, which were increasingly taking a back seat.

I began to understand the comment made to me by the chairman of Bradford City before a crucial match. Bradford were fighting relegation and desperately needed to beat us to survive at the expense of Grimsby Town, my boyhood team.

Meeting the Bradford chairman in their boardroom, I shook his hand and told him, "I don't envy you today, you must be feeling very nervous."

"It's all right," he told me by way of reply. "I have been to see the doctor and he has given me beta-blockers and Valium, so I should be OK."

"Heaven help me," I thought to myself, "if I ever get to the point that I need beta-blockers and Valium before I can go to a football match." However, the stress of going to QPR soon reached those proportions as the 1997-98 season ended with us avoiding relegation to the Second Division on the last day of the season, despite losing at home to Bury.

In stark contrast, Wasps were going from strength to strength. As they swept to the title in my first year in charge, the original idea was that we would play the major games against the bigger-name teams at Loftus Road, while hosting the lesser lights at the old ground in Sudbury. The Loftus Road experience went so well that we soon started playing all the games there.

In my second season, we played in the Heineken Cup and beat Toulouse 77-17, a 60-point victory against one of the biggest rugby union teams in Europe, at an ecstatic Loftus Road. With the ground at Sudbury surplus to requirements, we made arrangements to sell it for redevelopment. The previous Wasps committee had always advised us this would not be possible, yet after having two planning-permission applications turned down, we eventually won permission to develop the ground and sold it for close to £10 million, which allowed us to reduce Loftus Road PLC's rapidly escalating overdraft and stave off any financial threats to the two clubs for a year or so.

Perversely, QPR fans were always upset that Wasps were performing better than they were but little did they know that, without the income from the sale of the Wasps ground, the impending financial crisis at QPR would have been greatly accelerated.

The fans' dissatisfaction was growing as, under Ray Harford, QPR continued to languish at the bottom end of the table. I was beside myself with concern when I had lunch at Langan's Brasserie with Ken Bates who at the time still owned Chelsea, and David Mellor, the former MP for Putney and Tory cabinet member. We discussed the problems I was having and they suggested that maybe Vinnie Jones could play a role at QPR.

I was surprised by this idea but Bates and Mellor told me that on a recent Chelsea trip to Canada to play pre-season friendlies, Vinnie had galvanised team spirit and organised events for the players whilst they were off the pitch. They said that he was an all-round positive influence. He had since returned to Wimbledon, the club where he had made his name.

It seemed worth a try so David Mellor set up a meeting for Nick Blackburn and I to meet with Vinnie. We were both impressed by how he came over so I told Ray Harford and Clive Berlin to sign him. Instead they signed George Kulscar, an Australian player who they said could perform the same role. Quite why we signed Kulscar I have no idea, and things went from bad to worse.

Eventually, with relegation ever more threatening, I pulled rank, overrode everyone and said, "Sign Vinnie Jones" which we duly did. We paid Wimbledon £500,000, which even Vinnie still feels was grossly over-inflated. He asked to be made player/assistant manager as a condition of joining us, which I agreed to.

With Vinnie on board, we needed seven points from seven games to guarantee avoiding the drop. His QPR career got off to a great start when he scored a spectacular goal in his opening match at Huddersfield.

Yet it was becoming clear that the defining point of the season would take place at Maine Road when we played away against Manchester City, who were also struggling to avoid relegation. The loser was pretty sure to be condemned but a draw would have guaranteed QPR safety.

For so many reasons, including the fact that I always supported City when I was at university in Manchester, the match was an incredibly traumatic experience for me. I don't think I have ever witnessed a football game with so much drama and emotion. My mouth was so dry that I must have drunk a gallon of water during the 90 minutes.

As the teams ran out on the pitch, I saw a couple of City stewards chasing after Vinnie. It transpired that in the tunnel before the teams came out he had been in a fracas with City's star player Georgi Kinkladze, their skilful talisman from the former Soviet state of Georgia.

Straight from the kick-off, with City on the attack, Vinnie scythed down Kinkladze just outside the QPR penalty box. The referee went for his pocket. My heart was in my mouth because it seemed a pretty clear-cut red card. Vinnie has the record for the earliest red card in a football match, but fortunately, probably because it was so early in the game, Vinnie got away with a caution. However, from the resulting free kick, Kinkladze found the top corner of the net so we were a goal down inside a minute. What a dreadful start!

Halfway through the first half, drama unfolded at the other end when a City player passed the ball back to their goalie, Martyn Margetson, who picked it up about two metres off the goal line, resulting in a QPR free kick. Despite City planting all the 11 players on the line, Mike Sheron scored. Then City's captain, Jamie Pollock, scored the most amazing own goal, one that would have been goal of the year had it been in the opposition's net. So we went in ahead at half-time.

City equalised just after the restart. It was looking dire, and things got much worse when our key midfielder, Nigel Quashie, was sent off. City needed to score only once to avoid the drop, but in an amazingly tense finish QPR held on for a 2-2 draw.

The result proved just enough and QPR managed to avoid relegation the following weekend, on the last day of the season. Manchester City went down, despite winning 5-2 at Stoke on the same day. Many QPR fans voted for Jamie Pollock as their player of the season for his stunning own goal.

Worryingly, the 1998/9 season for QPR started off pretty much how the previous had finished. A couple of months in, following a 4-0 defeat away to Oxford United which Nick described as the worst team performance he had ever seen, we decided we had to sack Ray Harford. He actually resigned before he was pushed, with a piece of parting advice: "Whatever you do, don't make Vinnie manager."

I was inclined to agree with him. During the close season, Vinnie had made his acting debut in the hit London gangster movie *Lock, Stock And Two Smoking Barrels* produced by Guy Richie. London was covered with posters of Vinnie balancing two double-barrel shotguns on his shoulders and his life seemed to consist of first-night premieres and media appearances.

Vinnie didn't seem to have the time to commit 100% to the difficult job of managing QPR, and by all accounts he was also a divisive figure. Nick Blackburn and Clive Berlin told me that some players in the dressing-room would run through fire for Vinnie, while others were rather less enamoured of our hard man.

I was thus faced with the difficult task of telling Vinnie that we were losing Ray Harford but not giving him the manager's job. Vinnie was pretty upset with me at the time, although whenever I see him nowadays, living a fantastic life in Los Angeles, I remind him that his route to Hollywood might never have opened up had he taken on the management of a struggling Division One football team.

Instead, we appointed reserve-team coach Iain Dowie as caretaker manager and set about looking for a full-time replacement. The QPR fans often chanted the name of Gerry Francis, an iconic former player and captain who, as manager, had steered the club to fifth in the Premier League in its first season. I knew they would love him back.

Gerry, who recently resigned from managing Tottenham Hotspur, phoned me up, saying he wanted to talk to me about a musical on the life of Helen of Troy that he was hoping to co-produce with record producer Dave Mackay. We had several meetings about Helen of Troy, and whenever football came up, he insisted that he was not interested in a role at QPR. Nevertheless, I managed to persuade him to return as manager: I am still not sure today whether Helen of Troy was a reality or if it was a front for him to get back to QPR!

We lost our first five matches under Gerry who, furthermore, made it clear that Vinnie Jones was not part of his future plans. Gerry insisted that Nick Blackburn and I break the news to Vinnie that his contract was being terminated. This was nerve-racking and once again Vinnie was understandably upset.

We stuttered towards the end of the season and yet again found ourselves needing to win our last match, at home to Crystal Palace, to avoid relegation. Where was that Valium and beta-blockers? Luckily, we did so in style, thumping them 6-0.

The 1999/2000 season was a bit of a false dawn as we finished the season comfortably in 10th place and even dared to dream of a return to the Premier League. However, the following season, things took a marked turn for the worst.

Loftus Road PLC was well and truly running out of money. The cash from the sale of the Wasps training ground had been spent on paying off debt and running costs, and we were back to the point where only my personally guaranteeing loans and my supportive bank manager were keeping the club afloat.

Elsewhere, my divorce from Chelle was about to be finalised, with all the financial outlay that would involve, which meant that I was about to breach all my loan covenants. Something clearly needed to be done.

QPR had a couple of players that we felt would command decent transfer fees: midfielder Richard Langley and defender Clarke Carlisle. Both players were young, with a good future ahead of them. However, in February 2001, Rangers' season and our financial plans all came crashing down with a thud.

We had two home local derbies in quick succession. The first one was on a Saturday against Arsenal in the FA Cup, where we put on a brave show in the first hour but were routed 6-0. The fans were outraged, and rather than folk hero Gerry Francis, I became the target of their ire.

Three days later, we were at home in the league to a very strong Fulham side that was challenging for promotion with billionaire Harrods owner Mohamed Al Fayed's money behind them. After about 15 minutes, Richard Langley went down under a strong challenge, clutching his knee. It was blindingly obvious that he had ruptured his anterior cruciate ligament, which would require 12 months of recuperation.

They say lightning never strikes twice. Ten minutes later, in an identical situation, the exact same thing happened to Clarke Carlisle. In the blink of an eye, QPR had lost our best two players, and our only two saleable ones, and with it any chance of a financial lifeline. It would have been difficult to lose any player with the club struggling and needing all the help on the pitch, but at least selling one of them would have staved off any financial threat.

Fulham beat us 2-0 and the fans were baying for my blood. As the game neared its end, there were several attempts to break into the directors' box. Death threats started arriving in the post and over the internet. This was no fun any more and I decided I had had enough, resigning as chairman, although I still owned the club and I was the club's only source of financial lifeline. Nick Blackburn replaced me as chairman.

We lost both our next two matches 5-0, against Preston and Wimbledon. Understandably, Gerry Francis was by now also feeling the stress. If I did not want to be the chairman who was responsible for QPR being relegated to the Second Division, Gerry did not want it against his name either. He duly resigned too.

Nick Blackburn and I interviewed potential replacements in Steve Coppell, Dave Bassett and Steve Bruce but, in the end, partly on the advice of Gerry Francis, we gave the job to an ex-QPR player, Ian Holloway, who had done a great job at Bristol Rovers. Holloway – Ollie as he was known – was to prove a good manager, but it was too late for him to weave his magic that season and QPR were relegated to the third level of English football for the first time in three decades.

By this time, we were losing over £5 million a year. I worked out that it was costing me about £200,000 a match to watch Rangers play, which would have been an extortionate sum even if I had been enjoying myself and not sustaining abuse from the fans. Furthermore, with so much of the expense related to player wages, it was difficult to make any meaningful changes to improve the bottom line.

By now I had relieved myself of Clive Berlin and subsequently appointed as chief executive Simon Crane, who prior to working in sports marketing in America had been in the military. One of his ideas was to save £20 per game by reducing the quality of the wine served in the chairman's suite from mediocre to undrinkable. I felt that I would rather lose £200,020 per game and drown my sorrows in something drinkable!

I knew it was futile trying to save on the costs of such things as the flower arrangements in the executive boxes, when it was the players' salaries that were the real issue. My position was not helped by the fact that our rivals, Fulham, were owned by a multi-billionaire in the form of Mohamed Al-Fayed and shortly after Chelsea would be taken over by the even richer Russian oligarch Roman Abramovich. With reported losses at Stamford Bridge of over £1 million a week I imagine it could well cost Abramovich over a couple of million each time he watches Chelsea play, but he can afford it.

Nick and I were focused on trying to keep QPR alive financially. I had hit the wall and couldn't provide any further financing. We tried very hard to find a new owner, holding a series of meetings with various chancers, all of whom claimed to be worth millions, all of whom we met in the boardroom and all of whom eventually turned out to be tyre-kickers.

Meanwhile, my name was mud among the fans. I had recently lent the club £1 million to buy the training ground from British Gas pension fund, and now, to prevent the club going into administration, I bought it back myself at an inflated price of £2.5 million. Inevitably, this incensed the fans as they all imagined I had conducted some sort of underhand deal in order to line my pockets.

Someone even suggested that the training ground was actually worth £40 million for development purposes, and so I had to enter into several covenants concerning any potential profit I would make if the land were sold for development – despite the fact that it had been purchased for the club with my own money in the first instance. In actual fact, that land is now the training ground for Wasps. The trustees of the old Wasps amateur club bought it back a few years ago and I made a loss on the deal.

For the rest of the relegation season, I hardly went to any matches at all – I certainly avoided the home games, as the abuse aimed at me was way too stressful. I got into the habit on match days of playing tennis at the Queen's Club from 3 p.m. to 5 p.m. I would turn my phone on at the end of the match. If I had a dozen messages, I would know we had won. If I had no messages, we would have lost. Normally, there were no messages.

But with no other options available, we pursued some off-the-wall ideas. One was an approach from Pete Winkelman who was trying to put together a team to play at Milton Keynes. He was interested in buying QPR for this purpose, but we rejected this out of hand – QPR had too much history and legacy to go down this route, and belonged in west London.

The chairman of Wimbledon contacted us to suggest merging QPR and Wimbledon. Wimbledon had been relegated from the Premier League two seasons before but had a reasonable squad and were being bankrolled by two very rich Norwegians. However they had no stadium and were playing their home matches at Crystal Palace.

The idea was the team would be called 'QPR and Wimbledon', play in blue and white hoops and be bankrolled by the Norwegians. They had good players and money and QPR had a stadium and a fanbase. But before we could go any further, the news was leaked by a Wimbledon director and both sets of fans revolted. Instead, Wimbledon, with nowhere else to go, and with the rich Norwegians eventually pulling out, ended up being the team that fulfilled Pete Winkleman's dreams in Milton Keynes and became the MK Dons.

I must have been desperate when I approached John Madejski, the owner of Reading, about merging with them, and playing as QPR at the Madejski Stadium. I felt this could work rather well, as both teams played in the same strip, blue and white hoops. John understandably – and sensibly – dismissed the idea out of hand, leaving us no option but to accept that Loftus Road PLC would have to go into administration.

By now both David Hudd and Mark Rigby had resigned from the board: as professional accountants and surveyors, their careers could be severely damaged by a business of which they were directors entering administration. At that time there was no points penalty for a football club entering administration but for a rugby club, it was elimination from the Premiership, so we had to split the two clubs up. I bought Wasps out of Loftus Road PLC at a value of £2.5 million, somewhat less than I had originally paid for them, but a figure that represented their value at that time following the sale of their ground at Sudbury. This at least replenished the QPR coffers for a while. In future, both clubs would operate as separate entities.

At the same time Mohamed Al-Fayed decided that he needed to redevelop Craven Cottage to make the ground fit for Premier League football. This meant that Fulham would need to ground share for a couple of years and the only real option he had was to share at Loftus Road.

Fulham manager Jean Tigana refused to play there if Wasps were also in situ. He couldn't conceive how the pitch would take the wear and tear from two football teams and a rugby club. So, in order to make the thing work financially, and so that QPR could receive some income from Fulham, I moved Wasps out of Loftus Road, to accommodate Fulham.

We had a choice of the Kassam Stadium in Oxford or Adams Park in Wycombe, and although the Kassam is a wonderful ground and was our first choice, I could not agree a deal with the owner, Firoz Kassam. So we temporarily, in theory, relocated Wasps to Wycombe, where over the next few years Wasps enjoyed some of the most memorable moments in the life of any club.

Sadly, the last ever match that Wasps played at Loftus Road saw groups of QPR fans, who were travelling back from an away match at Wolves, descend on the ground to stage yet another protest. This led to me leaving Loftus Road, for the last time, via a side entrance with a police escort and with Janice and a terrified seven-year-old Holly at my side. It was to be many years before I ventured back to Loftus Road, although I have occasionally seen QPR play away, usually at the invitation of the directors of the away team.

I ended up writing off the bulk of my loans and leaving the club in the hands of the remaining directors, Nick Blackburn, David Davies and Ross Jones, who ran the club for almost three years. The last few turbulent years have seen QPR reclaim their place in the Premier League amidst a soap opera of constantly changing big-name owners but despite the funding from Tony Fernadez, the current incumbent, who incidentally once worked in the finance department of Virgin Records in London, the club are now back in the Championship (the old first division). I did eventually return to Loftus Road on the occasion of my son Tim's 40th birthday in January of 2013, to watch a goalless draw between Rangers and Manchester City which I felt was particularly poignant after all the drama and emotion at Maine Road several years previously. It was a bitter sweet moment.

As part of the deal when I relinquished the QPR chairmanship, I was given six seats in the Directors' Box for all future matches and the title of Life Vice President. I still hold the hope that one day – and in happier circumstances – I will be able to return regularly to Loftus Road.

CHAPTER 25

Sing It Back

Parallel to my time consuming commitments to both QPR and Wasps much was going on at Chrysalis across all the various areas in which we were involved. With the Pony Canyon deal concluded, Steve Lewis and I set about launching the Echo label in 1994, but tensions started to develop between us. Understandably, having brought in the $17.5 million investment from Pony Canyon, Steve felt he should have a major say in the way the label was run.

It soon became clear that his view of a record label was somewhat different from mine. My philosophy stemmed from what we had accomplished with Chrysalis Records, while Steve's was formed at Virgin – and the two companies had their own separate traits and characters. In addition, Steve had not been fundamentally involved in Virgin Records, but principally with Virgin Music.

My instinct was to start with a bang, a huge marquee signing to put a marker down, but Steve wanted to sign Julian Cope. I had nothing against Julian but he was hardly a major name by then. His hits had all been in the early eighties with The Teardrop Explodes, and by the mid-nineties he had diversified into writing books and developing an interest in paganism and megalithic monuments. A dictionary definition of a cult artist, he was never really going to be a major success, or the artist to launch the label in the spectacular fashion that I had in mind.

Steve had his way and *Autogeddon* by Julian Cope was the first album on Echo in July 1994. It reached number 16 in the album charts after we arranged an appearance on *Top Of The Pops* for an 'album performance' of 'I Gotta Walk', but it didn't give Echo the big splash I wanted. But Julian looked the part, with his head half shaved and wearing nothing but a tunic split down the sides.

Julian's next album, *20 Mothers*, did have a hit single in 'Try, Try, Try', produced by Ed Stasium, who played guitar and "sprinkled some fairy dusty on it", as Julian put it. Cope could make the occasional radio-friendly track but it wasn't what he was about any more and we pulled the plug after his next album, *Interpreter*, in 1996.

This rather flat start was typical of the annoyingly slow pace at which Echo was developing. Too many early signings turned out to be essentially vanity projects. Orang comprised Lee Harris and Paul Webb from Talk Talk, and were as self-indulgent and impenetrable as their previous band had been after its initial success in the eighties.

I was more excited by Melanie Garside, whose *Fossil* album received excellent reviews that compared her to Annie Lennox, but it just didn't work out. Denim were a quirky project led by Lawrence, the arch indie figure from Felt, yet their ironic take on glam-rock attracted no more than a knowing cult following who loved songs like 'The Great Pub Rock Revival' and 'It Fell Off The Back Of A Lorry'.

It was deeply frustrating but things improved when we signed Babybird in 1996. The band was built around Stephen Jones, a very prolific artist from Sheffield, who enjoyed a massive success with his first single, 'You're Gorgeous', a winningly twisted love song with an irresistible chorus that sold 400,000 copies and hit number three in the chart.

Unfortunately, 'You're Gorgeous' turned out to be a one-off for Babybird and not very representative of the lo-fi recordings he had made previously. He struggled to follow it up, although the *Ugly Beautiful* album became the first Top 10 album on Echo and 'Candy Girl' made the Top 20 in 1997.

In the way that some artists are, Stephen Jones was his own worst enemy and seemed determined to sabotage his career before it got off the ground. He upset *New Musical Express* by being highly critical of it at a London showcase gig – not a smart move as it had been one of his earliest and biggest supporters. He disappeared after a couple more albums, although I understand he has written two novels and has reformed the band – but it was yet another false start for Echo.

Thankfully, our next success had a little more stamina. Moloko were the trip-hop hued electro-pop couple of multi-instrumentalist Mark Brydon and Irish singer Róisín Murphy, who introduced herself to him at a party with the chat-up line "Do you like my tight sweater?" That became the title of their debut album for Echo in 1995 and we persevered with them after they had a minor hit the following year with 'Fun For Me'.

It paid off. In 1999 a club remix of Moloko's track 'Sing It Back' by German JD Boris Dlugosch was played to death in Ibiza and hit number four in the UK. They went two places better the next year with a similarly infectious club track, 'The Time Is Now'.

Mark and Róisín were initially in two minds about the success of 'Sing It Back' as Dlugosch's remix was so radically different from their original track. The duo were happy to accept the kudos but didn't want to include the remix on their next album, *Things To Make And Do*. We argued for weeks until they reluctantly agreed to add it as a final track: had they not done so, I doubt the record would have gone on to sell the 750,000 copies it achieved.

Sadly, Mark and Róisín then split up as a couple and made a difficult record dissecting their break-up. *Statues* was not at all what their club-going audience was looking for. More happily, Sky Sports snapped up 'The Time Is Now' as the theme for its Premier League broadcasts. As we had also signed both Babybird and Moloko to

Chrysalis Music Publishing we did well out of licensing their songs to movies, video games, TV shows and commercials. In fact, I believe 'Sing It Back' has appeared on more than 100 compilation albums.

Hewn from a similar electro-pop cloth to Moloko were Morcheeba, who had signed to Chrysalis Music at the start of their career in the mid-nineties and then joined Echo after making four albums for China and Warner Brothers. They never had major hits but we licensed their distinctive, mellow mood into countless ads, films and TV shows such as *Buffy The Vampire Slayer*.

Morcheeba's two albums for Echo, *The Antidote* in 2005 and *Dive Deep* in 2008, did well in Europe. *Dive Deep* included two wonderful guest vocals by Judie Tzuke, who had been signed to Chrysalis as a solo artist in the early eighties, which was a nice nod to the company's previous incarnation.

The rock band Feeder were another slow burn. Singer and guitarist Grant Nicholas and drummer Jon Lee were Welsh while bassist Taka Hirose came from Japan, a factor that helped Pony Canyon in its own market. Their post-grunge sound found favour with the readers of *Metal Hammer* and *Kerrang!*. Radio One playlisted their single 'High' in 1997, enabling them to break through to a new audience and their career went on an upward trajectory.

Each Feeder release did better than the previous one, with their third album, *Echo Park*, selling 400,000 copies and the single 'Buck Rogers' making the Top 5 in 2001. Unfortunately, tragedy struck at the start of 2002 when Jon Lee committed suicide while suffering from depression.

Grant and Taka made the difficult decision to continue as a group and the subsequent album, *Comfort In Sound*, reflected on Jon's passing and seemed to tap into the gentler side of Grant's writing. The album went platinum, with sales above 400,000 in the UK alone, as Feeder became the best-selling act on Echo. Their success even enabled the label to turn a small profit for the first time in 2003. After support tours to Stereophonics and Coldplay, Feeder looked to be on their way to the big league.

One senior move behind the scenes at Chrysalis was not a success. In 1996, Steve Lewis removed Tom Sturges who was running Chrysalis Music in America. Tom had a great pedigree, having worked at Chrysalis Music Publishing since 1985 and signed alternative rock bands Smashing Pumpkins and Tripping Daisy as well as OutKast, Montell Jordan and The Goodie Mob on the rap and R&B side. The Goodie Mob featured Cee-Lo Green who went on to join Gnarls Barkley and have a glittering solo career before re-signing with us. It was Tom who placed *I Knew You Were Waiting For Me* by Simon Climie and Dennis Morgan, with Aretha Franklin and George Michael in 1987, and also gave 'Where Do Broken Hearts Go?' to Whitney Houston.

Tom Sturges and I were pretty close, something that Steve Lewis was not used to in a business relationship. Personally I would have not agreed to let Tom go, but Steve managed to convince the group board during the time when I was having issues with the non-executive directors. Tom did himself no favours by naming the company to whom his songwriter wife, Antonina Damato, was signed as Tom Sturges Music. He went on to be Executive Vice President and Head Of Creative at Universal Music Publishing in the US.

To replace Tom, Steve brought in a friend of his, Leeds Levy, who had run MCA Music in the US. Leeds did a decent job of running the American company from an administrative standpoint, but I never saw him as the cutting-edge creative person that a creative independent company needs.

Around this time we started opening European offices for the publishing company. We'd had a major presence in Scandinavia since the purchase of Air Music there in 1975 and we also opened offices in Paris, Amsterdam and Munich. In 1999, we bought Global Music Group, the largest German independent company, from Peter Kirsten and created Global Chrysalis Music Publishing. We then launched Chrysalis Clip in Spain, a joint venture with Julio Guiu's Clippers Music, and since then Julio and I have become very close friends.

The same year we also launched Papillon, named after the French for butterfly, and therefore referencing Chrysalis. It was my idea, although we brought in old Chrysalis stalwart Roy Eldridge and his colleague Mike Andrews to run it. I wanted to start a label for what are now called heritage acts: established artists with loyal fanbases who were being dropped by major record companies and needed a home. Fittingly, we started with Jethro Tull and their album *J-Tull Dot Com*.

We also enjoyed a Top 5 album on Echo with *In My Life*, Sir George Martin's farewell record. It was an inspired collection of Beatles songs recorded by acts like Robin Williams, Goldie Hawn, Jim Carrey and Sean Connery as well as musicians such as Phil Collins and Jeff Beck. Connery's narration of *In My Life* was used for a major commercial throughout South East Asia for a real estate company, which Connery was not too pleased about, feeling the advertising agency had secured a voiceover without going through the usual channels. We had tried to reach Connery to tell him about it but were unable to do so before the deal had to be concluded, and when he found about it he was somewhat dismayed. We did receive a very large fee for it, however.

By 1999, Cliff Richard had been having hits for four decades on EMI, but the way he was treated epitomised the way the music industry had become obsessed with youth. He had recorded 'The Millennium Prayer', which blended the words of *The Lord's Prayer* with the tune of 'Auld Lang Syne'. Paul Deal, a Christian musician and songwriter, had come up with the idea but EMI didn't want to release it as a Christmas single.

I thought that was ludicrous and through Mike Andrews, who shared Cliff's religious beliefs, we offered to put the Cliff Richard track out on Papillon. We found that most radio stations wouldn't play 'The Millennium Prayer': not Radio 1, not Radio 2, not even the Chrysalis-owned Heart FM.

Cliff sang the track on a special *An Audience With Cliff Richard* show on ITV two days before we put the single out in November. It promptly became Cliff's 14th number one, and spent three weeks at the top in December. Cliff went on to have two more hits on Papillon with 'Somewhere Over The Rainbow'/'What A Wonderful World' and 'Let Me Be The One'.

Unfortunately, none of the other heritage acts on Papillon turned out to have a fanbase as dedicated as Cliff's. We signed The Human League, Terrorvision, Deacon Blue and Monaco and reunited with another former Chrysalis act, World Party, but all to no avail.

Conceptually, Papillon was a good idea, but it never really worked and we closed down the label in 2001. I'm not quite sure what went wrong as other labels like Proper and Cooking Vinyl have followed a similar business plan and made it work with some degree of success. As the consumption of music moves more towards the internet and downloading, increasingly heritage artists are able to do a great deal of this themselves and no longer have the need for labels like Papillon.

Our music publishing business remained a more secure and reliable source of income than our record company because of the innate differences between the two businesses. Whereas a record company makes almost 100% of its income from the sale of CDs and downloads, a music publishing company collects royalties on behalf of the songwriters for the use of their songs and thus has many more revenue sources.

Songwriters can earn money via songs being played on radio and television stations throughout the world, or licensed specifically for use in TV and radio commercials and in feature films. Furthermore, although a music publisher spends money finding and developing talent, he is not normally making albums, paying the production costs, shooting videos or paying artists tour support.

Creative publishers can put writers together and make magic. Procol Harum's 'A Whiter Shade of Pale' had come about when an enterprising publisher called David Platz at Essex Music teamed up piano-playing vocalist Gary Brooker and non-performing lyricist Keith Reid. Another publisher, Ray Williams, put together Elton John and the lyricist Bernie Taupin to create one of the most successful songwriting partnerships of all time.

Another example of a creative publisher doing his job well was 'Three Lions' by The Lightning Seeds with Baddiel and Skinner. When the Euro 96 football tournament was coming around, Jeremy Lascelles was aware that the FA would look to release an official tournament song.

Jeremy was amazed to learn that the FA was in talks with Black Grape to write and record the official song with the England team. Black Grape's singer was Shaun Ryder, a notorious drug abuser in his years with Happy Mondays. At the time the FA was waging a war against drug-taking in the sport, so Jeremy contacted the agent who was commissioning the song and gently pointed out the contradiction.

Jeremy suggested that Chrysalis Music had the ideal artist and writer for the gig: Lightning Seeds singer Ian Broudie, a football fanatic whose song 'The Life Of Riley' had been extensively used by *Match Of The Day* for its *Goal Of The Month* competition.

The FA was keen immediately as, unsurprisingly, was Ian. He was running very late on his next album for his label, Epic, and to its chagrin turned his attention instead to a Euro 96 anthem. He already had a song that he had half-written, which he played down the phone to Jeremy.

At that stage the tune had no lyrics, but the melody and the chorus were instantly memorable, and the song was quite light and whimsical – almost Beach Boys-like. Ian said that he could drop the key, change the tempo to make it more "laddish and sing-a-long", which he thought would work well.

We then had the inspired idea of asking Frank Skinner and David Baddiel to write lyrics and sing the song with him. Now Frank and David had no experience at all of songwriting or singing, but they were riding high at the time with their football comedy series *Fantasy Football League*. Their lyrics were brilliant, with "Thirty years of hurt/ Never stopped me dreaming" a particularly inspired line.

When 'Three Lions' was released, it was an instant hit, going straight into the charts at number one, but what no one had quite anticipated was the way the crowds at the England games adopted the song as a terrace chant. It became almost a national anthem for the country that summer, and is still to this day chanted – usually with adapted words – by football fans, not only in this country but internationally as well.

Incidentally, Black Grape did release their own record, called 'England's Irie', for which they had roped in ex-Clash frontman Joe Strummer, as well as actor Keith Allen. But they didn't stand a chance against The Lightning Seeds and 'Three Lions'.

In 2005 we put Dan Wilson of the American band Semisonic with The Dixie Chicks and together they wrote six tracks for the group's *Taking The Long Way* album, amongst them 'Not Ready To Make Nice'. Dan went on to collaborate with Adele and has three co-writes on her *21* album, including the arresting 'Someone Like You', which has since become a classic.

Another interesting Chrysalis Music Publishing signing was Rod Temperton. A Lincolnshire lad like me, Rod had written some fantastic songs such as 'Boogie Nights' for his group Heatwave and then 'Give Me The Night' for George Benson and 'Ya Mo Be There' for James Ingram and Michael McDonald.

Rod's big break had come in 1979 as a result of his friendship with Quincy Jones, who was producing Michael Jackson. They were struggling for songs and Quincy asked him to come up with a couple. Rod sent in three and thought no more of it until a few weeks later when he ran into Quincy. He asked him whether they were any good and was told they had all made *Off The Wall*: the title track, 'Rock With You' and 'Burn This Disco Out'.

The same thing happened with the next Michael Jackson album: *Thriller*. Again Rod submitted three compositions: 'The Lady In My Life', 'Baby Be Mine' and 'Thriller', the title track. He told me he was still coming up with the rap for Vincent Price on his way to the studio. The rest is history.

Despite the fact that Rod has spent most of his life either in Germany or in Los Angeles, he has never lost his broad Lincolnshire accent. A fascinating character, he takes a group of friends every year to an island in Fiji. He has become a close friend: his wife, Kathy, gets on particularly well with Janice.

The successes of Chrysalis Music Publishing enabled us to back some of our struggling writers to the hilt. If a record company won't fund the making of an album, publishers will sometimes step in. After David Gray lost record deals first with Virgin then with EMI, we kept him afloat. Jeremy Lascelles always believed in David's talent. He was the one who had signed him to Virgin in 1992 but, after three stiff albums, he had a hard time convincing Steve Lewis that David was worth persevering with and that we should give him a publishing deal when Warner/Chappell lost interest.

We kept David going and helped him to make *White Ladder* on a shoestring budget in 1998. The initial ambition was to recover the recording costs and sell enough copies in Ireland to allow David to continue touring there. *White Ladder* ended up selling over seven million copies worldwide, and reinvigorated the singer-songwriter scene and genre.

Like record labels, publishing companies make mistakes and there are those that got away. Our biggest blunder was probably The Spice Girls. Chrysalis Records and the Echo label had always looked for long-term artists with inherent and unique creativity, and we applied the same criterion to the writers that we signed to the publishing company.

The Spice Girls turned up in our building with Simon Fuller and caused quite a stir in Jeremy's office. Miming to a backing track of 'Wannabe', they stood on his desk and ended up sitting on his knee, not quite the sort of thing we were used to.

Nevertheless, they clearly had something, so we agreed a deal which involved an advance of £250,000. Before the paperwork was confirmed, however, they had made a similar visit to Windswept Music, run by our old alumnus Bob Grace. Windswept bid £300,000, and we were asked to top that with a bid of £325,000.

Steve Lewis refused and that was that. The Spice Girls signed a publishing deal with Windswept instead. We clearly should have gone the extra yard, but no one dared ask me for my opinion. Later, they speculated on what my reaction would have been had they suggested that they wanted to pay that kind of money for a group of five girls, only one of whom could sing, and whose involvement in the writing of their material was minimal!

However, sometimes A&R is about more than just what you hear: you can often smell a hit, even if the basic components are lacking. The Spice Girls were the antithesis of everything we stood for, but they were a lot of fun, and it would have been great to have had them around.

In 2001 Steve Lewis left the company. I was unable to agree terms with him when his contract was up and he chose to leave. During his time as CEO, Chrysalis Music had grown into the UK's top independent publisher, although credit was also due to Jeremy Lascelles and his team who had also been responsible for signing artistes such as Portishead, Leftfield and Skunk Anansie.

When Jeremy assumed full control, the first thing he did was to remove Leeds Levy from Chrysalis Music in the US and bring in Kenny MacPherson, a Scottish guy who had started out in artist management and had been living in America for years. He had many years of experience as a music publisher with Warner/Chappell, and came to us with a much more cutting edge, artist-friendly vibe.

To replace Jeremy as MD of Chrysalis Music UK we managed to poach Alison Donald to join us from Warner Music. This was to prove to be an inspired appointment, as Alison was responsible for much of the success of the UK company throughout the first decade of the 21st century.

She signed a variety of different artists, all of whom had great credibility and went on to generate huge income for the company, artists like the Yeah Yeah Yeahs, led by Karen O, and Gossip with Beth Ditto. She also signed two cutting-edge American acts, Fleet Foxes and Bon Iver.

They were joined by two extremely interesting and talented ladies, Laura Marling, a new age folk singer who writes poignant songs and whose second album somehow managed not to win a Mercury Music award despite clearly being the obvious candidate, and Rumor, an Anglo Asian girl with a very interesting background and a fantastic voice, a cross between Karen Carpenter, Sade and Norah Jones.

With the help of Ben Bodie we also signed to a songwriting deal the producer-artist Brian Burton, aka Danger Mouse. Teaming up with Cee Lo Green he had a huge hit with the song 'Crazy', a number one throughout the world and the first single in England to ever reach number one on downloads alone. We later signed Cee Lo as a writer just in time to take advantage of another huge hit with 'Fuck You', which had to become 'Forget You' on the radio.

Over in America the Grammy Awards of 2007 were a real highlight. Our writer Dan Wilson had worked with The Dixie Chicks on their album *Taking The Long Way*, which scooped five Grammys, including album of the year and song of the year for 'Not Ready To Make Nice'. The awards were controversial at the time as The Dixie Chicks had lost a large part of their country base in the States following lead singer Natalie Maines' announcement, at a concert at the Shepherd's Bush Empire, that they were ashamed to come from the same State as George Bush, i.e. Texas, and for his role in the Iraq War.

Jeremy and I also started to grapple with the fact that Echo was haemorrhaging money at an alarming rate. Apart from the year when Feeder came up trumps, Echo had never been profitable.

Why was this? The record business model was changing drastically. In 2005, Echo had what appeared to be a very exciting release schedule with albums by Ray LaMontagne, Feeder, Black Rebel Motorcycle Club and Morcheeba. It turned out to be the label's best ever year in terms of sales and turnover, and its worst in terms of losses: over £2 million.

The problem was that the major labels, Universal in particular, had changed the rules of engagement. If they got a sniff of success they spent so much money on marketing their records that smaller labels like Echo felt obliged to spend a comparable sum just to remain competitive.

Whilst this was Universal's way of trying to blow their major rivals out of the water, it couldn't care less – and maybe even liked it – if it also killed off the smaller independent labels. We couldn't compete, and it was at this point that we decided to change Echo from being effectively a mini-major into an incubator label, designed to help and develop artists signed to our publishing company.

One of the strengths of Echo as a record company was that we continued to take a long-term view, as we had with Chrysalis. We had already entered an era where the major labels had no patience with their acts, in part due to the level of their marketing costs. If a project did not connect right from the off, the act would be dropped.

Very few follow-up albums were made unless the debut had gone platinum or thereabouts. In that climate, it is very much to Echo's credit that we broke both Feeder and Moloko on their third albums. Had either band been signed to a major, they would never have made a second, let alone a third, album.

When we turned Echo into an incubator label, Feeder were still our most successful act but we knew they couldn't keep Echo afloat if too many other acts like Engineers, I Am Kloot or The Stands carried on losing money. It was the disappointing sales of Feeder's next album, *Pushing The Senses*, in 2005 that clinched our decision to downsize.

We cut a clever deal with EMI to distribute *The Singles* compilation by Feeder in the UK the following year. It was a joint venture, not a distribution deal, whereby EMI paid all the marketing costs – including several hundred thousand pounds of TV advertising – and we made an extremely healthy profit on sales in excess of 500,000 in the UK.

It was telling, however, that the next Feeder album, *Silent Cry*, was a disaster. It's surprising how often that happens after a group release a greatest hits album: people just assume it's the end of their career.

Functioning as a smaller, incubator label concentrating on artists who were signed to Chrysalis Music Publishing, Echo continued to be very artist-friendly and creative in our approach to how we developed the acts. The plan was to give an album a low-key indie release with a minimal marketing budget, develop the project to the point where there was a genuine underground buzz building, and then license the artist to a major for a substantial deal whereby we recovered our initial investment, split the balance of the advance with the artist, and continued to act as the creative conduit for them.

The marketing clout of the major would then, all being well, sell the album through in significant quantities, and we would make money on an override, and of course by virtue of being the publisher. We did this very successfully with three artists in particular: Ray LaMontagne, Nerina Pallot and Bat For Lashes.

Ray LaMontagne was living in the mountains of Maine, in New England, when we discovered him in 2004. He had worked as a carpenter and, with his beard and plaid shirts, he looked like one, but his music reminded me of Van Morrison in his *Astral Weeks* and *Moondance* prime. It had that soulful sweep, also reminiscent of the late Tim Buckley.

We financed the making of his *Trouble* debut which we released on Echo but licensed to BMG in the US, and next we brokered a deal for him to sign to 14th Floor Records, a Warner subsidiary in the UK. *Trouble* went on to sell half a million copies worldwide. Within a couple of years, in 2007, Ray LaMontagne was nominated for Best International Breakthrough Act at the BRITS and headlining the Royal Albert Hall.

After Nerina Pallot had been dropped by Polydor in 2004, Chrysalis Music Publishing helped finance her second album, *Fires*, which came out on her own Idaho label via Echo. It was subsequently relaunched by 14th Floor and sold close to 150,000 copies. Later, Nerina and her husband and co-producer, Andy Chatterley, wrote two songs for Kylie Minogue's *Aphrodite* album, including the title track.

We used pretty much the same strategy with Bat For Lashes, aka Natasha Khan. In 2006, we issued *Fur And Gold*, her debut, which saw her compared to Kate Bush and Björk. The next year, she moved to EMI and the album was nominated for the Mercury Music Prize. In 2010, Natasha went on to win the Ivor Novello Award for Best Contemporary Song with the haunting 'Daniel'.

Echo may have been a failure from a financial standpoint but it certainly wasn't from a creative one. And we weren't alone: I couldn't help but notice that all the music entrepreneurs from my generation who had sold their record companies in the nineties and started labels a few years later struggled in the harsher musical climate.

Jerry Moss and Herb Alpert of A&M fame closed down their new label Almo Sounds after a few years and Richard Branson's V2 venture also struggled, despite the success of Stereophonics and the discovery of Elbow, who only crossed over to the mainstream after signing to a Universal label. Chris Blackwell, who had helped us start Chrysalis in the late sixties under the Island umbrella, did better with the film than the music side of Palm Pictures, and Brown Punk, the label he launched with Tricky in 2007, was a resounding failure.

Of course it's always possible to buck the trend. Daniel Miller has been successful with Mute as have Laurence Bell at Domino and Simon Raymond and Bella Union. However, it is Martin Mills at Beggars Banquet who has really proved how a well-managed independent record company can still achieve the kind of success that was enjoyed by labels like Chrysalis, Island, A&M and Virgin in the seventies. Martin has stuck to the strength of his convictions and, amazingly, after years of successes with left-field indy acts has really hit the jackpot with Adele. He is a shining beacon in the difficult landscape which is now the record industry.

Artists like Adele, and the kind of artists I have always been involved with, are the complete antithesis of the karaoke clones that emerge from *The X Factor* and other reality TV shows. They write their own material and can sing without the aid of Auto-Tune: they don't rely on marketing and hopefully they will endure.

By 2010, Chrysalis Music Publishing controlled and administered 100,000 songs, both current and vintage. However, not every publishing deal worked out, even when they involved artists and writers who were already well established.

In October 2006, we signed Thom Yorke of Radiohead as well as Damon Albarn. Thom Yorke proved a good decision and we also thought we were on to a winner with Damon as he had been incredibly successful as the leader of two iconic groups: Blur and Gorillaz.

Unfortunately, the Damon Albarn publishing deal would become a major factor in the demise of the company. It was a very expensive signing for Chrysalis Music Publishing, by far the biggest we had ever made. The initial advance was £2.5m, with an added advance of £500,000 for each album project or £1m for a Gorillaz album.

Yet when we signed Damon, who was managed by Chris Morrison, former partner of Chris O'Donnell, to Chrysalis Music, we did not acquire any of his catalogue, only new songs. We suspected that in time there would be a Blur reunion, which would make the deal recoup in one fell swoop. As a backstop, we were also to receive the songs on the next but one Gorillaz album.

However, Damon became preoccupied with critically acclaimed esoteric projects that failed to generate any significant income. There was his The Good The Bad & The Queen, the side-group he formed with former Clash bassist Paul Simonon, Verve guitarist Simon Tong and the afrobeat drummer Tony Allen. Damon then wrote and recorded a Chinese opera, entitled *Monkey: Journey To The West*, which played to big audiences, especially at London's Covent Garden Opera House. However, neither of these projects did much to recoup the advance.

In addition, *Plastic Beach*, the second Gorillaz album, to which we did not have the rights, did not perform well compared to its predecessor, so by 2010 our ultimate backstop seemed to have disappeared. It was pretty obvious that we were looking at a bottom line write-off of at least £3 million.

A loss as heavy as this could wipe away much of the profit that the company might have made, which would not have been well received in the City. As a consequence, the share price would have been hammered and I would have come under even more pressure from the institutional investors to sell the company.

Despite this, I could not place any blame on Damon Albarn. He was only following his creative lights, and he was certainly not the only artist or writer to incur such large losses for us. Velvet Revolver, whose personnel included ex-members of Guns N'Roses and Stone Temple Pilots, had a similar situation in the States, although the figures were nowhere near so extreme.

There is always an element of 'win some, lose some' in our dealings with artists, and people like myself who have worked in the music industry all their lives find it easy to accept this. But it is not a concept that sits well with bankers and fund managers. It was becoming more and more difficult to engage the financial community in understanding how a company like Chrysalis functions – a constant war we were beginning to lose.

CHAPTER 26

Sports

If my experience with QPR rates as one of the biggest disappointments of my life and one of the most high-profile failures of my career, then my time with Wasps must rank as one of the greatest successes. In fact, I struggle to think of another owner of a sports team who achieved the same level of success that I managed in the 11 years I owned the team.

After the initial euphoria of winning the Premiership in my first season, 1996-1997, we had a couple of years of modest success before really hitting the high spots in the first decade of the 21st century. The Championship success in 1997 was followed by two back to back victories at Twickenham in the National Cup Final in 1999 and 2000 and another such victory in 2006, the first year the competition was open to Welsh clubs as the Anglo Welsh Cup.

However, it was the three consecutive Premiership Finals we won at Twickenham in 2003, 2004 and 2005 that set the tone, followed by yet another in 2008. Even more wonderful were the Heineken Cup Final victories in 2004 and 2007. Add to this a Parker Pen European Challenge Cup Trophy in 2003 and it amounts to 11 major trophies in 11 years. Some record.

During this time, Wasps were supplying almost half of the English National team, including five players in the squad the day England won the World Cup Final by beating Australia 20-17 after extra time in Sydney in November 2003.

I did initially fall lucky with Wasps, I inherited a very good director of rugby in Nigel Melville, good coaching staff and a reasonable executive structure, which we were able to improve over the years. In stark contrast to QPR, our problems off the pitch were few and far between.

Our own major scandal came when our club captain, Lawrence Dallaglio, was caught in a *News Of The World* sting in the spring of 1999. One of their reporters had contacted his then agent, Ashley Woolfe, passing himself off as an executive from an advertising agency acting on behalf of a client. He pretended they were keen to sign up Lawrence for a big advertising campaign and pay him £250,000 a year – ten times the amount that had been mentioned in a bona fide offer from Physio Sport, a subsidiary of Lever Fabergé.

Lawrence agreed to have dinner at Langan's Brasserie with another male reporter and an extremely attractive female reporter, supposedly the two marketing executives, who had been described as party animals. He went straight there from another engagement, a testimonial dinner with his Wasps team-mate, Scottish international Damien Cronin, and proceeded to have another dinner and a few drinks with the so-called marketing people and then accompany them to their hotel for more drinks.

During the course of the conversation, in order to come across as a bit of a player, Lawrence told a few tall tales about the drugs he might have taken as a teenager. He might even have claimed to have access to all the paraphernalia needed for a party, including copious amounts of cocaine.

A few weeks later, a bogus photo-shoot was arranged in what was turning out to be quite an elaborate sting. Again, drink was consumed and the conversation turned to drugs once more. They were trying to get Lawrence to talk about Will Carling and Princess Diana, with whom Will was supposed to have had an affair. Obviously, they recorded everything.

The penny only dropped on May 23, 1999 when Ashley Woolfe called Lawrence to inform him the story was splashed all over the front of the *News Of The World*. It went as far as falsely accusing him of dealing drugs.

Two days later, Dallaglio held a press conference at Twickenham. In case anyone had any doubts, he took a drugs test to prove he was clean, but he admitted his behaviour had been foolish and resigned the England captaincy. The RFU was obviously going to hold an inquiry.

Things worsened three weeks after the *News Of The Word* sting when the *Mail On Sunday* published its own 'exposé'. It claimed two people had seen Lawrence snorting coke in a London wine bar after a Wasps game. He had indeed been celebrating a win with his teammates there, but the rest of the story didn't stand up. The owner was adamant no drugs had been consumed on his premises.

Because this time Wasps was named in the story, Lawrence called me. I think to this day he appreciates what we did for him. The idea of the England rugby captain involved in a drugs scandal was not only a crisis for England, for Wasps and for Lawrence, but for the world of international rugby. Charles Levison and I went into overdrive.

We advised him to contact Gerrard Tyrrell at Harbottle & Lewis, who specialises in that type of litigation, to help resolve the issue. Together, they decided to sue the *Mail On Sunday*. Of course, the paper couldn't produce the supposed witnesses, an Australian and a Kiwi, who had been employed at the wine bar and had conveniently vanished. But the story dragged on. *The Mail On Sunday* agreed to pay Lawrence's costs and to run an apology (which only finally appeared in April 2001).

Meanwhile, the Rugby Football Union wanted to investigate both allegations. Ray Manock, a retired solicitor from Yorkshire, was the RFU disciplinary officer. Gerrard Tyrrell suggested George Carman

y and I together in the good days. This photo was taken for a major *Billboard* supplement on Chrysalis.

Talking to Diana, Princess of Wales, at the first ever Princes Trust Rock Concert at the Dominion in Tottenham Court Road, with Pete Townshend on my right and Tony Stratton-Smith on my left.

With George Martin and Paul McCarthy at a very early Brit Awards. I started the Brits, when they were originally called the BPI Awards, and then the British Record Industry Awards. DOUG McKENZIE

Nick Blackburn at Loftus Road, at the first game following my takeover of Queens Park Rangers FC. The happy times were lived! RICHARD YOUNG

Janet Street Porter at at MIPTV market in Cannes. Janet suggested we got married, as we shared so many similar interests. Who ws? It could have been fun!

My 68th birthday on the London Eye, with four gorgeous members of the family, left to right: Janice, Tina, Holly, me and Chloe.

At the 2013 MusiCares dinner in Los Angeles with Daniel Glass, Jerry Moss and Shep Gordon.

llecting my CBE at Buckingham Palace with Holly, Janice and Chloe.

ring his term as Prime Minister Tony Blair was a regular visitor to our Bramley Road offices in Notting Hill for appearances on LBC.

Janice and I with Bill and Alex Roedy at my 60th birthday party at Sketch in London. DOMINIC O'NEILL

Me with Tom on my right and Tim on my left at the same event. DOMINIC O'NEILL

ce and I at a reception at 10 Downing Street. REX FEATURES

Old friends. I first met Michael Gudinski over 45 years ago, and we have been mates ever since. This was taken in 2013 at London's River Cafe.

ebrating one of the many famous Wasps victories at ckenham with Lawrence Dallaglio.
RCHIVE/PRESS ASSOCIATION IMAGES

With NBA commissioner David Stern in my Sheffield Sharks basketball days.

With Janice outside the entrance to Rick's Café Americain for the Casablanca party in 2002 – an amazing night to celebrate her 40th birthday. RICHARD YOUNG

QC, who had a fearsome reputation, should put Lawrence's case. Our ability to secure his services was paramount to mitigating any further damage to Dallaglio's reputation.

Nigel Melville also went along, as did Gerrard Tyrrell. It was quite a formidable team for what was a bit of a show-trial, with 14 journalists in attendance. High Court judge Sir Oliver Popplewell was on the disciplinary panel alongside RFU Council members John Spencer and Chris Tuffley.

Carman highlighted the underhand tactics of the tabloid press and Lawrence got away with a slap on the wrist and a £15,000 fine for bringing the game into disrepute. He also had to pay £10,000 costs but it could have been far worse: he could have been banned from playing for a long time. He avoided any further punishment, any stain on his character soon faded and he resumed his illustrious career with both England and Wasps. Lawrence was even re-appointed England captain following Martin Johnson's retirement in 2004.

After the QPR debacle and the separation of the two teams I became Wasps chairman. As such I re-engaged with the regular meetings of the Premiership Rugby Club owners which I had attended initially when Sir John Hall chaired the committee. These were the early days of political confrontations between the owners and the RFU, who felt that the owners were hijacking professional rugby and wanting a greater degree of control. The battle between the owners and the RFU would rage for several seasons before a truce of sorts was reached.

By the year 2001, Sir John Hall had left the rugby arena and Tom Walkinshaw, the automotive magnate and racing car owner, took over the chairmanship. Tom had recently bought Gloucester Rugby club and at my first owners meeting under the new set-up, it became apparent that a sub-plot existed. I had been kept in the dark about negotiations that were well underway for some teams to split from the RFU to form a British League of both English and Welsh teams. The idea was that three of the existing Premiership clubs, including Wasps, would be cast adrift and replaced by two from Wales (Cardiff and either Llanelli or Swansea) and a team based in Devon or Cornwall.

I was flabbergasted at this discovery and immediately suggested a vote of no confidence in the chairman, as it was clear plans were afoot to discriminate against other components of the organisation. Some people certainly had the perception that Wasps were an unnecessary "extra team" cluttering up the rugby landscape. In part as a result of my obvious opposition to the proposal the whole scheme was ultimately dropped.

Tom Walkinshaw was not the only one to feel that Wasps were an unaffordable luxury, based as they were in west London. I was also approached by Cecil Duckworth, the owner of Worcester, who was interested in short-circuiting his team into the Premiership as the Worcester Wasps. Maurice Lindsay, from the Wigan rugby league team also approached me about moving to the DW stadium as the Wigan Wasps.

Luckily, after our initial skirmish, Tom Walkinshaw and I fell into a good relationship and became firm friends. However, we were to have one more run-in at the beginning of 2002 when Wasps were under-performing on the pitch.

Nigel Melville, our Director of Rugby, unexpectedly handed in his notice. I had been alerted on the grapevine to the fact that Nigel had been spotted entering an estate agent's office in Cheltenham. With Gloucester looking for a new coach, I put two and two together and assumed Tom and Nigel were scheming for Nigel to go to Gloucester. They both vehemently denied it and I accepted their denials.

I negotiated Nigel's severance agreement, despite my protestations that a married man with a family does not leave a good job with nowhere to go to, and, lo and behold, a few weeks later, he re-emerged as the new Director of Rugby for the West Country team. He has always denied that he had the Gloucester job lined up before he resigned from his position at Wasps and Tom Walkinshaw always denied that he was involved with attempting to poach Nigel

Melville. Frankly, I didn't believe either of them at the time, and still don't today.

Yet this unwanted development did us a favour in a way as Nigel, showing a degree of guilt, felt a huge responsibility to help us appoint a new Director of Rugby. He recommended Warren Gatland, the former New Zealand hooker, who had just been released from his job as coach for the Irish national team.

I met with Warren and effectively hired him on the spot, an appointment that seemed both natural and obvious. Despite success on the pitch, things had not worked out for Warren in Dublin. The committee of the Irish RFU had found Gatland's direct Antipodean manner not to their liking.

Warren is definitely someone who would call a spade a spade, and was not afraid to voice opinions that might upset the heirarchy. For example, he spoke his mind when the Irish team had to fly to Buenos Aires the day before a test match against Argentina and most of the better seats on the aircraft were occupied by officials rather than players. Another issue was his insistence that supposedly unbudgeted new fitness equipment could be made available if fewer committee members' wives flew to Rome for a fixture against Italy.

Warren Gatland turned out to be an inspired appointment for Wasps. He is a brilliant coach, a great organiser of his support team and an excellent, if authoritarian, man-manager of the players. With Warren Gatland as director of rugby we started what truly was a purple patch at Wasps; we went into a golden period in the history of club rugby.

Everybody says, and it is absolutely true, that the most important relationship in any sports team is that between the chairman/owner and the director of rugby/football manager. Warren, or 'Gats' as he is known, and I had an excellent relationship right from the word go: the epitome of a top-class rapport between chairman and manager.

Warren definitely knew how to handle me. He recognised that I knew very little about rugby, something I accepted, but he never admitted it. Nevertheless, he always listened to my recommendations on signing new players and usually we managed to make all the key decisions in tandem. There was an awful amount of mutual trust between us.

Most of the great players that we signed to Wasps in that era were joint decisions between Warren and myself and, in some instances, just as much at my suggestion as his. I could feel the bits that were missing from the jigsaw puzzle and I watched enough rugby to know where we might find those bits and I left the rest to him.

At the end of the season, at the board meeting where we started preparing for the following season, we discussed the various positions in the squad that needed strengthening and the players that we might recruit for these roles. We always went for the best players available. Second-best was not an option and whoever we wanted, we managed to get, including some very high-profile signings.

To my surprise, however, Warren said at the first meeting to discuss signings that he didn't want any new signings in the team and that the squad was good enough already. Instead, the few hundred thousand pounds we had set aside for increased salaries should be spent on fitness equipment and hiring extra backroom staff, a fitness coach and conditioning coach etc.

I was shocked and disappointed as I was keen to bring in two or three marquee signings to strengthen the team and add to the aura, but Warren was adamant and in the end I agreed. The fitness equipment and coaches would be a priority. Later on, we ended up signing the players I had suggested anyway. Warren admitted that his strategy was based on the fact that getting me to agree to the new signings would be easy but getting me to agree to fitness equipment and weights would be a bit of an ask, which is why he did it in the way he did, and ended up getting everything he wanted in the first place.

Another integral component of the Wasps team was Shaun Edwards, the backs coach. Shaun was a brusque northerner, a former rugby league scrum half who has become an outstanding rugby union coach. He and Warren formed a potent relationship, so much so that they later worked together with the Welsh national team.

Warren Gatland's management style could be brutal. Put one foot out of line, and your career could be over. There were players who, on the back of one bad game, wouldn't get picked again for 12 months. I'm not saying that Warren objected to the lads having a few beers at the appropriate times – that was all part of the culture – but it was very much "Take care of business or else".

Janice and I spent a lot of time with Warren and his wife, Trudi – who is also from New Zealand – and their two children, Brett and Gabby, who are of a similar age to Holly and Tina, including taking skiing holidays in Aspen each February. Trudi's brother played for the Aspen Gentlemen, one of the top rugby teams in the USA, and Aspen was a great place for the Kiwi clan to get together for a family vacation.

We had some great times there although, on one occasion, I very nearly killed Warren as I pointed him in the direction of a restaurant where we were meeting for lunch and told him to get some pace on in getting there, or he would not get up a hill. Unfortunately he failed to realise where the piste stopped and the concrete forecourt of the restaurant started, and saw it too late, ending up spreadeagled on the concrete in front of a host of other diners, with a few pretty nasty bruises as a consequence.

Throughout my 11 years at the helm, the Wasps squad read like a who's who of international rugby with a host of superstars and household names, all of whom made a tremendous contribution to the success of the team and the ethos of the club. Winning was the culture and nearly every game ended with us singing the Wasps victory song, 'Black And Yellow Bonnet', in the dressing room after the final whistle.

Besides Lawrence Dallaglio, other English internationals included Josh Lewsey, Stuart Abbott, Alex King, Simon Shaw, Joe Worsley, Fraser Waters and then later on Phil Vickery, Tim Payne, James Haskell, Tom Palmer, Paul Sackey, the French internationals Serge

Betsen and the hooker Raphaël Ibañez, Welsh legend Rob Howley, Irish scrum half Eoin Reddan, Scottish superstar Kenny Logan, All Black Prop Craig Dowd, the Samoan hooker Trevor Leota, the English wonder kid Danny Cipriani and Matt Dawson, the scrum half who played such a pivotal role when he fed Jonny Wilkinson for that drop goal in Sydney in 2003.

Moving to Adams Park in High Wycombe in 2002 initially proved an inspired choice. Apart from the 10,000 stadium capacity and the corporate boxes, the off-pitch facilities were excellent, including the changing rooms and rehab areas. The truth is that you need far better facilities for rugby than you do for football. You have more players and coaches and you need enhanced medical facilities, including a dentist's chair, which is used quite regularly at rugby matches.

Adams Park was absolutely perfect for rugby at that stage of its development. We were sold out most games and there was a great atmosphere. In fact, the move was so successful initially that, when Fulham moved out of Loftus Road, the decision was made that we would stay at Adams Park and Wasps in return paid a substantial sum to QPR to exit from the long-term ground-sharing agreement.

Initially, I continued funding the club 100% myself but within a couple of years of the move to High Wycombe, I received a letter from John O'Connell, a rugby and football fanatic, who incidentally was also a QPR fan. John had recently sold his business in the computer software industry and was keen to be involved with Wasps.

He joined as a junior partner initially, and helped carry the burden of financing the losses, which we managed to keep to a six-figure sum despite the superstar salaries we were committed to paying. John and I worked very well together. He kept me from overspending on recruiting players, was particularly strong on the structural, financial and sponsorship side, and allowed me to continue working with Warren Gatland on putting the best possible team out on the pitch.

Most of the other club owners felt that I had pulled off a miracle in going to High Wycombe. It was only several years later when attendances for rugby union grew well beyond the 10,000 point that we realised we were going to be at a disadvantage. London Irish, initially playing in front of a sparse crowd at the Madejski Stadium in Reading, were in a much better position as they could now accommodate 25,000 people. Harlequins, Gloucester, Northampton were close to 15,000 at their grounds. Leicester could host 20,000. Wasps at Adams Park had a ceiling of 10,000.

We tried hard to increase the stadium capacity, by seeking permission to build a new stand at the visitors' end, with extra corporate boxes, but the issue with the local council was always about the access road. They would not allow any change without a new road, on the grounds that evacuation would be difficult in the event of an aircraft crashing on the stadium, a disingenuous position to take when one considers the proximity of Twickenham to the Heathrow flight path. Try as we might, a new access road remained impossible.

Following the sale of Wasps' spiritual home at Sudbury, Wasps had moved to Twyford Avenue in West Acton to share the QPR training ground. We were able to create sufficient facilities for both clubs and everyone was able to benefit from some economies of scale in terms of the extra facilities that we added. The gym was converted into a state-of-the-art weights room, which was of tremendous advantage to Wasps.

Unfortunately, the footballers tended to shun the facility, and one sensed they were intimidated by the superb physiques and fitness levels of the rugby players. Although very fit, footballers do not usually share the same superman size torsos! But both sets of players got on well, were very supportive of each other and looked out for each other's results at the weekend. The training ground was a little basic in the accommodation it offered, but to my mind this was compensated for by the fact that it was so close to the trendy bars and restaurants of west London and, in many cases, to the homes of the players.

The first Heineken Cup victory in 2004, when we beat Toulouse at Twickenham, was one of the most exciting finals ever. We had already managed to get past Munster in Ireland at a sold-out Lansdowne

Road to win a place in the final; something that gave 'Gats' enormous satisfaction after his less-than-enjoyable spell coaching in Ireland. The result was Munster 32, Wasps 37. The game was regarded as one of the all-time classic rugby matches for its incredible intensity, and with the lead constantly changing hands.

In the final, we were up against Toulouse, perhaps the most dominant European rugby team of the modern era. The score was 20-20 with just a minute to go and Toulouse seemingly in the ascendancy, with extra time beckoning. My hunch was, had the game gone into extra time, Toulouse might well have prevailed. Their squad was probably stronger in depth than Wasps'.

Then Rob Howley, the former Welsh international scrum-half, produced a grubber kick down the touchline into the far left hand corner. The French international full back Clément Poitrenaud tried to shepherd the ball, to let it go into touch, rather than put it into touch himself and give Wasps a lineout close to his line. The ball never quite went into touch, instead bobbling over the try-line, Rob Howley pounced and dived on the ball to score a brilliant try in the last second of the match. The try was converted from the touchline by Mark Van Gisbergen to secure a brilliant 27-20 victory.

The only disappointment on the day was the hospitality, or rather hostility, that I and the other members of the Wasps board received from the RFU hierarchy. They always seemed to resent the fact that we were appearing so often at the temple of English rugby. It was almost like Wasps were making Twickenham our home ground.

Even when I was supplying and paying for almost half the English team, I was never ever afforded any hospitality at Twickenham. I happily pitched up like a member of the general public for a picnic in the car park and a seat in the stands.

I remember a famous quote from a member of the RFU board, when the idea of the Heineken Cup was first mooted: "What, clubs from different countries playing against each other? Who on earth would ever want to pay to see that?" It is now a competition that almost rivals the Six Nations for public interest, but unlike the Six Nations, the matches are attended by passionate die-hard rugby fans, and not corporate hospitality brokers.

The following weekend, doubtless making the RFU blazers even more unhappy, we were back at Twickenham again, this time to beat Bath and win the Premiership and complete a famous double.

At the end of the 2004/2005 season, following a third English Premiership, Warren Gatland decided that it was time for him and his family to return home to New Zealand. He had been away for several years and he and Trudi felt that their children should grow up spending more time around their family and grandparents.

Quite possibly, Warren had also decided he had achieved all he could do with his tremendous success with Wasps in both England and Europe. I believe in his mind, a major role with the All Blacks beckoned, or at the very least a head coach job in the Super 14 as a stepping stone to that particular objective. Unfortunately for him, no such opportunity was forthcoming and he ended up coaching one of the leading New Zealand teams, the Waikato Chiefs, in the domestic league.

Before long, Gats was tempted back to Great Britain by the Welsh RFU, where he has once again been an incredible success, leading Wales to two Grand Slams and the semi-final of the Rugby World Cup.

It was no surprise when Warren was appointed head coach of the British and Irish 2013 tour of Australia, recognising him as the outstanding coach in the northern hemisphere. His ability and will to take tough decisions remained as strong, and he faced hostility from the British press for dropping iconic Irish centre Brian O'Driscoll for the third and decisive test in Sydney. The result, an amazing win for the Lions by 41 points to 16, led to the side he coached becoming the first Lions team to win a series since 1997.

Warren's stock could not be higher in world rugby, yet despite the affection in which he is deservedly held in Great Britain I still believe that the ultimate accolade – coaching the New Zealand All Blacks –

will become the final cherry on the cake of the Gatland career, a role no Kiwi could ever resist.

Replacing someone of Warren's capability was always going to be a daunting task. Given Wasps' standing in Europe, we could attract the very best but we were anxious not to completely re-engineer the club. The choice was between revolution or evolution, substantial change or continuity.

The selection board to find the successful candidate was Charles Levison, John O'Connell and myself and we chose to go the evolution route and brought in the former Scottish coach, Ian McGeechan, who had been at the Northampton Saints.

'Geech', as he is nicknamed, settled into the role perfectly and we barely batted an eyelid as the success on the pitch continued. I enjoyed the same relationship with 'Geech' as I had with 'Gats'. We discussed every decision together and, more often than not, ended up making the right ones.

Ian McGeechan's management style was more laid-back than Gats'. He had been at Northampton Saints the year they were relegated from the Premiership to Division I. I remember asking Keith Barwell, the owner of Northampton Saints, about McGeechan's relationship with the players to which Keith replied: "The players loved him, even the year they got relegated, they still loved the coach." With 'Geech' the success continued and we won another English championship in 2008 and he too had his Heineken Cup in 2007.

Nevertheless, the second Heineken Cup final in 2007 was a very different affair from 2004. In Geech's second season in charge, we were up against Leicester Tigers, the pre-eminent club during the season. Leicester were firm favourites on the day, which also was to be the swan song for England's World Cup winning captain, Martin Johnson. The whole event was intended to be a brilliant celebration and send off for the iconic Tigers star. Yet things did not go according to plan. Wasps destroyed Leicester from the kick-off to the last minute, winning by 25-9.

As for me, the events leading up to the match and the after-match celebrations were bizarre to say the least. A couple of years previously, a majority stake in Wycombe Wanderers Football Club, which owned Adams Park, the ground at which we played our home matches, had been bought by Steve Hayes, a wealthy entrepreneur who had recently made a huge pot of money by founding and then shortly thereafter selling a loan business tailor-made for the internet called loans.co.uk.

Steve was also a big rugby fan and a good mate of Lawrence Dallaglio. He was also a very generous donor at the Wasps fundraising and charity initiatives that we ran. Soon after buying Wycombe Wanderers, he decided that he would also like to own Wasps.

Steve's first suggestion was that we combine Wasps and Wycombe Wanderers under a jointly owned umbrella organisation. I wanted nothing to do with that idea. I had been there once before with QPR and at least I was a QPR fan, not a Wycombe Wanderers fan. Steve then came up with an offer to buy the club, which I rejected. I had no wish to sell.

At the same time a series of stories started to appear in the tabloid press sport gossip columns that all was not well at Wasps, particularly with regard to the rather basic creature comforts at the training ground. I was concerned as to the provenance of these articles until someone told me that Max Clifford, the prominent PR man, was seated on Steve Hayes' table at the end-of-season awards dinner. Steve had apparently engaged Max to handle PR for him.

While I was away at York races in the middle of May there was a renewed attempt to buy the club in advance of the Heineken Cup final, an improved offer which this time I was prepared to consider. However, when I was advised that the offer would be available for 24 hours only and would be withdrawn were I not to sign an agreement within that time frame, I decided once again to say no.

I hate being pressured and in the midst of entertaining a dozen or so close friends at an important race meeting, I did not have time to do this anyway. I thought nothing more of it until I turned up on that Saturday evening at Hampton Court Palace as a guest of honour at a European Rugby Commission (ERC) pre-Cup Final dinner.

At that time, I was not in the habit of accessing my e-mails over the weekend, but Nigel Butterfield pointed out to me that there had been a barrage of e-mails emanating from the Hayes camp presenting me with another deadline for acceptance. The deadline had already passed without me being aware of the offer. It did not impair my enjoyment of the evening and I ended up making a rather lengthy and, I hope, humorous speech thanking our hosts for the event (and doing the whole thing in French, at that).

The following day, after the emphatic victory, I went to the car park to continue the celebrations with the Wasps players, staff and fans only to be told of some bizarre happenings in the press conference following the game. Despite the bulk of the national rugby journalists wanting to praise Wasps for their performance, there was one particularly obstinate journalist, apparently from a local Croydon newspaper, who insisted on asking Lawrence Dallaglio how Wasps were going to be able to compete with teams like Leicester, especially in view of the fact that its training facilities were spartan and that the club was underfunded.

It was hard to fathom the rationale behind this line of questioning. The players at the press conference were bemused at how this could have happened but it all seemed to make perfect sense to me. Fortunately, the real rugby journalists there were more committed to writing about the amazing team performance on the day. We had just upset the odds and beaten Leicester and this guy couldn't stop asking what appeared to be clearly pre-arranged questions.

Despite the fact that he had been thwarted in his attempts to buy the club, Steve Hayes was still keen to join the board. Eventually, John O'Connell and I decided to make him a third partner as a minority, 11% shareholder in Wasps, an arrangement that appeared to be a huge advantage to the club, especially with the extra financial muscle he would bring to the feast. But, whereas the partnership between John and I had always worked well, this was very much a case of two's company and three's a crowd.

Initially, 'Geech' was particularly pleased about the new arrangement and made a lovely speech at a pre-season event we held, explaining to all and sundry what a marvellous position the club would now be in. On the same evening as our final pre-season friendly, Windsor racecourse was hosting an evening meeting and I made arrangements to hire a large marquee in the very attractive paddock and provide hospitality for all the players, staff and all their other halves. It was a great way to start the season and something that I thought might become a regular event.

However, at the end of that season, having suffered increased losses, we recast the respective shareholdings, and ended up with a situation that was much closer to parity. Steve wanted the following year's event to be a sit-down dinner at the Hurlingham Club which would have cost substantially more and which John and I felt would not produce the same relaxed atmosphere as we had at Windsor.

This became a major issue between us and we stupidly fell out over it. In the end we compromised that we would take it in turns between the three of us to host the pre-season event. We could provide whatever we wanted in the way of hospitality, and pay for it ourselves.

We also crossed swords when Lawrence Dallaglio retired. Steve wanted him to be appointed to the board immediately. I refused. I was fully aware of the tremendous contribution Lawrence had made to Wasps and following his retirement he was given a major role with the club and a generous salary and support structure to go along with it.

However, I felt it was too soon for him to be made a director and to be responsible as one of the individuals to whom 'Geech', as the Director of Rugby, would be reporting. In his last couple of years as a player Lawrence had been affected by the severe injury he had sustained playing for the Lions at the start of their campaign in New Zealand when his ankle was broken in several places and his ankle ligaments torn. In fact, the injury was so severe that, had Laurence not been immediately airlifted to a specialist hospital, it might have been necessary to amputate his ankle and foot.

It naturally took him quite a while to recover, following which his place in the starting line-up was no longer secure. It was more difficult for him to sustain a performance for the full 80 minutes. I am not sure if there had been any issue between Lawrence and 'Geech' over this but I was concerned that, if that had been the case, it should not affect the running of the playing side of the club.

In any sports organisation, it is incredibly difficult if the person responsible for putting the team on the pitch is getting conflicting messages from more than one person, or from the board. I think it got to the point where Steve objected to my hands-on role and felt he should be in the position where he could have significant input on decision making.

I personally had no issue with Steve and certainly never fell out with him but it was clear at the beginning of the 2008/2009 season that Steve and John had stopped talking to each other. At the opening match, the Twickenham double-header against London Irish, a fellow director noticed this fissure and asked me for my opinion on it. I said it would not usually constitute a problem but it could prove very serious if there was a requirement for the board to make a difficult decision like changing the Director of Rugby or Head Coach.

Another issue we were at loggerheads over was the long-term future of the club. We had outgrown Adams Park but the alternative venues John and I were prepared to consider did not suit Steve's vision. He was committed to finding a new stadium in the Wycombe area that could accommodate over 20,000 for both Wasps and Wycombe Wanderers.

I had had a series of meetings with the local council over the years, and had grown despondent that the site for any such stadium would ever be forthcoming. I had accepted that a move to an entirely new location may be necessary. Steve could not agree to any such move, and believed he could meet his objectives by creating a stadium at the nearby Booker Aerodrome. My view was that the access was poor, planning permission would be virtually impossible, and the scheme would not get off the ground. A stand-off between us ensued.

Finding sites for new stadia in the prosperous Greater London area is a major problem that I also faced at QPR. Even with their immense wealth, Abramovich at Chelsea or Al-Fayed at Fulham have been unable to solve this problem

At a board meeting a few weeks later, Steve handed John and I an envelope each, which he told us to take away, look at and give him an answer. John said, "If that's an offer for my shares, then I am not interested." And he refused to take it. Out of interest I took my envelope and did open it later that evening to find that, in fact, the envelope addressed to me contained the offer intended for John.

John's shareholding was at a lower level than mine. I discussed the matter with him and told him that I felt the club was becoming unmanageable and that it was ceasing to be any fun, and that I was prepared to consider an offer.

I had been finding Wasps less fulfilling since the sad death of Charles Levison in June 2006 as he and I had been there right from the start. Charles' death was one of the saddest things that I ever experienced. I had travelled to Antigua for the family Easter holiday when I received a phone call on the Monday morning following my arrival from Charles's son-in-law telling me that Charles had had a massive heart attack at his house in Notting Hill and been admitted to the cardiological Department of St Mary's Hospital, Paddington.

Charles had suffered further heart attacks in the ambulance and, although the operation was a success he never came out of the coma. When I returned back from Antigua, I went to visit Charles and found it impossible to see a man who meant so much to me and of such huge energy lying there in that state. He eventually passed away three months later. With Charles' death, a part of my involvement with Wasps had died too. It was never quite the same afterwards.

Another offer from Steve arrived a couple of weeks after the first one. Sadly and reluctantly, I decided to accept it.

I had had 11 great years, having taken over the club when the sport was still amateur and Wasps were playing on what was not much more than a public park in Sudbury. Sure, it had cost me a lot of money, but I had enjoyed it enormously and to this day feel that I made a major contribution, not just to Wasps but to the whole sport of professional rugby in Europe.

The whole family were involved at every step along the way. My daughter Holly, who was no more than six at the time of our first Twickenham appearance, was always asked to be mascot and lead the team out at that great stadium. She was a real talisman. Wasps never lost a match at Twickenham when Holly was the mascot. Running out alongside Lawrence Dallaglio in front of 80,000 people is an experience she will remember for the rest of her life.

Sadly, my memories were somewhat impaired at my last official appearance at the end of season dinner for the 2008/09 campaign. On taking the stage to receive their awards several players spoke about how excited they were that Steve Hayes had taken over, implying that the club was in infinitely better hands now.

I was disappointed as I regarded most of the players as friends, some of whom had stayed over at Glebe House on several occasions when I had hosted shoots in which they participated.

One member of the team told me that the club had held a pre-dinner dinner, at which all the players who were to receive awards had been presented with a speech they were to make at the function expressing those sentiments.

Sadly things have not gone well for Wasps since my departure and in 2011/12 season they only avoided relegation by one point. Steve Hayes had told me that if he didn't take over the club, all the players would leave, but within a few months, many of the senior players had left anyway.

Steve announced he was leaving the club during 2012, and since then things on the pitch appear to have improved somewhat. I understand a new well-funded owner has recently come on board and the future of Wasps appears to be secured.

It is hard to say whether Wasps could have maintained the incredible run of success that they had achieved in my 11 years. Certainly it is hard to see them thriving again until they have escaped the restrictions of Adams Park and found a bigger stadium – and that is a lot easier said than done.

After I sold my major shareholding the club, with Steve's agreement, decided to create the position of Life President in recognition of all I had contributed to the history of Wasps, a role that I very much enjoy. There is a saying: once a Wasp, always a Wasp. Nothing could be more true.

I imagine that I lost around £20 million with my involvement in QPR and Wasps, and several million more with Wasps independently after the split, despite having financial assistance from John O'Connell and, for the last year, Steve Hayes.

So when the media clamour for investment from club owners, what exactly do they mean? The willingness to fund the losses that are inevitable when you put a championship-winning team on the pitch? That I did, and in spades! And ultimately, Wasps left an indelible mark on my life and my heart, one I will never forget.

CHAPTER 27

Come Back Around

The travails that caused me to put Loftus Road PLC into administration, downsize the Echo label and even threaten the future of the entire Chrysalis Organisation had looked impossible just a few years earlier.

In fact, throughout the second half of the nineties, Chrysalis was one of the top-performing media stocks in the UK. The apex had possibly come in December 1999, when I was in Australia with my family for the millennium Christmas. I had phoned Lisa Gordon in the London office to touch base. What she told me was astonishing.

The Chrysalis share price had shot through the roof, reaching over £3.50 per share, which at the time valued the company at around half a billion pounds and my personal shareholding at a staggering £175 million. Even going through an expensive divorce and funding a struggling football club, I suddenly felt very rich.

Such news brought with it an assurance that enabled me to make the occasional exorbitant splash and for the football World Cup in 1998 I bought a new boat, a Mangusta 80, and arranged for it to be berthed in the port of Bandol, near Marseilles, for the duration of the tournament.

As the boat had accommodation for only three couples, I also rented a five-bedroom villa up in the hills overlooking the harbour and secured eight tickets for every game at the Stade Vélodrome, the Marseilles stadium, and also for some matches further afield at Montpellier. At the time, Janice was still working at BA but managed to join us on her days off, and I commuted back and forth to London as and when necessary.

We invited a whole string of corporate guests and clients to France and I even traded in my Porsche for a Chrysler Voyager people carrier to transport everyone to matches. We held the most amazing dinner parties and barbecues long into the night back at the villa, and had days out on the boat when there were no matches taking place in our area. It could not have been more fun.

The highpoint was getting tickets at short notice for the England v Argentina quarter-final in Saint-Etienne. The game could not have been more exciting, with David Beckham getting sent off and England losing a penalty shoot-out 4-3. It was unfortunate that Charles Levison had forgotten where our hotel was, leading to a few hours driving around remote country lanes in the dark in search of it. But we laughed it off.

Time flies, and never was this more evident than later in 1998, when Chrysalis celebrated its 30th anniversary on September 18. To mark the occasion, I threw a huge media party, The Butterfly Ball, at a marvellous venue, One Great George Street in London's Westminster, a stone's throw from Parliament and Big Ben.

The Butterfly Ball was a glamorous occasion at which the whole of Chrysalis' – and, therefore, my – past life seemed to pass before my eyes. We had performances from members of Jethro Tull and Procol Harum as well as Leo Sayer, who flew in from Australia, and Arrow, who came in from Montserrat.

Terry Ellis helped me cut the cake along with Ian Anderson and Gary Brooker and other faces from the past and present included Anna Ford, Adam Faith, George Martin, Julia Bradbury and Jono Coleman, not to mention David Mellor, Janet Street-Porter and

Anneka Rice. Chrysalis has had some stupendous parties over the years but this was something special.

At the end of the same year, Janice and I hosted a fantastic family Christmas at Malthouse Cottage. Although we had only four bedrooms, we were able to accommodate everybody else in the Olde Bell Hotel. It had taken a while for my three children by Chelle to come to terms with their parents splitting up, but my newly enlarged family seemed to get on well and I even managed to hook up with Tom on his gap year by flying to see him in Bali after a trip to Australia on TV division business.

As part of the separation agreement, we were initially prevented from visiting Glebe House with our respective partners, although Janice and I still frequently went down to Gloucestershire on free weekends. We would stay in local hotels and I would join my tennis mates for a game, visit the stud to check on developments there, and have Sunday lunch with friends.

We also converted an old barn on the estate at Glebe House as a home for us, but eventually Chelle decided that she did not want Glebe House as part of the settlement. Janice and I were thus able to move in after the divorce was finalised. Having stood empty for a while, it had become rather dilapidated and required Janice to undertake a large degree of renovation.

For a few years, we lived between three houses, which could hardly be called normal, and was not ideal, but it meant the girls could stay at their school in Cookham. It was only when both Holly and Tina started at senior school that we were able to downsize to two properties, Glebe House and the apartment in Holland Park, where we still live today when we're in London.

After the blissful Malthouse Cottage Christmas of 1998, for the next year's millennium New Year, I took my entire family to Australia, including my sister Carol and her family. I rented both a house on Point Piper, in Sydney's Eastern suburbs, and another up in Palm Beach. We needed both houses to fit us all in, and this way we could have the best of both worlds.

As the new millennium dawned, the dotcom and media stock market boom was peaking and the Chrysalis share price was at its absolute height. Yet it was all *Monopoly* money. We did not try to sell the Chrysalis Group and no one tried to buy it at that price although it could have happened. Most of our businesses were doing well. We had the basis of all the old media: radio stations, television production, records, music and book publishing (about which more later). And we were actively involved in developing new media.

Of course, all of this would change as media valuations collapsed. The puff went out of the dotcom boom and the whole music industry went pear-shaped but I always felt that what we were doing in the area of new media could have been really successful if only we'd had a bit more understanding of the field. We were making some good moves but we didn't get it quite right – and we got our timing completely wrong.

Lisa Gordon was the corporate development director running that part of our business at the time. She is extremely sharp and shrewd and was very up to speed with what was going on in that space. I visited Silicon Valley in California two or three times with her and Marcus Leaver. It was a fascinating experience but, in all honesty, I was out of my depth and not particularly computer-literate at the time, though I roughly understood what the new businesses were supposed to be doing.

We decided that, rather than plunge recklessly into the online world, we would try to participate in early-stage developments, climb the learning curve and get to grips with the impact it could have on our existing businesses. Much more importantly, we were looking to back ideas and businesses where we could add value rather than just cash to things that had a resonance with our existing businesses. We also looked at initiatives that could be developed from within.

Lisa Gordon recruited Nick Fox, who had been a financial journalist with the *Sunday Telegraph* and the *Sunday Times* and was familiar with the new technology and venture capital sectors. He was the one who introduced the first initiative, our first step into the internet, when we acquired a stake in a start-up e-commerce software company called Taxi Interactive in 1998.

This was probably a typical tale of the era. Two brothers had developed Mytaxi.com, a personal online shopping tool. Essentially it was something similar to Google, the search engine developed by Larry Page and Sergey Brin in California. It was a virtual taxi that took you around the internet collecting information.

Mytaxi.com was part shopping portal, part comparison engine. The idea was that it was like jumping into a taxi and saying, "Take me to Debenhams": hence the name. We liked the idea of it, and the following year we increased our stake, as well as launching Chrysalis Radio Online and Rivals.net, a sports results service.

Our new media development was partly driven by the City's short-lived obsession with the internet. Throughout 1999, every time we did a presentation, the questions that arose would be about our internet strategy. It became obvious very quickly that, having been a highly rated media stock because we were perceived to be in strong growth areas, we were now in danger of being left behind without embracing the web in our presentations.

In January 2000, we did a share placing on the basis that we were getting involved in more internet-related activities. We went to the stock market and we issued 5% of new shares in Chrysalis and raised £26.8 million to specifically invest in those areas.

The problem was that when we raised the money it was almost at the height of the crazy levels that were being paid for start-ups. People had started internet companies in the second half of the nineties, sold them for a fortune in 1999, and, by 2000, everybody was coming into the business at highly inflated levels and with vast expectations.

Yet by that time, the pioneers had made the money. The newcomers moving into it were dealing with reality, which was nowhere near the level the perception had been. Businesses were buying ideas for a few million pounds from the people who had only just dreamt up the concept.

We felt that, since the City investors had given us the money, they would want us to do something with it. With hindsight, we would have been better off giving the money back to the shareholders or using it to invest in old media, but it was 'ring-fenced' specifically for investment in new media activities. We had to account for it separately and we were under pressure to spend it. We spent it all in a year.

Lisa Gordon was probably being over-sensitive to the fund manager environment from which she had emerged. In retrospect, confessing "We haven't found anything worth spending the money on and we will give it back to you" would have been a far better idea than rushing to spend it in the way we did.

Mytaxi.com and Rivals.net, a sports fan site, were both good ideas. We thought we were well positioned to get one of these off the ground and to do well out of it. In 2000, we also invested in Darker Than Blue, an online home for black music and youth culture founded by Everton Wright and Glen Yearwood. It was before the social networking revolution and ahead of its time: sadly, they lacked the ability to generate the business behind it.

We were behind the curve. To make money out of new media, we should have come up with these ideas and sold them on in 1998, instead of buying the businesses in the late nineties and then, as so often happened, closing them down in 2001.

Mytaxi disintegrated into chaos for the same reasons so many other fledgling internet businesses failed. People got carried away with the potential of any fantastic idea. Lisa Gordon took the Mytaxi brothers out to Silicon Valley to meet with Intel and a couple of investment banks and venture capitalists. She was trying to manage two young, bright individuals who had flair.

However, none of us really had a clue how to take it from A to B. The guy from the investment bank said: "This could be a billion dollar company." From that moment on, it all started to go horribly wrong. The brothers thought they were running a billion-dollar company when, in reality, they weren't. The potential was there but that wasn't enough. It was also about the team and the execution. The whole thing vanished into thin air. We ended up having to exit from Mytaxi.com after we had invested £1.3 million in it.

We backed four other internet businesses. Two were absolutely spot-on, even if they weren't fully realised. Keith Pringle, programme director at Chrysalis Radio, developed an idea called Ride The Tiger. It was effectively personalised radio designed to build up a profile of the listener. There is no doubt that Last.fm was a very similar concept, and that was sold to CBS for £140 million in May 2007.

We had a little more success with Rivals.net, the sports fan site. It was merged with its nearest competitor, 365.com, at the end of 2001, and then acquired by Sky in 2007.

Yet soon after the turn of the millennium, the City fell out of love with the internet as quickly as it had fallen in love with it two years earlier. Its attitude changed completely, and by the beginning of 2001 we were under huge pressure to get rid of anything related to the internet. There had been hugely expensive casualties out there, including Boo.com, a site that sold clothes and cosmetics and went into receivership in May 2000 after spending $135 million of venture capital. The City got badly spooked.

We had one or two germs of ideas and we should have had the balls to say to both the City and to our own non-executive directors that we wanted to pursue them. After all, Chrysalis Records grew by backing talent: we were never guaranteed a hit on everything we released. We just knew that out of 10 acts, one superstar would emerge to carry the rest – but like all record labels we never knew for sure which one it was going to be.

For a long time now Chrysalis had enjoyed such strong backing from the City that it was hard to deal with falling out of favour and our share price going the wrong way. There was one reason and one reason only: the City had closed its mind to the internet.

Looking back, we should have cut our losses sooner than we did. The most important lesson is to know when to quit. We could have prevailed with Ride The Tiger, which sat close to our core business and was absolutely the right thing to do. We had the raw intelligence to predict how the market was going to develop and the product people might want, but we didn't have the balls to pursue it.

We went from being heavily criticised for having no internet strategy to being compelled to demonstrate that we had a significant position. And then we were heavily criticised for having any exposure to web-related potential losses whatsoever, so we pulled the drawbridge up very quickly. The lesson: you can't run a business by responding to the City's short-termism.

Thankfully, despite the internet-related losses, I still had enough cash to put on the occasional big bash. We marked Janice's 40th birthday with a huge Hollywood-scale *Casablanca*-themed party at Glebe House. Inside an enormous marquee in the paddock in front of the house was a re-creation of Rick's Café Américain, the bar run by Humphrey Bogart in the iconic movie. We also had another marquee in the grounds of the house, where the pre-party drinks were served.

Most of the 250 guests thought they were in the main party venue until we opened up the vista to go into the second one, with Rick's logo emblazoned above the door which was approaching a path strewn with sand. The only problem was that everyone insisted on having their photograph taken in front of Rick's logo, delaying proceedings for the best part of an hour!

George Martin did a wonderful impersonation of *Casablanca* pianist Sam, who sings 'As Times Goes By' in *Casablanca* before a set from Björn Again, the Abba tribute band, got everyone on the dance floor. The party lasted until dawn, and some of the less 'rock'n'roll' guests may have been surprised by the contents of the hookah pipes, which we had arranged via my PA's contacts in Brixton.

Janice and I were very happy together, but we finally made the leap into marriage in rather inauspicious circumstances. One day in London I ran into a very attractive young lady called Jennifer who had left a successful career in the City to try her luck in the music business. Together with Nick Blackburn we went out to dinner at J Sheekey, a fish and seafood restaurant in Covent Garden.

Nick left early and the following morning I was in the office going through press clippings. This normally involved a quick glance before I threw them in the bin but I suddenly felt the need to reclaim an item that I had thrown away a few seconds previously, the gossip column from that morning's *Daily Mirror*. A short item ran: Who was the long-legged blonde with her arms draped around Chrysalis boss Chris Wright at J Sheekey's last night?

I went white. The phone rang. Richard Huntingford asked me, "What are you going to do about the story in the *Daily Mirror?*" Panic set in. I spoke to three friends, Richard, Nick Blackburn and Charles Levison: I got three separate bits of advice. One said: "Do nothing and hope it goes away." Another said: "Call up Janice and tell her in case she sees it." The third said: "Get on the next flight to Australia."

At the time Janice was sharing the school run with Carol Vorderman's mother, as Carol's daughter Katie and Holly were going to the same school. Carol's then-boyfriend was Des Kelly, at the time the deputy editor of the *Daily Mirror, so* it was obvious the Vorderman household would have the *Daily Mirror* and would see the story.

So I thought it best to tell Janice. I called her up and told her the whole story.

"Well, I think it's time we got married or that we decide we are going our separate ways," she replied.

The next day, I went out and bought her a huge engagement ring. That was the end of my second bachelorhood. I have to say it was probably about time.

Initially I imagined that Janice and I might have a wonderful wedding in an exotic locale but eventually we just decided to get married at the local registry office in Cirencester on a Friday in July. We didn't plan a reception as such but we invited about 100 close friends to come to lunch at Glebe House.

We put up a big marquee in the grounds and managed to keep the occasion secret from the guests. It was only when the guests arrived that they realised it was a special occasion and that, in fact, we had got married that morning. It was such a relaxed occasion. We partied until the early hours before leaving for a few days on the boat in Ibiza.

Another landmark occasion was my 60th birthday on September 7, 2004, which was an equally high profile but more sedate affair with 150 guests at Sketch in central London. We hired the stand-up comic Jimmy Carr for the occasion, though the indomitable Willie Robertson, God rest his soul, decided he could do a better job and rather embarrassingly proved this was not the case.

Nerina Pallot and Lucie Silvas, another singer-songwriter signed to Chrysalis Music, also performed. We even managed to have both Tim Rice and Andrew Lloyd Webber, who had been somewhat estranged, having a great time at the same table.

A rather grander occasion was Chloe's wedding at St Paul's Cathedral in September 2007, though the event was marred by the distressing news that Richard, my sister Carol's husband, had been diagnosed with pancreatic cancer. It was doubly disturbing that such a fit sports lover like Richard – he played golf to a handicap of one – should be so afflicted. He passed away a few weeks later.

After a boat trip down the Thames, the reception was held at the Hurlingham Club, the same venue where the reception was held after my marriage to Chelle in 1972. Sadly, the marriage lasted a little over a year – as I know only too well from my own life, there are as few guarantees of success in love as there are in the music business.

CHAPTER 28

Toujours L'Amour

The appointment of Philip McDanell to the position of group managing director may or may not have appeased David Puttnam and Tom Chandos and it may even have helped me create the time I needed to sort out the various problems with both QPR and Wasps, but Philip did not provide the dynamic leadership that the company required from a Chief Executive. Without the pressure from David and Tom I was able to more clearly see the necessity for making such an appointment. I can be an extremely obstinate person if pressured, but normally see a way to making difficult decisions if left to my own devices. So, it was with this in mind that we decided to let Philip McDanell go and commence a search for a Group Chief Executive to work under me as Chairman.

Once again Milena Djurkovic assisted me with the search. Clearly the outstanding candidate would be Richard Huntingford who had led the radio division with such great success and who ticked all the boxes in terms of the requirement to deal with the city and the ability to direct and motivate the staff.

Not wishing to enter a room with a choice of only one we did make a point of interviewing other candidates, one of whom was of some interest.

David Hockman had been chief executive of Polygram, soon to be Universal, Music. Famously, David flew to Stockholm to meet with Stig Anderson, the manager of Abba, and convinced him and his partners to sell the Abba catalogue to Polygram, one of the greatest music publishing acquisitions in history. This was before *Mamma Mia!* became such a huge hit in the West End, which re-invigorated the catalogue and introduced those wonderful songs to a new and younger audience. When Richard failed to agree terms with the recruitment committee of Charles Levison, non-executive director Geoff Howard Spink and I, we offered the position to David Hockman.

A press release was drawn up, photos taken, but of course the appointment required board approval. At the ensuing board meeting all hell broke loose. Not only did the other members of the board assume that Richard would be given the position but his number two in the Radio Division, Phil Riley, clearly expected to become the Chief Executive of that division. Eventually Richard was persuaded to compromise on his terms, which confirmed him the role, and I had the very difficult task of having to explain to David Hockman that our offer to him had been scuppered.

Richard and I developed an excellent working relationship which allowed the company to go from strength to strength. He was well liked and respected both internally and externally, and developed an excellent reputation for himself in the City.

Most Monday mornings Richard would drive out to Hurley, where I was living at the time, and we would play tennis – the matches were always competitive – and following that sit down for a few hours to plan the week's business.

One of the first initiatives Richard took was to suggest removing Mick Pilsworth from his position as Chief Executive of the Visual Entertainment division as it was now known and, with this layer of management gone, have all the various production company heads

371

report directly to him. This would give Richard more control of the financial performance of the division, and allay his concern about the bottom line figures not always matching the obvious successes we were achieving.

Over the years, the TV division had become one of the jewels in the crown of the Chrysalis Group and I was very pleased with the way things had developed. I always had the ability to rate a show in terms of how it would appeal to the general public, I understood the creative process and I knew how to engage and deal with creative people.

Of course, there are differences between TV directors and actors, on one side, and record producers, writers and musicians, on the other, but they have far more traits in common: an innate belief in their own creative ability, along with a degree of vulnerability about whether or not the public will accept that ability.

I have always considered it a big part of my job to be a bridge between the artist and the marketplace. I have largely been an enabler, helping people to turn their talent into something that could work commercially. I can also be realistic with creative people, whereas too often people are inclined to appease their egos and tell them how great they were. And I could build their confidence back up in times of doubt.

Furthermore, as I grew older and musicians were getting so much younger than me, it became easier for me to engage socially with the creative people within the television industry. In my fifties, I felt at ease in that environment, and I was keen to continue to build on our successes in the TV division. Selling it had never even occurred to me.

However, around the middle of the second week of January 2003, while I was in Antigua, Richard Huntingford phoned and asked me if I would be prepared to have dinner with Steve Morrison, whom I had known when he was a senior executive at Granada Television in Manchester. Richard explained that Steve was keen to buy our television division.

Although we were not interested in selling the business, Steve was nevertheless considering making an offer for it. However, he wouldn't do so until he'd met with me to establish whether or not he was wasting his time.

I was not remotely interested in hearing an offer for the television division, but I was perfectly willing to have dinner with Steve Morrison. Unfortunately, this was arranged for the evening that I returned from Antigua. Having just got off an overnight flight from the Caribbean, I was not at the top of my game.

I was aware of rumblings inside the company about selling the television division. It was very definitely not Richard Huntingford's baby. He was fundamentally preoccupied with the radio division and it was no great secret that, left to his own devices, Richard would have made Chrysalis a radio company and very little else.

Richard probably knew he would be fighting an uphill battle in persuading me to sell the music division, although he had even mooted that from time to time. We had considered a merger with Sanctuary, a publicly quoted company in a broadly similar space to us, since it was involved in artist management, music publishing and recording.

Yet I had always felt that Sanctuary was a castle built on sand – literally you might say, since part of its catalogue was the old Castle Communications reissue business which had been built up over the years by Terry Shand, who sold it to Sanctuary. I was so pleased that this idea had gone no further when I saw that a few months later Sanctuary went into administration and Universal acquired its catalogue. Had we gone into any kind of merger with Sanctuary, the institutional shareholders and myself would have ended up with a significant stake in return for our Chrysalis shares in a new, still publically quoted, joint venture company of dubious financial viability.

However, the sale of the TV business had been mooted from time to time on the grounds that it was a low-margin business and the

City didn't like it. That was partly of our own making, as when we reported our results to the City to my mind we tended to be negative about the TV business. It was also significant that, at the time, there were no publicly quoted television production companies.

I have always believed that gross margins are irrelevant unless you are selling nuts and bolts or washing powder. In order to value a business involved in the creative process, a great many other factors must be considered, including – and perhaps most importantly – the value of the copyrights and the sustainable long-term net income they will bring.

Although Mick Pilsworth had essentially built up the TV business, I had been greatly involved in it too. In fact, it's fair to say that the division had blossomed more after Mick left and Richard started managing it while reporting to me. Managing any creative business is difficult but the TV division was well run, with me taking the figurehead and major creative role, and Richard managing the bottom line.

Obviously, I was more emotionally involved in some parts of the TV business than in others. The sports broadcasting had always meant a lot to me, but I was less involved in Cactus TV and one of its projects, the British Soap Awards, which it instigated and which has become a major annual network show. As I never watched soaps, this was not something that particularly excited me.

However, the cream of our television business was Bentley Productions which Mick Pilsworth had started some time before with Brian True-May. Bentley Productions created and owned the rights to *Midsomer Murders* and by 2003, six years into its existence, the show's catalogue amounted to around 30 two-hour programmes that were regularly broadcast with multiple repeats in the UK and sold to more than 170 territories around the world.

Midsomer Murders was the most valuable copyright that the Chrysalis Group owned, even more important than any of our great songs. The shows were timeless: the episodes were not topical and could be repeated for 10, 20 or 30 years without appearing dated. Every new episode broadcast consistently rated in the Top 10 of the most-viewed programmes that week in the UK.

Brian True-May and I had become very close friends, especially after Mick Pilsworth left the company and the mantle fell on me to maintain the relationship on a personal level. Not only that, but Janice had become particularly friendly with Brian's wife, Maureen.

There was therefore a variety of differing emotional, personal and business reasons why I felt it made no sense to sell the TV division. Not only did it have strong, long-term asset value but, in part as a result of the good management that Richard Huntingford had instilled, it was making a profit of over £6 million a year.

Nevertheless, rather tired and jet-lagged I went to dinner with Steve Morrison and Richard at Clarke's restaurant. It became obvious, even before we'd finished our starter, that to a certain degree Richard seemed well down the road to doing a deal to sell the TV division of the company.

Conversations must have been going on between him and Steve for some time and basic terms appeared to have been progressed. Given my jet-lagged state, it was very difficult for me to do anything other than to sit quietly, appear interested and say that, under the right circumstances, I would be prepared to consider selling the company. When I left the restaurant I was clearly quite confused and taken aback at this somewhat dramatic development.

And I was in a difficult position. Richard was keen to expand the radio business and the company was already leveraged as much as was prudently possible. After the publication of the Communications Bill, there were radio stations coming on the market that we were interested in acquiring and we needed to build a war chest to prepare for this.

So the board met to discuss the proposal from Steve Morrison.

I was aware of all the facts on the other side of the argument: the City didn't like TV production at the time (although, within six months, that attitude would change), but it did like the radio division: in fact, that was the reason many of the shareholders had invested in Chrysalis shares in the first place.

At this point, Richard had amassed an enormous amount of credibility in the City. He always presented well and was regarded as a top-quality media executive. I knew that if the matter was put to shareholders rather than to the board, they would probably support a sale of the TV business to buy further radio stations. However, I just didn't see that selling it made any business sense. We would be receiving only £50 million for the asset-rich TV business, which was in any event making £6 million a year in profit. In the board meeting, I strongly advised against the disposal.

At the time, the directors who supported the deal besides Richard included Phil Riley, the chief executive of the radio division (for obvious reasons), Peter Lassman and Lisa Gordon, the corporate development director who also dealt with the City. The TV division had no chief executive to fight its corner. Jeremy Lascelles, head of the music division, was not even on the main board.

It was thus left to the non-executive directors and the finance director to mount any opposition and they all found it hard to make a decision. We asked David Murrell, a director with a chartered accountant's background, to value the assets from the copyright standpoint, which he appeared to be competent to do (although, of course, valuing any creative asset requires more than just an accountant's view).

In the end, perhaps for the first time ever, the board was forced to take a vote on the issue and Richard's argument held sway and won the day. In fact, I was the only director to vote against the sale. I was convinced it was the wrong decision and I insisted that the minutes recorded my opposition. I believed the company had taken a decision that it would eventually come to regret.

I was now in a very difficult situation. I was the chairman of a public company whose board had made a decision to dispose of its TV division and I had no alternative but to go along with it, otherwise, my position would have been untenable. I had a fiduciary responsibility to do that and I abided by that at every stage along the way to help conclude the deal, but it was not easy.

Most of the managers of the companies within Chrysalis Television were more than happy being part of the Chrysalis Group, and violently opposed to the transaction. In some instances, it was fear of the unknown; in other cases, there were sound practical reasons why they were not prepared to go along with it.

As the deal drew ever closer towards conclusion, my trenchant view meant that every time the other side came back to chip away at the price I could refuse. By doing so, I am sure we saved around £5 million of reductions that would have been forced on us if the board had not known that it would be a bridge too far for me.

However, Steve Morrison still had to reach agreements with the key executives or the deal would not complete. On the morning it was supposed to be signed, I was driving into the office from Hurley when I received a call from Richard to say that the negotiations between Steve Morrison and Brian True-May, the producer of *Midsomer Murders*, had totally broken down and that, unless they could be put back on track very quickly, the deal would be off. He wanted my advice. I was already prepared for this question as I had just had a call from Janice who had had Maureen True-May on the phone saying there was no way that Brian was ever going to agree to the deal with Steve.

I explained concisely to Richard exactly what Steve Morrison should do in order to get the deal back on track: get in his car, drive out to Pinewood Studios, where Bentley Productions was based, to see Brian True-May, and eat humble pie by agreeing whatever terms he proposed. Meanwhile, the other key television executives started celebrating that fact that the deal had apparently been scuppered. By contrast, when I arrived at the Chrysalis office, there was a general air of despondency around the group management team that the deal was off and would not be revived.

Amazingly, Steve did everything that I suggested and, by putting a tremendous deal on the table, managed to talk Brian around. By the end of the afternoon, to the despair of the other members of the TV division management, the deal was back on track and ready to be signed.

With the backing of a private equity group, Steve Morrison was attempting to use Chrysalis Television to achieve a consolidation of independent television producers. He added Mersey Television, the producer of the soap *Brookside*, Lion Television, which made the reality TV programme *Castaway* for the BBC, and Company Pictures, the team behind the comedy-drama series *Shameless*, and renamed the company All3Media.

Two or three years later, Steve was able to re-market and sell half of the company to US venture capitalist Permira. That deal valued All3Media at £320 million, including debt, which gives you an indication of the way the value of TV companies had been revised upwards by City analysts and investors within a few months of the sale of Chrysalis Television.

Soon afterwards, two or three other television production companies went to the market to float and were all hugely successful. One of them was Shed Productions, Eileen Gallagher's company, which made *Bad Girls* and *Footballers' Wives* for ITV. The other was RDF Media, the television production company behind *Wife Swap*.

The City used to regard television production companies as a low-margin, low-return business. It attributed its own fresh enthusiasm for television to a change in regulations which allowed producers to keep control of their overseas rights. However, we had always controlled our rights: the truth was that the City did not understand the way Chrysalis Television operated.

To this day, despite all the erosion of value with media industry assets, the one area that has not been eroded is television production. Elisabeth Murdoch sold her production company, Shine, to her father's News Corporation for £415 million. Even very small companies sell at really high multiples.

When we sold Chrysalis Television, there was some concern that *Midsomer Murders* might not continue and was a franchise that could have a short shelf life. These fears proved groundless. It remains in production, with around seven or eight episodes being made a year. The library now has over 250 hours of programming.

Midsomer Murders alone has made back the acquisition price many times over, and has made both Steve Morrison and Brian True-May very wealthy. It will continue to make money as the shows will no doubt run and rerun for many years into the future.

We used the money from selling the TV division to pay down debt and, in May 2005, bought Century 106 in the East Midlands from GCap Media, which had to sell because of competition concerns. It became the third station of the Heart network, rebranded Heart 106, in August 2005.

Had we gone on to acquire more stations with the proceeds from selling the TV division, it might not have been such a bad deal. But we had reached a point in time when the value of any radio station was being bid up to unbelievable levels in what was essentially a land grab.

There was limited radio real estate available as fewer and fewer new licences were being awarded. As the major radio players sought to expand, the value of any independent assets that came on the market escalated enormously.

Furthermore, the sale of the TV division had several other consequences, not least the way it adversely affected my working relationship with Richard Huntingford, which until that time had been excellent. Although we ran the business together successfully for several years afterwards, our relationship was never quite the same.

I think that Richard knew he would have had a problem persuading me to sell the TV division and so had to work very hard behind the scenes to achieve his objectives. I am sure he felt he was acting in the best interests of the company at the time, but he knew he would have struggled to achieve his aims acting any differently.

In hindsight, it is clear to me now that rather than selling Visual Entertainment we should have sold the radio business and used the proceeds from selling the radio division to build up the TV division.

Had we done so, with the way things have turned out, I believe the company would have been so successful we would still be around today as a major media rights owning group. The value of radio assets has since fallen markedly as, arguably, they were never really worth the prices that were being paid for them.

As the TV deal was closing, the other side broached the subject of a non-compete clause that would bar me, and Chrysalis, from re-entering the television business for three years, which was normal practice. This I was not prepared to accept, which I think they were surprised about. I had enjoyed my involvement in the television business enormously, it had become a big part of my life and I was keen to continue.

Nevertheless, although I had made many friends in that area, it was never ever going to be a substitute for my involvement in the music business. My reputation remained primarily as a music person. If I ever turned up at MIPTV, the television conference in Cannes, I would know very few people and very few people would recognise me. Whereas, when I attended Midem, the music conference in Cannes, the opposite was true. That was the world I had always moved in.

Even so, following the sale of Chrysalis Television, I started exploring other areas where I could involve myself in TV production or distribution. I had a series of conversations with Jeremy Fox, an old friend and accomplice, about what opportunities existed. Unlike me, Jeremy had worked in television all his life, and eventually he came up with a couple of opportunities.

One was the purchase of a small film, television production and distribution company called Portman Film & Television, which had run into financial difficulties. We ended up buying it and used it as a base to rebuild a new television company. Portman came with some problems, however. Its principal business was as a small independent film sales company, a difficult area for a small operator, as I knew well from my Chrysalis days. It was always difficult acquiring the films or repertoire to sell, particularly without paying substantial advances. It was a business that, once we bought the company, we ultimately exited.

We did take on the distribution rights to *Doc Martin*, a comedy drama series featuring Martin Clunes as an eccentric London-born Cornwall-based doctor. I felt it had some elements of *Midsomer Murders* and the potential to become a long-running series: it had a star celebrity lead actor and was set in a quintessentially English village background.

One of my first jobs after we acquired Portman was to go down to Cornwall to visit the set, meet Martin Clunes and have dinner with him and his wife, Philippa Braithwaite, who co-produces *Doc Martin*. The programme achieves huge ratings on ITV1 and has since been sold to almost as many global territories as *Midsomer Murders*, though in some countries it is being re-made in foreign-language versions.

We also helped fund and distribute a similar series called *Kingdom* with Stephen Fry playing the part of a country lawyer. This series was set in the Norfolk countryside and also sold well internationally, but despite those two successes, Portman was ultimately sub-scale and we ended up merging it with a similar operation called ID TV, which was owned by Patrick McKenna's company, Ingenious Media.

As a result, Ingenious Media became the largest shareholder in what became the Digital Rights Group. Our relationship with Ingenious was complicated and became fraught. Certain terms of the deal were too heavily slanted in it favour and a few years later it chose to remove Jeremy Fox as chief executive with the intention of ultimately disposing of the company. However, on June 13, 2013, DRG was sold by Ingenious Media to Modern Times Group (MTG), a Swedish Company, and Fox was re-hired as CEO of the new entity.

Although my involvement has obviously been behind the scenes, I have always enjoyed appearing on television. I contributed to several of the *Top 10* series we made for Channel 4, usually talking about some of the Chrysalis acts that fitted the genre covered in the programme, such as Jethro Tull in the progressive show, or Ultravox in the eighties New Romantics one. These shows were incredibly well researched and rather tongue-in-cheek, with presenters like Bill Bailey and Boy George, and became a mainstay of the Channel Four Saturday night schedules in the early 2000s.

During my involvement with QPR and Wasps, I appeared on all kinds of sports programmes on radio and on television. The fact that our offices were very close to BBC Television Centre in west London meant that they could get hold of me quite easily.

A weightier TV appearance came in 1995 when I was profiled in the *Millionaires* series on Carlton Television, but in 2004, the BBC did a much more in-depth job when it devoted a whole hour to Chrysalis in an episode of *Ruby Does The Business* presented by Ruby Wax. Ruby really seemed determined to find out what made me tick, although it was not something I felt comfortable doing. In fact I was approached initially about the show as a promotional opportunity for the radio stations.

On two separate occasions, the BBC screen-tested me for *Dragons' Den*, the entrepreneur-seeking reality TV programme. The first time, they set up a meeting at my office two or three hours after I had got off a long-haul flight from Australia. I had specified that I would do no more than a simple meeting that day, but they still turned up with all the cameras. On the second occasion, I went up to Television Centre. Because they didn't take it any further, I assume that I failed both auditions. They also had an idea for a charity request version show similar to *Dragons' Den* which I did a pilot for over the course of a few days. I thought it went very well but the producer left the BBC soon after.

Having wanted to be a journalist or broadcaster when I was at school, I enjoyed my flirtation with broadcasting, such as it was. Sadly, in these youth-obsessed days, I think that is as far as it can go. I am beginning to be too old to do anything on television, although radio may still be within my scope. Nowadays, I have a good face for radio, as the famous phrase goes.

Chrysalis had also entered the book publishing business in 1998. Initially, this came about because I mentioned to Peter Lassman, who was running Lasgo Chrysalis, that its core business of distributing and exporting CDs and DVDs could well be a declining area of activity. Peter was extremely competent at running the business and I felt he should look for other areas to add on to Lasgo that might be more sustainable.

Lasgo started trading in books in much the same way as it bought and sold CDs and DVDs, and this soon became quite a significant part of its business. The possibility of us buying Ramboro, a book remainder company, was mooted as it seemed as though such a move would complement the Lasgo distribution business.

We appointed John Needleman, the original owner of Ramboro Books, to head the new books division, reporting to Peter Lassman. Unfortunately, the book-remainder company also owned a mainstream book publisher so we became, by stealth, a publishing company.

To compound the problem, in 2001, we decided to expand this area of business by making a number of acquisitions. We bought up a series of small and not so small independent book publishers, including Batsford, Brassey's and Pavilion, all of whom seemed to have fallen on hard times, plus Collins & Brown, an illustrated book company which was quite substantial. The rationale was that Chrysalis Books would reduce the overheads and make them profitable once again.

Most of the companies published illustrated, so-called coffee-table books, and covered a variety of non-fiction genres: DIY, interiors, mind and body, architecture, military and children's books. The division also included the Jeremy Robson-led Robson books which specialised in biographies.

Robson had published the Michael Winner books and a rather controversial tome entitled *The Assassination Of Robert Maxwell: Israel's Superspy* by Martin Dillon and Gordon Thomas, which posited the theory that the late Robert Maxwell had been an agent for Mossad, the Israeli intelligence service, and had been assassinated after attempting to blackmail them.

It was a riveting read and proved one of Robson's most successful titles, with three reprints within a few weeks of its publication in the

UK in 2002. The book also made headlines when an employee at Carroll & Graf, its US publisher, showed it to Isabel Maxwell, one of his daughters, pre-publication, despite a confidentiality clause. Isabel used it to attack the authors in *The Jewish Chronicle*.

Chrysalis Books existed for seven years, between 1998 and 2005. The division was never starved of investment and in fact the management on the whole found it easy to get the consent of the board for large speculative ventures. It's amazing to think how intelligent businessmen could take such a confident view of what was to us a new area of activity. Their vision was clearly impaired by the fact that they obviously felt publishing books was a safe, risk-free, conservative business, unlike investing in songwriters and rock groups. At the same time, the Music Division was being starved of investment on the grounds that it was a highly speculative business. There were a great many similarities between the two businesses except, of course, we had a huge amount of expertise in the music area, and we had very little in books.

In 2002, Chrysalis Books published 643 titles across 14 imprints and had a staff of around 100 people. Turnover was £ 33.9 million and, in theory, the book publishing division declared an operating profit of £3 million. Everything appeared to be going well.

However, on one of my annual visits to York races, I decided to stop off in Leeds and visit our warehouse and was shocked to find acres on acres of books stacked up and gathering dust. I was also astonished that no one from the company, apart from myself, had registered any concern over this.

I was seriously alarmed, but despite my uneasiness I was continually assured that the book division was performing well, and that it was making bottom-line profits even though the cash-flow numbers seemed far from positive.

It soon became clear that we had a huge problem on our hands. We had been buying up a lot of imprints that were not profitable when we acquired them and nothing that we could do to manage them was going to turn their fortunes around. The profits we were declaring did not reflect the cash position. The performance of the division should have been judged much more on its cash flow than the bottom-line profits, and the cash-flow situation was horrendous.

The books division became a major drain on the business and inevitably, it soon started showing not just cash-flow losses but bottom-line losses too, stretching into the millions. It required a great deal of management time to address the issue.

After a full review of the operation in 2002, John Needleman, who had been charged with building Chrysalis Books, left the company under a cloud and we appointed Marcus Leaver, who had been the group's corporate development director, to sort out the problems.

Throughout 2003, we had a strategic rethink and restructured the whole division. This involved a number of redundancies, re-evaluating the stock and reducing the number of imprints from 17 to eight. Following a loss of £3.6 million in 2003, Chrysalis Books generated a loss of £2.1 million in 2004.

We found it impossible to sell Chrysalis Books and by the end of 2005 the only option was to give it away to the management team who were prepared to take it on. The division was hived off and became Anova Books, a new venture headed by Robin Wood. Our foray into book publishing had been an unmitigated disaster. The total losses incurred during the period amounted to some £35 million. The sad thing was I could see it all happening from the time I visited the warehouse in Leeds.

On a far more positive note, 2005 saw a major landmark in my life. One day as I was driving back from Goodwood races, I called my PA in the office to see if there was anything I needed to know about. We discussed a few issues, confirmed some appointments and then in passing she told me we had received a letter in the post. She read it out in a matter-of-fact tone. It informed me that I had been awarded a CBE in the Queen's Birthday Honours List.

Before the ceremony at Buckingham Palace, I was informed of the event's protocol. I was to step forward to meet the Queen when invited, receive the medal, speak when spoken to, and step away backwards when dismissed.

I was being given my honour amongst a host of other people and couldn't help but think it must be an extremely tedious procedure for the Queen. I thought I would try to make my part of the ceremony a bit more interesting for her, and imagined us chewing the cud about horse racing and comparing notes on Crime of Passion and Heights of Fashion.

My turn came, and I stepped forward from the line.

"And what do you do?" Her Majesty asked me.

"Well, I've had a career in the music business, television production, and I own radio stations," I told her. "And, like you, I'm a keen race horse owner and breeder."

I eagerly awaited her riposte.

"Oh," said the Queen. "Very varied."

And that was it. My moment was up. I was so dumbfounded by Her Majesty's low-key reaction that I totally forgot about backing away from her, and instead turned around and strode off. It was very special to meet our Head of State but the encounter had not gone as I had imagined, or had hoped. I feel great embarrassment about it to this day.

CHAPTER 29

Trouble

The death from a heart attack of Charles Levison in July 2006 had left a big hole in my life. Unfortunately, I found it impossible to replace him within the company.

Charles had been at my side from the early nineties throughout the huge expansion and development of Chrysalis. He was a wonderful counsel. He was a great enabler, an enthusiast but practical with it. He became deputy chairman of the Chrysalis Group, and had the office next door to me in the Chrysalis building. It got to the point where I would seek his advice on everything, both business and personal, and he likewise with me.

Charles had become a completely indispensable figure in my life and helped me make good decisions – plus, of course, at other times he helped me make bad decisions. I still wonder exactly what he would have made of what was about to happen to Chrysalis Radio.

Following the disposal of Chrysalis Television, there had been much debate around the boardroom table about demerging Chrysalis Radio from the music division. This became known as Project Cavalier but it never got off the ground and was in any case superseded when we decided that radio had nowhere to grow anyway, resulting in the eventual sale of the division.

Richard Huntingford and Phil Riley felt that the progress of the radio division was being impeded by my reluctance to sell the music division in order to fund further radio acquisitions. Nor was I keen on the idea of issuing shares at a very low price compared to break-up value, as I did not want to accept the punitive nature of any dilution in my shareholding of the Chrysalis Group.

I guess I was suspicious that the radio division management was driving the initiative. However, when you took a step back, you realised that historically Chrysalis had always been valued on the sum-of-its-parts basis. At some point, shareholders would want to test the reality and see if the music publishing division really was worth £200 million and whether our radio assets were worth £200 million, to use ball-park figures.

A demerger of the divisions would have realised real cash and underpinned the values on the sums-of-the-parts basis. Richard and Phil's ambition was to do what Global Radio eventually did and become a consolidator, rather than a 'consolidatee'. Indeed, for a couple of years, we tried to go down that route.

By 2005, Chrysalis had become the third biggest commercial radio operation in the country, behind Capital and EMAP. We had Heart in London – perhaps the largest and biggest independent radio station in Britain, having overtaken Capital as number one in London – as well as Heart in the West Midlands, Galaxy stations covering all of Yorkshire, the North East, Manchester and Birmingham, and LBC in London, broadcasting two different programmes on AM and on FM.

Try as we might, we had failed in our countless attempts to add to this. We had been unsuccessful in further applications for newly advertised licences and the radio land grab was still continuing apace in the country as a whole. As the advertising of new large radio stations ground to a halt as the map and the dial filled up, the existing operators started looking at their competitors in order to further expand and consolidate.

The first move was when Capital Radio merged with GWR to create GCap in 2005. This gave the new group an enormous number of stations outside London, where it had not been particularly strong. As part of this transaction, for monopoly reasons, it had to divest itself of a couple of stations which we attempted to buy but we were outbid by the Guardian Media Group, the radio division arm of *The Guardian*.

Meanwhile, I was receiving numerous phone calls from – and getting into conversations with – other operators about the possibility of acquiring Chrysalis. I had a series of meetings with Sir Robin Miller, chief executive of EMAP. I did not share these conversations with the Chrysalis management, as I didn't want them to think that I might be interested in, or even entertaining the idea of, selling the radio division.

By now, radio had become the main focus of the company but, with the industry consolidating, we had to sustain ourselves and make sure we remained one of the three major players. The idea of buying the Guardian Media Group radio business arose on our agenda. Despite the £50 million cash we had received from selling the TV division, because of our previous radio acquisitions we were operating the company with quite a considerable amount of debt.

We entered conversations with *The Guardian* to buy its stations. I personally valued Real Radio and Jazz FM, which would soon be renamed Smooth, at something less than £100 million but the management of Chrysalis Radio was so keen to acquire them that it was almost prepared to pay whatever it took.

In the end, it seemed like a figure of £125 million would buy them but I was uncomfortable at this level. We stretched the bidding to £115 million, with bonus payments to increase the payment to £130 million on certain performance figures. The Guardian Media Group board met to consider the offer and all the indications were that the deal had been agreed with management and would be rubber-stamped. We were therefore rather taken aback when they decided to reject it.

These were still the heady days before the 2007 run on Northern Rock when the value of everything had soared to unbelievable levels. We sat in board meetings at Chrysalis during which figures north of £400 million were being mentioned as the value for the existing Chrysalis radio business.

With hindsight, a value of that magnitude was clearly unsustainable, certainly based on the cash flow generated and profits achieved by the radio business. Yet, amazingly, some stations were changing hands on multiples based on this level. Clearly it had to come to an end at some point and I became firmly of the opinion that were we able to sell our radio business at anything close to this inflated figure, it would be in the best interests of all the shareholders, including myself. I was reluctant to move this conversation forward because I knew I would get little or no support from inside the company although I had shared those thoughts with Charles Levison.

However, at the end of July 2006, a few weeks after Charles passed away, I took a Friday afternoon phone call from Sir Bob Phillis, the chief executive of the Guardian Media Group. He asked me if we would consider selling our radio business.

"Yes," I replied, "at the right price. How much?"

Phillis asked me to give them the weekend to think about it and promised to call on Monday with a figure. On that Monday morning, we had a management meeting in the boardroom at Bramley Road. Before going up to my office, while still with Richard Huntingford, I called my PA to check on my phone calls to find that Bob Phillis had indeed called me back. "Can you get him back and put me through?" I asked her, and then told Richard: "Bob Phillis is going to make an offer for the radio business."

Richard was shocked. I had sprung this one on him in a very similar way to how he had surprised me about the sale of our TV interests three years earlier.

I had thought about it over the weekend and I had decided that if the offer was more than £200 million, I would bite Bob Phillis' hand off. I knew this was a long way from £400 million, the number which had been mooted in the past, but it still felt to me much closer to the true valuation. Bob Phillis came on the line.

"What's your number?" I asked him.

"£225 million."

I knew we were close to a deal. "Thank you very much," I said. "I'll get back to you."

Richard was taken aback. He felt the stations were worth £300 million, certainly on the basis that we had bid around £115 million for *The Guardian*'s own stations not that long ago. I was concerned that the economic environment was deteriorating and I would certainly not have paid anything like that for the *Guardian* stations in 2006.

Richard asked me to go back with a figure of £300 million for the Chrysalis radio division, which I was not comfortable doing, although one assumed that if *The Guardian*'s opening offer was £225 million, they might possibly have been nudged up a little, maybe as far as £250 million.

Before we could proceed, Richard brought up the subject of him receiving a disposal bonus on the sale of the business, with some justification since radio had been his baby and a division that he had nurtured for several years. I was not opposed to Richard benefitting from the sale but it took us some while to agree on terms. When we did so, because of the level of the remuneration, I explained it had to be subject to the approval of the remuneration committee of the Chrysalis board.

On that basis, professional advisers were hired and Richard and I left to go on our respective holidays, in his case to Barbados and in mine to the boat in France which was by now a brand new Mangusta 92, both of us assuming that the deal would progress during August. Two or three weeks later, with Richard and I both back from vacation, I asked what progress had been made, only to be told none whatsoever. One set of professional advisers had apparently been away for the earlier part of the holiday, and when they had returned, the second set had in turn gone away.

I was very concerned, particularly as I would have expected someone from inside Chrysalis to have told me they were struggling to get meetings together to push things along. I called Bob Phillis, who was equally worried that no progress had been made. Sadly, in the meantime Bob had been diagnosed with cancer, and though he showed signs of recovering, he eventually died in December 2009.

Because of his illness, Bob was relinquishing his post as chief executive of Guardian Media Group to be replaced by Carolyn McCall, now the CEO of EasyJet. Bob promised to call Carolyn and get things back on track. Carolyn called me and we hastily arranged a meeting at the Chrysalis office between Richard, myself, Carolyn and Nick Castro, the group finance director at Guardian Media Group.

With the figure of £225 million on the table, Richard began to explain why the business was really worth £300 million, to which Carolyn McCall replied that, if anything, the financial environment had weakened in the intervening period during August and they should be negotiating the figure down. Richard countered with: if it's not £300 million or very close, then you might as well leave right now.

The *Guardian* pair got up to leave, I managed to persuade them to stay, and we agreed that we would involve other senior management of both companies to get to a fair valuation so the deal could progress. But once again no progress was made, and *The Guardian* eventually withdrew its offer.

By November, the realisation dawned upon us that Chrysalis Radio really had limited opportunity to expand any further. It was likely to become subscale and maybe we should review our options in terms of the sale of the business. I was concerned as to who else would be able to buy it as, for regulatory reasons, it would have been difficult by this point for either EMAP or GCap to devour the whole of Chrysalis without having to divest some of their other stations.

Richard and the management remained convinced that the natural bedfellow of the company was *The Guardian*, as it would combine the third and fourth largest radio operators with no regulatory issues, and that they would be waiting in the wings ready to pounce as soon as we pressed the start button. I called Carolyn McCall to tell her of our plans, only to be told: "Chris, if you put Chrysalis Radio up for sale, I can guarantee you that *The Guardian* will not be one of the bidders." My gut feeling was to believe her.

When I reported this to the rest of the board, the view seemed to be that she was bluffing. However Carolyn was true to her word, and as we went into the sales process for the radio division one glaring absentee from the bidding was the Guardian Media Group.

Later on, when the process was completed, I asked Carolyn why this was. She replied that from the time of the first meeting with Richard in the Chrysalis office, she knew Richard would ensure that Chrysalis radio would not be sold, and certainly not at a realistic price, so it would be pointless even bidding.

So we entered into the disposal process, euphemistically called a strategic review, of Chrysalis Radio with the most obvious buyer absent from the room. This didn't mean to say we didn't have numerous other offers, but it became clear that the offers we were about to receive were not going to be in excess of £200 million.

In the midst of all of this, in February 2007, I went to Los Angeles for the Grammy Awards and as I got off the plane at LAX I found I had a voicemail message from Michael Tabor. I was intrigued.

I knew Michael primarily from horseracing, as he is one of the partners with John Magnier and Derek Smith in the Coolmore racing operation, one of the biggest horseracing owners in the world. For a second, I thought maybe I had a horse he wanted to buy, but it didn't take me long to realise that none of my horses would have featured very high on his radar screen.

Michael called me again and said that he had a consortium that was interested in entering the bidding process for Chrysalis Radio. He added that Denis Brosnan, an Irish businessman, the founder of the Kerry Group food company, who was also involved in horse racing but not under the Coolmore banner, would be handling negotiations.

I arranged for Denis to be added to the list of recipients of the offer documentation and he and I agreed to meet when he was over for the

Cheltenham Racing Festival in the middle of March. But progress with the Michael Tabor/Denis Brosnan bid became very lethargic, principally because the Chrysalis advisers and management did not take them seriously. The general perception was that they were just some people I had met via horse racing.

In fact, Michael Tabor's interests went way beyond racing. He had amassed a large portfolio of different businesses but his son Ashley had more of a flair for the music business and was already operating as an artist manager and a small music publisher. Ashley may well have been the driving force behind the interest in acquiring Chrysalis Radio.

When the final bids were in, although there were four or five different offers, including one from EMAP for the bits of the group it felt it could acquire without having a monopolies problem, the best bid in terms of execution risk, price etc was the bid from the Tabor-led consortium, and terms were duly agreed.

The price was around £170 million, some way below the £225 million *Guardian* offer from the previous summer, and considerably down on the £400 million plus price tag that had been mentioned a couple of years previously. I should say that the level of the offer was only just above the point at which the board would have rejected it.

In hindsight, had we said no, heaven knows what problems we would have created for ourselves, because we were highly leveraged at the time. When the financial crash occurred in 2008, we could have been left with a huge problem. Beyond that, one shudders to think of the scenario had we been successful in acquiring the *Guardian* stations a couple of years previously for around £125 million, all of which we would have needed to service by debt.

Indeed, the fact that Guardian Media Group valued its radio stations at around £120 million in 2011 but has since sold them to Global Radio for £70 million puts a different complexion on the aforementioned figures. In actual fact, we achieved a good price for Chrysalis Radio and realised value for our shareholders.

Unfortunately, Richard's disposal bonus on the sale of the radio division, which he and I had agreed, was still subject to board and shareholder approval. When it came time for the board to debate it, the remuneration committee considered it was set at a level with which they were uncomfortable and suggested they would approve it only if the shareholders approved it first.

I am not sure if anyone expected this would be a problem, but when we sought shareholder approval for the package, we ran into an enormous amount of hostility from different shareholders for various reasons. Some said that they had never agreed to disposal bonuses. Others thought the level was too high, and in the case of some shareholders who had only just acquired Chrysalis shares, they couldn't see why a bonus of that level was justified. We realised we would struggle to secure the necessary consent.

Richard blamed me for this, but there was little I could do about it at the time. Richard and I had been very close friends, tennis partners, we had holidayed together, and now we had ended up in this sorry, acrimonious situation. It was a major shame: Richard had devoted a great deal of his professional life to Chrysalis, he was an excellent executive, and had contributed enormously to the success of the company. It was sad for him to be leaving under such circumstances.

In hindsight, I should have personally been more proactive in ensuring that the *Guardian* deal did progress, regardless of Richard's feelings, and perhaps also I should have stuck to my beliefs on the subject of the sale of the TV division. To be fair, with the change in management between Bob Phillis and Carolyn McCall, who knows at what level the *Guardian* deal would ultimately have closed, but one has to assume the figure would have been in excess of £200 million.

On June 25 2007, it was announced that Heart, along with its sister stations LBC, Galaxy and The Arrow, our digital station, were to be sold for £170 million to what was to become Global Radio.

When the stations were sold, although I was convinced it was the right thing to do from a business standpoint, it was nevertheless a very sad moment for me emotionally. Still, I was delighted that the stations were sold to someone in Ashley Tabor, who I knew was a radio buff. I knew he would love, cherish and develop both the stations and the business, and look after the staff, all of which he has managed to do.

At first, the new owners continued to operate the stations from the Chrysalis building. Only after Ashley went on to buy GCap Media, the former Capital Radio group and Classic FM the following year, and merged much of it with the old Chrysalis Radio, did he choose to move out of the building to the Capital offices in Leicester Square.

The downside of this was that Chrysalis' Bramley Road base began to resemble a morgue. It was hard not to think back with affection to the days when the building regularly rattled with visits from everyone from pop stars to prime ministers. The company had lost an important component, and this would have profound consequences for the Group. In short, it would never be the same again.

CHAPTER 30

The Time Is Now

In the end-of-the-millennium years of the dotcom bubble and absurdly inflated values for Chrysalis Radio, and when music publishing assets were valued at 20 times the net publishers share, the overall business environment in which we were operating had appeared to a large extent healthy and buoyant. This was all to change with the global financial crisis of 2007 and 2008.

The first inkling this was coming came in October 2007 when the run on Northern Rock made headlines in the UK. Had we been smart, we might have seen gathering on the horizon the storm clouds that were to shake the financial world 11 months later with the collapse of Lehman Brothers in the US. I guess we were too busy reorganising Chrysalis to really take much notice of the impending global crisis.

With the sale of the radio business completed in July 2007, we refocused the company on what remained: primarily Chrysalis Music, with music publishing as its core activity, the Echo label, and Lasgo Chrysalis.

A large proportion of the Chrysalis core management structure had been involved in the radio business and the diminished group did not require a chief executive of Richard Huntingford's stature. It was always his intention to leave following the radio sale, and he departed at the end of that September, with the issue of the disposal bonus still unresolved. In fact, it was only after legal proceedings were commenced that we reached a settlement acceptable to both sides.

The question of ongoing management requirements also applied to group finance director Michael Connole, who had recently taken over from the stalwart Nigel Butterfield, though he and Clive Potterell, the long serving company secretary, stayed on until they both secured roles at Global Radio. They and others like the corporate communications director Harriet Finney had worked for the company for many years and found they had no role left, though Harriet remained on a part-time basis because we still had a requirement to report results to the City.

Jeremy Lascelles became group chief executive but there was a question mark over the second most important role of the company, that of group finance director. I recruited Andy Mollett, formerly chief financial officer of EMI Music Publishing, who had left because he had had problems dealing with the hierarchy in New York.

Andy had previously been finance director of Ginger Media, the Chris Evans-owned company, and the founding finance director of Virgin Radio, where he had spent eight years. He was also on the board of Channel 4 as a non-executive director so his appointment made a lot of sense.

The new management team consisted of Jeremy Lascelles, Peter Lassman at Lasgo Chrysalis, Andy Mollett and myself. We had to decide if Chrysalis was sustainable as a small public company, and then justify that position to the City.

When we sold the radio division, our original intention had been to pay out the bulk of the net funds, almost all of the £170 million, to the shareholders, which would have benefitted myself as the largest shareholder. Richard Huntingford, in particular, recommended this.

However, Andy Brough, the fund manager at Schroders, the largest single and the longest standing shareholder in the company, having been involved with Chrysalis for some 20 plus years, counselled against this. He told us it would be crazy to pay out the bulk of the profits from the sale of Chrysalis Radio and saddle the ongoing company with an enormous amount of debt, so we took the decision to pay off all but £20 million of the debt. That gave the ongoing Chrysalis a reasonable chance of success.

We had to position ourselves with the institutional shareholders and work out the level of overhead we could carry. Having stripped out a layer of management, we had to reduce costs and salaries wherever possible. Initially, the salary package that was reduced, without compensation, was mostly mine. It was much easier to negotiate with myself than anyone else, but there was also pressure from inside Chrysalis for me to do this in order for the company to be sustainable. The logic ran that I was now chairman of a smaller company, so why should I carry on receiving the same amount of money?

In the autumn of 2007, we presented our plans to the institutional shareholders. We expected a few problems but thought that Andy Brough would be supportive as he had been involved every step of the way with the sale of the radio division, and the metamorphosis of Chrysalis Group PLC into what was now Chrysalis PLC.

Some of the shareholders were indeed supportive, some less so, but enough gave us hope we would be able to remain as the largest British independent and the only public quoted music company. With the uncertainty already hanging over EMI, we may even have ended up being the largest British music company of any description.

The last meeting of an exhausting round of institutional meetings was at Schroders with Andy Brough and on that day we were joined by Mark Lyttleton from BlackRock, who had around a 4 or 5% shareholding in the company. They both seemed to listen intently to our plans for restructuring and we felt the meeting had been a success.

So we were completely taken aback a few days later to receive a call from Keith Anderson, the Co-Head of Corporate Broking at our brokers, Investec. Andy Brough had phoned him to say he was no longer prepared to support Chrysalis and wanted the company to be sold. This came as a huge shock as it was totally out of the blue.

Frankly, if we were now to put the music division up for sale it would have made far more sense to have sold the whole Chrysalis Group in one go a few months earlier and not have had to implement the round of redundancies and the complicated and expensive restructuring process. However, without the support of the shareholders, we knew that there was very little we could do to preserve the company's independence.

Possibly what happened was that, following our meeting, Mark Lyttleton must have told Andy Brough something along the lines of: "This is going nowhere. It's not sustainable. Let's get it sold, and cash in our chips." Or maybe both fund managers were anxious to create liquidity as financial markets began to worsen.

For a while, the financial landscape for a sale of Chrysalis seemed as healthy as ever. Although sales of CDs were continuing to decline as a consequence of downloading, music publishing remained flavour of the month in the City. Synchronisation revenues from use in commercials and film were increasing and performance income was also rising as more and more radio and television stations and even internet sites paying royalties came on stream.

No one had foreseen that the demise of the record industry would have a negative influence on music publishing. In fact, music publishing was the one resilient area of the music industry. Funds were flooding into it as it was seen as a 'sexy' investment.

Over the previous couple of years, banks, pension funds and private equity firms had been buying or setting up small music publishing companies. Babcock and Brown, the private equity firm based in Australia, had bought the Spirit Music Group, and was building it up. The Commonwealth Bank of Australia had started First State Music and was actively buying up copyrights. The Ontario Teachers pension fund in Canada had started Ole Music Publishing and Lehman Brothers backed EverGreen Copyright Acquisitions.

The industry giant Universal Music Group had recently bought BMG Music Publishing, the music publishing division of Bertelsmann Music Group. Following the sale, Bertelsmann, in conjunction with the private equity fund KKR, started a new operation called BMG Rights Management.

Given the popularity of music publishing with financial institutions, a successful sales process for a catalogue of the quality of Chrysalis looked a cast-iron certainty. As there seemed to be no alternative, we had to accept the company would be sold and we engaged Jonnie Goodwin who had recently sold his own boutique bank, LongAcre, to Jeffries, a New York based merchant bank, to do so.

I was deeply unhappy about this. It was not my decision and I was being forced into it. Had I had the resources to take the company private or to have bought it myself, I would have tried to do so. But a process of this nature was surrounded with regulatory problems.

If you own close to 30% of a public company and then buy enough shares to take you over the 30% threshold, you are legally bound to make an offer at the same price for the remaining 70%. I simply couldn't have found the money personally to buy the 70% of the Chrysalis shares that I did not own.

As we expected, there was an enormous amount of interest in Chrysalis Music both from the major music publishers and also from smaller companies looking to make acquisitions. Everybody was beating a path to our data room. The only question mark seemed to be over the identity of the eventual buyer.

Universal Music Publishing Group appeared the least likely suitor because, with its acquisition of BMG Music Publishing, it had reached a level where it would have found it difficult to gain EC regulatory approval to buy a catalogue the size of Chrysalis Music.

In fact, Universal had to sell off Rondor UK, the British arm of the publishing company founded by Herb Alpert and Jerry Moss, to get the BMG Music Publishing deal past the European regulators. Chrysalis had bid for Rondor UK when it was being divested but we were outbid by Imagem Music, owned by the Dutch pension fund ABP, yet another institution which became involved in music publishing with this deal and made other acquisitions subsequently. Imagem then entered the bidding for Chrysalis.

Warner/Chappell Music also made an offer for Chrysalis Music but the initial favourite seemed to be EMI Music. However, Bug Music, a large independent publishing company based in Los Angeles and owned principally by Spectrum, a Boston private equity fund, headed by Brion Applegate who lives in San Francisco, also came into the picture, as did the French conglomerate Lagardère.

At Christmas 2007 I went away to Antigua as usual, maintaining close contact with the office, and expecting the process to be completed by the end of February 2008. On my return in January, I attended Midem in Cannes where negotiations continued apace, by which time Lagardère had emerged as the front-runner.

Lagardère, a major French conglomerate with extensive media interests, had invested in Because Music and Because Editions, a label and a small music publishing division run by Emmanuel de Buretel, who was well known to Chrysalis as a top-class independent operator for his success in establishing the French acts Air and Daft Punk internationally during his time at EMI/Virgin.

Emmanuel saw Chrysalis as a big acquisition, something to take him from being an independent operator in France to a major player on the world stage. He had some excellent ideas on how the company would expand and most of the Chrysalis staff would have had an ongoing role, which would not have been the case had the company been taken over by EMI Music with its own infrastructure. It seemed a perfect fit.

We set a target price of £2 a share, which was a reasonable figure at the time. On February 5, 2008, I went to Paris for the day to have lunch with the principals from Lagardère, including Jean-Marie Messier, who used to call himself the Master of the World. In 2011, Messier would be found guilty of embezzlement and divulging misleading information during his tenure as Vivendi Universal Chief

Executive a decade earlier. The lunch was convivial and appeared to go well.

A board meeting was held at Jefferies' offices in London the following afternoon to review the bids and approve the sale of the company. We all congregated there to, in theory, rubber-stamp the deal with Lagardère. However, when the meeting started, I was shocked when Jonnie Goodwin announced that when he reached the point of soliciting a final offer from Lagardère, he had been told it had decided to pull out of the process entirely.

We were all astounded. I wondered if, the previous day in Paris, I had said something wrong that might have made them change their mind, but it transpired it had nothing to do with our lunch whatsoever. The reality was that we were seeing the first stages of the contraction in the financial markets that was to plunge the world into recession a few months later.

As a result of this and the ongoing domino effect affecting all companies, Chrysalis Music went from having numerous offers above the asking price at the end of January 2008 to a series of bids whose value eroded on a daily basis. We had been hoping to achieve as much as £2.25 a share but we quickly reduced our targets and accepted that we would possibly have to settle for something closer to £1.90 a share.

Privately, the board had agreed that £1.85 would be the benchmark below which we would not be prepared to drop. We revisited our preliminary conversations with Bug, which did not have access to the same amount of funds as some of the others and had been struggling to get to our price, and told the company there was now an opportunity for it at a level that may be attractive. I would be prepared to roll over my shareholding into a new Spectrum/Bug/Chrysalis entity. This would make the deal more feasible from their standpoint.

Later that February, I went to Los Angeles to allow Bug to undertake due diligence on Chrysalis, and myself on Bug, since I would be buying into the joint entity. A merger with Bug had the benefit of putting two large independent publishers together under the same ownership. We both had US operations but Bug's international set-up was relatively small compared to ours and the bulk of the Chrysalis staff outside of America would have secured a role with the ongoing company.

Harbottle and Lewis was appointed to do the legal work, and the partner responsible decided that my daughter, Chloe, now a member of the team there, would be part of the process. However, after a couple of days, the due diligence we were undertaking on Bug suddenly dried up. Our team of lawyers and accountants were not exactly thrown out of the office but it became apparent that their presence poring over Bug's contracts and financial information was not particularly welcome.

My communications with the principals at Bug also became a little less cosy. In hindsight, I can only assume that they felt they did not have the funds available to proceed with the deal even at the now reduced target price of £1.90.

After people dropped out of the process one by one, it left only EMI Music as the one apparently firm bidder. I flew to New York and met with Roger Faxon, the chief executive officer of EMI Music, to discuss various strategies post-acquisition. Again, Andy Mollett and the members of my team who were engaged in the day-to-day due diligence started to notice a sea change in the attitude of EMI. It began quibbling over the smallest issues that had very little relevance to the overall value of the company.

Indeed, EMI was backpedalling at a rate of knots. When the eventual offer came in, it was not north of £2 a share or even £1.85 a share, our new minimum price, but £1.55 a share, well below even our worst expectations.

I'm still not sure why EMI offered £1.55 a share. I rather suspect that the impending worldwide financial situation meant that EMI had decided it didn't have the money to fund a deal at any price and so it had to extricate itself from what could become an embarrassing situation. The best way of doing that was to offer a price it knew we would definitely not accept.

Clearly, had we agreed to sell at £1.55 or at any price, given what happened to EMI in the subsequent months, it's highly unlikely that it could have completed the deal. Nevertheless, we decided to turn down its offer.

We still needed the support of Andy Brough at Schroders, so we trotted off to see him. Thankfully, he felt we had conducted a very well organised sales process, that we had done our best to sell the company, and that, in the end, we couldn't get the price we wanted and had rightly taken it off the market. He was in total agreement with our position.

Two or three months later, in September 2008, came the collapse of Lehman Brothers, which almost brought down the entire world of finance.

With hindsight, had we set out to sell the music publishing company at the same time that we sold the radio division in July 2007, we would certainly have achieved a successful sale and at a higher price than we subsequently achieved. Indeed, had we started the process a couple of months following the sale of radio, and found a buyer by November or December 2007, instead of February or March 2008, the outcome would undoubtedly have been the same: a sale at around £2 a share.

It was not to be, and we were to remain an independent company for the next couple of years. But the sales process had taken almost a year, which was very debilitating for the whole group, the staff and the artists signed to Chrysalis Music. Managing the business was not easy under these circumstances. It became impossible to sign new writers, especially if they had other options, because rival publishers would argue that Chrysalis was about to be sold and they would be better off signing with them.

I knew it would take us some time to recover from the damage. I also decided that, whatever happened in the future, we would not go into another protracted sales process, and any future negotiations must be handled outside of the public glare. Should someone come up with the right offer, it would be considered privately.

We were anxious to make up for lost time and we set out to start replenishing our roster of writers. We were also aware that being a small public company could ultimately be unsustainable in the long term, especially with some shareholders deciding to sell their stake regardless of the share price or our performance.

Following the financial crash, when the values of most companies reduced significantly, the Chrysalis share price had dropped to 55p in January 2009. I bought some shares at that price, as did members of my family, although I was restricted because I was pretty close to the 30% mark, especially if that ruling was deemed to include the shares held for my three elder children through a US-based trust.

To my surprise and concern, our second largest shareholder, the Fidelity Special Situations fund, previously run by Anthony Bolton, decided to sell its 12% stake at these ridiculously low levels. Had we been aware of its intentions, I imagine we could have sought a friendly buyer for them.

Unfortunately, the Fidelity shares were acquired by a combination of North Atlantic Value Trust and the Guinness Peat Group: two funds with a reputation for being difficult and activist shareholders. They didn't buy shares because they liked what a company was doing, and they appeared to know little about our particular industry. The strategy was to buy shares and then increase their holding to reach the point where they could agitate for the company to be disposed of, thereby making a quick capital gain. That didn't bode well for the future.

On the quiet, I was still on the lookout for approaches for an outright sale of Chrysalis as an independent entity to someone prepared to privatise the company and keep it going in its existing form. I was aware, of course, that any new owner would in all likelihood ask me to step down, which was something I was totally prepared to accept.

The most interesting approach came from a new LA-based fund that wanted to develop music assets. It was fronted by Phil Quartararo, who was well-known in the US as one of the most successful record company promotion people throughout the nineties and the noughties. He was a short man but a big personality. He had teamed up with a small private equity company who felt it could come up with the funds to buy Chrysalis and was considering making a tentative offer in excess of £2 a share.

In February 2009, I flew out to LA to see them and we arranged an afternoon meeting. Our conversations were unofficial, off the record, so I was staggered to be woken up in my hotel room at 4 a.m the following morning by Jonnie Goodwin, who told me that the Chrysalis share price had risen sharply that morning and that the stock exchange panel had been in contact to insist we make an announcement to the City and say we were in talks for disposal of the business.

There was no reason why anybody in London should have known about this meeting. We were a long way from having anything to announce so I could only assume someone from the other side had leaked the story. Having to make another public statement was annoying as it once again unsettled the staff and the creative community.

I always doubted the LA fund had the infrastructure or the money to complete the deal and sure enough it was soon put on ice, because the principal's wife had sustained an accident falling off a horse.

In the meantime, following the aborted merger of the spring of 2008, I had kept in touch with the principals at Bug. In September 2009, Tom McGrath, Bug Music's Chairman, and James Quagliaroli, Spectrum's CEO, came to London and we had lunch to discuss the state of the music industry.

Both Bug and Chrysalis had been unsuccessful in buying any rights of substance because BMG Rights Management, the new Bertelsmann/KKR operation, always appeared to get there before us. For instance, it had bought Crosstown Songs, the US publishing company run by Robin Godfrey-Cass, an experienced English publisher, which both Bug and Chrysalis had looked at.

Tom McGrath and I came up with a new formula for a Bug/Chrysalis merger. Bug/Spectrum would have to come up with the money to buy out the institutional shareholders in Chrysalis and I would roll over my shareholding into the new joint company. I would be executive chairman and the senior executive roles would be shared between the two companies.

This appeared to me to be the best solution because it would resolve the shareholder problem, as they would have been bought out at a price acceptable to them, and certainly in excess of the £1.55 offered by EMI before the world financial markets collapsed. I was really excited by this new opportunity.

We had extensive conversations through September and October and the deal was progressing well. In November, I went to Los Angeles to have lunch with Brion Applegate, the principal of Spectrum, whom I had not met before, to dot the i's and cross the t's of the deal and work through any of the operational issues left to be resolved. We were scheduled to meet at Craft, a well-known restaurant in Century City.

Janice dropped me off at noon and I joined Tom McGrath and Jim Quagliaroli. Brion Applegate was late and, as soon as he arrived, both he and Jim Quagliaroli excused themselves to take calls on their cell phones. Tom was getting agitated as both were on their respective calls for a while, but I was relaxed about the whole thing. Although I did suspect that they may have been on the phone to each other!

Eventually, we sat down for lunch. Brion Applegate had regularly spent summer vacations in Europe so we exchanged pleasantries and stories about different resorts. We then discussed my art collection, in which he seemed to be particularly interested.

I was aware there was a limited time for the lunch so I suggested we move on to some of the operational issues but Brion said not to worry about that, we had years ahead of us being in business together, and there would be plenty of time to discuss matters of that nature. When Janice came to pick me up, I told her I thought the deal was off and immediately called Jonnie Goodwin to express my fears. He reassured me this was not the case. I also spoke to Tom McGrath about the bizarre nature of the conversations. He told me that, to the contrary, Brion was really happy, and had enjoyed the lunch enormously. After we flew back to London, the merchant bankers and lawyers continued to work on the deal diligently to complete the paperwork.

Fortunately we had been able to keep the negotiations secret and the share price had not moved. And despite my scepticism, Jefferies remained convinced the deal was progressing and expected it to close. Then, at the end of November, I received an email from Tom McGrath requesting a conference call the following day, a Friday. Sure enough, when Tom and Jim called, they admitted they had not been able to find the funds to complete the transaction. The deal was off.

We were now back to square one with none of the problems solved, and seemingly no solution in sight.

Throughout this process, I had been thinking for some time about strengthening the main board of the company. We didn't have anyone who could really help us navigate through issues with the City. Additionally, Geoff Howard-Spink, who had been a non-executive director for 10 years, was required to resign because, after having served that length of time, he was deemed to be no longer impartial.

I suggested to David Hudd that he should fulfil this role. I had known David for several years. He had been on the board of Loftus Road PLC and had also been chairman of two different leisure companies: Kunick, which had bought Allied Entertainment, the company co-owned by Harvey Goldsmith; and Vardon, which owned the London Dungeon. By now, he was chairman of the Falkland Islands Company, which had a similar shareholder base to Chrysalis. I thought it would be a very good move to have him join the board.

Before agreeing, David said he wanted to meet all the other directors, make sure he got on with them, go through all of the company accounts and reports and satisfy himself that the company was indeed being run for the benefit of all the shareholders and not just the executives.

He also asked to meet the key shareholders to ensure he had their support. I don't think I've ever appointed a non-executive director who was so diligent in his approach to joining the board of a public company although, ultimately, he did not join.

At the end of January 2010, I found myself back in Los Angeles for the Grammy Awards and scheduled a meeting with Jim Quagliaroli and John Rudolph, the chief executive officer at Bug Music, to rake over the coals of the deal that had been aborted and see if there was any scope for further conversations between us.

If Bug didn't have the funds to buy out our institutional shareholders, we might instead be able to engineer an all-share merger between Bug and Chrysalis, with Spectrum owning 35% of the business, me owning about 20% and the institutional shareholders being downgraded pro rata. The merged entity would still be a public company but it would effectively be controlled by Spectrum.

This was a possible solution, but it did not thrill me and I doubted it would be acceptable to the institutional shareholders, as they would be moving from a situation where they had one private individual owning just under 30% of the company and owning the rest of the company themselves, to one where a private fund would own 35% and I would own 20%, meaning that together we would effectively control the company between us. It would also give them less control over whether the company could be disposed of.

I wasn't even sure I wanted to do it myself, as I would be left in a minority position, whereas, as things stood, I still had some control of the situation and of any possible exit route. I left LA and flew off to Aspen for my annual skiing holiday with the family at the beginning of February, thinking this deal would evaporate.

On arriving in Aspen, I was astonished to be told that a huge number of Chrysalis shares were being traded and that the main buyer was the North Atlantic Trust, although a few were also bought by the Guinness Peat Group. I suspected they were in conversation with each other. The share price was shooting up. I spoke to Keith Anderson at the corporate broking firm Investec, and mentioned my concerns that they were buying shares on misinformation, as I knew no deal was imminent.

Coincidentally, the very diligent David Hudd was at the same time doing his round in the City of leading shareholders. The first person he went to see was Christopher Mills, an Old Etonian banker who was an heir to the Bertram Mills circus fortune, who had built up JO Hambro Capital Management and North Atlantic Value very successfully.

Initially, Mills thought the meeting was to discuss the Falkland Islands company. To some extent it was, but David explained that the main reason he was there was to talk about Chrysalis, as North Atlantic was a shareholder and he was planning to join the board.

The other matter David Hudd wanted to specifically discuss with Christopher Mills was the fact that Chrysalis had recently decided to try to buy First State Music from the Commonwealth Bank of Australia. It was a sizeable acquisition and we didn't want to go too far down the line without knowing we could get shareholder approval for it, although we were convinced that Andy Brough at Schroders was prepared to support us.

I am not sure how much David managed to convey about our plans because Mills immediately exploded.

"My patience is exhausted," he told him. "I have had enough of Chrysalis. It's a lifestyle company run by Wright and the management for their own benefit. I am not prepared to tolerate it any longer. I want the company sold and I want it sold immediately."

He ended this rant with a bombshell: "I know about the Bug deal and I want to make sure it happens."

When David Hudd relayed this to me, I was staggered for several reasons: one, we clearly had a major shareholder problem; two, there wasn't a Bug deal any more; three, how did Mills know there might have been a Bug deal when I had discussed it with no one?; and four, why had Mills been continuing to buy shares? Because if he had been doing so, surely he was using insider knowledge. This would be highly illegal, and with very serious penalties.

I immediately called an emergency telephone board meeting to discuss this. I spoke to Investec and to Jefferies, the merchant bank. I was very concerned that the shares were being traded illegally and I had no idea from where Mills was getting his information.

I believe a conversation took place between Mills and Keith Anderson from Investec. I also recollect sending an e-mail myself expressing my horror and to keep Anderson in the loop. Mysteriously, if I did, that e-mail has subsequently disappeared. We also reported Mills to the Financial Services Authority (FSA), which took no action against him.

The following day was a Saturday, and I understand that the principals from Bug spent most of the day on the telephone with lawyers from Freshfields Bruckhaus Deringer, Mills' lawyers, discussing the situation, which was fraught with legal issues of great magnitude.

Slowly, I pieced together what had happened. It transpired that Christopher Mills had found himself at the same conference as Tom McGrath. Most likely, Mills had asked Tom what he did and, on finding out he was the chairman of Bug Music, had probably suggested he buy Chrysalis.

Tom might have admitted he'd been trying to do just that for a while, which would have triggered interest from Mills. If Bug was trying to buy Chrysalis, he would make sure there were no obstacles in the way of the transaction. What he didn't realise was that Bug couldn't find the cash to buy Chrysalis. He might even have felt that, if Bug was a few million pounds short, he could provide the funds to bridge the shortfall.

Furthermore, I had absolutely no idea why Christopher Mills was allowed to buy such a significant percentage of the company's shares without anyone questioning him. I had always thought this is why there are rules against insider dealing.

The situation was so serious that I cut short my vacation and immediately flew from Aspen back to London. The first thing I did was to go and see Andy Brough at Schroders to brief him on the situation. He was completely supportive and not in any way in cahoots with Christopher Mills. At least we knew we had a way to deflect the flak we were getting. Andy also understood there was no opportunity to make a deal with Bug.

Christopher Mills was also agitating on the non-executive director front. He was insisting that Rory Macnamara, a traditional banker director, join the Chrysalis board as non-executive director. Obviously, our choice all along had been David Hudd. We went to see Andy Brough and explained the situation to him, asking him who he would prefer.

Instead of choosing between Hudd or Macnamara, Brough suggested Adam Driscoll who had started the MAMA Group, a company that owned artist management agencies and live venues including the Hammersmith Apollo in London. He had sold MAMA to HMV the previous year.

Andy thought Driscoll would be an ideal choice as he came from a similar music business culture to Chrysalis. We were able to go back to the shareholders and say we weren't prepared to accept Rory Macnamara, and we eventually appointed Adam Driscoll to the board.

However, Jeremy Lascelles received a message on the morning of March 9 from Rory Macnamara to say that Mills was still agitating and wanted to talk to us. Jeremy called Christopher Mills. A fraught conversation opened with a predictable exchange of hostilities.

"We are putting two people on the board and we are going to get the Bug deal done," said Mills. Jeremy replied that we understood his point of view and we were already prepared to accept a change in the non-executive director we would appoint. With this in mind, out of courtesy, we had already met with Rory Macnamara.

Jeremy also explained that, from our perspective, there were now three candidates for the non-executive directorship: Rory Macnamara, Adam Driscoll and David Hudd. Mills stressed that all three major institutional shareholders, i.e. North Atlantic Value, Guinness Peat Group and Schroders, were totally opposed to David Hudd.

When Jeremy asked Mills how he knew about our negotiations with Bug, Mills replied that Jeremy had no need to know, but he admitted he was also aware that we had discussed a deal with Bug two years earlier. He added that Bug needed £50 million to put on the table, and that he could come up with £35 million of that. If I rolled over £15 million of my equity, then the deal could take place.

When Mills opined that we were hindering the deal by putting too high a price on the value of the Chrysalis shares and said some of our terms "made him laugh", an intrigued Jeremy asked what he meant. Mills specified our suggestion that the new company should be called Chrysalis. Jeremy pointed out that it was agreed between both parties and a no-brainer: anyone in the industry knew the Chrysalis brand was far stronger than Bug's.

Mills claimed I had asked for a "put option" to buy all the shares in the company long-term on an agreed formula – which was, and always would be, impossible. Jeremy explained that this had never been discussed between the parties.

Mills replied that in that case someone was telling lies and that it was unlikely to be Tom McGrath, whom he thought a lot of. This was the first time that Mills admitted that he had any kind of relationship whatsoever with Tom. When Mills ventured that McGrath was a "fine, upstanding, believable individual", Jeremy pointedly replied: "No comment."

When Mills complained about us reporting him to the FSA, accusing him of insider trading and "putting the wind up Bug", Jeremy said that we were equally unimpressed to find out he had been talking to Bug behind our back and had not had the courtesy to inform us of his conversations. Mills conceded that he should have called us.

Jeremy stressed that, contrary to what Mills believed, our agendas were fundamentally the same. The Chrysalis Board had been seeking a resolution to the ultimate ownership of the company in the best interests of all the institutional shareholders, including him, and had been conducting this in a very diligent manner without resorting to a For Sale sign outside the building. He added that Bug was not the only game in town, that we were exploring different opportunities, and ironically stressed that he did not intend to tell Mills any details.

"That would make you an insider, wouldn't it, Christopher?"

Mills admitted that it was important for him not to be made an insider because it would impair his ability to continue buying shares. He then said that, regardless of any other choices, he wanted Rory Macnamara on the board because he was an expert at executing the disposal of the company. Jeremy replied that was the role of Jefferies, our merchant bank and professional adviser, which was charged with securing a sale of the company.

Mills then launched into a tirade against Jefferies, claiming its limitations were obvious as it had failed to conclude a deal to sell the company for the last two years. Jeremy reminded him that, over the past two years, the financial climate had been the worst in living memory and in any event, Jefferies was working on a success-fee basis only and was therefore financially incentivised to secure a sale of the company.

Jeremy stressed his scepticism about the likelihood of a positive resolution to the Bug deal, given that three previous attempts had failed. Mills was forced to agree that it was not Chrysalis' fault when Bug had pulled out of the deal due to its inability to fund it.

Nevertheless, Mills still felt we were asking too much for Chrysalis. He would have been prepared to sell the company for a lot less. Jeremy told Mills that the price we were discussing with Bug would be acceptable to all the shareholders, and added that I was prepared to roll over the bulk of my shareholding into the new vehicle with Bug to get the deal done, which constituted an enormous gamble on my part.

Jeremy agreed with Mills that there was a compelling reason to put the two companies together. That wasn't the issue. The issue was whether Bug and Spectrum could deliver on the funding and get the deal done. Mills then told Jeremy that he did not want Chrysalis to make any acquisitions in the short-term so that our credit lines could be used to fund any possible deal.

With the mood now far more amiable, Mills then invited Jeremy to his office for a one-on-one meeting with him and they agreed to meet for breakfast the next day. I decided this would be the wrong thing to do, especially without the presence of an adviser, and Jeremy excused himself and cancelled the meeting.

Once again, we had managed to overcome a particularly tricky situation but it did not mean the issue was going to go away. It was becoming increasingly debilitating to me personally having to continually fight fires over shareholder issues whilst maintaining good relations with the other fund managers.

Meanwhile, Andy Brough was taking an entirely different view. He wanted us to stop being defensive and forget about selling the company. He said he would support us and he wanted us to go on the front foot, be aggressive, and expand outside of the music publishing area, to buy music venues and festivals.

That was an option we were prepared to consider, except I was concerned about the long-term viability of some of the areas he suggested we could move into. Vince Power, previously of the Mean Fiddler organisation, had recently floated a company operating festivals, which ultimately failed. I would have loved Chrysalis to be a consolidator but I had to be realistic.

In parallel to the Bug talks, I had been having some informal conversations with Lord Hollick, whom I had met some years previously, when he was chairman of Anglia Television. Clive Hollick was now a consultant at private equity firm Kohlberg Kravis Roberts (KKR), the financial partner to BMG Rights, the new Bertelsmann venture in music rights management. I knew from him that BMG would be interested in buying Chrysalis.

In theory, that wasn't my preferred route. I was still trying to preserve the company's autonomy rather than effectively dispose of it. We had one of the best catalogues around, a great reputation and staff, and we were performing extremely well. But at least I was now aware a deal with BMG Rights could be in the offing if necessary. Clive stressed BMG's reputation for not overpaying but it did have the money so you knew that a deal would complete – something which had not happened with anyone else so far.

I was by now becoming increasingly weary of looking for a solution. In June 2010, I had lunch with media analyst Claire Enders, the founder and principal of Enders Analysis, a British research company that looks at trends in the media industry.

We talked about the music industry in general, and the numbers Enders was about to release showing an ever-increasing decline in CD sales, especially in America. Claire came out with some very bleak projections for the future.

In the US, it was becoming more difficult to find anywhere to buy a CD. The music stores that had once been located in the main retail areas were now not even on the side streets but had almost vanished altogether. The continued decline in CD sales would mean that hardware manufacturers would stop manufacturing CD players. The automobile companies had already stopped putting CD players in cars.

She predicted things were going to continue to deteriorate. She made the point that the sales of CDs would diminish to such an extent that it would impact on publishing companies' revenues as well as those of record companies, and this decline would never be replaced by revenues from downloading, most of which is illegal anyway. Although record or CD sales used to account for 70 to 80% of the publishing revenues in volume and this was now down to about 30 or 40%, it was still a sizeable chunk of revenues.

She also said that, following the last recession the world's financial markets were still in a very fragile state, that we were not out of the woods, and that there could well be another recession in 2011/2012 – which was to prove correct. On the bright side, there was still confidence in the music publishing business.

Eventually she cut to the chase: "Chris, if you are really considering selling the company, my advice would be to do it now rather than wait," she advised. "You never know what the landscape may be like in a couple of years: a sale may not be possible. Now you have a chance and there are buyers around. Funding is available, but it may not last."

I took on board what she said because it made sense. Whereas I knew that BMG Rights might potentially buy Chrysalis, I also knew that EMI was basically for sale and Warner Music could be for sale. If BMG Rights was able to buy EMI Music or Warner/Chappell Music, acquiring Chrysalis may disappear from the company's radar screen altogether.

However, I was still not prepared to throw in the towel quite yet and I continued to talk to Bug to see whether the hybrid arrangement to pay off the shareholders, take the company private and merge the two businesses had some traction.

Towards the end of July 2010, we convened a Chrysalis board meeting at Glebe House. We had decided to sell the office building in Bramley Road to tidy up the company's assets ahead of any deal, and because the new owners were refurbishing the premises the boardroom was unavailable.

In light of developments, the board took the decision to resolve the position of the company by the end of the year. We had three options open to us.

1) An outright sale to BMG Rights, where the price achieved might be limited but the execution risk was the smallest. However, as BMG had its own infrastructure, opportunities for the Chrysalis management and staff would be limited.

2) The Bug merger. We hoped some of the institutional shareholders would roll over into the new entity, and the others would take cash, but it still required an element of financing which could be difficult to achieve.

3) We were also seriously discussing a private equity acquisition of Chrysalis. We explored a couple of possible partners for this but without either of them really showing the ability to conclude a deal.

Eighteen months previously, we had hired as a consultant Andrew Kitchen, who had built up Spirit Music, the music publishing asset for Babcock & Brown, the private equity firm based in Australia. When it was hit by the worldwide recession, he helped it liquidate its assets in 2009.

Kitchen was now working for us acquiring catalogues. He had helped us buy into First State Music, which was effectively owned by the Commonwealth Bank of Australia. Because some major pension funds co-owned the catalogue, we felt it might be a good way forward as those funds could effectively take over Chrysalis if they so desired.

Unfortunately, by this time the value of music publishing assets had already started to reduce significantly. The catalogues they owned were no longer worth the price they had been bought at, and the banks who had invested heavily in such assets were beginning to regret doing so. Even so, we were able to engage in conversations with a couple of interested funds.

When the board met in Gloucestershire, we decided that the Bug option had a big question mark attached to it. We had been down the aisle with Bug three times and, each time we got to the altar, no one could find the ring. But the marriage still had the most appeal.

Ultimately, we decided private equity was probably unlikely to be the solution, with the attendant execution risks. Therefore, taking on board Claire Enders' advice, we thought a deal with BMG Rights while the opportunity existed might end up being our only real option.

I was still intent on finding another outcome, and planned to continue to do so. But in the end it was the ubiquitous Christopher Mills who was to land the most telling blow.

Jeremy Lascelles phoned me at 7.30 on a Friday evening at the beginning of October saying he'd had just taken a call from Brunswick, our corporate PR company. It was asking if we wanted to comment on a story that James Ashton, the *Sunday Times* City editor, was intending to run that Sunday describing a shareholders revolt at Chrysalis.

According to the story, shareholders were banding together to put pressure on us to sell the business so they could realise the value in their shares. If we refused to immediately announce that the company was to be sold, they would call an extraordinary general meeting to vote off the existing board members and replace them with those of their choice who would deliver a sale.

I suspected that Christopher Mills might be behind this. I immediately contacted Jonnie Goodwin, who managed to get hold of James Ashton and succeeded in convincing him to pull the story on the basis that, the following week, I would give him an exclusive interview to discuss exactly what was going on at Chrysalis.

Even though we were genuinely considering potential offers and seriously thinking about disposing of the business, the last thing I wanted was a story in the *Sunday Times* saying we were under pressure from shareholders to sell the company. It would have totally removed my negotiating ability, and I could well have had to settle for a much lower price. It was imperative that we killed the story, or at least managed it to avoid another crisis.

When I met James Ashton, I explained to him that we were indeed exploring our options and that Chrysalis would not necessarily continue in its present form. I made sure that the story James Ashton ran stressed that I was the one considering the sale of the company.

I would rather have said I had no intention or wish to sell Chrysalis, and that it was only the one institutional shareholder – Mills – who was trying to agitate for such an outcome. That would have been the truth but I couldn't go public because it would have affected my ability to negotiate the best deal for the shareholders. In a way, by adopting his strategy Mills was shooting himself in the foot. He should be thankful that I conducted the disposal process in such a way that we were able to maximise value for him and the other institutional shareholders.

BMG Rights Management came up with a proposal of £1.60 a share, well below our expectations but 5p higher than the deal we had turned down from EMI a couple of years earlier. At least we could go to our shareholders and tell them that we were delivering a better price than we could have secured last time.

I flew to Los Angeles and had lunch with Brion Applegate and the Bug guys to tell them of my decision. They belatedly tried to come up with another proposal. Unknown to me, Simon Fuller had been discussing an investment in Bug, which would have helped the financing of a Chrysalis deal. It was too late: by now Chrysalis had entered into a period of exclusivity with BMG Rights.

BMG had an incredible amount of resources to throw at the process. It was easy to see how it had been so successful buying up companies. It had a team of about 50 people working on it and managed to complete the due diligence in a few weeks. It was focussed on being in a position to announce the deal on Thanksgiving Day in the States, when all the competition was otherwise occupied. The deal closed on November 26, 2010, three years after the process had originally started.

I can't say it was the happiest day in my life. I acted professionally and spoke to all the staff, who were totally shocked by the news. I explained that it could be a good deal for everybody and that they would be in a stronger position to sign new artists as there would no longer be any uncertainty hanging over the company.

I expected many of them to keep their jobs. Thankfully, with a few exceptions, that is exactly what happened.

When I look back at the sale process, I have to question the role of bankers and fund managers in the whole exercise. It used to be the case that funds invested in companies they believed in, and saw the value of their investments rise as the company developed and performed. If they lost confidence they would sell their holdings.

Nowadays, the stock market has become more of a casino. Apparently the average length of time a fund holds a share on the New York Stock Exchange is around 20 seconds. Even for longer-term holders often the best route to a quick profit is to force a disposal of the company, regardless of how well the business is doing. It did not just happen with Chrysalis, but with many other well run British companies too, like Cadbury, which suffered the same fate.

Some of the staff at Chrysalis who lost their jobs had been with the company for over 20 years, the best part of their working lives. They and the many artists had no say in a decision made to secure a healthy profit for bankers who, in many cases, had invested in the company's shares less than a year before.

Few people question matters of this nature, but it was the subject of the Proclaimers' song 'Letter From America' many years previously. Most of the major British companies are now foreign-owned, including, amazingly, those that control our basic infrastructure, like transport, water and electricity. The quick profit for a banker dictates the agenda, to the exclusion of all other principles.

Soon after BMG Rights acquired Chrysalis, Christopher Mills sold his investment company to an Australian group for £160 million. I believe Mills received £60 million personally, and is currently worth £200 million according to the *Sunday Times* rich list.

Still, on the whole, I bought into the BMG Rights acquisition. I knew certain staff would lose their positions, including Jeremy Lascelles, because BMG had its own CEO, Hartwig Masuch, but many others would keep their jobs.

I was concerned about the Chrysalis name disappearing but I managed to negotiate a commitment that the company in the UK, the US and Scandinavia would be called BMG Chrysalis for at least three years. There is no guarantee that the name will live on after that period, but I think it has a great deal of value.

As you would expect, I had mixed emotions about the sale. It is only natural. This was a very poignant moment. It was definitely the end of an era, not just for me but for a certain type of British music company. Not long after the sale of Chrysalis EMI Music was sold to Universal.

For too long, though, I had felt like King Canute trying to turn the tide back. I had the feeling that I was the last man standing of a certain generation of mavericks. Chris Blackwell, Jerry Moss and

Richard Branson had all sold their music companies. The only one I spoke to following the sale was Jerry Moss, who sympathised with my situation, but reassured me I had made the right decision.

For more than four decades, Chrysalis had been my life's work. I had started the company in 1967 with Terry Ellis in a bedsit in Shepherd's Bush. Our early success had exceeded my wildest dreams and had lasted many years. I had managed to reinvent the company by diversifying into radio, television and book publishing. I had taken an enjoyable, if occasionally fraught, detour into the world of sport.

We had launched the careers of many superstars and flown the flag for British music throughout the world and now, with the sale of EMI, there is no longer a British flag bearer in an area where the country has excelled on the global stage for five decades. Had we not been a public company with institutional shareholders, we would still be in business today, and maybe for years to come.

The very essence of a music company, or indeed any rights-owning company, does not sit well in that environment. There are too many imponderables, too many variables that can change or affect your figures. The creative process is not easy for a banker to understand, and things take time to mature. Time is not a commodity that bankers can understand. As a result there are no longer any publically quoted music companies. That is why Chrysalis no longer exists. It's a huge pity.

Epilogue

Looking back, it has been an incredible journey. When I was growing up in Lincolnshire, sitting on a tractor ploughing fields, I could never have imagined that my life would end up being so rich, so rewarding, and so full of amazing memories.

I have watched such stellar performers as Janis Joplin, Led Zeppelin, The Doors, The Who and Jimi Hendrix from the side of the stage, and was incredibly fortunate to work with some exceptionally original and ground-breaking acts like Jethro Tull, Procol Harum and Blondie – to pick three absolute one-offs – who enjoyed lengthy and hugely successful careers with Chrysalis.

I learnt the ins and outs of the music industry from such legendary figures as Bill Graham, Peter Grant, Tony Stratton-Smith, Chris Blackwell, Jerry Moss, Clive Davis, Mo Ostin, Ahmet and Nesuhi Ertegun and George Martin. I cannot overstate the inspiration they were to me.

I was lucky to have lived through the late sixties and early seventies, a golden period that saw a real blossoming of musical talent, especially in Britain. Like the Renaissance, the period when painters, sculptors and architects benefitted from the patronage of rich potentates, the rock explosion of the late sixties and early seventies was founded on a community that extended throughout Western Europe and North America, and for whom music was the single most important thing in their world. Music dominated the lives of the baby-boomer generation. Radio and television were tightly controlled and very much in their infancy. There was no such thing as social media.

The landscape of the late sixties and early seventies was uniquely conducive to music becoming the countercultural force to what had gone on before. Music became the common bond within that counterculture. Back then, the greatest thing you could do was buy an album, sit down and – with or without smoking a joint – listen to it.

Over the following decade and a half, together with Terry Ellis, whose role in the creation of Chrysalis cannot be overestimated, we competed with our kindred spirits Chris Blackwell and Richard Branson and arguably achieved a better strike rate per release than either. Between 1976 and 1991, when our acts sometimes topped the albums and singles charts simultaneously, it seemed we could do little wrong.

Chrysalis occupied a unique place in the music industry. We had a certain cachet, we were cool, we could be quirky and off the wall, but we were able to attract critical acclaim and deliver commercial success in any genre, from blues to progressive, heavy metal, via folk, pop and punk.

And, much like Island had helped us flourish in the late sixties, we served as the umbrella company for the next generation of British labels in the eighties, Go! Discs, China, and Beggars Banquet in particular, not to mention the wonderful Glass Note label in America, headed by our old alumnus Daniel Glass in the current century.

In the nineties, we reinvented the company and punched above our weight, simultaneously creating one of the top three radio station groups in the UK, and developing the first super-indie television production company.

Unfortunately, at least from my point of view, the music scene has now changed beyond recognition. Nowadays we are wholly preoccupied with communicating electronically, joining social networks and using the latest technology. Music is just another element in that entertainment and communication mix, with nothing like the importance and urgency it had when I decided to throw in my lot with Ten Years After.

The changes in technology have scattered in their wake my beloved vinyl albums and their 20-minutes-a-side, and even crippled the longer CD format which emerged in the mid-eighties. With downloading and streaming, fans without the patience to listen to what seems at first like a weak track five can now skip on to track six at the push of a button.

This is a shame. Even albums as good as *Bridge Over Troubled Water*, *The Dark Side Of The Moon* and *Graceland* include tracks you may like a little less than others but they are important to the album because they create the light and shade. We seem no longer willing to accept shade, only light – but how often has the shade turned out to have the same merit in the long term? Tragically, as a format, the album is breathing its last.

In this respect, I am a dinosaur left over from the old music business. The industry has changed enormously. It is not the business I grew up in.

The current era of single track downloads and streaming makes it difficult for an artist to create anything really special. And the problem is exacerbated by illegal downloads which have sapped the income from record companies to the extent that they no longer have the funds to invest in developing long-term careers for artists, and instead seek out only the overnight, often fleeting, successes.

The old model of A&R-oriented executives finding artists, nurturing them through two or three albums and helping them gain exposure by touring around the world and playing to audiences who have never heard of them until they eventually develop and break through to millions, is almost unsustainable. I say almost as, fortunately, there is still room for great bands to develop over a period of time, like Muse, Snow Patrol and Elbow, as well as innovative hip-hop artists like Jay Z, Kayne West and Eminem, and much credit is due to those who discover and nurture them.

At the same time, talent shows like *The X Factor, Britain's Got Talent, American Idol* and *The Voice* introduce to the public unproven performers who are manipulated, marketed and have their looks and personalities changed overnight. Whoever thought *Viva Forever*, a musical based on the disposable material of The Spice Girls could sustain in the West End in the same way that musicals based on the music of Queen and Abba have done was clearly misguided.

In today's high-exposure, quick-fix, quick-access, single-track download world, it is fairly easy to take TV show contestants and turn them into the artists of the moment. Of course, they will never become the artists of tomorrow, or often even next year, and you are left with a catalogue that has no lasting cultural, never mind monetary, value.

The quick fix is thus more expedient than putting resources into developing the new Beatles, U2 or Coldplay, and that way of thinking is even starting to affect music publishing. Thankfully, you still have the occasional exception, like Adele selling over 25 million albums, but I suspect it will be a very long time before anything on that scale happens again. Hopefully I'll be wrong.

As you grow older, you may get wiser but you still need a great deal of help in terms of A&R. It's a young person's business. At the age of 67, I have reached my limit in manning the front line where new talent is discovered and signed. I have to accept that those with their finger on the pulse are out in the clubs and pubs and venues seeing how the artists are communicating with the fans. I was there once, running one of my own in Manchester, but it's a young man's game at the sharp end, always will be.

What is my legacy? Foremost, my role at the forefront of the great British rock invasion of the US, and founding and building one of the three or four biggest independent record companies in the world;

and, following the sale of the record company, creating one of the largest media companies in the UK.

You can go anywhere in the world and, as you jump in a taxi, hear performances by Chrysalis artists, or switch on the television and watch an episode of *Midsomer Murders*, a detective series Chrysalis Television developed many years ago.

But, in other ways, I am not leaving behind that great a legacy after all. In 1991, Chrysalis Records became part of EMI, the last major British record company, which has now itself disappeared in all but name. Chrysalis Music, the publishing company, lives on through BMG Chrysalis but there is no guarantee this will continue, or my role within it.

Some of the artists with whom I have been involved are becoming distant memories for many, even if others, like Jethro Tull, The Waterboys and Sinéad O'Connor are still touring and recording. It's heartening to tune in to radio stations the world over and hear Blondie, Spandau Ballet or Huey Lewis & The News on a daily basis.

I was never fortunate enough to work with anyone of the calibre of Bob Dylan or The Beatles, The Rolling Stones, Paul Simon, Bob Marley or Queen, but I relish the fact that the publishing deal we gave David Bowie four decades ago supported him at a crucial stage in his life and set him on his way to becoming a global superstar.

Many great people in the past have accomplished a lot more than me and I know how easy it was for their legacy to disappear; just look at Steve Ross of Warner Communications. I am under no illusions that the legacy I have produced will last beyond a couple of generations at the most.

So what was it all for?

You come into the world with nothing, and you leave with nothing, save your reputation, the value of which cannot be measured in monetary terms, so you had better make sure that you enjoy your journey through it. That doesn't mean to say that you lead a life of pure hedonism, because that is too shallow. You lead a life of accomplishment and achievement but, when it's over, you can't take it with you and you can't look after it.

I hope that there are enough people out there, from the students at Manchester University who enjoyed the gigs I used to put on, all the way through to fans of Wasps who loved seeing their rugby team beat the other teams in Europe, who feel they have a little to thank me for.

Maybe for me this is it, maybe not, who knows? My life demonstrates how you never know what's around the corner, which path you decide to take when you reach a major crossroads. Maybe there is a volume two, or at least a few more chapters, maybe there is even that elusive mega artist out there only waiting to be discovered and nurtured.

In the meantime I have a wonderful family with Janice, my wife, and five incredible children, Tim, Tom, Chloe, Holly and my step-daughter, Tina. I have a great deal to remind me how lucky I have been and how full and rewarding my life still is.

Beyond that, I'm reminded of a story Procol Harum lyricist Keith Reid wrote for the band. It's called 'Glimpses Of Nirvana', the opening section of the suite *In Held 'Twas In I* on their second album, *Shine On Brightly*. It's also included on *Procol Harum Live In Concert With The Edmonton Symphony Orchestra*, the group's most successful album and a jewel in the Chrysalis catalogue.

In the song, the main character, a pilgrim, goes to see the Dalai Lama. After he has first spent five years in contemplation he is ushered into the Dalai Lama's presence and asks him the meaning of life.

The Dalai Lama has an answer.

"Well, my son, life is like a beanstalk, isn't it?"

Index